SUMMARY

The Theological Department in Yale College was established September 10, 1822, with the selection by the President and Fellows of Nathaniel W. Taylor as Professor of Didactic Theology. His colleagues during the period 1822-1858 were Eleazer T. Fitch, Chauncey A. Goodrich and Josiah W. Gibbs.

Of the students who attended the Theological Department in Yale College during this period, almost three-fourths were natives of New England; about nine-tenths were college graduates, over two-thirds of whom came from Yale; less than two-thirds became ministers, one-fourth of this group settling in the "West"; almost four-fifths of those who became ordained were Congregationalists; and a little less than one-fifth obtained one or more honorary degrees.

The course of study was largely administered in the form of lectures, and remained almost entirely static throughout the period in respect to arrangement and content. The subject of Church History was entirely neglected; Theology was overemphasized.

Of the libraries available, the College Library was most frequently consulted, the majority of books withdrawn being of a theological nature. The Libraries were treated as depositories and were opened only a few hours each week and then for the withdrawal of books. No official reading room was provided.

The Student Societies appear to have been the best medium for the expression of student opinion and initiative. The Rhetorical Society was, however, dominated by the perennial presidency of Dr. Taylor. The Society for Christian Research used methods of investigation worthy of the twentieth century.

Of the contemporary conditions and events, theological discussion and controversy dominated religious thought, and the Theological Department through its Professors contributed to an advancement in the development of New England Theology. The life of the churches was marked by repeated revivals. The outstanding social movement was the opening of the "West". In comparison with the last named interest, Foreign Missions occupied a secondary position in the minds of the Faculty and students.

A decided lack of administration was an outstanding feature of the Theological Department in Yale College during this period. There was no Dean of the Theological Faculty. This Department suffered with the Law and Medical Departments from the attitude of the officials of Yale College who looked upon them as appendages of the Academic Department. The evolution of the University belongs to a later period. The funds of the Theological Department were so neglected that the provisions made for indigent students, building equipment, and the salaries of Professors, were quite inadequate.

The last decade of the period under review witnessed a sharp decline in student attendance. Causes, other than the lack of funds, were the failure on the part of the Faculty to realize that in the area of religious thought the theological emphasis had changed to one of a Biblical nature, and the fact that each of the Professors was growing old and no provision was made for his honorable retirement. So pronounced was the decadence of the Theological Department that only by the greatest labor and sacrifice were the friends of the Department, after an eleven-year struggle, able to rescue it from extinction and to restore it to its former position.

- PREFACE -

The history of the Divinity School of Yale University has been marked by the inheritance of the tradition and theology of New England, a connection with a venerable College and great University, and a Christian faith characterized by a progressive orthodoxy. The Yale Divinity School was established in 1822 as the Theological Department of Yale College. Its first and leading Professor, Nathaniel William Taylor, completed his work in 1858. In this last year was appointed the first Professor of a New Faculty which was to supplant Dr. Taylor and the three colleagues who had served with him. The period 1822-1858, therefore, constitutes the first era in the history of Yale Divinity School.

In writing a history of this era the author has endeavored to give as complete a picture as possible of the entire environment which surrounded the students of the Theological Department during this period, and of the characteristics of the young men themselves as revealed in their student activities and in their records as alumni. In the pursuit of this purpose the history of ministerial education at

Yale College prior to the establishment of the Department has been reviewed for a better understanding of the traditions and experience inherited by the Faculty and students of the period 1822-1858. In the main body of the work those several parts which make up the life of a seminary, the personnel and administration, the facilities for instruction including the libraries and student societies, and the contemporary conditions and events which influenced the manner in which the Theological Department trained the students, have been investigated and recounted. The whole has been subjected to a critical examination for the light which may be thrown upon educational principles and policies of permanent value for theological education.

    For aid in the making of this study I am chiefly indebted to Dean Luther Allan Weigle of the Yale Divinity School, who first suggested the limits and scope of this work, and has been my constant advisor. I wish to express my obligations to Dr. Hugh Hartshorne of the Divinity School for valuable assistance at many points, and to Drs. J. W. Tilton and John S. Brubacher of the Department of Education for helpful criticisms on the manuscript.

    The author has been fortunate in that almost all of the source materials for this study were found in the Sterling Memorial Library where the efficient services of Miss Anne S. Pratt of the Reference Department, Miss Emily Hall and Mr. G. M. Troxell of the Rare Book Room, and Mr. T. R. Barnum, curator of the Yale Memorabilia, and their assistants, have made that Library a most delightful and profitable place in which to pursue such a study.

I am grateful to my wife, Eunice Fowler Wayland, for the preparation of the statistical tables found in this work.

TABLE OF CONTENTS

PART I

THE BACKGROUND AND ORIGIN OF THE THEOLOGICAL DEPARTMENT

Chapter I	Page

Religious Education in Yale College 1701-1822 ... 4

    Beginnings of the Provisions for Higher Education in New England 4

    The Founding of the Collegiate School of Connecticut 6

    The Course of Study 1718-1745. 15

    The Administration of Rector Cutler 1719-1745. 19

    Rector William's Administration 1725-1739. 22

    President Clap's Administration 1739-1766. 24

    Three Methods for the Training of Ministers. ... 30

    Naphtali Daggett as Professor of Divinity. ... 37

    The Administration of Ezra Stiles 1777-1795. 40

    President Dwight's Administration 1795-1817. 46

Chapter II

The Establishment of the Theological Department in Yale College. 51

    Demands of Students and Faculty for a Theological Department 52

	Page
Major Factors which precipitated a Need for a Theological Department in Yale College	55
The Events of the Year 1822 Resulting in the Establishment of a Theological Department	72

PART II

PERSONNEL AND ADMINISTRATION

Chapter III

The Faculty 1822-1858. 77

    Nathaniel William Taylor 79

    Eleazer Thompson Fitch 89

    Chauncey Allen Goodrich. 97

    Josiah Willard Gibbs 106

Chapter IV

The Students 1822-1858 119

    Enrollment 120

    Birth places of the students 124

    Colleges Attended. 127

    Professions Followed by the Alumni 130

    Denominational Affiliations of the Alumni. 136

    Honorary Degrees Obtained by the Alumni. 142

Chapter V

Administration of the Theological Department 149

    Relation to Yale College 150

	Page
Relation to the President and Fellows of Yale College	154
Relation to the President.	156
Administration of the Theological Department by its Faculty.	158
Administration of Finances	160

PART III

FACILITIES FOR INSTRUCTION

Chapter VI

The Purpose and Plan of the Course of Study . . .	172
The Purpose of the Course of Study.	173
The Plan of the Course of Study	176

Chapter VII

The Administration and Content of the Course of Study.	183
The Academic Year	184
The Size of the Classes which met for Study . .	185
Sources for an Investigation of the Course of Study.	186
The Course of Study	188
The Junior Year	188
The Middle Year	200
The Senior Year	211
Professor Fitch's Sermons	220
Examinations	222

Chapter VIII

The Libraries 226

    The College Library 227

    The Extent to which Theological Students
        Used the College Library 232

    The Libraries of the Several Societies . . . 241

    The Moral and Rhetorical Library 248

    Comparative Use of All the Libraries
        by the Students 253

    Plans for the Improvement of
        Library Facilities 255

    Illustrations Concerned with the
        Libraries 258

Chapter IX

The Student Societies 290

    The Rhetorical Society 291

    The Society of Inquiry Respecting Missions . . 302

    The Society for Christian Research 305

PART IV
CONTEMPORARY CONDITIONS
AND EVENTS

Chapter X

Theological Controversies 313

    New England Theology Prior to the Year 1820 . 315

    The Controversies of N.W. Taylor and
        his Colleagues 322

	Page
The Establishment of the Theological Institute of Connecticut	336
The Dow Incident	337
The Wider Influence of the New Haven Theology	340

Chapter XI

The Theological Department and the Community	347
The City of New Haven 1820-1860	348
The College Square 1820-1860	352
Relations between the College and the Town	358
Sunday Schools In New Haven and in Yale College	361
Revivals of Religion in Yale College and in New Haven	366

Chapter XII

Missions: Home and Foreign	377
Organizing for Home Missions	378
The Theological Department and Home Missions	383
Organizing for Foreign Missions	393
Evidences of Interest in Foreign Missions by the Students	399

PART V
CRITICAL EXAMINATION
AND SUMMARY

	Page
Chapter XIII	
The Close of the Period	406
Financial Problems	409
Religious Thought Changed from a Theological to a Biblical Emphasis. .	409
The Faculty in Their Declining Years	416
Chapter XIV	
The Significance of the Period.	428
BIBLIOGRAPHY	447

LIST OF TABLES

Table		Page
I	STUDENT ATTENDANCE AT THE THEOLOGICAL DEPARTMENT IN YALE COLLEGE DURING THE PERIOD 1823-24 to 1857-58.	121
II	GEOGRAPHICAL DISTRIBUTION OF THE BIRTH PLACES OF THE ALUMNI OF THE THEOLOGICAL DEPARTMENT OF YALE COLLEGE WHO WERE STUDENTS DURING THE PERIOD 1822-1858; ARRANGED BY CLASSES	125
III	DISTRIBUTION OF COLLEGES ATTENDED BY STUDENTS WHO WERE MEMBERS OF THE THEOLOGICAL DEPARTMENT OF YALE COLLEGE DURING THE PERIOD 1822-1858; ARRANGED BY CLASSES	129
IV	PROFESSIONAL DISTRIBUTION OF THE ALUMNI OF THE THEOLOGICAL DEPARTMENT OF YALE COLLEGE WHO WERE STUDENTS DURING THE PERIOD 1822-1858; ARRANGED BY CLASSES.	131
V	GEOGRAPHICAL DISTRIBUTION OF MINISTERS AND TEACHERS WHO WERE STUDENTS IN THE THEOLOGICAL DEPARTMENT OF YALE COLLEGE DURING THE PERIOD 1822-1858; ARRANGED BY CLASSES	134
VI	DENOMINATIONAL DISTRIBUTION OF THE ALUMNI OF THE THEOLOGICAL DEPARTMENT IN YALE COLLEGE WHO WERE STUDENTS DURING THE PERIOD 1822-1858; ARRANGED BY CLASSES	143
VII	HONORARY DEGREES GRANTED TO MEMBERS OF THE THEOLOGICAL DEPARTMENT OF YALE COLLEGE WHO WERE STUDENTS DURING THE PERIOD 1822-1858; ARRANGED BY CLASSES	145
VIII	NUMBER OF STUDENTS OF THE THEOLOGICAL DEPARTMENT USING THE LIBRARY OF YALE COLLEGE AND THE NUMBER OF BOOKS WITHDRAWN	234
IX	THE TYPE OF BOOKS WITHDRAWN FROM THE LIBRARY OF YALE COLLEGE BY STUDENTS OF THE THEOLOGICAL DEPARTMENT	237
X	USE MADE OF THE LIBRARY OF THE LINONIAN SOCIETY BY THE STUDENTS OF THE THEOLOGICAL DEPARTMENT IN YALE COLLEGE	245
XI	USE MADE OF THE LIBRARY OF THE SOCIETY OF BROTHERS IN UNITY BY THE STUDENTS OF THE THEOLOGICAL DEPARTMENT IN YALE COLLEGE	247

LIST OF TABLES (Continued)

Table		Page
XII	USE MADE OF THE LIBRARY OF THE MORAL AND RHETORICAL SOCIETY BY THE STUDENTS OF THE THEOLOGICAL DEPARTMENT IN YALE COLLEGE.	252
XIII	COMPARISON OF THE PERCENTAGE OF INCREASE AND DECREASE IN THE NUMBER OF MEMBERS IN THE CLASSES OF THE SEMINARIES AT ANDOVER AND AT PRINCETON WITH THE THEOLOGICAL DEPARTMENT AT YALE COLLEGE DURING THE PERIOD 1825-1874; IN GROUPS OF FIVE CLASSES.	407

LIST OF ILLUSTRATIONS

Illustrations		Page
1	THE FUNDS OF YALE COLLEGE	162
2	ESTIMATES OF INCOME OF THE THEOLOGICAL DEPARTMENT FOR THE ACADEMIC YEAR 1851/2	168
3	THE COURSE OF INSTRUCTION IN THE THEOLOGICAL DEPARTMENT IN YALE COLLEGE ACCORDING TO THE CATALOGUE OF THE OFFICERS AND STUDENTS OF YALE COLLEGE 1820-51	189
4	AN EXAMPLE OF A "THEOLOGICAL" LIST OF BOOKS WITHDRAWN FROM THE LIBRARY OF YALE COLLEGE	260
5	AN EXAMPLE OF A "THEOLOGICAL TEXT" LIST OF BOOKS WITHDRAWN FROM THE LIBRARY OF YALE COLLEGE	262
6	AN EXAMPLE OF A "THEOLOGICAL-GERMAN" LIST OF BOOKS WITHDRAWN FROM THE LIBRARY OF YALE COLLEGE	263
7	AN EXAMPLE OF A "THEOLOGICAL-VARIED" LIST OF BOOKS WITHDRAWN FROM THE LIBRARY OF YALE COLLEGE	264
8	AN EXAMPLE OF A "VARIED" LIST OF BOOKS WITHDRAWN FROM THE LIBRARY OF YALE COLLEGE.	266
9	AN EXAMPLE OF A "THEOLOGICAL" LIST OF BOOKS WITHDRAWN FROM THE LIBRARY OF YALE COLLEGE (H LARGE LIST)	268
10	BOOKS WITHDRAWN FROM THE LIBRARY OF YALE COLLEGE DURING THE THREE YEARS OF A THEOLOGICAL COURSE	271
11	TWENTY BOOKS MOST FREQUENTLY WITHDRAWN FROM THE LIBRARY OF YALE COLLEGE BY THE STUDENTS OF THE THEOLOGICAL DEPARTMENT DURING THE YEARS 1834-35 to 1838-39	273
12	TWENTY BOOKS MOST FREQUENTLY WITHDRAWN FROM THE LIBRARY OF YALE COLLEGE BY THE STUDENTS OF THE THEOLOGICAL DEPARTMENT DURING THE YEARS 1839-40 to 1848-49	275
13	TWENTY BOOKS MOST FREQUENTLY WITHDRAWN FROM THE LIBRARY OF YALE COLLEGE BY THE STUDENTS OF THE THEOLOGICAL DEPARTMENT DURING THE YEARS 1849-50 to 1857-58	277

LIST OF ILLUSTRATIONS (Continued)

Illustration		Page
14	TWENTY BOOKS MOST FREQUENTLY WITHDRAWN FROM THE LIBRARY OF YALE COLLEGE BY THE STUDENTS OF THE THEOLOGICAL DEPARTMENT DURING THE YEARS 1858-59 to 1867-68	278
15	BOOKS WITHDRAWN FROM THE LINONIAN LIBRARY BY A STUDENT OF THE THEOLOGICAL DEPARTMENT IN YALE COLLEGE	281
16	BOOKS WITHDRAWN FROM THE BROTHERS LIBRARY BY A STUDENT OF THE THEOLOGICAL DEPARTMENT IN YALE COLLEGE	283
17	BOOKS WITHDRAWN FROM THE BROTHERS LIBRARY BY A STUDENT OF THE THEOLOGICAL DEPARTMENT IN YALE COLLEGE	285
18	BOOKS WITHDRAWN FROM THE MORAL AND RHETORICAL LIBRARY BY A STUDENT OF THE THEOLOGICAL DEPARTMENT IN YALE COLLEGE	287
19	BOOKS WITHDRAWN FROM THE MORAL AND RHETORICAL LIBRARY BY A STUDENT OF THE THEOLOGICAL DEPARTMENT IN YALE COLLEGE	288
20	THE COLLEGE SQUARE (ABOUT 1845)	353

PART I

THE BACKGROUND AND ORIGIN OF THE THEOLOGICAL DEPARTMENT IN YALE COLLEGE

Chapter I   Religious Education in Yale College

Chapter II   The Establishment of the Theological Department

CHAPTER I

RELIGIOUS EDUCATION IN YALE
COLLEGE 1701 - 1822

RELIGIOUS EDUCATION IN YALE COLLEGE, 1701 - 1822

Beginnings of the Provision for Higher Education in New England

The traditional New England pride in ancestry is perhaps best substantiated by the educational attainments of the famous first settlers of Massachusetts Bay. Beginning with the arrival of the Massachusetts Bay Company in June, 1630, the Puritan colonists numbered many leaders who were graduates of the universities of England. During the years 1636-47 there was definite educational activity in the Colony in connection with the establishment of a public school, a printing press, and a college. Before this period was over at least ninety university men had emigrated to New England. Almost three-fourths of these were from the University of Cambridge, known as a special stronghold of Puritanism from the middle of the sixteenth century onward. Up to the time when Harvard graduates were ready to take up the work, there had been some threescore ministers regularly inducted into Massachusetts pulpits; and certainly not more than half a dozen of these lacked university training.[1] It is not surprising, then, to find

---

1. F. B. Dexter, The Influence of the English Universities in the Development of New England, Proceedings of the Massachusetts Historical Society, Vol. XVII (February 1880) p. 340.

in the records of the General Court of Massachusetts Bay for October 28, 1636, that "the Court agreed to give 400^t towards a schoole, or college, whearof 200^t to bee paid the next yeare, and 200^t to bee paid when the worke is finished, and the next Court to appoint wheare and w^t building".[2]

One of the members of the committee which was named to carry into effect the vote of the General Court of Massachusetts Bay, fixing a college at Newtown, later designated as Cambridge,[3] was the Rev. John Davenport.[4] Davenport had arrived in Boston on the 26th of June, 1637, intending to establish a colony of his own. Rejecting all invitations for settlement elsewhere, he decided in March 1638 upon Quinnipiac, on what is now known as Long Island Sound, as the place where an independent republic might be established. A formal purchase of land from the Indians was made there in November and December of that year. The civil government was formally established on June 4, 1639.[5] The name of the town was changed to "New Haven" on July 1, 1646.[6]

As early as December 25, 1641 an ordinance declares that "Itt is ordered thatt a free schoole shall be sett up in this towne, and our pastor Mr. Davenport together with

---

2. Records of the Governor and Colony of Mass. Bay in New England, printed by order of the Legislature, ed. by Nathaneal B. Shurtleff, (1853) Vol. 1, p. 183.
3. May, 1638. Ibid., p. 235.
4. 20 November, 1637, Ibid., p. 217.
5. Records of the Colony and Plantation of New Haven, from 1638 to 1649. Transcribed and ed. in accordance with a resolution of the General Assembly by Charles J. Hoadley (1857), pp. 11-18.
6. Ibid., p. 40.

the magistrates shall consider whatt yearly allowance is meete to be given to itt out of the com͞o stock of the towne."[7] Just ten years after the founding of the New Haven Colony, the General Court in New Haven gave power to a select committee of the town "to consider and reserve what lott they shall see meette most commodious for a colledg, which they dessire maye bee sett up so soone as their abillitie will reach thereunto."[8] For some reason the work was halted, and it is not until May 22, 1654 that mention of a college is again made in the Records.[9] A year later, May 21, 1655, Davenport, and his associate in the ministry, Mr. Thomas Hooke, "spake much to incourag the worke, after which the men hereafter named were desired to goe to the several planters in this towne and take from them what they will freely give to this worke."[10]

At a meeting of the Court, June 21, 1660 Davenport[11] urged[12] the establishment of a grammar school and a college.[13] As trustee under the will of Edward Hopkins, Davenport made over to the Court a claim on that estate for a legacy to be used in the establishment of these two schools. After a

---

7. Records of Colony and Plantation of New Haven, from 1638 to 1649, op. cit., p. 62.
8. 23rd of March 1647/8, Ibid., p. 376.
9. "New Haven Town Records, 1649 - 1662, Ancient Town Records," Vol. 1, New Haven Colony Historical Society, (1865) ed. by F. B. Dexter, pp. 213, 214.
10. Ibid., pp. 241, 242.
11. New Haven Town Records for July 4, 1655, Ibid., p. 246.
12. Mr. Davenport's address on this occasion is given in full by Jonathan Trumbull in The History of Connecticut, (1818) Appendix No. 21.
13. New Haven Town Records, op. cit., p. 457.

fitful beginning, the Hopkins Grammar School began a continuous history in 1664, but the turn of public affairs in the union of the Colony with Connecticut and the consequent disappointment of Davenport with this union, and his departure from New Haven for Boston, worked against any progress in the founding of a college.

In the meantime, the college at Cambridge, begun in the same year as the New Haven plantation, received such patronage as this settlement could afford to give to so distant an institution. There were among the founders of the New Haven and Connecticut Colonies proportionately fewer university men than in Massachusetts but before the establishment of the Collegiate School of Connecticut, nearly sixty students from these colonies went to Harvard, making one-eighth of the whole number of her graduates. Almost a third of this group, more than from any other two towns in the list, came from New Haven.[14]

The Founding of the Collegiate School in Connecticut

Further attempts at the establishment of a college in Connecticut in 1698, 1699, and 1700, have been described by Benjamen Trumbull,[15] and Professor James L. Kingsley.[16] For

---

14. F. B. Dexter, "The Founding of Yale College", The papers of the New Haven Colony Historical Society, Vol. 3, 1882, p. 3.
15. History of Connecticut, Vol. 1, pp. 472-474.
16. "A sketch of the History of Yale College in Connecticut," Quarterly Register, Vol. 8, (1835) pp. 14, 15.

a long time the year 1700, which, according to tradition, witnessed the dedication of books for the founding of a college, was considered the beginning of the school.[17] Professor Henry Bowditch Dexter says that "this venerable and beautiful tradition. . . . has undoubtedly some basis of truth but can hardly be accepted in detail."[18] He preferred to accept, as the birthday of the college, the date of the granting of the charter for the establishment of the Collegiate School, which he believed to have occurred on the sixteenth day of October, 1701. Yale University now recognizes this date as the authentic one.[19] In this charter are named as trustees ten clergymen, among whom the most active in the establishment of the school were Mr. James Pierpont of New Haven, and Mr. Samuel Andrew of Milford. These ten ministers were the most influential in the Colony of Connecticut, and were all, with the exception of the Rev. Thomas Buckingham, graduates of Harvard College. The plan of the Collegiate School in Connecticut differed appreciably in only one respect from that of Harvard College.

----

17. Prof. Kingsley states in the work cited in the preceding footnote, p. 15, that "this act of depositing the books has ever been considered the beginning of the college." On August 14, 1850, President Woolsey gave "An Historical Discourse - One Hundred and Fifty Years After the Founding of that Institution."
18. "The Founding of Yale College", op. cit., It is in this document that Professor Dexter enters into the discussion of this problem in detail, and his conclusion is reflected in most of his several works concerning the beginning of the college.
19. The Bicentennial of the founding of Yale College was celebrated in 1901 with extensive programs and pageants, and the erection of Bicentennial buildings, etc.

In 1636 the founders of the latter, coming fresh from Oxford and Cambridge, followed these great universities in the provision for a body of resident fellows. But between 1636 and 1700 the old recollections had passed away, and in keeping with the lowly term, "collegiate school", resident fellows are not mentioned in the charter of 1701.[20]

The statement that the founders designed that the school should have the aspect of a theological seminary is probably an exaggerated one.[21] The charter records that several well-disposed persons were desirous of endowing a Collegiate School "wherein youth may be instructed in the Arts and Sciences who thorough the blessing of Almighty God may be fitted for publick employment both in Church and Civil State."[22] The chief professions of the day were those connected with the Church and the State, and the greatest need was felt in these areas. Furthermore, there was not a great distinction between the two fields since ministers had been, from the beginning, very active in the affairs of town and colony. Special professional training was little considered, it being customary for the prospective minister, doctor, or lawyer to study, for a few months usually, with

---

20. The Charter of 1745 speaks of "Fellows", but with an entirely different connotation from that which the word possessed in the early seventeenth century.
21. Pres. Clap, in the interest of defending the right of the college to set up a religious society within its borders describes the college as "a society of ministers for the training up of persons for the work of the ministry". Chancellor Kent gives a similar argument for the same purpose, in his pamphlet published in 1754, on The Religious Constitution of Colleges, especially of Yale College.
22. The Charter of the Collegiate School of Connecticut, 1701.

his father, or some friend who had attained success in the profession which he himself wished to follow. The classical curriculum, burdened with an emphasis on "logick", was considered the *sine qua non* for the gentleman, lay or clerical. The conception of a professional school did not evolve until near the beginning of the succeeding century.[23] However, it would be most strange, in view of the very important place which religion enjoyed in the life of the times, if this group of ministers had not designed that this school should have a religious basis of the type which was in keeping with their convictions, and that it should be an institution wherein a worthy group of ministers might be prepared to take their places in the leadership of ecclesiastical affairs in the Colony. The religious turn which the first founders intended to give the course of study in the Collegiate School of Connecticut appears in the account of the first act of theirs on record after the charter of the school was granted.

> "Whereas it was the glorious publick design of our now blessed fathers. . . . to propagate in this Wilderness, the blessed Reformed, Protestant Religion, in ye purity of its Order, and Worship. . . . We their unworthy posterity lamenting our past neglects of this Grand errand, and Sensible of our equal Obligations better to prosecute ye Same end, are desirous in our generation to be serviceable thereunto – Whereunto the liberal, and Religious Education of Suitable growth is under ye blessing of God, a chief, and most probable expedient. . . . Do in duty to God, and the Weal of our Country undertake in ye aforesd design." (24

---

23. See pp. 63-65.
24. Proceedings of the Trustees, November 7-11, 1701. MS.

At this meeting the Rev. Abraham Pierson was elected as Rector of the School, and among the "Sundry orders and determinations with respect to the Rector For the time Being and his work",[25] were:

> "The s^d. Rector shall take Especial Care as of the moral Behavior of the Students at all Times so with industry to Instruct and Ground them well in Theoretical devinity and to that End Shall neither By Himself nor by any other person Else whomsoever allow them to be Instructed and Grounded in any other Systems or Synopses of Divinity than such as the s^d Trustees do order and appoint But Shall take Effectual care that the s^d students be weekly in such seasons as he shall see Cause to appoint Caused memoriter to recite the Assemblies Catechism in Latin & Ames's Theological theses of which as Also Ames's Cases, He shall make or Cause to be made from time to time such Explanations as may be (through the Blessing of God) most Conducive to their Establishment in the Principles of the Christian protestant Religion.
>
> That the s^d Rector shall also Cause the Scriptures Daily (Except the Sabbath) morning and Evening to be read by the Students at the times of prayer in the School according to the Laudable orders and usages in Harvard College making Expositions upon the same, and upon the Sabbath Shall Either Expound practical theology or Cause the Students non Graduated, to Repeat Sermons, & in all other ways according to his best discretion shall at all times studiously Indeavor in the Education of s^d students to Promote the power and Purity of Religion and Best Edification & peace of these New England Churches."

The influence of Harvard College is seen in the declaration of the trustees that in lieu of there being no code of laws for the School the Rector or tutors "Shall make use of the orders and institutions of Harvard College for the instructing & Ruling of the Collegiate School."

---

25. Proceedings of the Trustees, date cited (Division III), p. 3.

In making recommendations concerning the drafting of a charter Samuel Sewall and Issac Addington, writing from Boston in 1701,[26] state: "We on purpose gave your Accademie as low a name (Collegiate School) as we could that it might the better stand in wind and weather". The first score of years in the history of the institution were in keeping with this lowly title of "Collegiate School". The poverty of the school was natural in view of the condition of the Colony at that time. Small as the institution was, it seems to have represented great effort on the part of its supporters. There were in Connecticut in the year 1700, but twenty-eight towns. The population, variously estimated,[27] but which was probably about 20,000, was scattered, exhausted by Indian wars, with little commerce, and depending for subsistence almost wholly on the cultivation of the soil.

At a meeting of the Trustees, September 30, 1702, it was agreed that the Collegiate School be settled in the town of Saybrook, but the salary given to Rector Pierson was so

---

26. October 6; 2 pp., MS.
27. Connecticut pursued in her colonial history the policy of hiding her strength; so far as might be consistent with general truthfulness, she preferred to make no exhibit of her actual condition. Absolute accuracy is, therefore, impossible. Professor Kingsley in his "History of Yale College", Quarterly Register, Vol. 8, p. 16, agrees with Benjamin Trumbull, in his History of Connecticut, Vol. 1, p. 4, that there were 14,000 to 15,000 people in the colony in 1700. Professor Dexter, in "Estimates of Population in the American Colonies", reprint from Proceedings of American Antiquarian Society for October, 1887, in his Historical Papers, p. 161, 162, states that after an investigation of the tax reports in the Colonial Records, he believes twenty thousand to be a correct estimate.

small that he was forced to continue his residence in "Kennelworth". The students, therefore, repaired to Killingworth for instruction and the commencement exercises were held in Saybrook. The members of Pierson's parish were not at all pleased [28] with the arrangement, and the cause of the school seems to have suffered no less than the work of the Church.

The first commencement was held at Saybrook in September, 1702, when four young gentlemen, who had before been graduated at Harvard, and one other who had been privately educated, received the degree of Master of Arts. The first student in the Collegiate School, Jacob Hemingway, was graduated at Saybrook in 1704. He entered the institution as a regular member in March, 1702, and continued alone under the instruction of Mr. Pierson until September of the same year. At this time, the number of students being increased to eight, they were put in different classes, according to their previous acquirements, and Mr. Daniel Hooker of Farmington, a graduate of Harvard College, and grandson of Rev. Thomas Hooker, the first minister of Hartford, was elected tutor. Mr. Hooker, however, was soon displaced [29] by Mr. John Hart, who had attended Harvard

---
28. Letter of Abraham Pierson to the Inhabitants of Killingworth, September 21, 1705, with the answer of the town, from a copy in the Killingworth Town Records, in the Documentary History of Yale University, ed. by F. B. Dexter, (1916) pp. 51, 52. At a town meeting, November 7, 1706, it was voted that the town is "not willing to allowe that the School should be keept hear as it has been". op. cit., pp. 54, 55.
29. Proceedings of the Trustees, September 15, 1703.

College for three years and had graduated alone from the Collegiate School in Connecticut in 1703. For the next three or four years the School continued on the plan whereby the students were taught in Killingworth, and Commencements were held at the meeting house on Saybrook Point. This unhappy arrangement was cut short by the sudden death of Rector Pierson in March, 1707.

Little is known concerning Mr. Pierson,[30] but he seems to have been greatly respected by his contemporaries. President Clap, who was contemporary with some of the first graduates of the Collegiate School says that he "was a hard student, a good scholar", and that "he instructed and governed the infant college with general approbation; and composed a system of natural philosophy, which the students recited for many years".[31]

As soon as possible after the death of Mr. Pierson a pro-tempore Rector was named--the Rev. Samuel Andrew, of

---

30. In letter written to President Stiles, July 22, 1788, in answer to an inquiry, Deacon Abraham Pierson professes to know little concerning his great-grandfather, depending largely upon an "elderly lady's descriptions" for his information. However, it is known that he was the son of Rev. Abraham Pierson, who emigrated from England and was the first minister in Branford, in the Colony of New Haven. The elder Pierson removed from Branford, in protest of the union of New Haven and Connecticut Colonies, and began the town of Newark in New Jersey. The younger Pierson graduated from Harvard in 1668. He afterward settled in the ministry as colleague with his father in Newark. After the death of the latter the son remained as minister, until, some controversy having arisen on the subject of Presbyterianism, he removed to Killingworth, in Connecticut, where he remained until his death. Thomas Clap, Annals of Yale College (1766), pp. 12-14.

31. Ibid., p. 14.

Milford--and the Senior Class of that year migrated to his house. The remainder of the student body was instructed in Saybrook by two tutors. Mr. Andrews presided at the Commencement at the latter place and acted as referee in important disputes. The location of the School had not been designated in the charter and local animosities grew up in regard to its location. The institution was suffering greatly from the uncertainty of being without a definite home and a regular Rector. The most important single contribution to the continuance of the School during these years was the arrival in 1714 of about one thousand books, which had been collected from benefactors in England by Jeremy Dummer.[32]

The granting of permission by the Connecticut General Assembly for the erection of a college building precipitated a crisis with regard to the permanent location of the School. The friends of the College were divided into three groups, one urging that the school remain in Saybrook, another arguing for a removal to Hartford, and the third desiring that New Haven be made the permanent site of the institution. After much controversy, those who favored New Haven were victorious. The majority of the trustees resided in that vicinity, and the largest contribution for the school had been raised in New Haven. The trustees, at their meeting

---

32. A list of the Boocks given to the Colledge of Connecticut in New England with names of Benefactors, collected by Jeremy Dummer. London 15 January 1712/13, MS. 42 pp. Mr. Dummer was the agent of Connecticut at the British Court.

of October 17, 1716, voted that the School be removed to New Haven.[33]

The institution then received benefactions from several donors, among whom, Governor Elihu Yale was outstanding in the generosity of his gifts. At the Commencement, held at New Haven, September 12, 1718, which seems to have been a happy one, the Trustees ordained that the "College House shall be called by the Name of its Munificent Patron, and shall be named Yale-College".[34]

The Course of Study 1718 - 1745

Excepting for the brief mention in the Records of the Trustees for November, 1701, of that portion of the studies which were of a theological nature, there is no definite record of the course of study pursued in the school during the first eighteen years of its existence. It is supposed that, in keeping with the order of the Trustees, of the same date (1701), the plan of study as found in Harvard College was largely followed.[35] President Clap states that "about the time the College was fixed at New Haven, a short Body of Laws was drawn up which was usually transcribed by the Scholars at their Admission."[36] The oldest known manuscript

---

33. Proceedings of the Trustees date cited.
34. Letter of the Trustees to the Hon. Elihu Yale, September 12, 1718.
35. See p. 10. The fact that all of the Rectors and President Clap were graduates of Harvard would be of great influence in regard to the plan of the course of study.
36. Annals of Yale College, (1766) p. 42.

laws of the College, now extant, bear the date A.D. 1718, and are probably copies of, or are very similar to, the first edition.[37]

The first statute declares that those who would be admitted to the institution shall in their examination "be expert in both the Greek and Latin Grammar, as also in construing Grammatically resolving both Latin and Greek authors, and in making good and true Latin".

The course of study is described as follows:

> "17. In the first year after admission, on the four first days of the week, all students shall be exercised in the Greek & Hebrew tongues only; beginning logick in the morning at the latter end of the year, unless their Tutor see cause by reason of their ripeness in the tongues to read logick to them sooner. They shall spend the second year in logick with the exercise of themselves in the tongues; the third year principally physick; and the fourth year metaphysicks & mathematticks, still carrying on the former studies. But in all classes the last days of the week are perpetually allowed for Rhetorick, oratory, & Divinity, & in teaching both tongues and arts; and such authers are to be used as do best agree with the Scriptures, wherein the Special care of the Rector & Tutor is to be exercised & their Direction attended."

The law just preceding this one in the same code will best describe the studies in Divinity:

> "16. All undergraduates shall, after they have done reciteing Ethicks on Frydays, recite Wollebius Theologie, and on Saturday mornings thay shall recite Ames Theologicall Theses in his medulla, and on Saturday evenings the Assemblyes Shorter Chateohisme in Latin, & on Sabbath morning attend the explication of Ames' cases of Conscience."

---

37. Orders and Appointments to be observed in the Collegiate School in Connecticut. Henry Allyn, His Book, Anno Domini, 1718. MS., 15 pp.

Another law[38] ordains that "all undergraduates shall publickly in the Hall repeat Sermons in their courses, & also Bachelors; and be constantly examined on Sabbath Evenings, Att Evening Prayer." And again,[39] "all undergraduates (except Freshman who shall read English into Greek) shall read some part of the Old Testament out of ye Hebrew into Greek in the morning, and shall turn some part of the New Testament out the English or Latin into Greek att evening att the time of recitations before they begin to recite, whereby skill may be obtained in the original tongues."

The influence exerted by Harvard College upon the Collegiate School in Connecticut, is further evident in a comparison of the laws of the Collegiate School, just reviewed, and the laws of Harvard College for 1655,[40] both in regard to the text and in reference to the customary use made of the laws by each student. Young men, on entering Harvard, were required to obtain a copy of the laws, each student acquiring one for himself.[41] At the Collegiate School in Connecticut, in addition to this requirement it was specified that each student transcribe his own personal copy of the laws.[42] A comparison of the text of the Laws

---

38. Orders and Appointments observed in the Collegiate School in Connecticut, op. cit., Law No. 15.
39. Ibid., Law No. 14.
40. Copy of the Laws of Harvard College, 1655, with an Introduction by Samuel A. Green, Cambridge, John Wilson and Son, 1876. (Pam.) 11 pp.
41. Ibid., p. 3. (Introduction)
42. Law No. 26.

of Harvard College for 1655 and those of the Collegiate School for 1718 reveals such a striking similarity of phraseology and actual identity of clauses and even sentences, that it seems very probable that the Harvard Laws greatly influenced the compiler of the statutes for the Connecticut school. The order in which the different matters for legal action are recounted is quite similar.[43] However, a striking difference between the two codes is found in the omission in the Connecticut laws of the Harvard requirement for the Bachelor degree which reads: "Every Scholar that upon proofe is able to read extempore the pentateuch of (or?) the new testament into latine out of the originall tongues" is granted a degree.

These laws for the Collegiate School, of the year 1718, which so nearly resembled the Harvard code of 1655, remained almost entirely unchanged until they were revised by President Clap in 1745.[44] It appears, therefore, that the course of study and the general life of the School, in so far as the laws influenced it,[45] must have remained almost static.

---

43. The laws are numbered differently, however. In the code of the Collegiate School there is no division of subjects, and, therefore, the laws are numbered from one to twenty-six without a repitition of numbers. The Harvard Laws are divided into three major parts, with eight, eleven, and nine laws numbered in each section.
44. The MS. Laws of 1720, 1721, 1727, 1728, (the last in Latin) are almost identical in every respect with those of 1718.
45. It is quite apparent from an examination of these laws that they are designed to control every area of the student's activities in the institution.

The Administration of Rector Cutler
1719 - 1722

After the location of Yale College was definitely settled upon as New Haven, and the institution had received some substantial gifts, its greatest need was a resident rector.[46] Accordingly the trustees, in March, 1719, elected Rev. Timothy Cutler, a minister of Stratford, Connecticut, to this office. In regard to the new Rector, Jonathan Edwards, then a Junior in the College, writes in July, 1719:

> "I take very great content under my present tuition, as all the rest of the scholars seem to do under theirs. Mr. Cutler is extraordinarily courteous to us, has a very good spirit of government, keeps the school in excellent order, seems to increase in learning, is loved and respected by all who are under him, and when he is spoken of in the school or town, he generally has the title of President." (47

While a pastor in Stratford, Connecticut, the Rev. Mr. Cutler had been honored by a request to preach before the General Assembly in Hartford.[48] Again, on October 18, 1719, he delivered a sermon to the Assembly, convened at

---

46. At a meeting of the Governor and Council of Connecticut rumors of the decadence of the College were discussed. The cause of student rebellion and desertion was laid to the "Insufficiency of the young Tutors, and the Council recommended to the Trustees of the College that a resident Rector be appointed. Colonial Records, Vol. 6, pp. 98-102, printed, Hartford, 1872.
47. Jonathan Edwards' Works, ed. by Edward Hickman (1840) Vol. 1, pp. lix-lx.
48. The Firm Union of a People Represented, New London, T. Green, 1717. (Pam.) 65 pp.

New Haven.[49] The fact that both sermons were printed at the expense of several of the gentlemen who heard them was an additional compliment.[50]

However, rumors concerning Cutler's unfitness for the Rectorship were confirmed the day after Commencement, on September 13, 1722, when the following letter was presented to the Trustees of the College:

> "Reverend Gentlemen:
>
> Having represented to you the difficulties which we labor under, in relation to our continuance out of the visible communion of an Episcopal Church, and a state of seeming opposition thereto, either as private Christians, or as officers, and so being insisted on by some of you (after our repeated declinings of it) that we should sum up our case in writing; we do (though with great reluctance fearing the consequences of it) submit to and comply with it: And signify to you that some of us doubt of the validity, and the rest are more fully persuaded of the invalidity of the Presbyterian ordination, in opposition to Episcopal: and should be heartily thankful to God and man, if we may receive from them satisfaction herein, and shall be willing to embrace your good

---

49. *The Depth of Divine Thoughts*, New London, T. Green, 1720. (Pam.) 2 pp. and 38 pp.
50. President Stiles writes in his Literary Diary, (MS.) under the date of May 24, 1779: Rector Cutler was an excellent linguist--he was a Hebrician and Orientalist. He had more knowledge of Arabic than I believe any man ever in New England before him, except President Chauncey and his Disciple the first Mr. Thatcher. Dr. Cutler was a good Logician, Geographer, & Rhetorician. In the Philosophy and Mettaphysics and Ethics of his Day or juvenile Educ[a] he was great. He spoke Latin with Fluency & Dignity & with great Propriety of Pronunciation. He was a noble Latin Orator--as I learned from my father who was educated under him. . . . He was of a commanding Presence and Dignity in Government. He was a man of extensive Readg in the academic Sciences, Divinity, & Ecc. History.

counsels and instructions in relation to this important affair, as far as God shall direct and dispose us to it.

> Timothy Cutler
> John Hart
> Samuel Whittelsey
> Jared Eliot
> James Wetmore
> Samuel Johnson
> Daniel Brown " 51

Mr. Brown was a tutor in Yale College, and the rest were young ordained ministers, all graduates of the school. At this time there was not an Episcopal Church or clergyman in Connecticut. The only town in which there was an Episcopalian family was Stratford. The persons who were uncertain of the validity of Presbyterian ordination were Hart and Whittelsey. Accordingly in October following, at a meeting of the Trustees in the College Library, at which Governor Saltonstall presided, the question was argued, Rector Cutler and Mr. Johnson being the leading advocates for Episcopacy, and Governor Saltonstall the chief exponent of the Presbyterian ordination.[52] The result was, that only Mr. Johnson stood with the Rector and the Tutor in resolving to withdraw from the Congregationalists; Mr. Wetmore followed them a few months later, while the other three found their scruples quieted by the arguments, or by the persuasions of the great majority around them.

---

51. "Some Original Papers Respecting the Episcopal Controversy in Connecticut, MDCCXXII", Collections of the Massachusetts Historical Society, Vol. 2., Second Series, pp. 128, 129.
52. Letter of John Davenport and Stephen Buckingham to Increase and Cotton Mather. op. cit., Vol. 4, Second Series, pp. 297-301.

On the next day, at a special meeting of the Trustees, it was voted, that the Trustees, "in faithfulness to the trust reposed in them, do excuse the Rev. Mr. Cutler from all further service as Rector of Yale College." Mr. Brown's resignation of his tutorship was also accepted;[53] and it was provided that all future rectors and tutors should, before their appointment was complete, declare to the Trustees

> "their assent to the Confession of Faith owned & consented to. . . . at Saybrook Septr 9th, 1718, & confirmed by the Act of the General Assembly and shall particularly give Satisfaction to them of the Soundness of their Faith in opposition to Armenian & prelatical Corruptions or any other of Dangerous Consequences to the Purity & Peace of our Churches." (54

Rector Williams' Administration 1725 - 1733

The Trustees were unable to secure a resident Rector for the next four years and an arrangement was made for a succession of temporary rectors to reside in rotation at the College.[55] Finally in 1726, on September 13, the Rev. Elisha Williams was formally introduced into the Rectorship.[56]

---

53. Mr. Cutler, Mr. Brown and Mr. Johnson, sailed from Boston the November following for England, and were ordained in March of the next year. Mr. Brown died of smallpox a short time after his ordination. Cutler was Rector of Christ Church in Boston from 1723 to 1756. See Mr. Cutler's funeral Sermon preached, August 20, 1765, by Henry Carver The Firm Belief of a Future Reward a Powerful Motive. Boston, 1765, 24 pp. See especially pp. 18-24.
    Mr. Johnson later became the first president of (1754-1763) Kings College (Columbia) in New York. The latest most complete work which has been accomplished with regard to Mr. Johnson, is the editing of his papers by Herbert and Carol Schneider; New York, Columbia University Press, 1929. 4 Vols. A total of 2267 pp.
54. Proceeding of the Trustees, October 17-22, 1722.
55. Ibid
56. Proceeding of the Trustees, September 13, 1726.

Mr. Williams was born in Hatfield, Massachusetts, August 24, 1694. He graduated in 1711 from Harvard College. While the location of the Collegiate School in Connecticut was being debated, during the years 1716-1718, he tutored some refugee scholars at Wethersfield under the authority of two Trustees who favored Hartford as the suitable place for the School. In 1718 he was a member and clerk of the Connecticut Assembly. In 1721 he was ordained pastor of the Church in Newington. He filled his chair as Rector of Yale College with great "usefulness & honor"[57] from 1726 to 1739. He resigned the Rectorship on account of failing health. He was later a Member of the General Assembly, and a Judge of the Supreme Court of Connecticut.

Although Mr. Williams seems to have been a successful teacher and administrator as Rector of Yale College,[58] it appears that little of importance happened during his term of office with the exception of Bishop Berkeley's donations of a farm at Newport, Rhode Island,[59] and of a large number of valuable books amounting in all to about a thousand, of which eight hundred and fifty were given at one time in the year 1733.

---

57. President Stiles' Literary Diary, May 24, 1779. MS.
58. President Stiles, in his Literary Diary, under May 24, 1779, writes: "Mr Rector Williams was a good classical Scholar, well versed in Logic, Metaph. & Ethics, & in Rhetoric & Oratory. He presided at Commencement with great Honor--he spoke Latin freely and delivered Orations gracefully and with animated Dignity. While a boy I heard him make his Valedictory Oration at the Commencement 1739 when he resigned the Chair. He was a Man of Splendore!"
59. Proceedings of the Trustees, December 20, 1732.

President Clap's Administration
1739 - 1766

On the resignation of Rector Williams the Rev. Thomas Clap, minister of Windham in Connecticut, was chosen his successor, and held office for twenty-seven years, until 1766.

The Great Awakening and Yale College

Soon after he entered upon his office began the religious revival known as the Great Awakening. The Rev. George Whitefield had arrived in Rhode Island, from England, on September 14, 1740. On the 23rd of October, he reached New Haven. He was well received in the town on this his first visit.[60] In 1741, however,

> "Mr. Davenport, of Southhold, on Long Island, who had been esteemed a pious, sound and faithful minister, but now became zealous beyound measure; made a visit to Connecticut, and preached in New Haven, Branford, Stonington, and various other places; and went on as far as Boston. He gained an unrestrained liberty to noise and outcry, both of distress and joy, in time of divine service. He promoted both with all his might, raising his voice to the highest pitch, together with the most violent agitations of body. . . .
> His brethern remonstrated against these wild measures, and represented to him, that he must be under the influence of the wrong spirit; but he persisted in his measures. . . . He was complained of, and brought before the General Court of Massachusetts, and was dismissed, as not being of a sound mind.
> His conduct had a pernicious influence on the people, and seems to have given rise to many errors."[61]

---
60. Benjamen Trumbull, History of Connecticut, Vol. 2, p. 153
61. Ibid., pp. 160, 161.

The excitement was so intense and the fear for the best interests of the College was so great that the Connecticut General Assembly took cognizance of the "unhaple clercomstances of the Colege" and noted that "Sundry of the Students of s^d Colege have us the rever^d Rector Informeth us by the Instigation persuation & example of others, fallen into Several Errors in principal and disorders in practice."[62] The Committee of the Assembly which was investigating this matter recommended that the Rector, Trustees and others concerned in the government and instruction of the College. . . . prevent the students from receiving instruction "of Such as would prejudice theire minds against the way of worship and Ministry Established by the Laws of this Government." The Committee further recommended that the Assembly grant to the college sufficient funds for the obtaining of, "a meet person" to instruct the scholars.[63]

In his zeal for the protection of what he believed to be the correct theological tenets, President Clap expelled David Brainerd, partially[64] because he had disobeyed the

---

62. Report of a Committee of the Connecticut General Assembly, on a Passage Relating to Governor Law's Speech, May 13, 1742, with the action thereon, (From the original in the State Library); <u>Documentary History of Yale University</u>, ed. by F. B. Dexter, pp. 355, 356.
63. <u>Ibid</u>, pp. 356, 358. The recommendation was passed by both Houses of the Assembly.
64. The other fault charged against Mr. Brainerd was his refusal to make a public confession, which was very often the punishment meted out for the first offense against several laws, for certain words which were dropped in private conversation derogatory to the religious character of Mr. Whittelsey, a Tutor.

Rector in going to a "separate" meeting.[65] Three years later occurred the expulsion of John and Ebenezer Cleaveland. These brothers, during their vacation from the College, had attended, with their parents, services which were conducted by a layman.

Upon their return to school they were called to account by the faculty. They were required, on the penalty of expulsion, to confess publicly their error. Since they declined to do this, the threatened expulsion was carried out.[66]

In 1745 the Rector and Tutors of Yale College made a declaration against George Whitefield, "his Principles and Designs", to the effect that "It has always appeared to us that you and other <u>Itinerants</u> have laid a <u>Scheme</u> to turn this generation of ministers out of their places. . . . and to vilify and subvert our Colleges, and to introduce a Sett of Ministers into our Churches by other ways and Means of Education".[67]

---

65. Jonathan Edwards, <u>Life of David Brainerd</u>, (1765) pp. 18-20.
66. Their conversations with the Rector and Tutor Whittelsey, at various interviews prior to the expulsion, were written down by the elder of the two brothers. A copy of the record was given, by his grandson, the Rev. Mr. Cleaveland of New Haven, to Professor George P. Fisher. In Appendix No. 10, connected with his <u>History of the Church of Christ in Yale College</u>, Professor Fisher has published the most important portion of these records. (1858)
67. <u>The Declaration of the Rectors and Tutors of Yale College in New Haven against the Reverend Mr. George Whitefield.</u> Boston, T. Fleet, 1745. (Pam.) 15 pp.

The Establishment of the Professorship of Divinity

By about 1746 President Clap's zeal for a strict Calvinism caused him to become more and more dissatisfied with the preaching of the pastor of the First Church in New Haven, the Rev. Joseph Noyes, who was thought to be an Arminian in sentiment; and whose style of preaching was felt to be not as forceful and animated as it should be.[68] On December 28, 1741, a number of the congregation of the First Church in New Haven had presented a memorial to the Ecclesiasticl Society of that Church stating, "We have, by wrong and sorrowful experience, found, that the preaching and conduct of the Rev. Mr. Noyes, has been in great measure unprofitable to us, and that we have also reason to think that he differes from us in some points of faith. Therefore we desire. . . . to be a distinct society".[69] The result was the establishment of the "North Church" in New Haven.[70]

President Clap decided to form a distinct congregation within the walls of the College, and made every effort to

---

68. Since Mr. Noyes was a member of the Corporation of Yale College, President Clap published no statement concerning him. In his Annals of Yale College (1766), written after Rev. Noyes' death Mr. Clap allowed himself the further latitude of stating that, at the time the students were made into a separate congregation "the College was in danger of being infected with Errors", p. 61.
69. Samuel W. S. Dutton, History of the North Church in New Haven, (1842) pp. 6, 7.
70. Dutton, op. cit., pp. 31-33.

secure funds to this end. In 1746, the Hon. Philip Livingston of Livingston Manor, a member of His Majesty's Council for the province of New York, having had four sons educated at the College, gave the sum of twenty-eight pounds, ten shillings sterling, to the President and Fellows to be used as they should deem most for the advantage of the Institution. The money served as the beginning of a fund for a Professorship of Divinity, and President Clap wrote to Col. Livingston: "We have taken the most Effective Method which lay in our power, that your name might be Remembered and Honored in this College in all succeeding generations."[72] However, on account of a lack of funds, it was nine years before this chair was finally established.

In view of President Clap's former fervor in censoring those who would form new churches in the Colony, and his extreme severity in dealing with students who attended "separatists" meetings, it was natural that he would be accused of grave inconsistency when he led in the establishment of a separate church in the College Hall. The controversy became more bitter with each succeeding year so that the last few years of President Clap's life were spent in great unpopularity. Rev. Benjamen Gale[73] was the chief

---

71. Thomas Clap, The Religious Constitution of Colleges, especially Yale College, (1754), (Pam.) p. 10.
72. April 22, 1746; MS. 1 p. See also Minutes of the President and Fellows, April 16, 1746.
73. Mr. Gale's first pamphlet gave in substance his case, which was argued and reargued later, The Present State of the College of Connecticut Considered, 1755, 21 pp.

antagonist, and so strenuously did he attack the policy of the College that the General Assembly was influenced to the point of failing to give to the College its annual bounty, beginning with the year 1755. President Clap's chief argument was that the original end and design of Colleges was to instruct, educate, and train up persons for the work of ministry, and that such a society must necessarily be of a higher order than an ordinary church. He cited councils, and creeds as authorities for such statements; and the colleges of England as examples of institutions having a church in a college.[74]

In September, 1755, the President and Fellows voted that Mr. Naphtali Daggett, who had been ordained as a Presbyterian minister in the town of Smithtown, Long Island,[75] be invited to the Professorship of Divinity in Yale College. On the 3rd of March, 1756, the President and Fellows met, and proceeded to examine Mr. Daggett as to his principles of religion. The Rev. Mr. Daggett wrote out for their approval a "Confession of Faith",[76] which contained four pages of statements in regard to doctrines and propositions which he denounced as erroneous. On June 30, 1757, the Church of Christ in Yale College was established, with the new Professor preaching a sermon, and the President reading the acts of the Corporation governing the life of the Church.[77]

---

74. The Religious Constitution of Colleges, especially Yale College, (Pam.) pp. 1, 10-12.
75. On September 13, 1751, Naphtali Daggett, Smithtown Records, MS., p. 3.
76. MS. 15 pp.
77. MS. among Professor Daggett's papers, 2 pp.

The preceeding day the President and Fellows had received a petition signed by the Tutors and several students, stating their desire "to attend upon the ordinance of the Lord's Supper under the administration of the Rev. Professor and to walk together in stated Christian communion".[78]

The duties of the Professor of Divinity are described by President Clap in his "Annals of Yale College", in the Appendix, which is entitled, "The Present State of the College, Method of Instruction, and Government, etc.":[79]

> "The Professor of Divinity preached Sermons in the Chapel, every Lord's Day, in the course of a Body of Divinity, Doctrine, & Practice, & occasional discourses & Lectures, at other times; & frequently gives private counsel and Instruction."

These services rendered by the Professor of Divinity were intended to be of special value to the graduates of the College who remained in residence for an indefinite number of years in order to prepare themselves for the ministry. This date then marks the first official provision for postgraduate study in Yale College.

Three Methods for the Training of Ministers

The custom of licensing young men to preach, by a formal or informal association of ministers had come into vogue

---

78. Minutes of the President and Fellows, June 29, 1757. Records of the Church of Christ in Yale College, 1757-1817, MS., pp. 4 and 5.
79. p. 80.

gradually in the early part of the eighteenth century, and Cotton Mather, in his "Ratio Disciplinae",[80] in giving an account of the "Discipline and Practice in the Churches of New England", decries the custom indulged in by careless ordaining councils in bringing unfit young men into the ministry, and states that a Boston Convention of Ministers has recommended that each candidate be examined in what "Authors in Theology he has read; and that he should particularly make it evident that he has considerately read, Ames his Medulla Theologiae: (Or, some other generally allowed Body of Divinity)."[81]

Prior to the establishment of the Professorship of Divinity in Yale College in 1755, the special training required of a prospective minister was obtained by the graduates of this institution in one of three ways. In his "Biographical Sketches of the Graduates of Yale College, with Annals of the College History",[82] Professor Franklin B. Dexter gives information, varying in completeness, concerning 321 clergymen who graduated from Yale College during the years 1702-1755.[83] Only seventeen of these 321 graduates, were ordained and began their ministry without further preparation than the college training which they had received in New Haven. Three hundred and four, or 94.7

---
80. Ratio Disciplinae Fratrum Nov-Anglorum; Boston, 1726, 210 pp.
81. Cotton Mather, op. cit., p. 117.
82. Six Volumes, 1702-1815. New York, Henry Holt and Company, 1885, 1896, 1903, 1907, 1911, 1912.
83. Vol. 1, passim, Vol. 2, 1746-1755.

per cent of the 321 graduates, are reported as having "studied divinity" subsequent to their college course. The amount of time spent in this study seems to be unknown in most cases, but according to the records, the time which elapsed between college graduation and the beginning of preaching averaged a little more than two years and seven months for each individual. Thirty-five, or 11.1 per cent of the 304 students who continued their studies after graduation, are reported as having done so as residents at Yale College.[84] The remainder, or 269 young men, pursued theological studies in the homes of resident ministers, twelve being tutored by their fathers. The graduates of Yale College who became clergymen, then, prepared for this profession by means of college training only, or enjoyed additional instruction as resident graduates, or studies in the homes of ministers.

1. College Training Only

Those who began their profession immediately after college graduation depended upon the course of study which

---

84. If all the facts were known the figure for those who studied as graduates at Yale College would probably be somewhat higher. The records of the attendance of the resident graduates appears to have been wholly neglected during these years. The lowly state of the school during its early years would tend to keep the attendance of graduates at a small figure. Also there seems to be no doubt but that in the majority of cases the young men preferred to study with some resident minister. Nathaniel W. Taylor writes (see p. 49 of this study) that in 1807 it was the fashion . . . to be licensed to preach in a few months or even weeks after graduation from college.

has been outlined above. And although in the first half century of the college, theology was favored, the course of study appears to have been in all its branches, unless logic be an exception, of a meagre nature. The preparation for admission was small, and the final examinations, before the receiving of the first degree, were given orally in the presence of the whole class.[85] It appears from the Laws reviewed above, that little more was done in Hebrew and Greek than to read the Psalter and a portion of the New Testament in the original tongues. Dr. Stiles, a graduate of the class of 1746, neglected the Hebrew since he did not intend to be a minister, and was able to take with him from college so little knowledge of that language, that at the age of forty-one, when a pastor at Newport, he began the study of the rudiments of it afresh under the tuition of Jewish rabbis whom he had befriended in that place.[86]

2. Theological Study with Resident Ministers

The great majority of the graduates, it has been seen, pursued further theological study with resident ministers. Those ministers who were connected with the rise of the "New Divinity", as the Edwardean theology, the system favored by the revival preachers was termed, became so popular, as private instructors of the young men who resorted to them,

---

85. The Diary of David McClure, with notes by F. B. Dexter, (1899) p. 18.
86. Abiel Holmes, Life of Ezra Stiles, (1789) pp. 128-131.

that their homes often took on the aspect of a small seminary. The modification of the traditional doctrine by this new school of theology awakened the curiosity of young men, and promoted discussion and inquiry. There was a new style of thinking and a new type of preaching; and this gave rise to a new form of instruction. Joseph Bellamy, one of the Edwardean group, graduated at the age of sixteen, and had begun to preach when he was only eighteen.[87] When he was thirty-one years of age, "his abilities, as a divine, became more conspicuous; and young gentlemen, who were preparing for the gospel ministry, applied to him as a teacher. He continued to be eminently useful, in this branch of his work, till the decline of life induced him to relinquish it."[88]

The course of study offered by Bellamy followed this plan:

> "After some conference, on religious subjects, with those who applied to him for instruction, by which he might learn their abilities, and cast of mind, he commonly gave them a number of questions, on the leading and most essential subjects of religion, both natural and revealed, in the form of a system. . . a long list of theological doctrines are given here . . . With a system of questions, similar to this, before his pupils, he directed their reading to such books on those leading topics as treat them with the greatest perspicuity and force of argument; and usually spent his evenings in examining into their improvements, solving difficulties which they had found. . . . After which, he directed them to write on each of the questions before given them, reviewing those parts of the authors which treated on those subjects. These dissertations

---

87. *Joseph Bellamy's Works*, published by Stephen Dodge, 1811, p. 31.
88. Ibid., pp. 33, 34.

of his pupils were submitted to his examination. He pointed out where their arguments were insufficient, and substituted others more suitable in their place. . . . he lead them to write on several of the most important points, systematically in the form of sermons. . . . discoursing occasionally on the various duties, trials, comforts, and motives of the evangelical work."(89

These theological instructors were all pastors, busy in their parishes and having the habit, customary with the group, of indulging in itinerate preaching. The effect of such a situation on the amount and quality of instruction obtained by the young men is illustrated in the case of Samuel Hopkins' term of study with Jonathan Edwards:

". . . . before he commenced preaching, he remained with his teacher less than four months, and it is known that during this period his teacher was often from home on missionary tours. . . .
After he had spent more than three additional months with Mr. Edwards. . . . Hopkins commenced a school in the village of Northampton, and at the same time prosecuted his studies, but at the end of four weeks was seized with a rheumatic affection, and was compelled to change his residence. Thus he spent a little more than eight months in the bosom of Mr. Edward's household, and in the enjoyment of his rich instructions". (90

3. Post-Graduate Study at Yale College

A third group of Yale College graduates of the years prior to the establishment of the Professorship of Divinity in 1755, remained at the College in order to gain further preparation for the ministry. There does not appear to have been any definite record as to their number, probably largely on account of the fact that their term of study was

---

89. Joseph Bellamy's Works, op. cit., pp. 34, 35.
90. Samuel Hopkins, Works (1852), with a Memoir of his life & Character, pp. 23, 24.

indefinite and the course of study no less so.[91] Following the example of Harvard College, provision was made in the statutes of Yale College for the instruction of resident graduates in theology. The earliest existent Laws of the College, those of 1718, ordain that "all undergraduates shall publickly repeat in the Hall Sermons in their courses, and also Bachelors."[92] The Laws of 1745,[93] which are the first to differ appreciably from those of 1718, state:

> "7. That all Resident Masters and Bachelors should constantly attend Prayers and Lectures or other Public Discourses in the Hall upon Penalty of having the Privilege of the library taken from them.
>
> 8. That all Resident Bachelors shall Dispute in the Hall under the President once a Week or Fortnight, as the President shall appoint upon Penalty Four Pence for every Neglect without Sufficient Reason.
>
> 9. The President may Order and Direct the Resident Bachelors, or Undergraduates to make Analysis in the Hall or any Other Scholastic Exercises upon Suitable Subjects for their Tryal and Exercise of their Skill and learning."

---

91. Professor Kingsley in his "History of Yale College", *Quarterly Register*, Vol. 8, (1836) page 207, says, "From the establishment of the professorship of Divinity in 1755, and probably from a much earlier time there had been generally at the college a class of resident graduates who were pursuing the study of theology." Professor George P. Fisher in his "Historical Address" given at the Semi-centennial of the Theological Department in Yale College, in 1872, quotes this statement of Professor Kingsley, and adds nothing further. Other historians of the School, including Chancellor Kent, President Woolsey, and Professor Dexter, either make a similar statement, or ignore the problem. The reason for these general statements or omission of statement is undoubtedly due to a lack of original sources in the form of College records.
92. Law No. 15.
93. MS., 28 pp.

The privilege afforded resident graduates appears, then, to have consisted in practice in debating and in the preaching of sermons, in attending public lectures, and in borrowing books from the College Library.

Naphtali Daggett as a Professor of Divinity

Beginning with the year 1755 the Yale undergraduates and resident graduates were accustomed to hear two sermons, preached each Sunday by Professor Daggett in the regular performance of his duties as Professor of Divinity. Professor Daggett was a native of Attleborough, Massachusetts. He was born September 8th, 1727; and was graduated from Yale College, winning the Dean Berkeley prize for scholarship, in 1748. The Rev. Mr. Jonathan Trumbull, a graduate of Yale College in 1759, writes in his History of Connecticut, that "the Professor was an instructive and excellent preacher; his sermons were enriched with ideas and sound divinity; were doctrinal, experimental, and pungent. He was acceptable to the legislature, clergy, and people in general." [94] Of sixty-nine of his original manuscript sermons, at present in the archives of Yale University, thirty-two are designated as having been preached in Yale College, most of them bearing dates signifying that they were preached on six different occasions, at

---

94. Vol. 2, p. 326.

about four year intervals. Although the collection is far from complete the addresses may be arranged into groups, each group having a common subject, and bearing consecutive dates, thus constituting a series of sermons.[95] Although he was installed as Professor of Divinity in the midst of bitter controversy concerning his own position and between the three theological parties existent at the time,[96] he avoided preaching on any controversial matters. He continued in his office for twenty-five years, until his death, which occurred after a short illness, on November 25, 1780.

In his Literary Diary President Stiles writes concerning Professor Daggett:

> "He has been Professor of Divinity in the College for 24 years, preached constantly in Chapel on Ldys, but never before delivered a Theological Lect. on a Weekday." (97

> "Considering vacations, he would be called to preach at College phps 40 Sabbaths a year at most; one quarter might be supplied by exchanges &c, so that 60 or 70 Sermons p. ann. would suffice. And 280 or 300, and especially 450 would be an ample Supply of the 4 years Revolution." (98

> "And from 1755 to his Death for 25 years he has officiated as Professor of Divinity or rather Minister of the College Church, for he usually preached only on Ldsdy & seldom lectured on week days." (99

Whatever aid the Professor of Divinity rendered resident

---

95. e.g., a series on one's relation to his neighbor, on "The Eternity of God", "The Omnipotence of God", "The Omnipresence of God".
96. See pp. 24, 25, 26.
97. Literary Diary, June 10, 1779.
98. Ibid., December 26, 1780.
99. Ibid., February 3, 1780.

graduates who were pursuing theological studies at the College must have been limited by this lack of regular weekday lectures, and a dependence upon Sunday sermons which were in danger of becoming less valuable through their continued repetition.

President Clap's Administration Concluded

President Clap grew more unpopular with students and people until "In the Spring of the Year [1766] the prejudices of the scholars ran to such a height that a petition to the Corporation for his dismissal was signed by all the classes. The Corporation met & the President resigned his Office"[100]. He died six months later, on January 7, 1767. President Stiles writes of him:[101]

> "Mr Clap tho no classical Scholar, was however of a stronger Mind than Mr Williams and surpassed him (as well as all the Presidents in Harv. Coll. & in all American Colleges) in Mathematics, Philosophy, and Astronomy. His reasoning powers were good and well improved. He had a singular Talent with little Reading of gaining great Knowledge, & became at length acquainted with almost every subject in the whole Circle of Literature. . . . He was not boisterous or noysy, but still quiet contemplative determined resolute firm immoveable - even to absolute Depotism. Not properly haughty, but sic volo sic jubeo was inwrot in his Make. This rendered the latter part of his Presidency uncomfortable. He was very strenuous for Orthodoxy: and had he been a Cardinal or a Pontiff he would have supported with the Inquisition and Arms: He was

---

100. Diary of David McClure, with notes by F. B. Dexter, p.9.
101. Literary Diary, May 24, 1779.

infatiquable in Labors both secular & scientific for the good of the College." (102

The Administration of Ezra Stiles 1777 - 1795

In October 1766 Professor Daggett was appointed President pro tempore, and continued in that office for over ten years, until April 3, 1777. On September 11 of that year the President and Fellows chose as President of the College the Rev. Ezra Stiles, who had been pastor of the Congregational Church in Newport, Rhode Island since 1755. He had graduated at Yale in 1746. At his request he was also elected Professor of Ecclesiastical History. It was his plan to give a four-year series of lectures on this topic; all classes were expected to attend them once each week.[103]

Almost from the beginning of his presidency the College suffered from the trials of the Revolutionary War. In his Literary Diary, under the date of November 6, 1777, President Stiles notes that the student attendance had fallen from 180 in 1776 to 125 in 1777. In 1779, December 16, he writes:

---

102. In his Miscellaneous Papers, (MS.) President Stiles writes concerning the Literary Character of President Clap, at length, pp. 292-306, paying him many compliments for which he claimed he had reason. He was President Clap's amanuensis, and was intimately acquainted with him for thirteen years. In a paper read before the New Haven Colony Historical Society, November 25, 1889, Professor F. B. Dexter pays President Clap many high tributes as a literary man, and as an administrator who did much for Yale College.
103. Literary Diary, November 8, 1781.

"Broke up College & dismissed the Students till the end of Winter Vacation viz. till Feb. 1, 1780. Necessitated to this because the Steward is unable to provide Commons with Continental Currency now in rapid Depreciation, having fallen near a quarter 3 weeks or a month past."

He writes in his diary under the date of June 24, 1779:

"Yesterday I put the Senior Class into President Clap's Ethics, or Moral Philosophy.[104] It was printed just before his death, and has been sometimes recited by the classes. Afterwards President Edwards on the will was recited; this giving offence was dropt.[105] And through the confusion of the times the Seniors have recited no ethics for several years."

One of the greatest disturbances of this period occurred when the British attacked and occupied the town of New Haven, on the 5th and 6th of July, 1779. Professor Daggett, in a fervent effort at aiding in the defense of the city, received wounds which hastened his death,[106] and incapacitated him for regular service during the remaining fourteen months of his life.

In March, 1781, President Stiles, in search of a Professor of Divinity, invited Rev. Samuel Wales, the minister

---

104. An Essay on the Nature and Foundation of Moral Virtue, and Obligation, New Haven, 1765, (Pam.) 68 pp. Its brevity is such that it probably required the class only two or three weeks to complete the study of it. In a letter to Dr. Greenough, May 28, 1765, MS. 2 pp., President Clap compliments his work by writing: "I think [it] contains the first Principles of True Religion, and so far as these Principles are received, Arminianism Will necessarily fall."
105. He does not state whether Edwards' work offended him, or the students. It may have been difficult for the scholars, but probably the professor suffered offense. He was at a disagreement with the theology of Edwards and his school. See pp. 394-418 in President Stiles' Miscellaneous Papers, Vol. 1, MS.
106. President Stiles gives a rather detailed account of the events of July 5 and 6, accompanied by a diagram and explanatory remarks; under the date of July 5, 1779.

of Milford, Connecticut, to preach in the College Chapel. Mr. Wales replied: "I had rather preach in almost any other place than the College Chapel, but in obedience to your request will engage to exchange with Mr. Atwater at the time proposed, extraordinaries excepted". [107] A letter accepting the Professorship was not written by Mr. Wales until May 15, 1782. [108] On June 12, he was installed in the office of Professor of Divinity and presented his "Confession of Faith" to the President and Fellows giving his "full & free assent to the Westminister Confession of Faith & to the Confession of Faith adopted by the Churches of this State, as containing the most essential and principle doctrines of Christianity." [109]

Twenty-six of his sermons, in the original manuscript form, are at present in the Yale University Library. An accompanying note, very evidently in his own hand, bears this notation: "Mostly systematically & mostly 3 times preached in the Chappel. Nov. - 91."

Samuel Wales was born in Raynham, near Taunton, Massachusetts, in March, 1747/8. Graduating at Yale College with the class of 1767, he taught in Dr. Wheelock's Indian School in Lebanon, and was a Dean Berkeley scholar and tutor at Yale during the term 1768-1769. In 1770 he had been ordained as pastor of the First Church in Milford,

----

107. Letter of April 2, 1718, in President Stiles Literary Diary, under April 4, 1781.
108. MS. 1 p.
109. MS. 7 pp.

Connecticut. On June 2, 1782, he gave his first "theological lecture" in the Chapel; on June 9, President Stiles writes that he "gave great satisfaction" as a preacher.[110] It may be gathered from frequent notations in his Diary to that effect, that President Stiles was much pleased with Professor Wales' efforts. Mr. Wales is described as intellectual and imposing in his personal appearance, as grave in his deportment, and as combining in his religious character a warm emotional spirit and a sincere devotion to sound principles. He belonged to the new school of ministers, which set a high value on literary culture, and hence possessed the graces of style that were missed in his predecessor, Mr. Daggett. President Stiles expressed the opinion[111] that if health permitted he would outrank "Mr. Dwight and Mr. Emmons as a preacher and theologian."[112] In the fall of 1783 he was first seized with a nervous disorder,[113] which continued upon him until his death.[114] From April to October, in the year 1786, he made a voyage to Europe for his health. Only temporary relief was attained by this rest and he grew steadily worse until he was kept from the pulpit the last two years of his life. On May 7, 1792, he relinquished part of his salary because of his in-

---

110. Literary Diary, June 2, 1782; June 9, 1782.
111. Ibid., August 11, 1787.
112. This opinion was probably influenced by his dislike of Messrs. Dwight and Emmons, see p. 45.
113. According to Dr. Stiles, Literary Diary, December 3, 1785, April 11 and 12, 1786, etc., Professor Wales suffered very severely and painfully from epileptic convulsions.
114. President Stiles, Literary Diary, February 21, 1794.

ability to serve his office, stating that these funds should be used to pay those who substituted during his frequent absences.[115] At the Commencement in September, 1793, he resigned his Professorship. During all this time of his disability his duties fell, for the most part, upon President Stiles.

Further responsibility had come to President Stiles, when Professor Nehemiah Strong, whose position had been precarious at this time because of his alleged "Loyalist's" sympathies,[116] resigned his Professorship of Mathematics and Natural Philosophy; and under date of January 2, 1782, President Stiles writes in his Literary Diary:

> "Professor Strong having resigned his Office, I read a public Lecture in the Chapel this afternoon upon Natural Philosophy. I purpose not constantly but frequently to fill the Chair of Math. & -- Nat. Philosophy."

This professorship was vacant for thirteen years, until within a few months of Dr. Stiles' death.[117]

President Stiles, therefore, in addition to his regular duties as administrator, and as instructor of the Senior Class, was called upon to bear the burden of the only two professorships in the school, and this during the trying days of the Revolution. Also it is apparent from the notations written in his Literary Diary for these years that

---

115. MS. 1 p.
116. President Stiles, Literary Diary, November 14, 1781.
117. In October 1794, Josiah Meigs, a graduate of Yale College in 1778, was chosen as Professor of Mathematics and Natural Philosophy. Minutes of the President and Fellows, October 7, 1794.

irregularity was the rule in respect to his Ecclesiastical Lectures, and even in regard to the functioning of the undergraduate courses. However, President Stiles seemed to be fitted for such trials since he differed from his predecessor, Mr. Clap, in that he had less of a dogmatic and dictatorial spirit,[118] and as a result his term suffered no disrupting theological controversies nor student rebellions.

There is evidence that President Stiles made some, though probably spasmodic attempts to aid resident graduates in their study of theological subjects. In 1732, he writes in his Literary Diary:

> "I attended a theological Exercise with Sir Atwater, Sir Channing and Sir Stebbins, Students in Divinity. They each read a Dissertation - the subject was the Evidences of Revelation, or the divine Inspiration of the Scriptures. Last Saturday it was, the Proof of the Existence or Being of a God. That appointed for next Saturday is the Doctrine of the Trinity. But I intend to devolve this upon Professor Wales."[119]

> "At IV P.M. I attended in the Library a theological Exercise with three Graduate Students in Divinity for two hours & a half. At Eveng prayer I expounded the Confession of Faith in the Chapel."[120]

---

118. In a letter to Bishop Whittlesey, written from Newport, March 6, 1770, (before he came to Yale, Stiles states that he felt that Mr. Clap's weakness was his theological dogmatism and says, "It is my opinion best to leave the Disputes about the new Divinity and the restricted Baptisms to be discussed chiefly among the Anti-Old Lights. Let them alone, they will settle it among themselves. Let Mr. Mills and Mr. Hopkins dispute it out, without interesting ourselves in a metaphysical Controversy so befogged, that it remains difficult, rather impossible to ascertain to the public, when the Victory is gained." Stiles Miscellaneous MS. Vol. 1, p. 394.
119. June 29.
120. July 6.

After serving Yale College for eighteen years in the capacities noted above, President Stiles died May 12, 1795, being sixty-eight years of age.

The Administration of Timothy Dwight
1795 - 1817

When Mr. Stiles had been elected President of Yale College by the Corporation in 1777, some of that group had voted in favor of Mr. Timothy Dwight, at that time a youthful tutor in the College.[121] In the meantime Dwight had gained a high place as a leader in ecclesiastical affairs in Connecticut, and cultivated not only an extensive acquaintance and intercourse with the Congregational Clergy of New England, but with "many in the Presbyterian Church in New York and the States farther south."[122] The Rev. Mr. Dwight was inaugurated as President of Yale College in September, 1795.

At the time of his accession to the presidency infidelity was fashionable and prevalent in the College. Forensic disputation was an important exercise of the Senior class,[123] and the young men had not been allowed to discuss controversial questions, e.g., the inspiration of the Scriptures. President Dwight encouraged free discussion on any problem

---

121. President Stiles, Literary Diary, November 20, 1777.
122. Theology Explained and Defended in a Series of Sermons, by Timothy Dwight, with a Memoir of the Life of the Author, (written by his sons) (1818-19) p. xxi.
123. Laws of Yale College, 1795, Chapter III.

chosen by the students, and by this gesture and his own forcefulness of personality and pungency of argument won the young men to the Christian viewpoint. He also greatly aided the development of more respect for religion by abolishing pecuniary fines, which were administered for failure to attend meetings in the College Chapel.

With the coming of Timothy Dwight to the presidency of Yale College, the "New Divinity", as the group following Jonathan Edwards' theology was termed, gained the ascendancy in Connecticut. This was the group which President Clap opposed during his term of office,[124] and the system of theology which President Stiles held in derision.[125] Indeed, some looked upon Dwight's coming to the presidency with alarm. The writer of a pamphlet entitled, "A View of the New England Illuminati",[126] asserts that:

> "Birth, education, elevation, and connections have placed Doctor Dwight at the head of the .... Illuminati. Active, persevering, and undaunted, he proceeds to direct all political, civil, and ecclesiastical affairs. Science, he forsakes, and her institutions he prostrates, to promote party, bigotry, and error. ... He is seeking to establish the Edwardean system of doctrines and discipline, from the pride of his grandfather's (President Edwards) talents and fame; while few indeed of the deceased gentleman's descendants believe in his tenets."

---

124. See pp. 26, 27.
125. Stiles, Miscellaneous MS., Vol. 1, pp. 394-418.
126. p. 17, The full title is: A View of the New England Illuminati: who are Infatigably engaged In Destroying the Religion and Government of the United States; under a feigned regard for their Safety, - and under an Impious abuse of True Religion. The author derisively names this group of men after the Illuminati Societies of Europe.

In September 1793, the Corporation having perceived that the Rev. Samuel Wales would never be able to resume his duties as Professor of Divinity, elected Dr. Lathrop of West Springfield, Massachusetts, to the office.[127] He declined the call. After the accession of Dr. Dwight to the presidency, several attempts were made, without success, to fill the vacancy. The duties of the place continued to be discharged by the President, at the request of the Corporation, annually repeated, until the year 1805, when he consented to take the Professorship of Divinity, in connection with the office which he had first chosen. Previous to this time, he had preached on Sunday mornings, from brief notes, the sermons comprising his theological system. These he now wrote out and delivered to successive generations of students in four-year cycles, until the end of his life. These sermons constituted his "System of Theology", and were printed under the title: "Theology, Explained and Defended, in a Series of Sermons".[128] President Dwight was in the direct line of that group of divines, including Jonathan Edwards, Samuel Hopkins, Joseph Bellamy, Nathaniel Emmons, Stephen West, Nathaniel W. Taylor, and E. A. Park, who were responsible for the rise and progress of the "New England Theology", probably the

---

127. Stiles, Literary Diary, September 12, 1793.
128. Timothy Dwight, op. cit., On pp. xxvi, xxvii, the editor of the works states: "In the prosecution of his duties as Professor of Divinity, he early began to deliver the lectures in these volumes."

most indigenous influential system of theology in American Church History.[129]   Concerning his interest in post-graduate study in theological education, his amanuensis, Nathaniel W. Taylor, wrote in a letter to William B. Sprague:[130]

> "He always advised and even urged young men, - when the fashion was to be licensed to preach in a few months, or even weeks, after they were graduated, to remain and study Theology, at least one or two years. It was in compliance with his counsel that I did so, though it was a thing nearly or quite unprecedented, and though my classmates and even ministers, regarded it as time and labour little better than lost. But Dr. Dwight in his views of this subject was greatly in advance of most of his contemporaries. To him I think is preëminently to be traced the great progress of theological education, especially in New England, for the last thirty or forty years."

Dr. Dwight was an Honorary member of the Massachusetts Historical Society, of the New York Historical Society, and of the American Antiquarian Society. He was a Visitor of the Theological Seminary at Andover, Massachusetts; President of the Connecticut Academy of Arts and Sciences, of the Connecticut Religious Tract Society, of the Foreign Mission Society of New Haven County.[131]

President Dwight died January 11, 1817. Although he did not live to see his hopes and plans for an expansion of theological instruction at Yale College fulfilled, by sheer force of personality and greatness of character, he did

---

129. See Chapter X of this study.
130. February 20, 1844; printed in Mr. Sprague's Annals of the American Pulpit, Vol. 2, p. 161, 162.
131. Calvin Chapin, A Sermon at the Funeral of the Rev. Timothy Dwight, footnote No. 1, p. 35.

much to produce such men as Moses Stuart, Lyman Beecher, and Nathaniel W. Taylor.

With the appointment of Professor Jeremiah Day to the Presidency, and the election of Rev. Eleazer Thompson Fitch as Professor of Divinity, began a new epoch in the history of Yale College, in which the Theological Department of that school had a part.

CHAPTER II

THE ESTABLISHMENT OF THE THEOLOGICAL
DEPARTMENT IN YALE COLLEGE

THE ESTABLISHMENT OF THE THEOLOGICAL DEPARTMENT IN YALE COLLEGE

Demands of Students and Faculty for a Theological Department

In the year 1822, fifteen young men, most of whom were to graduate from Yale College in that year, petitioned the Faculty that they might be organized into a theological class.[1] This request was recognized and supported in a statement[2] submitted to the Prudential Committee,[3] by the Professor of Divinity in Yale College, Eleazer Thompson Fitch. He pointed out that in accordance with the laws of the college it was his duty to attend to the instruction which has been requested of him in this application. "His chief embarrassment in the discharge of this duty, has arisen from the present advanced state of theological

---

1. Resolution of the Faculty of Yale College to the Corporation, 1822, MS., p. 1.
2. A Statement Submitted to the Prudential Committee by the Professor of Divinity in Yale College April 23, 1822. The original MS. seems to have been lost. The copy used here is bound, with other documents of an official nature, in a volume bearing the name of Mary C. L. Fitch, the wife of Prof. Fitch, upon its flyleaf. It bears an attestation, by Professor George E. Day, as to its genuineness. W. C. Fowler, Origin of the Theological School of Yale College, Hartford, 1869. 26 pp. (Pam.)
3. The following gentlemen constituted the Prudential Committee: President Jeremiah Day, Rev. John Elliott, Rev. Calvin Chapin, Hon. David Tomlinson.

instruction."[4] "Another embarrassment arises from the state of his health."[5] His present duties as College pastor and preacher are all he can bear, so he cannot be expected to instruct in the several branches of theology. So pressing is the situation that,

> "The question which arises on this statement, & wh. he respectfully submits to the Committee is the following: Shall exertions be made to add a new professor to the college who shall take a part in the education of theological students, & the duties of the Chapel; or shall the education of students in theology be wholly discarded from the college?"[6]

Against the adoption of the later alternative, he argued from the history of the college, "its primitive design", from all it had accomplished in the work of educating ministers. It seemed to him to be unbelievable that they could "wholly discard a theological department so clearly intended by the founders to be the chief pillar and ornament of the college".[7]

He further pointed out that "the support of a theological department interferes not with existing theological

----

4. The Professorship of Divinity had been established in 1755, and, as was evident from the review of the provisions for theological education given in Chapter I of this study, no additional facilities for such education had been developed in Yale College since that date.
5. E. T. Fitch, op. cit., p. 18.
6. Ibid., p. 19.
7. Ibid., p. 22.

institutions"[8], not in regard to any claim of precedence which these schools might have upon public patronage, since training for the ministry was "the most precious branch of instruction in the estimation of the founders." Nor, in regard to the number of scholars, would there be interference with other schools, since statistics concerning the ministerial students in the colleges of New England revealed that a larger group were anticipating theological education than could obtain such training in the existent seminaries. He further stated that the facilities obtainable at Yale College were capable of supporting a theological department, and that such a department would be advantageous to the college and to the community.[9]

The students' Petition to the Faculty and Professor Fitch's Statement to the Prudential Committee were supported by a Resolution of the College Faculty addressed to the Yale Corporation.[10] This group of professors included, besides President Day and Professor Fitch, Professors James L. Kingsley, Benjamin Silliman, and Chauncey A. Goodrich. They responded to the proposition in much the same spirit as that evidenced by Professor Fitch. They pointed out that it was "inconsistent with the dignity of the College and the interests of the Church to attempt to sustain a system of instruction in theology which cannot but prove inadequate

---

8. E. T. Fitch, op. cit., p. 23.
9. Ibid., p. 18.
10. MS. 6 pp.

to the increasing demands of the public."[11] The needs of the New West, the increased number of theological students in the colleges of New England, and the crowded condition of the seminaries, were reviewed.[12] Their sincerity in the matter is best shown in the freedom with which they offer their own services:

> "On deliberate consideration the Faculty have found that this object can be attained only by the additional services of a Professor devoted to the Theological Class; to be aided in the Department of Hebrew criticism, by the Professor of Languages; In Sacred Rhetoric by the Professor of Rhetoric and Oratory; and in Greek Criticism and Systematic Theology by the Professor of Divinity.[13]

Major Factors Which Precipitated a Need For a Theological Department in Yale College

A crisis, then, seems to have arisen in regard to theological instruction at Yale College. This state of affairs appears to have been influenced by certain major factors:

1. Secularization of the Yale College Curriculum

Gradually with the progress of knowledge, and in accordance with the demands of the times, studies other than theology were added to the college curriculum, placing this study in a less prominent position. The course of study

---

11. Resolution of the Faculty of Yale College, op. cit., p. 2.
12. Ibid., p. 5.
13. Ibid., p. 3.

offered, first in the Collegiate School in Connecticut, and afterward in its successor, Yale College, during the years 1701-1745, remained almost entirely static.[14] But when Rev. Thomas Clap assumed the presidency, since he stood high in his day for attainments in mathematical sciences,[15] it was natural that he should give an impulse to these branches of study. Such appears to have been the case if we may rely on his account of the matter in his history written in 1766, the year of his resignation. He writes in the appendix to that work:[16]

> "In their first year they learn Hebrew, & principally pursueth study of the languages, & make a Beginning in Logick, & some parts of Mathematicks. In the second year, they study the Languages, but principally recite logick, Rhetorick, Oratory, Geography, & Natural Philosophy: and most branches of Mathematicks: Many of them well understood Surveying, Navigation, and the Calculation of Eclipses; and some of them are considered Proficient in Conic Sections & Fluxions. In the Fourth year they principally study & recite Metaphysicks, Ethicks, & Divinity.[17] . . .
> . . . . The President frequently makes public dissertation upon every subject necessary to be understood to qualify young gentlemen for (the) various stations and employments (of civil life,) such as the nature of civil government, the civil Constitution of Great Britain, the various kinds of courts.[18]

A comparison of the laws of 1728 with this account[19]

---

14. See p. 18.
15. See p. 39.
16. Annals of Yale College; the Appendix is entitled, "The Present State of the College; Method of Instruction & Government, etc."
17. Ibid., pp. 80, 81.
18. Ibid., p. 82.
19. See pp. 16, 17.

reveals that mathematics has come to occupy some of the space, which was given at first to logic.

Prior to the Revolution, the English Language and Literature was almost wholly ignored.[20] Latin was kept up as the linguistic medium in rendering excuses for absences, in syllogistic disputes, and in much of the intercourse between officers and students.[21] In 1776 the Seniors petitioned that Mr. Timothy Dwight--then Tutor--might instruct them in rhetoric, history and belles lettres. Dr. Dwight wrote poetry and endeavored to instil in his students a love for their mother tongue.[22]

During his presidency, Dr. Ezra Stiles received a letter from Mr. Silas Deane in which the latter decried the omission of the study of modern languages in the colleges in America and in Europe and offered to solicit for funds in France for a Professorship of the French language in Yale College.[23] President Stiles consulted the influential men of his acquaintance concerning the matter, and although some feared that the introduction of this language might be a means whereby French infidelity would enter the College, the majority favored the plan.[24] However, there is no record

---

20. The Catalogue of the Library of Yale College, 1742-43, lists 2600 volumes, with only 2 titles on English Grammar. MS.
21. Laws of the Collegiate School in Connecticut and of Yale College, 1718-1745. MS.
22. The Conquest of Canaan, an Epic Poem was finished, when he was twenty-two years of age, in eight books. It was enlarged and published in 1785 in eleven books. It was reprinted in London in 1788. In 1794 he published a poem in seven parts - "Greenfield Hill".
23. Stiles, Literary Diary, August 21, 1778; Mr. Deane's letter is given in full under the date of July 29, 1778.
24. Literary Diary, August 22, August 24, and September 30, 1778.

that definite steps were made to take advantage of Mr. Deane's offer.

The progressive spirit of Dr. Dwight, evidence of which was given in his leadership in the introduction of an appreciation of the English language into the curriculum, combined with more settled conditions and a returning prosperity, made his administration one in which the course of study was greatly expanded.

In the year 1789, a small sum was given by the Rev. Dr. Salter, of Mansfield, Connecticut, for the encouragement of oriental literature, which had, contrary perhaps to present popular opinion concerning the course of study in that day, been grossly neglected during the preceding years.[25] Mr. Ebenezer Grant Marsh was appointed instructor in this branch of study. In 1801, the corporation voted to institute a professorship of law. It was not their design to furnish undergraduates such instruction in this department as might qualify them for the bar--a plan wholly inconsistent with the requisite attention to the other branches of the collegiate course--but to give occasional lectures on the several provinces of legal study.[26]

The new branches of natural science were introduced, when in September, 1802, the corporation voted that such a

---

25. The meagreness of the instruction in Hebrew has been noted above, see p. 33. An examination of the Laws of the institution reveals that before 1789 the reading in Greek was limited to that of the New Testament. Other oriental languages are not mentioned.
26. J. L. Kingsley, "A Sketch of the History of Yale College," Quarterly Register Vol. 8, (1836) p. 202.

professorship should be instituted; and Mr. Benjamin Silliman, at that time a tutor of the college, was elected professor of "chemistry & natural history". Professor Silliman served the college for fifty years, and was a pioneer in his field.[27] Another step was taken in the direction of professional education, when, in 1806, the Corporation took measures to establish a course of medical lectures.[28] In October, 1810, an act was passed by the Connecticut Legislature regulating the joint action of the Medical Society and the Corporation of Yale College in establishing and conducting a medical school. In 1813, under four newly elected professors,[29] the lectures commenced "under very favorable auspices";[30] and the legislature, in May, 1814, made a grant to the institution of thirty thousand dollars, to aid in effecting its objects.

Among the other improvements in the condition of the college, undertaken at the same period, was the enlargement of the library and of the philosophical and chemical apparatus. Another new professorship was established, in September, 1817, when the Corporation elected the Rev.

---

27. T. D. Woolsey, *Discourse Commemorative of Benjamin Silliman*, (1864) p. 23.
28. The first plan whereby provisions for professional education would be given in Yale College seems to have been formulated by President Stiles in 1777. See his diary under date of December 3, 1777.
29. The medical professors, and the chairs to which they were appointed at this time were: Aeneas Munson, Professor of Materia Medica and Botany; Eli Ives, Adjunct Professor in the same department; Nathan Smith, Professor of the Theory and Practice of Physic, Surgery, and Obstetrics; and Jonathan Knight, Professor of Anatomy.
30. J. L. Kingsley, *op. cit.*, p. 20.

Chauncey A. Goodrich, who had been tutor in the college, Professor of Rhetoric and Oratory.[31]

2. Revival of Thought and Life in the Churches

A second influence favorable to the establishment of theological seminaries, particularly the one at Yale College, was the awakening of the churches to a new life beginning about 1734. The low state to which religion had fallen prior to the preaching of Jonathan Edwards upon "Justification by Faith" in Northampton, in this year, and the leadership afforded by him and his followers in the revival of religious life has been noted above. The rise of the "New England Theology" which constituted a revival of religious thought and acted as a doctrinal basis for the new style of preaching, has also been briefly reviewed.[32] The leaders of these concomitant movements, prior to the year 1822, were Jonathan Edwards and his two immediate friends Joseph Bellamy and Samuel Hopkins; and the later representatives of the same impulse, Stephen West, John Smalley, Jonathan Edwards the Younger, Nathaniel Emmons, and Timothy Dwight. Seven out of eight of these men were graduates of Yale College, the exception, Jonathan Edwards the Younger, being educated at Princeton College probably because his father had been made President of that institution shortly before his death. Timothy Dwight was the only one of the

----

31. Minutes of the President and Fellows of Yale College. MS.
32. See pp. 33, 34.

group who was born outside of Connecticut, and he became the president of Yale College. The work of these men influenced theological education in two ways. First, as independent thinkers, they engaged in several controversies with opposing parties. Jonathan Edwards was active in attacking the Arminians on the one hand and defending his new views from the ultra-conservative Calvinists on the other. His two friends, Bellamy and Hopkins, took up the task of extending and developing the new views of truth which he had more suggested than formulated. Before Hopkins had ceased his labors, the controversy with the original Universalists, in which the younger Jonathan Edwards was the leader, was in full course. Then came, with the beginning of the nineteenth century, the Unitarian controversy, with its attendant development of an anthropological emphasis in theology. Such an atmosphere of controversy stimulated theological study, discussion, and debate. Each minister was expected to have definite opinions and reasons therefor. Leaders felt the need of a school of some sort to insure the dissemination of the "true doctrine". The manner in which young men flocked to the homes of these theologians, and the impetus which this school of doctrine gave to a renewed interest in theological education, and the part which they played in the training of the graduates of Yale College has been noted above.[33]

In the second place the revival movement under the

---

33. See pp. 33, 34, 35.

leadership of these men was directly responsible for a great increase in the membership of the church, and in the number of young men devoting themselves to the ministry, and for the expansion of religious work in general. In the Resolution[34] petitioning the Corporation that a Theological Department be organized, the Faculty of Yale College declared that there were three hundred students in the colleges of New England who were desirous of theological training, and that they had so increased that the existent seminaries could not care for them.[35] The appeal of the Corporation[36] for funds for the establishment of such a department estimated the figure at four hundred and stated that one hundred such students were graduating from the colleges each year.[37]

3. "The Appeal of the West"

An additional demand was made upon the Churches of New England with the opening of the Mississippi Valley after the Louisiana Purchase in 1803. The manner in which the Faculty of Yale College sensed the "Appeal of the West" is indicated in their resoultion to the Corporation, in 1822, reviewed above, requesting that a Theological Department be established in the College:

---

34. MS. 6 pp.
35. Resolution, op. cit., p. 6.
36. The Present Situation of Yale College, June, 1822, MS. 12 pp. Probably written by President Day.
37. Ibid., p. 6.

"The period at which we are called to this decision is one of peculiar interest. A large portion of the United States, rapidly advancing in population and wealth, are destitute of a regularly educated ministry. To Christians of the present age is committed the momentous decision, what character shall be impressed on those using institutions and habits which will decide the future destiny of millions. Shall ignorance, vice and fanaticism overspread the most fertile and extensive part of our Country, or the pure gospel of Christ with its innumerable blessings be transmitted to remote generations? This question is pressed with peculiar urgency on the Churches of New England. Among us the Spirit of God is raising up great numbers of young men who may be called forth and prepared for the ministry of reconciliation. Among us are most of the colleges of the United States - the means of education are at hand - multitudes of pious youth are offering themselves to the service of the Lord, while hundreds of infant churches in our Western Settlements demand their aid. (38

4. Rapid Development of Professional Schools

The first twenty years of the nineteenth century constitute a period in which professional schools grew apace, and it was particularly marked by the establishment of theological seminaries. The first American law school was founded at Litchfield, Connecticut in 1784 and discontinued in 1833. A course of lectures in law was delivered in the College of Philadelphia in 1791 by James Wilson, but his work was discontinued before the close of the second course. In 1797 James Kent made a similar attempt at Columbia, but he gave only one course of lectures. The Harvard Law School, established in 1817, was the earliest school in the country

---

38. Resolution, op. cit., pp. 3,4.

connected with a university and authorized to confer degrees in law. The Yale Law School was established in 1824.

At the time of the American Revolution, in a population of 3,000,000, there were probably about 3500 physicians in the colonies, of whom it is estimated that not more than 400 had received medical degrees. In New England the clergyman was often the only available physician. Two medical schools were organized in the colonies, the Medical College of Philadelphia in 1765, and the medical department of King's College, in 1768. Harvard Medical School was organized in 1782, and Dartmouth Medical College in 1797. Twelve medical schools were established between the years 1801 and 1825.[39]

Meanwhile the provisions for the professional education of ministers were greatly increased by the establishment of separate schools of theology. In 1721 the Hollis Professorship of Divinity at Harvard College had been established[40] with Rev. Edward Wigglesworth as its first incumbent. The control of this chair and that of mathematics, as well as the presidency, was the subject of contention between the high Calvinists and the more liberal group in Eastern Massachusetts throughout the eighteenth century, with the latter gradually becoming more powerful. This chief position of theological influence in Massachusetts became vacant again in 1803, and was filled in 1805, after a sharp contest,

---

39. Professional Education in the United States, prepared by Henry L. Taylor and James K. Parsons, edited for the Paris Exposition 1900, Vol. I, p. 350.
40. Benjamin Pierce, History of Harvard University, (1833) pp. 96-100.

by the appointment of Rev. Henry Ware. It was generally understood, and soon became certain, that he was a Unitarian. It was, therefore, felt that Harvard would no longer be a suitable place for the education of orthodox ministers. It had also been the desire of the Hopkinsian group that a seminary should be established for the propagation of their views. Accordingly the "Old Calvinists" and the Hopkinsians united in the founding of Andover Theological Seminary at Andover, Massachusetts, in 1808.[41] The Harvard Professorship of Divinity was enlarged into a Theological School in 1816.[42] In view of President Dwight's connection with its establishment,[43] and the importance of the school to New England Congregationalism, the founding of Andover Seminary was probably of greatest influence in the beginnings of provisions for theological study at Yale College.

But Andover was not the first separate theological school. The Dutch Reformed Church established the first separate seminary in America at Flatbush, Long Island, New York, in 1774.[44] In 1812 the Presbyterian Church in the United States of America, after two or three years of study of the needs, organized at Princeton, New Jersey, its first

---

41. Memorial of the Semi-Centennial Celebration of the Founding of the Theological Seminary at Andover, (1859, Pam.) pp. 70-84.
42. Addresses delivered at the Observance of the 100th Anniversary of the Establishment of the Harvard Divinity School, (1917, Pam.) pp. 8-12.
43. See pp. 67-69.
44. "Historical Discourse", Centennial of the Theological Seminary of the Reformed Church in America, (1885, Pam.)

school for ministers.[45] On February 25, 1814, a Charter was granted by the Legislature of Maine for the incorporation of the "Maine Charity School",[46] which institution very soon took the name of "Bangor Theological Seminary". It was the second separate theological school organized by New England Congregationalists. The first Lutheran Seminary in the United States was established as Hartwick Seminary in Ostego County, New York, April 17, 1816.[47] In 1817 the General Convention of the Protestant Episcopal Church in the United States established the General Theological Seminary in New York where instruction was first given in 1819.[48] The Seminary was removed to New Haven in 1820 but was reopened in New York in 1822. The Baptist Theological Seminary, State of New York, was established by the act of the Legislature on April 15, 1817.[49] On August 16, 1818, the Synod of Geneva, New York, voted to found Auburn Theological Seminary,[50] and this Presbyterian school received its first students October 11, 1821.

Of the nine theological seminaries which were established between the years 1800 and 1822, and lived until the end of

---

45. Extracts of the Minutes of the General Assembly, printed in the Centennial Celebration of Princeton Seminary, (1912) pp. 1-8.
46. C. M. Clark, History of Bangor Theological Seminary, Original Charter reprinted, (1916) pp. 21-23.
47. Memorial Volume of Hartwick Semi-centennial Anniversary, (1867), pp. 175-181.
48. Plan of the Theological Seminary of the Protestant Episcopal Church of the United States, (1820) pp. 5-7.
49. Constitution of the Baptist Theological Seminary, New York, (1818) p. 6.
50. John Quincy Adams, History of Auburn Theological Seminary, (1918) p. 43.

the century, the founding of the six reviewed above was influential for the beginnings of provisions for study in divinity at Yale College, on account of the denominational kinship or geographical proximity of these schools.

5. Dissatisfaction with Contemporary Methods of Theological Education

Growing out of the above influences there seems to have been an increasing realization, on the part of those connected with Yale College, faculty and students, that the old methods of theological instruction by a resident pastor, or by a Professor of Divinity, were wholly inadequate for the contemporary religious needs. To President Dwight, whose successful efforts in the substantial enlargement of the college curriculum has been noted, probably belongs the credit for suggesting and recommending the expansion of the provisions for theological instruction in Yale College.

In a letter, sent to Dr. William B. Sprague,[51] Rev. Nathaniel W. Taylor wrote concerning President Dwight:

> "When I was his amanuensis, he told me that he had long had it in his heart to extend the means of a thorough preparation for the ministry in this College; that in consequence of his wishes on this subject, his eldest son, Timothy Dwight, Esq., of this city, had then appropriated a certain stock in trade, with its profits, to the establishment of a Professorship of Theology in the College. It was this which resulted in the present extended theological department. I think he did much, though I cannot say how much, in

---

51. February 20, 1844, printed in Sprague's *Annals of the American Pulpit*, (1857) Vol. 1, pp. 161-164.

getting up the institution at Andover. I remember well that I was with him when the project was started. Doctors Morse and Spring came from Massachusetts to consult him on this subject, when the first donations were offered for the purpose. I heard much of their conversation with him. He entered into the subject with the deepest interest, unfolding his views of the advantages and necessity of such an institution; and seemed to exult as an eye witness of its great and blessed results. The gentlemen were evidently greatly influenced by his views in their determination to go forward with the enterprise. I remember his stating to them his own plans in regard to extending the means of theological education in this College; and particularly of his saying that, should the time come when this should be done, and the graduates of Yale should be induced to pursue theological study here, it must not be considered as interfering with their undertaking."

In his sermon, at the opening of the Theological Institution at Andover, September 28, 1808,[52] possibly preached in answer to the complimentary request of the above gentlemen, President Dwight reviews the grave dangers, to religion and to the state, which arise from an ignorant ministry. He congratulates the founders of the proposed seminary in that professors will be established in "the five great divisions of theological education: Natural Theology, Christian Theology, Sacred Literature, Ecclesiastical History, and the Eloquence of the Desk."[53] He continued by saying:

"It is hardly necessary for me to observe, that each of these branches is sufficiently extended, and various, to demand, and to exhaust, the utmost talents of a single man; or that the instruction in each, which will be highly profitable to students in Theology, may advantageously employ the whole time, and labours, of the most learned Professor.

---

52. A Sermon Preached at the establishment of the Theological Institution at Andover. Boston, 1808. 38 pp.
53. Timothy Dwight, op. cit., p. 11.

In this country, hitherto, such students, after having completed a regular course of Collegiate education, have generally, and necessarily been placed under the tutelage of parochial Ministers. An individual, in this case has furnished all their professional instruction; and that while encumbered by the superintendance of a parish, and the labour of writing, and preaching, two sermons in a week. Of this subject I speak with confidence, because I speak from experience; and cannot but have learned, in this way, the embarrassments, inseperable from a course of instruction, so interwoven with other perplexing concerns. Were an Instructor ever so competent: it would be impossible for him to communicate the knowledge which ought to be considered indispensible.(54

President Dwight was elected as one of the members of the Board of Visitors at Andover Seminary,[55] which body was responsible for the management of the institution. He served in this capacity during the remainder of his life.

It appears that a demand by students for a more extended opportunity for the study of theology at Yale College took definite form four years before the establishment of the Theological Department in the year 1822. Mr. W. C. Fowler, who had graduated from Yale College in 1816, writes

---

54. Timothy Dwight, op. cit., pp. 11, 12.
55. The Constitution and Associate Statutes of the Theological Seminary in Andover, (1808) p. 59.

about 1869,[56] of his coming to New Haven, in the spring of 1817, in order "to make plans to enter Andover Seminary." He accidentally met Samuel B. Ingersoll, who persuaded him to join him in an interview with Professor Fitch, the Professor of Divinity, concerning the possibility of their studying theology under his tutelage. Professor Fitch was pleased at their request and granted it. After the Commencement of the second term the students requested one of the tutors to invite Professor Kingsley to give instruction in Hebrew. He complied with their request. Some

---

56. Origin of the Theological School of Yale College, 26 pp.
    The title is ambitious--the Theological Department was not originated with the events recounted by Mr. Fowler. Suspicion is also thrown upon this source by the essayist's style and the apparent braggadocio air of an elderly man priding himself at having been a pioneer in the establishment of an institution. No other independent source telling of the existence of a "school" has been discovered. However, there appears to be evidence that the account is true, at least in general. The facts given by him do not conflict with those found in catalogues and histories of Yale College. Mr. Fowler's work, used as a source in this study, is in the form of a pamphlet bound with books of an official character in a volume bearing the name of Mrs. C. L. Fitch, the wife of Professor Fitch, upon the flyleaf.
    The account of Mr. Fowler's life given in "Biographical Sketches of the Class of 1816" contains the following: "After his graduation he taught a family school one year in Farquier County, Virginia, was Rector of Hopkins Grammar School in New Haven one year; was Tutor in Yale College nearly five years; was appointed by the Connecticut Alpha of Phi Beta Kappa Society orator for 1823; studied theology in New Haven under Professor Fitch; was ordained in the ministry August 31, 1825, in Greenfield, Mass., where he remained two years; was eleven years Professor of Chemistry and Natural History in Middlebury College; was five years Professor of Rhetoric in Amherst College. . . . In 1845 editor of the "University edition of Webster's Dictionary"; author of three volumes composing "Fowler's Series of English Grammar", the first being entitled, "The English Language in its Elements and Forms".

months later Mr. Fowler was delegated by his fellows to invite Professor Goodrich to tutor them in elocution and in the composition of sermons. Mr. Fowler was, at that time, rector of the Hopkins Grammar School, situated on the corner of Temple and Crown Streets, and invited the group to meet in that school. By the year 1818 their numbers had increased to twelve, they were enjoying the teaching of three great professors, and had a regular place of meeting. Mr. Fowler states [57] that the class was particularly interested in taking up with Professor Fitch the science of Biblical Criticism, or Exegesis, [58] "a term that was beginning to be current". The idea that the language of the Bible was to be interpreted as any foreign language was a new and fascinating one. Three of them also struggled together in the translating of a German work on Biblical Criticism. Mr. Fowler remarks [59] that the clergy of New Haven and neighboring districts were much interested in their enterprise and encouraged it.

Since Mr. Fowler was a Tutor in Yale College he may have been quite influential in the circulating of the petition, mentioned above, for a theological class, composed, for the most part, of the graduates of the class of 1822.

These factors, then, were influential in bringing about

---

57. W. C. Fowler, op. cit., p. 3.
58. This "Exegesis", which is also called "Biblical Criticism", was of a grammatical nature, sometimes accompanied by a bit of textual criticism.
59. W. C. Fowler, op. cit., pp. 8, 9.

the series of events happening in the year 1822 which resulted in the petitions for the establishment of the Theological Department of Yale College.

Events of the Year 1822 Resulting in the Establishment of a Theological Department

Taking cognizance of the students' Petition to the faculty, Professor Fitch's Statement to the Prudential Committee of the President and Fellows, and the Resolution of the Faculty addressed to the President and Fellows as a group, this last body proceeded to attempt to raise funds for the establishment of a Theological Department in Yale College. Only very recently, on May 7, 1822, this body had, in making its annual report to the General Assembly of the State of Connecticut, requested financial aid.[60] In this "Memorial" the Corporation compares the condition of Yale College with similar institutions in the country, and states that "Cambridge University in Massachusetts,.... has an annual income, (including the amount paid for tuition by the students) of more than 45,000 dollars; a sum nearly equal to our whole productive capital".[61] A treatise upon the advantages of the College to the State follows. The Report of the Committee of the General Assembly concerning this request,

---

60. To the Honorable the General Assembly of the State of Connecticut, now in session in New Haven. The Memorial and Statement of the President and Fellows of Yale College. 7 pp.
61. Ibid., pp. 3,4.

after reviewing the financial needs of the school (which it seems to recognize as being of large proportions) concluded by recommending to the Legislature "that at present it would be inexpedient to make the grant desired."[62]

Having failed in obtaining funds from the General Assembly, the appeal for financial aid was made to the people, particularly those friends of the College residing in New Haven. In this document[63] much is made of the financial returns gained from the presence of the College in the city, and of the additional monetary value which would result from the establishment of another department. It was pointed out that "the <u>ordinary</u> expenses of the College have exceeded its whole income during the last five years; by the sum of $450. each year, accumulating a debt of $1800 against the remaining fund.[64] The dangers to religion, to the State, and to the city, if the College should decline are enumerated. There is an appeal for two definite needs: the establishment of a Theological Department, and the enlargement of the Library. In regard to the former it was affirmed that the Theological Department of Yale College could expect a goodly portion of the one hundred ministerial candidates graduating each year from the colleges of New England, and that the applications already made to Yale

---

62. <u>The Report of the Committee to whom was referred the Petition of the President and Fellows of Yale College</u>, 3pp.
63. <u>Statement of the Present Situation of Yale College</u>, June, 1822, MS., 12 pp. Probably written by President Day.
64. <u>Ibid</u>., p. 1.

College are numerous and pressing.[65] A fund of $20,000 was declared "indispensable" for the establishment of an additional Professorship in Theology.[66]

The subscriptions appear to have been given rapidly, for, following the last word of this Appeal is the statement: "Subscriptions have been secured from the following persons. . . .", beneath which statement is written the signatures and amounts of the donors, with names of the Faculty heading the list with substantial gifts. The Minutes of the President and Fellows for "the 10th Day of Sept." give the conditions under which the money and property were given. These requirements included the specifications that the funds be "kept distinct from all other property belonging to the College, and should never be blended" and that every Professor in this chair must give his assent to the ecclesiastical discipline of the State which was affirmed in 1708.

A bit of paper[67] bearing the date of September 10, 1822, bears witness to the zeal of Professors Goodrich and Fitch in pressing forward the establishment of this Professorship without delay. It is a note given by them to the President and Fellows: bonded by Mr. Timothy Dwight, binding themselves to pay to that group of men the five thousand dollars yet needed, if other subscriptions did not make up that deficit. Each man had already given large sums, but performed this deed in order that the establishment of the Professorship should not

----

65. Statement of the Present Situation of Yale College, p. 8.
66. Ibid., p. 9.
67. 1 sheet, 2 pp.

be further postponed.

That very same day, September 10th, the Minutes of the President and Fellows contain the following, "voted that whereas Eleazer T. Fitch and Chauncey A. Goodrich have agreed for the balance", the body will proceed to establish the Professorship of didactic theology." The unanimous election, to this office, of Rev. Nathaniel W. Taylor, pastor of the First Church in New Haven, followed.[68] It was further "voted that the Prudential Committee, and the Professors of Divinity and didactic theology, establish the course of instruction and necessary rules and regulations for the management of the theological department for the ensuing year". The Theological Department in Yale College had officially begun.

---

68. Professor Fitch wrote a "Memorial to the First Church in New Haven", (MS. 22 pp.), pointing out the great need of expansion in theological education, and Mr. Taylor's fitness for leadership in such an undertaking. He sympathized with them in their probable great loss, but urged them to accept his resignation.

PART II

PERSONNEL AND ADMINISTRATION

Chapter III The Faculty 1822 - 1858
Chapter IV   The Students 1822 - 1858
Chapter V   Administration of the Theological Department

CHAPTER III

THE FACULTY 1822 - 1858

THE FACULTY 1822 - 1858

It will be noted in a succeeding chapter that the lecture method was predominant in the classroom procedure in the Theological Department in Yale College during this period of its history. This situation, and the fact that it was a time when the value of a school was judged almost wholly by the merit of the men who were responsible for its leadership in instruction, make an examination of the faculty important for an understanding of the curriculum. The four gentlemen[1] who constituted the Faculty of the Theological Department in this period were as remarkable in their differences from one another as they were in their individual mental characteristics. After a brief note has been given concerning the cultural background of each professor, and the experience which had been his before becoming a member of the theological faculty, an endeavor will be made to discover the man himself as he lived in the minds of his students. For any opinion that may be

----

1. Professor J. L. Kingsley who was the instructor in Hebrew, 1822-24, is not counted in this group. That it was a temporary arrangement was understood. He gave his services without remuneration. He was Professor of Languages and Ecclesiastical History in the Academic Department of Yale College. Mr. George E. Day, who graduated from the Theological Department in 1836, and remained as Instructor of Sacred Literature, thereby assisting Professor Gibbs, for three years, 1838-1841; is also not to be considered as one of the regular Faculty in the review in this Chapter of the Professors of the Theological Department.

expressed concerning these professors only those sources prepared by these students[2] will be used. These sources are found to be of several types. Some are in the form of "memoirs" of the professors, some are contained in the autobiographies of the students, others in the histories of the Theological Department, and still others in the private correspondence of the students. Direct quotations will be used for special purposes only, since these accounts are very similar, even in respect to details.

Nathaniel William Taylor

The central figure in the Seminary, in the minds of the students, was Dr. Taylor. This was not due merely to his intellectual powers, but was owing in some degree to the fact that the taste of the time turned strongly in the direction of metaphysical theology.

Nathaniel William Taylor was born at New Milford, Connecticut, on the 23d of June, 1786. He was the son of Nathaniel, and Anne (Northrop) Taylor. His grandfather, the Reverend Nathaniel Taylor, was for fifty-three years pastor of the Church in New Milford. He had graduated at Yale College, and for twenty-six years, from 1774 till his

---

2. The authors of these sources and the years spent in the Theological Department are: S. G. Buckingham, Theological Department, 1835-1836; Horace Bushnell, 1832-33; George E. Day, 1835-38; Samuel W. S. Dutton, 1835-38; Timothy Dwight, 1830-33; George P. Fisher, 1849-50; William L. Kingsley, 1844-49; Benjamin N. Martin, 1837-40; Peter Parker, 1831-34; J. M. Sturtevant, 1828-29; I. N. Tarbox, 1841-44; Theodore D. Woolsey, 1823-25.

death in 1800, was a member of its Corporation. He was wealthy for the times, and especially for a minister, and educated two of his sons at Yale College. Professor Taylor's father was a farmer. Young Taylor was fitted for college in Bethlehem, a town near New Milford, in the family school of the Reverend Dr. Azel Backus, then pastor of the Church in Bethlehem, and afterwards President of Hamilton College.

Taylor entered Yale College in 1800, when he was fourteen years of age, but was compelled to abandon his studies for a time on account of a disease of the eyes. He reëntered the following year, and he was again obliged to return to his home for the same reason. He made another trial three years later, in 1805, and was able to continue his scholastic duties, though at a disadvantage, and graduated in 1807.

His early religious experience as recorded in the language of the time was as follows:[3]

> "He became interested in religion during his Junior, or third year in College. He was convicted of his sinfulness very deeply and most painfully--so painfully that Dr. Dwight, his spiritual adviser, feared that his reason would be deranged. He soon became a decided servant of Christ, though his belief that he was, and

---

3. S. W. S. Dutton, A Sketch of the Life and Character of Rev. Nathaniel A. Taylor, (1859?, Pam.) pp. 5, 6.
  Mr. Dutton was a student in the Theological Department 1835-1838. He was minister of the North Church in New Haven for the rest of his life, 1838-1866, and was well acquainted with Dr. Taylor. Dutton's account is quoted at two points in this sketch in order to preserve a vocabulary largely lost to the present generation and one necessary to describe the spirit of the times.

> his consequent hope in the forgiving mercy of God, were feeble. . . . His hope of salvation . . . . was not strong, owing perhaps to the type of instruction and experience which he had in his revered teacher, Dr. Dwight, who was never strongly confident of his good estate. Indeed, Dr. Taylor, through life, was not accoustomed to express confident assurance of hope, though he had a degree of hope which gave him, for the most part, peace and joy. He had a very clear view and deep sense of his own unworthiness and imperfections, and a strong conviction and fear of the deceitfulness of the human heart, and these, united with some error or undue severity of judgment with regard to his full and habitual compliance with the terms of grace, prevented his feeling of full assurance of hope."

During the year after his graduation young Taylor was employed in the family of Hon. Stephen Van Renssellaer, of Albany, as the private tutor of his son. Several months of this year he spent in Montreal, where he devoted himself to the study of the French language. He then, in 1808, became a student of theology with President Dwight for four years, an unusually thorough and protracted course for that period. For two years Taylor was a member of Dr. Dwight's family, acting as his amanuensis, and writing down, at his dictation, most of the sermons which compose his "theological system."

Dr. Dwight's influence upon young Taylor is told by the latter in a letter written to the Reverend William B. Sprague,[4] February 20, 1844:

> "I know of more than one who has succeeded well in life, because, through Dr. Dwight's influence he was led to a suitable appreciation of his own powers. I can speak on this point somewhat from experience. I came to College very young; my health failed; and I lost three years from study. When I came the last

---

4. Printed in Sprague's <u>Annals of the American Pulpit</u>, Vol. II, pp. 161-164.

time, (for I entered three different classes,) it was rather to gratify my parents, than with any expectation or intention of being a scholar; for, though I had previously felt an intense interest in study, I had by that time entirely lost it. . . . I had abandoned the thought of either doing or being much in future life. In my Senior year, I read an exercise before Dr. Dwight, an argument on the question--"Is virture founded in utility?"--a question in which he always felt a peculiar interest. To those who preceded me he said, "Oh, you do not understand the question;" but when I had finished my argument, he remarked with great emphasis,--"That's right," and added some other commendatory remarks which, to say the least, were adapted to put a young man's modesty to rather a severe test. But it certainly had one good effect--it determined me to make intellectual efforts, which, otherwise, I probably never should have made. . . . When I received a call to the church in this city, which I, in every suitable way, tried to avoid accepting, Dr. Dwight was very anxious that I should accept it. I told him frankly my principal objection. You know the great popularity of my predecessor in that pulpit; and I told Dr. Dwight that, if I were settled there, I could expect nothing else than that I should be dismissed within a year. . . ."Believe me", said he, "I have no fears of the issue, and I know much better what you can do, than you know yourself." After I was settled, I was occasionally at the end of the matter as to sermons,-- not exactly sermons, but such sermons as I was willing to preach. "Why", said he, "you are in as bad a plight as President Edwards said he once was, when he could not find another text in the Bible on which he could make a sermon." . . . . After a while I got over these fits of despondency, and no one can tell how much I owe him for it."

As a result of these years of personal contact, Professor Taylor considered himself the spiritual and theological child of President Dwight, pointing out, in the midst of controversy, that his theology was grounded on that of his teacher.[5]

In 1811, after Moses Stuart had accepted a professorship at Andover Seminary, Taylor had become Stuart's successor in the pastorate of the First Church in New Haven. His ministry was one of unusual prosperity. He preached with a fervor that strengthened the church,[6] and brought fame to himself. A new height was reached in the years 1820 and 1821, when an "unprecedented revival of religion" occurred under his leadership.[7] He had already shown himself to be a theologian of no mean ability.[8] It was natural, then for those interested in the expansion of theological instruction in Yale College, to turn to this successful pastor, and disciple of President Dwight.

Professor Taylor, therefore, came to Yale, in the year 1822, at thirty-six years of age, with the experience of a successful preacher and theologian. But he did not relinquish preaching when he accepted the Professorship of

---
5. e. g. A pamphlet written by Professor Taylor: An Inquiry into the Nature of Sin as exhibited in Dr. Dwight's Theology. A letter to a Friend by Clericus, New Haven, Hezekiah Howe, 1829; pp. 43.
    Also in the preface to the "Concio ad Clerum" which was thought by his opponents to be most heretical, Dr. Taylor states that he is "not aware. . of any departure in any article of doctrinal belief, from his revered instructor in theology, the former President of the College."
6. The present edifice was built during his pastorate; in 1814.
7. C. A. Goodrich, "A History of the Revivals of Religion in Yale College", Quarterly Register, Vol. 10, (Feb. 1838) pp. 303, 304.
8. His Regeneration the beginning of Holiness in the Human Heart, 1817, 40 pp., had drawn much criticism and acclaim. He carried on controversial correspondence on theological questions in 1816, and in 1822; the latter being an attack by him on Professor Norton's Views of Calvinism, in the Christian Spectator, Vol. 4, (1822) pp. 299-318.

Theology. He was seen in some pulpit every Sunday almost without interuption for a long course of years. To the congregation of which he had been pastor he continued to preach, at the invitation of their committee on various occasions until the installation of Leonard Bacon as pastor in the year 1825. When the Third Church in New Haven was formed, (1825) he preached for them the greater part of the time for nearly four years, until their first pastor was ordained. During most of the next year (1830) he addressed the congregation of the North Church in Hartford. The Pulpit of the North Church in New Haven Taylor supplied a large part of the time during the interval of four years and a half (1831-1835) between the pastorates of Rev. Mr. Merwin and Rev. Mr. Sawyer.

His first lectures had little of the formal accuracy of expression, or of the systematic completeness of thought, which distinguished those of subsequent years. "His earlier students used to declare that it was only in the glowing discourses of those first years of his instruction, that the whole fire of his genius showed itself."[9] According to his students, Dr. Taylor was an original thinker of a high order. "He had a creative mind and was fitted to be a founder of a new system, whether of theology, or of philosophy."[10]

As he sat in his professorial chair in the lecture-room

---

9. Benjamen N. Martin, "Nathaniel W. Taylor", in Yale College, A Sketch of Its History, ed. by W. L. Kingsley, Vol. II, p. 34.
10. Timothy Dwight, Memories of Yale Life and Men, 1903, p. 25.

he had a commanding personality--his head and face being indicative of greatness and his eyes had a bright and penetrating quality which reflected clearness of insight. His confidence in the conclusions he reached was strong, and his announcement of them was emphatic. He seems to have been a combination of argumentative lecturer and preaching-teacher. When in the course of his lectures on Revealed Theology, he came to the subject of election, he did not call his discourses lectures, he termed them "Sermons." However, his appeal, first of all, was always to the understanding, and not to the emotions. His greatest scorn was reserved for those writers in theology who were "too lazy to make definitions", which he declared to be the "severest labor of the human mind." Though he possessed a dogmatic air, he freely encouraged the inquiries of his students, and even their objections, and gave ample opportunities for discussion.

> "The manner and degree in which Dr. Taylor regarded truth. . . . was a radical characteristic, affecting all his thinking, and all his teaching, whether by lecture or pen, by sermon or conversation. Truth, or the reality of things--this, in his view, is fundamental. Nothing is reliable which does not rest on this. . . . He admired and exulted in the adaptation of the mind to truth. . . . This confidence in the truth and in the capability of men, under the divine guidance and assistance, to know it and defend it, to use it and be blessed by it, Dr. Taylor imparted to his pupils. He taught them to be thorough and independent thinkers--to call no man master, and to go for the truth themselves to its sources, and especially to the law and to the testimony. . . ."[11]

He invariably concluded his lectures with the potent

---

11. S. W. S. Dutton, A Sketch of the Life and Character of Rev. Nathaniel W. Taylor, pp. 9, 10.

formula, "Now I will hear you;" and then the discussion broke forth. One would make an inquiry or suggest an objection; and the professor would answer with the fullest argument and the clearest elucidation--so it seemed to his students. He was ready in argument, and quick in repartee, and had an unfailing fund of humor; and often the second hour would draw to a close, and another class would enter before the discussion had concluded. Professor Taylor continued the instruction in theology until within a few weeks of his death, in March, 1858.

An Annotated Bibliography of the Writings of Nathaniel W. Taylor.

Manuscripts

1. Letter to Rev. Benjamin Trumbull, September 10, 1813. 1 p.

2. A Sermon, "no. 226, Glorifying God", October 1816. 16 leaves. Cover also bears the following notes: Yale College 1816; New Milford, March 1817. A manuscript note by Noah Porter, dated June 7, 1873, on the first page of the sermon attests to the authorship of the sermon.

3. Letter to President Day, New Haven, December 5, 1820. 1 p.
   Recommending Elias Brewer for aid from the American Education Society.

4. Declaration of Faith and Signature at his entrance on the Professorship of Didactic Theology, December 31, 1822. 1 p.

5. Letter to President Day, reporting his success in soliciting funds for Yale College; Hartford, January 20, 1826. 2 pp.

6. An Explanation (4 pp.) and a Statement addressed to the President and Fellows of Yale College

(4 pp.) defending himself against the accusation of teaching heretical doctrines in the Yale Theological Department, New Haven; August 21, 1834.

7. Autograph Essay on Virtue; May 4, 1840. In "Sacred Wreath".

8. Resignation of his Professorship of Didactic Theology, Yale College, July 13, 1857.
"Such are my age and infirmities. . . . ."

Publications

1. Regeneration the beginning of holiness in the human heart. A sermon, New Haven, 1816. 19 pp.

2. Man, a free agent without the aids of Divine Grace, New Haven, 1818. 18 pp.

3. "Review of Norton's Inaugural Discourse." In the Christian Spectator, February, 1821. Vol. 3, pp. 74-83. Anonymous.

4. Review of Professor Norton's Views of Calvinism From the Christian Spectator. February, 1821. New Haven. 1823, 30 pp. Anonymous.

5. A Sermon, addressed to the Legislature of the State of Connecticut, at the Annual Election in Hartford, May 7, 1823, Hartford, 1823. 43 pp.

6. Concio ad Clerum. A Sermon delivered in the Chapel of Yale College, September 10, 1828. New Haven, 1828. 38 pp.

7. Essays on the Means of Regeneration, first published in the Quarterly Christian Spectator, for 1829, in four articles, pp. 1-44, 209-235, 481-509, 691-712. Anonymous. These were written as a Review of, and in answer to Rev. Gardiner Springs Dissertation on the Means of Regeneration; New York, 1827. 50 pp.

8. An Inquiry into the Nature of Sin, as exhibited in Dr. Dwight's Theology. A Letter to a Friend, by Clericus. (With remarks on an Examination of Dr. Taylor's and Mr. Harvey's Views on the same subject) New Haven, 1829. 43 pp.

9. Review of Dr. Tyler's Strictures upon an article in the Christian Spectator, on the Means of Regeneration--First published in the Christian

Spectator for March, 1830. New Haven, 1830.
56 pp. Anonymous.

10. A Review of Dr. Wood's Letters to Dr. Taylor, on the Permission of Sin. Together with remarks on Dr. Bellamy's Treatise on the same subject. First published in the Quarterly Christian Spectator, for September, 1830. New Haven, 1830. 50 pp. Anonymous.

11. "Case of the Rev. Mr. Barnes." In the Quarterly Christian Spectator for June, 1831, Vol. 3. pp. 292-336. Anonymous.

12. "The Biblical Repertory on the Doctrine of Imputation". In the Quarterly Christian Spectator for September, 1831, pp. 497-512. Anonymous.

13. "Correspondence between Rev. Dr. Taylor and Rev. Dr. Hawes". From the Connecticut Observer. 1832. 8 pp.

14. Reply to Dr. Tyler's Examination. Boston, 1832. 24 pp.

15. Remarks on Propagated Depravity, and Sin as the necessary means of the greatest good. First published in the Quarterly Christian Spectator, for September, 1832, as a review of Dr. Tyler's Remarks on Dr. Taylor's Letter. New Haven, 1832. 40 pp. Anonymous.

16. "Reply to Dr. Tyler (on the Doctrine of Decrees, the Doctrines of Propagated Depravity, etc., and the Doctrine of Irresistable Grace)". In the Spirit of the Pilgrims for December, 1832, and January and February, 1833, vol. 5, pp. 669-94, and vol. 6, pp. 5-18, 65-84.

17. Review of Spring's Dissertation on Native Depravity. First published in the Quarterly Christian Spectator. New Haven, 1833. 20 pp. Anonymous. From the Spectator for June, 1833.

18. A Letter, on the subject of his late discussion with Rev. Dr. Tyler. First published in the Quarterly Christian Spectator for September, 1833. New Haven. 24 pp.

19. He was also the author of the Reply to the President (pp. 5-12), in the following:

The New Haven Memorial to the President, protesting against the use of the United States Army to enforce the bogus laws of Kansas; the Answer of President Buchanan; and the Reply of the Memorialists (New Haven, 1857) 12 pp.

After his death were published:

20. Practical Sermons. New York, 1858. pp. 455.
Containing thirty-two sermons, written during his early ministry.

21. Lectures on the Moral Government of God. New York, 1859. 2 vols., pp. xiii, 417; viii, 423.
With Introduction by his son-in-law, President Porter.

22. Essays, Lectures, etc., upon select topics in Revealed Theology. New York, 1859. pp. viii, 480.

23. An Address delivered at the funeral of Dr. Noah Webster, May 31, 1843.
In Professor William C. Fowler's Essays, Hartford, 1876. pp. 62-71.

Eleazer Thompson Fitch

For the first two years Professor J. L. Kingsley instructed in Hebrew, and Professor Fitch in the Greek of the New Testament. In 1824 Professor Gibbs was appointed Professor of Sacred Literature for the Theological Department. Professor Fitch continued to give instruction in Homiletics. Though his chief task was that of the college minister, he greatly influenced the school throughout the years of his connection with it; 1822-1863.

Eleazer Thompson Fitch was born on the New Year's Day of 1791, in New Haven, Connecticut. He was the playmate and schoolmate of Chauncey A. Goodrich, and later his colleague in the Theological Department. They attended Hopkins

Grammar School together, and graduated with the same class from Yale College. Mr. Fitch's outstanding achievement in college was in Geometry. He missed Chapel but once in the four years; and those were the days when Chapel, in the winter-time, began before dawn. After graduating from Yale he attended Andover Seminary and remained there to be an assistant to Rev. Ebenezer Porter, the Professor of Homiletics. He was also associated with Rev. Jeremiah Evarts in conducting the "Panoplist", a popular religious periodical of the day. In 1817 Ebenezer Porter was called to the Livingston Professorship of Divinity in Yale College. Upon his refusal, the Corporation turned to his assistant, Mr. Fitch. Fitch was only twenty-six years old at the time and it was, indeed, a severe test for the powers of any minister, to be asked to equal the demands of a cultured audience of professors and students who had either listened to the discourses of President Dwight, or heard of them from their fathers and friends. He was, however, regarded as a young man of remarkable ability and promise, and the President and Fellows seemed assured of his being able to fill the chair of Divinity in the College. That he himself felt differently in this regard is apparent from a letter written to President Day,[12] very evidently sent in answer to the one informing him of his appointment, wherein he speaks much of his own weakness, and says that he feels that he will be able to prepare only one sermon each week, and suggests that

---

12. Andover, August 4, 1817, MS. 4 pp.

the Church Committee use "exchanges" for the evening services. Another letter,[13] ostensibly one written to the President in answer to the one received in reply to the above epistle, he further dwells on his own shortcomings. He says,

> "The question has come to me at a period in which I am considerably oppressed with ill health and feel less confidence in myself than usual. . . . I am a bruised reed; shall easily be broken; and shrink at the thought of being crushed at once. If I go I need allowance from my fellowmen, and special assistance from heaven."

He promised to meet President Day in Cambridge in order to consult with him concerning the matter.

He was elected to the chair upon his own terms of preaching but once a week, but according to the following minute the President and Fellows seem not to have been particularly pleased with his request:[14]

> "Mr. Eleazer Thompson Fitch, the Professor of Divinity Elect having signified to the Committee a desire that for the past four years he is in office, he may be excused from preaching in the Chapel more than half time and he having renewed a similar desire in his letter of acceptance, this Board is of the opinion that such an arrangement is inconvenient and impracticable--they entertain the hope that by the aid of occasional assistance and exchanges, he will be able to discharge the duties of the office without inconvenience."

This reticence on the part of Dr. Fitch in pushing forward to any task which was his to perform, appears to have been, for him, an outstanding and very noticeable characteristic. It seemed to be an intense nervousness, or nervous

---

13. Andover, August 19, 1817, MS., 2 pp.
14. Minutes of the President and Fellows of Yale College, September 9, 1817.

intensity, which interfered with his steady and quiet working power. For this reason, the composition of sermons occasioned him great mental and physical strain, and he always felt unable to speak before large audiences extemporaneously, or without a fully prepared manuscript. Yet, while this impediment was noticeable, it was so overcome by his ability as a metaphysician and a poet, that the difficulty was sometimes forgotten. A returning graduate best expresses what seems to have been the opinion of the group:

> " He began with the same half-embarrassed, half-awkward way; and fumbled at his Bible-leaves, and the poor pinched cushion, as he did long before. But as he went on with his rusty polemic vigor, the poetry within him would now and then warm his soul into a burst of fervid eloquence, and his face would glow, and his hand tremble, and the cushion and the Bible-leaves be all forgot, in the glow of his thought, until with a half-cough and a pinch at the cushion, he fell back into his strong but treadmill argumentation. (15

It was considered altogether possible, by his students in Homiletics, that if the Rev. Professor should one day come to class without his manuscript, he would be wholly unable to utter a word. Yet "his brief series of lectures on Homiletics were considered at the time and for the time to be unsurpassed in merit."[16]

As a theologian and controversialist, Dr. Fitch was the help-meet of Professor Taylor. It was his preaching of two discourses in 1826 on the nature of sin that first brought

---

15. I. K. Marvel (Donald G. Mitchell), Reveries of a Bachelor, (1877) p. 229.
16. George P. Fisher, "Historical Address" Semi-centennial Anniversary of the Divinity School of Yale College, May 15 and 16, 1872, p. 18.

the suspicion of many that all was not well theologically[17] at the Yale school.

Professor Fitch seems to have surpassed his fellows in the variety of excellent mental gifts which he possessed. He was a theologian, a metaphysician, a preacher, a poet, and a musician.[18] He also possessed mechanical skill, and was a lover of nature. "Considered in the full measure and the variety of his powers, he had no superior among the eminent scholars and teachers who were associated with him. I believe this to be the judgment of those who were most thoroughly acquainted with the whole circle of men."[19]

Professor Fitch resigned the Professorship of Divinity in Yale College in 1852, and the Professorship of Homiletics in the Theological Department in 1863, and died in the year 1871.

An Annotated Bibliography of the Writings
of Eleazer Thompson Fitch

Manuscripts

1. Letter to Professor S. J. Hitchcock, Andover, June 22, 1815. 2 pp.
   New York money depreciated in Massachusetts: he wished to exchange it for Hartford bank-notes.

2. Two letters to President Day and the Yale

---

17. See Chapter X, pp. 324, 325.
18. He was influential in obtaining the first organ for the College Chapel. His love for music is exemplified in his lecture, Music as a Fine Art published soon after his death; 1872, 36 pp. He also actually composed the music for a song, Take Heed, which is now existent in its 2d edition.
19. Timothy Dwight, Memories of Yale Life and Men, pp. 77, 78.

Corporation, concerning the offer made to him of the College Professorship of Divinity. Andover, August 4 and 19, 1817.

3. Memorial presented to the 1st Church and Society in New Haven, on the call of Rev. N. W. Taylor to the chair of Didactic Theology in the Yale Theological Department. 1822. 21 pp.

4. Letter to President Day, Concord, N.H., October 20, 1822.
   Professor Fitch begs to be excused for being late for the beginning of the school year. His wife is ill and unable to travel.

5. Letter to President Day concerning a proposal to conduct a religious meeting on Saturday evenings. New Haven, March 3, 1827. 7 pp.

6. Letter to his brother-in-law, Rev. Seth Bliss, concerning a revival in New Haven; New Haven, March 21, 1831. 3 pp.

7. Autograph Moral; April 20, 1840.
   In "Sacred Wreath".

8. Letter to Isaac Bird, New Haven, May 12, 1842. 3 pp.

9. Letter to a committee of the Faculty, on his proposed resignation of his professorship of Divinity. June, 1852. 28 pp.

10. Letter to Yale Corporation resigning his Professorship of Divinity. July 13, 1852. 4 pp.

11. Letter to the Yale Corporation resigning his Professorship of Homiletics in the Theological Department, July 28, 1863. 1 p.

12. His own account of his Sermons, (1-367), from 1814-1856. In 3 volumes. Each volume in two parts.
    Part I Enumeration
    Part II Chronological Table of Preaching

Publications

1. The Minister presenting his people to Christ: a Sermon preached at the Ordination of the Rev. Joel H. Linsley, as pastor over the Second Congregational Church and Society in Hartford, Conn., February 25, 1824. New Haven, 1825. 40 pp.

2. A Sermon preached at the Funeral of the Rev. John Elliott, D. D. New Haven, 1825. 19 pp. Dr. Elliott died in December, 1824.

3. Two Discourses on the Nature of Sin; delivered before the Students of Yale College, July 30, 1826. New Haven, 1826. 46 pp.

4. "Defense of the Two Discourses on the Nature of Sin against a Review of them in the Churchman's Magazine for November, 1826". Christian Spectator, Vol. 9, January 1827, pp. 17-21.

5. An Inquiry into the Nature of Sin; in which the views advanced in Two Discourses on the Nature of Sin", are pursued; and vindicated from objections, stated in the Christian Advocate. New Haven, 1827. 95 pp.

6. Sermons: "The Repentance of Peter, Mark xiv, 72; and, The Duty of Reproof, Eph. v, 11", National Preacher, vol. 2, (September 1827), pp. 49-64.

7. National prosperity perpetuated. A Discourse delivered in the chapel of Yale College; on the day of Annual Thanksgiving: November 29, 1827. New Haven, 1828. 34 pp.

8. "Review of Erskine on the Gospel", Quarterly Christian Spectator, vol. I, (June, 1829), pp. 289-306.

9. Liberal Christians, helpers to the truth: a Sermon delivered in the Centre Church, New Haven, on the Anniversary of the Female Education Society of New Haven; July 1, 1829. New Haven, 1829. 28 pp.

10. "Review of Tyler's Lectures on Future Punishment," Quarterly Christian Spectator, vol. 1, (December, 1829) pp. 598-624.

11. "Review of Fisk on Predestination and Election", Quarterly Christian Spectator, vol. 3, (December, 1831), pp. 597-640.

12. "Divine Permission of Sin", Quarterly Christian Spectator, vol. 4, (December, 1832) pp. 614-60. also published separately with title, A vindication of the divine purpose in relation to the existence of sin. New Haven, 1832. 48 pp.

13. "An Address, delivered in the Centre Church, New Haven, December 4, 1833, at the Funeral of

Martha Day". In the <u>Literary Remains of Martha Day</u>. New Haven, 1834. pp. 55-70.

14. "A Translation and Exposition of Romans ix, 22-24," <u>Quarterly Christian Spectator</u>, vol. 7, (September, 1835) pp. 382-92.

15. <u>An Account of the Meeting of the Class which graduated at Yale College In 1810, held at New Haven, August 18, 1840</u>. New Haven, 1840. 14 pp.

16. "(Review of The Works of) Nathanael Emmons, D. D.", in the <u>New Englander</u>, vol. 12, pp. 217-63, (April, 1855)

17. "Sermon: The mode of preaching the Gospel that is adapted to success; Acts xiv, 1." <u>National Preacher</u>, vol. 37, (July, 1863) pp. 169-85.

18. "A Statement submitted to the Prudential Committee, by the Professor of Divinity in Yale College". Dated April 28, 1822. In W. C. Fowler, <u>Origin of the Theological School of Yale College</u>, 1869. pp. 17-26.

After his death the following were published by his son:

19. <u>Sermons, practical and descriptive, preached in the pulpit of Yale College</u>. New Haven, 1871. pp. vii, 365.
    Containing twenty-three sermons, composed from 1816 to 1847.

20. "Music as a Fine Art. Its history--its productions--the elements of its beauty. A Lecture", <u>New Englander</u>, vol. 31, (October, 1872) pp. 689-725.

Chauncey Allen Goodrich

The member of the Faculty of this period, who with Professor Fitch, had the principal share, as was noted above,[20] in the establishment of the Theological Department, was Chauncey Allen Goodrich. He did not become officially connected with this Department until 1839, when he was made the Professor of Pastoral Charge, but he worked for the interests of the theological school so continuously that the Faculty almost considered him as one of themselves from the first.

Chauncey Allen Goodrich was born in New Haven, October 23, 1790. He spent almost every year of his life in that city and died there. After fitting for college, partly at Hopkins Grammar School and partly with Rev. Dr. Perkins, of West Hartford, he entered Yale College in 1806 and graduated with honor in 1810. He was at once chosen Rector of Hopkins Grammar School, and there remained until 1812, when he became tutor in Yale College. At the same time he studied theology with President Dwight and found time also for the preparation of a Greek Grammar. Mr. Goodrich founded this grammar on that of a Dutch scholar, Casper Louis

---

20. See pp. 74, 75.

Hachenberg, the best within his reach,[21] and by successive corrections and improvements made a work which was used as a textbook, in Yale and elsewhere, for nearly a quarter of a century.[22]

In 1816 he accepted one of three calls to the pastorate, that one which came from Middletown, Connecticut. In this same year he married Julia, the second daughter of Noah Webster.

His service at Middletown was of short duration, for "certain gentlemen of the state"[23] gave funds to the Prudential Committee of Yale College for the establishment of a Professorship of Rhetoric and Oratory, and Mr. Goodrich was elected to that office.[24] In the pursuit of his duties he taught all four classes in the College, those in the last year receiving what appears to have been his most valuable instruction. In this course he led the seniors in a critical study of the best orators of the last two centuries. He later published a large volume on **British Eloquence, Embracing the Best Speeches of the Most Eminent Orators**, which was[25]

---

21. President Woolsey, in his Commemorative Discourse on the Life and Services of Professor Goodrich, (1860) states that "the helps at that time accessible for the study of... [Greek] were exceedingly meager. The German philologists, Buttmann and Matthiae, had either not published their leading works or these were wholly unknown in this country, and the very indifferent Westminister Grammar was the one in common use." p. 7.
22. Lessons in Greek Parsing or Outlines of Greek Grammar, New Haven, Duwle and Peck, 1857. 27th edition. iv, 138 pp.
23. Minutes of the President and Fellows of Yale College, July 22, 1817. MS.
24. Ibid., September 9, 1817.
25. 947 pp., 1852.

well accepted, being published again, in 1870, about ten
years after his death. It was also his appointed duty to
prepare the many orators for the Commencement exercises and
frequent exhibitions which were then customary. So strenuously did he labor that in the year 1825 his health began
to fail. He offered to resign, but the President and
Fellows replied by "relieving him from duty for one year"
upon "full pay".[26]

It was noted above that Professor Fitch had requested
that he be relieved from many of the duties connected with
the pastoral work of the College. It was Dr. Goodrich who
voluntarily took upon himself the responsibilities of a
college pastor. He conducted the Sunday evening service for
young men each week, and his rhetorical ability seems to
have been enjoyed continually by them. A greater work was
done by him in personal contact. It was he whom generations
of college and theological students have pointed out as the
dynamic force behind the many revivals which visited Yale
during his connection with the institution. There is not
much detailed information now existent concerning his own
personal part in these movements, for he himself is the
chief authority on the history of revivals in Yale College.[27]

It appears that Professor Goodrich had conceived for
Dr. Taylor a warm personal friendship, so that when the
latter's theological views were made the object of attack,

---

26. Minutes of the President and Fellows, September 14, 1825.
27. "A History of Revivals of Religion in Yale College", American Quarterly Register, 1838, pp. 289-301.

Mr. Goodrich purchased in the year 1828 the Christian Spectator,[28] which had begun as a monthly, and made it a quarterly, in which the views which had come to be called "Taylorism" were defended by the New Haven theologians. As long as it was considered important to continue the discussions, Professor Goodrich conducted the Spectator, receiving the support of Dr. Taylor, Dr. Fitch, Dr. Lyman Beecher, and others, till in 1836, when the object proposed was thought to have been accomplished, he allowed the magazine to pass out of his hands.

Dr. Goodrich was not a wealthy man, but he was thrifty, and by systematic saving was able to become one of the largest benefactors of Yale College, and especially of the Theological Department. Accordingly, in 1839, feeling the need of a Professor of Pastoral Charge for that department, he offered to give $5,000, and agreed to interest himself in procuring other subscriptions which would enable the Corporation to establish this new chair. Rev. Joel Parker, pastor of the Broadway Tabernacle, in New York, was invited to accept the responsibility but declined "in the interest of the church" he was serving.[29] Mr. Goodrich was then finally persuaded to accept the professorship.[30]

It appears that the regular duties to which Dr. Goodrich

---

28. There is extant a brief circular proposing the establishment of this periodical, which bears the signatures of the original subscribers, many of whom were officers of the College. Printed and MS., 4 pp.
29. Personal letter, Joel Parker to Jeremiah Day, January 29, 1839. MS., 4 pp.
30. Minutes of the President and Fellows of Yale College, July 20, 1839.

was now called were such as his past life had well qualified him to accomplish. He brought to the criticism on the composition and delivery of sermons, the rhetorical practice and judgment of the eighteen years which he had spent in his former professorship. For leadership in the practical side of the pastoral work he was prepared by the years of difficult service of this kind in the College, which work he continued to do. In fact, his transfer to the Theological Department changed his approach from that of a strict disciplinary professor, which had formerly made him unpopular, to one who could more freely approach the students. It is significant, that in the student-printed pseudo-Catalog for 1852-53,[31] in which almost everything and everyone was subjected to comical ridicule, Professor Goodrich's name and title was left unchanged, and was preceded by an asterisk which referred one to the bottom of the page, where "Amicus" appeared.

His qualifications for the new professorship were enhanced by his interest in the great religious societies of the time. The Temperance Society, the Society for the Promotion of College Education in the West, the Tract Society of New York, of which he was one of the most active directors, the Bible Society, and most of all the American Board of Commissioners for Foreign Missions--all claimed his time and energy. His scholarship found expression in the repeated

---
31. Catalogue of the Officers and Students of Yale College, revised edition, Springfield, Massachusetts. 35 pp.

revision of Noah Webster's English Dictionary, which task became his at the death of his father-in-law, and occupied much of his time during the last twenty years of his life. Though his talents were many, the one that seems to have meant most to his students was an unusual quality of hopeful and joyful Christian graciousness.[32]

Professor Goodrich continued his lectures on the Pastoral Charge until the day of his death, February 17, 1860.

An Annotated Bibliography of the Writings of Chauncey Allen Goodrich

Manuscripts

1. Two Letters to S. J. Hitchcock, October 2, 1810. 2 pp.
    He is busy at the Grammar School (Hopkins) and will be unable to watch over the conduct of a college student.
    October 10, 1810, 1 p. His roommate Ellsworth will also be unable to accept the task.

2. Ten Letters to President Day, Hartford, London, etc., 1815-39.
    Hartford, May 24, 1815, 1 p. Concerning examination of a student about to enter Yale College.
    Durham, April 13, 1816, 1 p. Concerning campaigning for funds for the American Educational Society.
    Hartford, June 29, 1819, 1 p. Mr. Wickham is ill and will be unable to teach next year.

---

32. The happy combination of good humor and consecrated, untiring hard work which were mingled in his character is well depicted in a personal letter of his to Mr. Benjamin Curtis in which he at first laughs with Mr. Curtis at the latter's misfortune in being a bachelor, and later writes, "I am absolutely so weary that I can scarcely hold a pen, having been engaged in continual speaking from 8 this morning to 5 (the present hour) with the exception of an hour at dinner".

On a trip through Europe--for his health--he wrote in description of the journey:
    Havre, October 30, 1825, 4 pp.
    Marseilles, January 10, 1826, 3 pp.
    London, May 20, 1826, 4 pp.
    London, August 22, 1826, 4 pp.

From New York, April 9, 1828, 3 pp. He writes of success in obtaining funds for the Professorship of Sacred Literature. He appends a personal note for Mrs. Goodrich.

Lexington, Kentucky, May 5, 1835. He describes his journey thither from New Haven, including the towns and cities visited en route.

New Haven, August, 1839, 2 pp. Professor Goodrich desires President Day to examine a statement concerning the Theological Department about to be printed in the Quarterly Christian Spectator.

3. Letter to Benjamin Curtis, April 28, 1828, 3 pp.
"Mr. Porter has got the start of Mr. Chauncey and Mr. Woodbridge and Mr. Curtis, and has brought home a pretty wife."

4. Letter to Mr. Otis Baker giving his opinion of the use of the translations in the study of Latin and Greek, Yale College, April 22, 1830, 1 p.

5. Two Letters to Professor E. Loomis, New Haven, 1830-32.
    July 22, 1830. Examination and Criticism of Mr. Loomis' "piece" (oration).
    March 24, 1832. Professor Goodrich requests Mr. Loomis to be the agent for the Quarterly Christian Spectator at Andover.

6. Creed at the entrance on the Professorship of Pastoral Charge in the Yale Theological Department October 23, 1839, 4 pp.

7. Autograph poetical quotation, signed also by Julia W. Goodrich. October 6, 1840, in "Sacred Wreath".

8. Three Letters to E. C. Herrick, 1844-53.
    Yale College, February 6, 1844, 1 p. Concerning ordering of books for the Library.
    Bristol, August 21, 1850. Concerning a letter of credit Goodrich gave his own son.
    Hartford, July 4, 1853, 1 p. Buying of railroad stock.

9. Letter to Mrs. Mathew R. Dutton on the death of her brother. New Haven, December 30, 1847, 3 pp.

10. Letter to President Woolsey, asking a degree for John P. Bigelow. 1 p. 1849.

Publications

1. Elements of Greek Grammar, taken chiefly from the Grammar of C. F. Hachenberg. New Haven, 1814, viii, 318 pp.

2. A Letter to the Rev. Harry Croswell, A.M., on the subject of two publications, entitled "A Serious Call", and "A Sober Appeal". New Haven, 1819. 12 pp.

3. Lessons in Greek Parsing; or outlines of the Greek Grammar, divided into short portions, and illustrated by appropriate exercises in parsing. New Haven, 1831. iv, 138 pp.

4. Lessons in Latin Parsing; containing the outlines of Latin Grammar, divided into short portions, and exemplified by appropriate exercises in parsing. New Haven, 1832. viii, 197 pp.

5. "Narrative of Revivals of Religion in Yale College from its commencement to the present time", American Quarterly Register, Vol. 10 (February, 1838), pp. 289-310.

6. Revivals of religion. Chapter 8 in Book 5 of Robert Baird's Religion in the United States of America. Glasgow, 1844. pp. 442-84.

7. Can I conscientiously vote for Henry Clay? New Haven, 1844. 4 pp.
    An anonymous defence of a Christian's support of Clay.

8. What does Dr. Bushnell mean? From the New York Evangelist. Hartford, 1849. 28 pp.
    An anonymous hostile criticism of Dr. Horace Bushnell's "God in Christ".

9. Select British Eloquence; embracing the best Speeches entire, of the most eminent Orators of Great Britain for the last two centuries; with Sketches of their lives, an estimate of their genius, and notes, critical and explanatory. New York, 1852. vii, 947 pp.
    Based on his College lectures.

10. "(Review of volumes 1, 2.) Sprague's Annals of the American Pulpit", New Englander, Vol. 15 (May, 1857), pp. 169-84. He had himself contributed to Vol. 1 (pp. 506-13) an article on his grandfather.

11. A Letter to the Secretaries of the American Tract Society, written in behalf of the Rev. Jeremiah Day, D.D., LL.D., Eleazar T. Fitch, D.D., and others. New Haven, 1858. 16 pp.
    On the policy of the Society in regard to publishing on the subject of slavery.

Long after his death was printed:

12. The Excursion (New Haven) 10 pp. (Y.C.
    A poetical jeu d'esprit, in commemoration of the excursion given by the Messrs. Joseph E. Sheffield and Henry Farnam, on the completion of the Chicago and Rock Island Railroad in 1854.

During his editorship of the Quarterly Christian Spectator, Dr. Goodrich made many contributions to its pages; the following may be mentioned:

Vol. 1, pp. 200-04 (March, 1829), "Letters from a Traveller on the Continent of Europe" (being his own observations in France, during a tour for health in 1826); pp. 343-84 (June 1829), "Review of Taylor and Harvey on Human Depravity" (in conjunction with Rev. Noah Porter); pp. 674-92 (December, 1829), "Review of Dana's Poem before the Porter Rhetorical Society in Andover, and Review of Daniel Wilson's edition of Willberforce's Practical View."

Vol. 2, pp. 61-70 (March, 1830), "Review of Wilson's Lectures on the evidences of Christianity"; pp. 380-84 (June, 1830), "Brief Notice of Dr. Tyler's Vindication"; pp. 608-21 (December, 1830), "Letter from a Traveler on the Continent of Europe"; pp. 720-50, "Review of High Church and Arminian Principles".

Vol. 3, pp. 75-85 (March, 1831), "Review of Robbins' Ancient and Modern History"; pp. 162-68, "Remarks on Protestant and the Biblical Repertory, respecting the doctrine of Imputation"; pp. 495-97 (September, 1831), "Review of the Child's Book on the Soul."

Josiah Willard Gibbs

The last of the four professors of this period, the Professor of Sacred Literature, was, according to his contemporaries,[33] in the strictest sense the scholar of the Faculty. Professor Gibbs' attitude toward his work is well shown by a statement of his written in a book of personal memoirs called "The Sacred Wreath",[34] and bearing his signature, and the date, October 6, 1840. He writes:

> "It is not, in my view, the duty of the sacred interpreter to sacrifice the unity of the Science to the harmony of revelation, much less to the preconceived dictates of human philosophy. There is real faith and piety in the directions of Dr. L. J. Rickert, a late German theologian.
> ' "Employ all the proper means in your power, to ascertain the true sense of the writer; give him nothing of thine; take from him nothing that is his. Never inquire what he ought to say; never be afraid of what he does say. It is your business to learn, not to teach.' "

Josiah Willard Gibbs, Professor of Sacred Literature from 1826 to 1861, was born in Salem, Massachusetts, April 30, 1790. He was the third son of Henry Gibbs, a graduate of Harvard College, and traced his ancestry in England to Sir Henry Gibbs, of Honington, Warwickshire, whose son Robert Gibbs, came to Boston between 1657 and 1660. J. W. Gibbs

---

33. George P. Fisher, "Historical Address", pp. 3-30, and James Hadley, "Professor Gibbs as a Scholar and Teacher", pp. 82-86, in Semi-centennial Anniversary of the Divinity School of Yale College (1872); Timothy Dwight, Memories of Yale Life and Men, pp. 265-277; George E. Day, "Josiah Willard Gibbs", in Yale College, ed. by W. L. Kingsley, Vol. II, pp. 37-40.
34. In the Rare-Book Room, Yale University Library.

entered Yale at an early age, and was graduated in the class of 1809. After teaching school in his native town, Gibbs was called to a tutorship in Yale College, where he remained from 1811 to 1815.[35] He then removed to Andover, where Professor Stuart's work in Biblical study had gained great attention, and devoted himself to sacred literature, and especially the study of Hebrew and cognate languages. In the preface to the edition of Professor Stuart's Hebrew Grammar, issued in 1821, the assistance of Mr. Gibbs is acknowledged, and Professor Stuart further states that he has urged Mr. Gibbs to translate Gesenius' <u>Manual Hebrew Lexicon</u>, feeling that he is capable of offering a distinct contribution to the knowledge of Hebrew in this work.[36]

In 1824 Gibbs was recalled to Yale College as Librarian and was allowed to give instruction to the undergraduates and theological students in classical literature, at their own expense.[37] In the year 1826 he was officially established in the Professorship of Sacred Literature in the Theological Department.[38] There seems to have been some difficulty in the matter of his salary, particularly at the

---

35. The letter which he writes to President Day accepting the tutorship has a friendly postscript concerning family affairs. Salem, November 7, 1811, MS. 4 pp.
36. Hebrew Grammar, 1821, p. vii.
37. Minutes of the President and Fellows, September 8, 1824.
38. <u>Ibid.</u>, September 12, 1826.

beginning and near the end of his term as professor.[39]

Professor Gibbs was a scholar most evenly balanced in his judgment, and hesitant in the utterance of his opinions; a scholar so disposed to give weight to both sides of the question in every case, and so indisposed to pronounce categorically for either side, that dogmatic men might even be ready, at times, to call him timid. His colleagues, Drs. Taylor and Goodrich, though in the highest degree friendly to him, were never quite able to appreciate his position--the condition of mind which pertained to his very nature, and was established in strength and permanency of his studies. They were men who felt, by reason of their mental constitution and habits, that definite conviction in all cases of questioning was to be reached, or nothing could be accomplished. Indecision was a state of which they were intolerant. They had little patience for such an attitude. Timothy Dwight writes, "I remember hearing Dr. Taylor say on one occasion--half jocosely, of course--'I would rather have ten settled opinions and nine of them wrong, than to be like my brother Gibbs with none of the ten settled.'"[40]
The fact is that Professor Gibbs, as a genuine exegetical

---

39. Statement of agreement to pay sums for the Professorship of Sacred Literature in the Theological Department; with signatures (and small amounts), January 1829; 3 pp. MS.
 A note by Professor Gibbs concerning obtaining arrearages in his salary, August 25, 1830; and September 7, 1830; MS. 2 pp.
 Minutes of the President and Fellows of Yale College, August 14, 15, 16, 1849.
40. Memories of Yale Life and Men, p. 266.

scholar of a high type, felt bound to look calmly at all the possibilities of interpretation.

In the classroom, Professor Gibbs was quiet and not self-assertive, yet faithful and painstaking. He had patience for the slow progress of his students. He was a man of few words, and these few seemed to have been chosen for the purpose.

> "The students were the jury, and he took the place not of the advocate, but of the judge. Upon every litigated point that came up, he spread before them the facts and authorities on either side, but on them was imposed the necessity of concluding upon the verdict........
> This, at least, is true, that under Mr. Gibbs there was no way of thinking vicariously, by adopting, without reflection, the opinions of the teacher. Though not possessing that magnetic power which inspires dullness itself, and which belonged, in an extraordinary degree, to Professor Stuart, he still rendered very important services to the classes under his care. But the amount of benefit they received, depended largely upon themselves. He required the stimulus of an active and inquisitive class, to call him out. . . .
> This activity and skill on the side of the pupil, were the more requisite, since his own taste and habits led him, when left to himself, to dwell with an equal pleasure upon great things and little things--upon vital questions in the interpretation of Scripture, and the minor matters of criticism." 41

It was foreign to his nature to refer to his own acquisitions, especially with any feeling of complacency; but he felt satisfied with his knowledge of the Hebrew. With cognate Semitic dialects he was also acquainted, in particular with their grammatical peculiarities. In the Greek and Latin, and the Greek of the New Testament he was thoroughly versed.

---

41. George P. Fisher, A Discourse Commemorative of the Life and Services of Josiah Willard Gibbs, (1861) pp. 17, 18.

Besides the two principal languages of modern Europe, he had explored various other languages, with particular reference to their syntax, and their relations to each other. He loved words, and most of the years of his life were spent in this type of study. His interest was in lexicography. While still at Andover[42] he had prepared a Hebrew and English Lexicon,[43] and later intended to translate the entire work of Gesenius. He had completed about one-third of his task, incurring no little expense for special kinds of type,[44] et cetera, when Professor Robinson published a similar work, making the production of the work he had planned unnecessary. He then turned to the study of philology.

Professor Gibbs' major interests are depicted in that part of his personal correspondence now existent.[45] These manuscripts fall rather clearly into two major categories: those connected with his contributions as a philologist, and those concerned with foreign missions.[46] The first group is filled with letters from professors and laymen from all over

---

42. A letter written by Mr. Gibbs from Andover to President Day, January 25, 1819, speaks of Harvard's having helped him financially in his work, and expresses appreciation for the patronage of the Corporation and of President Day.
43. Edited, with Improvements from the German works of Gesenius, Andover, 1824. viii, 656 pp.
44. In his personal papers, under "Oriental Types", are listed sixteen cases of several different kinds of type, including English-Hebrew of various grades, Arabic, Syriac, and Samaritan. These were designated as his personal property.
45. 399 different pieces, the majority of which is made up of personal letters.
46. See the Annotated Bibliography of Professor Gibbs' writings for a more detailed description of his correspondence.

the United States and from foreign lands. For example, his opinion is asked concerning the interpretation of the first chapter of Genesis; concerning the correct translation of the Lord's Prayer; concerning some point in German etymology; et cetera. In this category are found letters from missionaries, giving him bits of American Indian vocabularies, or those of people of a foreign land. He also possessed lexicographical material concerning the languages of several negro tribes,[47] which he obtained from slaves in New York, and on a more romantic occasion from a group of mutinied negroes who had found their way to New Haven, after killing most of their crew. These black men were unable to tell their story until Professor Gibbs, after learning the numerals and other elemental words in their language, found a negro in Lew York who could act as their interpreter.

A large part of his correspondence is concerned with the Morrison Education Society of Canton, China. The Committee representing this Society in New Haven and the surrounding district, were Professors Goodrich and Gibbs, and Professor Benjamin Silliman. Several letters are concerned with the recommendation of young men as missionaries, others in regard to funds to be raised, and still others about the condition of the mission in China.

It will be noted later that the committee on foreign missions in the Society for Christian Research, composed of

---

47. These were later published--"A Giss or Kissi Vocabulary, a Voi or Vay Vocabulary, and a Mendi Vocabulary", American Journal of Science, Vol. 38 (New Haven, 1839), pp. 41-48.

theological students, invariably had as its chairman, Professor Gibbs. His nature was not that of an ardent propagator of the faith, but he seems to have worked for the foreign cause in the quiet manner that was his.

Professor Gibbs continued his lectures on Sacred Literature until his last illness in the year 1861.

An Annotated Bibliography of the Writings of Josiah Willard Gibbs, Sr.

Manuscripts

1. Letter to President Day, Salem, Massachusetts, November 7, 1811. 1 p.
    With reference to beginning of tutorship in Yale College.

2. Letter to President Day, respecting his translation of Gesenius' Hebrew Lexicon, Andover, January 25, 1819. 1 p.

3. Notes concerning his own salary. August 25, 1830 and September 7, 1830. 1 p.

4. Autograph Quotation, October 6, 1840.
    In "Sacred Wreath".

5. Recommendation of Cyrus Brewster for honorary B.A., New Haven, August 14, 1841. 1 p.

6. Plan of a Reading Room for Foreign Periodicals in Yale College Library, October 1845, 2 pp.

7. Scheme of Classification of topics with reference to purchases for the Yale Library, 1846. 2 pp.

8. Reminiscences of Professor J. L. Kingsley, 5 pp., and a list of his writings, 3 pp. (1861)

9. Correspondence and Private Papers, totaling 266 pieces, which may be catalogued as follows:

    I. Concerning Languages

        1. Letters from Foreign Missionaries, giving information concerning the various languages of the countries in which they are laboring. 12 in number.

2. Letters from Fellow-Scholars, and other persons, requesting information concerning certain philological questions. 89 in number, including: five letters from Mr. Joseph Henry of the Smithsonian Institute at Washington, seven pieces from Professor E. A. Park of the Andover Theological Seminary, five letters from Mr. W. W. Turner of New York City, and ten from Professor J. E. Worcester of Cambridge, Massachusetts.

II. In connection with the Morris Education Society (for Foreign Missions).

   1. Letters written concerning appointees. 21 in number.

   2. Letters from missionaries in China under the auspices of this Society. 23 in number.

III. Miscellaneous Correspondence.

   1. Personal Letters. 42 in number.
   2. Concerning students enrolled in the Theological Department. 10 pieces.
   3. Letters from publishers and editors of periodicals. 27 in number, including ten from Mr. David N. Lord of New York City.
   4. Letters from former students. Five in number.
   5. Eight Letters requesting recommendations for some position.
   6. Five Letters concerning the affairs of the Theological Department.
   7. Two business letters.

IV. Copies of Letters written by Professor Gibbs.

   1. Letter to S. J. Hitchcock, Esq., Salem, July 8, 1820. 1 p.
   2. Two Letters to J. Robert Morrison Esq., New Haven, June 26, 1843, 2 pp; September 5, 1843. 1 p.
   3. Letter to the Trustees of the Morrison Education Society, New Haven, October 15, 1845. 2 pp.
   4. Two Letters to Professor Joseph Henry, New Haven, November 10, 1849, 4 pp.; November 27, 1852, 2 pp.
   5. Letter to I. N. Tarbox, New Haven, July 14, 1851. 2 pp.

6. Recommendation of O. M. Smith for his entrance into Andover Seminary, July 27, 1858. 1 p.

V. Miscellaneous Papers, fifteen in number; the most important of which are:

1. The Lord's Prayer in the Choctaw Language. 6 pp.
2. Confession of Faith of Mr. D'Israel, a Jew, June 1843. 4 pp.
3. Three Lists of the members of three Academic Bible Classes, November 1, 1850; February 9, 1851. 3 pieces.
4. Account of the Oriental Types in a rack belonging to Josiah W. Gibbs, now in the printing office, 60 Chapel Street, New Haven. 1 p.
5. A List of Writers on the Orthography of the English Language. 2 pp.
6. Names of those examined and licensed to preach by the New Haven East Association, July 19, 1852. 1 p.
7. Melek Taus of the Yazides. 4 pp.

Publications

1. Catalogue of the Library belonging to the Theological Institution in Andover. Andover, 1819. 161 pp. Without the compiler's name.

2. A Hebrew and English Lexicon of the Old Testament Including the Biblical Chaldee, from the German works of Professor W. Gesenius, Andover, 1824. viii, 715 pp.

3. A Manual Hebrew and English Lexicon, including the Biblical Chaldee. Designed particularly for beginners. Andover, 1828. iv, 211 pp.

4. Selections from the Holy Scriptures; intended as Sabbath Exercises for Children. Part I.--Devotional Extracts from the Book of Psalms: accompanied with short notes and questions. New Haven, 1830. viii, 88 pp. Part II, consisting of moral extracts, was never published.

5. Philological Studies with English illustrations. New Haven, 1857. vii, 244 pp.

6. A Latin Analyst on modern philological principles. New Haven, 1858. viii, 150 pp.

7. <u>Formation of Teutonic Words in the English Language.</u> New Haven, 1857. viii, 139 pp.

He also contributed extensively to periodicals: the following examples may be specified:

<u>American Journal of Science and Arts,</u>

    Volume 24 (April, 1833), pp. 87-96: "On the Orthography of Hebrew words in the Roman character".

    Volume 33 (January, 1838), pp. 324-28, and Volume 41 (July, 1841), pp. 28-31: "Contributions to English Lexicography".

    Volume 34 (July, 1838), pp. 334-47: "Table of Greek Correlatives, with explanations".

    Volume 37 (July, 1839), pp. 112-15: "Greek Conjugations".

    Volume 38 (January, 1840), pp. 41-48: "Gissi or Kissi, Vai or Vey, and Mendi Vocabularies".

    Volume 39 (October, 1840), pp. 255-62: "Characteristics of the Language of Ghagh or Accra".

    Volume 41 (July, 1841), pp. 32-39: "Origin of the Names of Beasts, Birds, and Insects".

    Volume 45 (July and October, 1843), pp. 96-102: "On the Adverbial Genitive Case in English"; pp. 284-92: "Greek Verbal Roots in English".

    Second Series, Volume 6 (September, 1848), pp. 206-09: "English Prefixes derived from the Greek".

<u>Quarterly Christian Spectator,</u>

    Volume 6 (March, 1834), pp. 156-59: "On the Biblical Use of the word Son".

    Volume 9 (March and September, 1837), pp. 109-134, 415-34: "Historical and Critical Views of Cases in the Indo-European Languages".

<u>American Biblical Repository,</u>

    Second Series, Volume 2 (July, 1839), pp. 166-74: "Natural Significancy of Articulate Sounds"; (October, 1839), pp. 480-85: "Biblical Criticism and Remarks".

Second Series, Volume 11 (July, 1845), pp. 441-46:
"Notes on the Septuagint Version of Psalms i, ii".

Third Series, Volume 2 (April, 1846), pp. 360-63:
"The formations of Compound Words".

Bibliotheca Sacra,

Volume 9 (January, 1852), pp. 220-22: "Notice of Brewer's Patmos and the Seven Churches";
pp. 226-27: "Notice of Ferguson's Palaces of Ninevah and Persepolis".

Volume 11 (October, 1854), pp. 836-39: "Notice of Curtius on Comparative Philology".

Volume 13 (July, 1856), pp. 665-67: "Correspondence on the use of Dii and Deus, etc."

Volume 14 (April, 1857), pp. 425-27: "Correspondence on Hebrew Parallelism, Vocalic Harmony, and Mammon".

Volume 16 (April, 1859), pp. 302-09: "Philological Studies, on the Latin Negation, and on Interrogative Words in the Indo-European Languages".

American Quarterly Register, Volume 15 (November, 1842), pp. 170-75: "Analysis of the English Interrogatives"; "Disguised verbal roots in English".

New Englander,

Volume 1 (January and July, 1843), pp. 140-41: "Resemblance of certain Languages to the Latin"; pp. 434-39: "On Vowel Changes in the English Language".

Volume 10 (February, May, and August, 1852), pp. 102-08: "Messianic Prophecies"; pp. 300-08: "Catholic Complaints, against the Early Protestant Versions of the Scriptures"; pp. 433-37: "The Jewish Kabbala"; pp. 472-74: "Scientific Miscellany: On the Particle But".

Volume 11 (May, 1853), pp. 320-24: "Scientific Miscellany On Guna and Vriddhi".

Volume 15 (May and November, 1857), pp. 242-49: "The Use of Testament for Covenant": pp. 666-74: "Critical Miscellanies".

Volume 16 (August, 1858), pp. 691-95: "The Ante-Mosaic Origin of the Sabbath, and Septuple times in the Pentateuch".

Volume 17 (May, 1859), pp. 489-528: "Common Version and Biblical Revision".

Volume 18 (February and May, 1860), pp. 220-29: "Hints on Lexicography; pp. 429-40: "Common Schools and the English Language".

Journal of the American Oriental Society,

Volume 1 (1849), pp. 360-73: "On the Mandingo and the Sasu Dialects".

Volume 2 (1851), pp. 125-34: "Characteristics of the Peshito Syriac Version of the New Testament".

Volume 3 (1853), pp. 235-40: "The Jews at Khaifung-fu in China"; pp. 469-72: "Remarks on Grout's Essay on the Phonology and Orthography of the Zulu and kindred Dialects", pp. 502-03: "Melek Taus of the Yezidis".

Volume 4 (1854), pp. 444-45: "The so-called Nestorian Monument of Singan-fu".

David N. Lord's Theological and Literary Journal,

Volume 3 (1851), pp. 446-48: "The Advent".

Volume 4 (1851), pp. 82-91: "Philological Contributions".

Volume 9 (1856), pp. 167-68: "Proverbial Phrases in the New Testament".

American Journal of Education, Volume 2, pp. 198-202, and Volume 3, pp. 101-24 (1856-57): "Philological Contributions".

American Journal of Education and College Review, Volume 2 (1856), pp. 53-58: "List of two hundred Latin verbal roots found in the English language".

He published the following translation:

An Essay on the Historical sense of the New Testament. By G. C. Storr, Boston, 1817. iv, 92 pp.

He contributed largely to two editions (1850-1855) of Professor W. C. Fowler's English Grammar.

He furnished the Rev. Dr. Sprague in 1854 with a brief memoir of the Rev. Samuel Willard (Harvard 1659), which is printed in the <u>Annals of the American Pulpit</u>, Volume 1, pp. 164-67.

CHAPTER IV

THE STUDENTS 1822 - 1858

THE STUDENTS 1822 - 1858

Enrollment

Two young men constituted the entire enrollment of the Theological Department of Yale College during the first year of its existence, 1822-23.[1] They were graduates of Yale College and were registered in the Junior Class of the Theological Department. They continued their studies for three years and were members of the first graduating class of the Department in 1825. In the second year, 1823-24, there were six students in the Junior Class and seven in the Middle Class. During the year 1824-25, seven Juniors, four Middlers, and five Seniors were in attendance. This was the first year in which all three classes were represented.

Table I, which appears on the following page, records the enrollment of students in the Seminary in groups of five years each for the thirty-five years now under observation, that is, during the academic years 1823-24 to 1857-58.[2] The total number, 1684, refers to the total enrollment for these years. Only 815 different students enrolled during this period, but of course many of them stayed for two, three, or

---

1. General Catalogue of the Students of the Theological Department in Yale College (1838), p. 6.
2. The school-year 1822-23 has been omitted in the interest of obtaining a number of years equally divisible by five. It has been noted that only two students were in attendance during this year.

TABLE I STUDENT ATTENDANCE AT THE THEOLOGICAL DEPARTMENT IN YALE COLLEGE DURING THE YEARS 1823/24 to 1857/58

Years	Juniors Total	Juniors Yearly Average	Middlers Total	Middlers Yearly Average	Seniors Total	Seniors Yearly Average	Three Classes Total	Three Classes Yearly Average	Resident Graduates Total	Resident Graduates Yearly Average	Total Total	Total Yearly Average
1823/24 1827/28	63	14.4	43	8.6	28	5.6	134	26.8	5	1	139	27.8
1828/29 1832/33	63	14.4	84	16.8	81	16.2	228	45.6	17	3.4	245	49
1833/34 1837/38	113	22.6	105	21	92	18.4	310	62	18	3.6	328	65.6
1838/39 1842/43	77	15.4	134	26.8	101	20.2	312	62.4	40	8	352	70.4
1843/44 1847/48	60	12	100	20	95	19	255	51	38	7.6	293	58.6
1848/49 1852/53	47	9.5	65	13	59	11.8	171	34.2	39	7.8	210	42
1853/54 1857/58	38	7.6	33	6.6	23	4.6	94	18.8	23	4.6	117	23.4
1823/24 1857/58	461	13.1	564	16.1	479	13.6	1504	42.9	180	5.1	684	48.1

more years, and their annual registrations are included in this larger figure. The enrollment of each of the three classes and also of the Resident Graduate Class is shown. This last group, which was comparatively small, was composed of those students who had completed their course in this or some other seminary and who registered in the school for the purpose of pursuing further studies. Some of them were pastors in nearby parishes.

It will be noticed from this Table I that during the first twenty years covered by this study, the enrollment at the Theological Department increased with each five-year period, but that during the last fifteen years the number enrolled declined rapidly. As a matter of fact, the last five-year period had a yearly average in attendance which was less even than the first five-year period, there being an average enrollment of only 23.4 students during the years 1853-54 to 1857-58, as compared with 27.8 students in the first five years. The peak of student enrollment came during the period from 1838-39 to 1842-43, when there was an average of 70.4 students in attendance during each year. The single academic year during which there was the largest student attendance was that of 1837-38, when 82 students were registered.

These figures include the Graduate Class, but the proportions are the same if only the total number of students registered in the Junior, Middle, and Senior Classes is considered. An examination of the four five-year periods between 1828-29 and 1847-48 shows that the average enrollment of these classes rises rapidly from 45.6 to 62, and then to 62.4, whereupon it drops suddenly to 51. This rapid rise in attendance and the equally rapid decline is most interesting in the light of the theological controversies which were going on at that time and in which the professors of the Theological Department played a leading role. In Chapter X of this study it will be noted that the most active period of this controversy was the ten years between 1828 and 1838, although the final debate between Professors Tyler and Taylor dragged on for some years after the latter date. During these years when young men were warned concerning the heresy of the "New Haven Theology" they seemed to have been encouraged rather than discouraged in their attendance at the Theological Department of Yale College. This increase in attendance during the years 1833-34 to 1842-43 is particularly noteworthy in view of the fact that an avowedly rival Seminary was established at East Windsor, Connecticut, in the year 1833.[3]

Table I also shows that the highest average for any one class in a five-year period is that of the Middle Class during the years 1838-39 to 1842-43, which had an average of 26.8 students each year. An examination of the yearly average for each class for the whole thirty-five year period under observation reveals that the Middle Class averaged 16.1 students in attendance each year, the Senior Class 13.6 students, and the Junior Class 13.1 students. This would

---

3. See Chapter X, pp. 336, 337.

indicate that young men came from other seminaries to the Theological Department of Yale College and joined the Middle and Senior Classes in such numbers as to offset the decline in enrollment which usually occurs in the more advanced years. Particularly is this true for the Middle Year; and the explanation probably lies in the fact that that year was almost entirely devoted to the study of Systematic Theology under the leadership of Professor Nathaniel W. Taylor, a principal in the theological controversies of the time.[4]

The average number of students in attendance each year during the entire period was 42.9 for the Junior, Middle and Senior Classes, or 48.1 when the Graduate Class is also included.

Birthplaces of the Students

The distribution of the birthplaces of the 815 different students in attendance at the Theological Department of Yale College during the first thirty-six years of its history, is given in Table II on the following page. The data have been arranged in five-year groupings of graduating classes, except that the figures for the years 1859 and 1860 contain data concerning only those members of these classes who were in attendance during the academic year 1857-58, which year

---

4. See Chapter X, "Theological Controversies".

TABLE II GEOGRAPHICAL DISTRIBUTION OF THE BIRTHPLACES OF THE ALUMNI OF THE THEOLOGICAL DEPARTMENT OF YALE COLLEGE WHO WERE STUDENTS DURING THE YEARS 1822-1858 ARRANGED BY CLASSES

CLASS	TOTAL	CONNECTICUT		MASSACHUSETTS		PENNSYLVANIA		MAINE		NEW HAMPSHIRE		VERMONT		NEW YORK		NEW JERSEY		OHIO		ILLINOIS		MISCELLANEOUS	
		NO	PERCENT	NO	PERCENT	NO	PERCENT	NO	PERCENT	NO	PERCENT	NO	PERCENT	NO	PERCENT	NO	PERCENT	NO	PERCENT	NO	PERCENT	NO	PERCENT
1825-1829	66	47	71.2	13	19.6	1	1.5					3	4.5	1	1.5	1	1.5						
1830-1834	111	65	58.5	21	18.9	1	.9	2	1.8	2	1.8	5	4.5	10	9.0	1	.9	2	1.8			2	1.8
1835-1839	167	73	43.6	28	16.7	2	1.1	6	3.5	3	1.7	10	5.9	30	17.9	2	1.1	4	2.3			9	5.3
1840-1844	169	74	43.1	41	24.2	3	1.7	3	1.7	11	6.5	2	1.1	25	14.7	2	1.1	2	1.1	1	.5	5	2.9
1845-1849	140	58	44.4	24	17.1	7	5.0	4	2.8	4	2.8	1	.7	21	15.0	2	1.4	3	2.1			16	11.4
1850-1854	95	38	40.0	12	12.6	3	3.1	1	1.0	6	6.3	2	2.1	14	14.7	4	4.2	4	4.2	1	1.0	10	10.5
1855-1858	67	25	37.3	11	16.4	6	8.9	2	2.9	2	2.9			12	17.9			1	1.4			8	11.9
1825-1858	815	380	46.6	150	18.4	23	2.8	14	2.2	28	3.4	23	2.8	113	13.8	12	1.4	16	1.9	2	.2	50	6.1

closes the period of this study.[5] This does not mean that all of these men actually graduated from the seminary, but for convenience they have been listed by "classes"; that is, the year in which they were supposed to graduate. This follows the procedure used in the bulletins of the school.

Of the sixty-six students in the first five classes, 1825-29, only three men were born outside of New England and forty-seven (71.2%) were natives of Connecticut. However, the percentage of students whose birthplace was Connecticut grows less with each succeeding group of graduating classes, until in the final period it amounted to only 37.3 per cent.

The classes which contained the largest percentage of students from Massachusetts were those of 1840-44, when forty-one out of 169 students (24.2%) were natives of that state. The state of New York reached its maximum proportional representation in two separate periods, the classes of 1835-39 and of 1855-60, the percentage being 17.9 in each case.

Although an examination of Table II reveals that the numbers and percentages of students from each state fluctuate greatly from one period to the next, there appears to be a gradual increase in the percentage of those who came from

---

5. Table No. I was based upon the annual Catalogue of Yale College, with the exception of the academic years 1822/23 - 1825/26, for which years data was obtained from the General Catalogue of Students of the Theological Department in Yale College (1838). The rest of the data found in the tables discussed in this chapter were obtained from the Eighth General Catalogue of the Yale Divinity School (1922), which is the first issue to give complete information concerning the alumni who were students during the years 1822-1858.

outside New England. This was probably due in part to the widening recognition of the seminary following the scattering of its alumni, and in part to the increasing facilities of communication and transportation concomitant with the growing industrialization of the states.

Taking the period 1822-23 to 1857-58 as a whole, the 815 students in attendance came from the following states: Connecticut, 380 (46.6%); Massachusetts, 150; New York, 113; New Hampshire, 28; Vermont and Pennsylvania, 23 each; Maine, 18; New Jersey, 12; Ohio, 16; Illinois, 2; miscellaneous, including those from southern states and foreign countries, 50. Of the entire group, 599, or almost three-fourths were natives of New England. This majority was doubtless due not only to geographic proximity but also to the fact that the school was almost entirely devoted to the interests of the Congregational denomination, whose membership lay largely in this territory. This feature will be discussed in a subsequent section.

Colleges Attended

The course of study given in the Theological Department of Yale College assumed a college education as a prerequisite, although college graduation was not made a requirement for entrance into the school.[6] Table III contains the record of the distribution of colleges which had been attended by

---

6. Principles and Regulations of the Theological Department in Yale College (1832), Chapter III, Statute 2. MS.

the 782 students of the period studied for whom information is available on this point. These data are arranged in five-year periods by graduating classes.[7] All of the men designated as alumni of the various colleges were graduates of those institutions with the exception of twelve.[8] Of these 782 students, 706, or almost exactly nine-tenths had attended some college and 682 (88.7%) were college graduates. For seventy-six of the students, there is no evidence that they attended any college, which is not remarkable in view of the wide-spread custom of private teaching in those days.

Yale College was the alma mater of 483 (71.7%) of the 782 students for whom information of this kind is available. From a comparison of Table I and Table III it will be noted that, as one might expect, the percentage of the alumni of Yale College decreases in the periods of largest attendance, and with the exception of the classes of 1855-60, increases with the periods of smallest attendance.

There was no other college that compared with Yale in the number of alumni sent to the Theological Department. Amherst College sent 31 men; Union College 29; Dartmouth 17; Middlebury 15; Princeton 10 and Harvard 7. From an examination of Table III a decrease in the alumni of the eastern

---

7. See Table III on the next page.
8. The class-groups during which these twelve men attended the Yale Theological Department and the colleges from which they came are as follows: 1830-1834, one - Yale; 1835-1839, one - Datmouth; 1840-44, four - Yale, Hobart, Yale, Williams; 1850-1854, two - Yale, New York University; 1850-1854, two - Madison, Missionary Institute of Illinois; 1855-1860, two - Yale, Brown.

TABLE III   DISTRIBUTION OF COLLEGES ATTENDED BY STUDENTS WHO
WERE MEMBERS OF THE THEOLOGICAL DEPARTMENT OF YALE COLLEGE
DURING THE YEARS 1822-1858; ARRANGED BY CLASSES

CLASS	TOTAL	YALE NO.	YALE PERCENT	PRINCETON NO.	PRINCETON PERCENT	HARVARD NO.	HARVARD PERCENT	UNION NO.	UNION PERCENT	DARTMOUTH NO.	DARTMOUTH PERCENT	AMHERST NO.	AMHERST PERCENT	MIDDLEBURY NO.	MIDDLEBURY PERCENT	MISCELLANEOUS NO.	MISCELLANEOUS PERCENT	NON-COLLEGE NO.	NON-COLLEGE PERCENT	PERCENT OF COLLEGE MEN FROM YALE
1825-1829	66	44	66.6	4	6.0			2	3.0	1	1.5	2	3.0	3	4.5	6	6.0	6	9.2	73.3
1830-1834	107	71	66.3	1	.9	1	.9	3	2.8	6	5.6	5	4.6	1	.9	13	12.1	10	9.3	73.1
1835-1839	155	88	56.7	3	1.9	1	.6	11	.6	2	1.2	5	3.2	8	5.1	22	14.1	14	9.0	62.3
1840-1844	168	88	52.3			5	2.9	13	7.0	4	2.3	7	4.1	2	1.1	31	20.0	18	10.7	58.6
1845-1849	137	95	69.3	2	1.4			1	.7	3	2.1	5	3.6			20	14.5	11	8.0	75.3
1850-1854	88	50	56.0					1	1.2	1	1.2	4	4.5	1	1.2	24	27.2	7	7.9	61.7
1855-1860	66	47	71.2					1	1.5			3	4.5			6	9.0	10	15.1	63.9
1825-1860	762	463	61.7	10	1.2	7	.8	32	4.0	17	2.1	31	3.9	15	1.9	119	13.9	76	9.7	65.4

colleges, with the exception of Yale and Amherst, will be
noted. This is true of Princeton, Harvard, Bowdoin, and
Dartmouth. Of the first three colleges named there was not
a single alumnus among the members of the graduating classes
of 1850 to 1860; and no alumnus of Dartmouth is found in the
last group of classes, 1855-60. In these same years,
1855-60, Yale College alumni made up 83.9 per cent of the
college men in the student body for those years, this being
the largest percentage of domination by a single college in
any of the class-groups.

Professions Followed by the Alumni

Eleven of the alumni of the Theological Department in
Yale College during the first thirty-five years of its history died before they had entered upon a profession.[9] There
is no information available about the occupational choice of
thirty-five others. Data are given in Table IV concerning
the professional distribution of the remaining 768 alumni of
the school for the period being studied. It will be noted
that 91.8 per cent of this number served in some profession
or other which was specifically devoted to religious interest. Of these 768 men, 480, or a little over three-fifths,
may be classified as ministers who spent the major portion
of their lives as pastors of local churches throughout the
country. This was consistently the favorite profession, the

---

9. See Table VI, p. 143.

TABLE IV PROFESSIONAL DISTRIBUTION OF THE ALUMNI OF THE THEOLOGICAL DEPARTMENT OF YALE COLLEGE FHO WERE STUDENTS DURING THE YEARS 1822-1858; BY CLASSES

CLASS	TOTAL	MINISTER		TEACHER		TEACHER AND MINISTER		GENERAL RELIGIOUS WORK		BUSINESS		FOREIGN MISSIONARY		DOCTOR OR LAWYER		POLITICAL SERVICE	
		NUMBER	PERCENT	NUMBER	PERCENT	NUMBER	PERCENT	NUMBER	PERCENT	NUMBER	PERCENT	NUMBER	PERCENT	NUMBER	PERCENT	NUMBER	PERCENT
1825-1829	67	44	65.6	7	10.4	7	10.4	7	10.4	1	1.4	1	1.4			3a	
1830-1834	108	64	59.2	8	7.4	9	8.3	14	12.9	5	4.6	6	5.5	2	1.8	1a	
1835-1839	150	99	66.0	17	11.3	11	7.3	10	6.6	8	5.3	1	.6	4	2.6	3a	
1840-1844	155	102	65.8	11	7.0	8	5.1	14	9.0	9	5.8	5	3.2	4	2.5	2	1.2
1845-1849	135	81	60.0	15	11.1	8	5.9	14	10.3	5	3.7	7	5.1	4	2.9	7a	
1850-1854	91	53	58.2	7	7.6	5	5.4	6	7.6	8	8.7	7	7.6	3	3.2	1	.7
1855-1860	62	37	59.6	11	17.7	1	1.6	6	9.6	4	6.4	2	3.2	1	1.6	3a	1.0
1825-1860	788	480	61.3	76	9.8	49	6.3	71	9.3	40	5.2	29	3.7	18	2.3	4 18a	.5

a. In political service as a secondary profession; not counted in totals.
b. Engaged in literary pursuits all of his life.

percentage of students choosing it being more than half in every five-year group and rising to 66.9%, or about two-thirds, in the class group of 1835-39.

Seventy-six of the students became teachers. One group of alumni, forty-five in number, spent their years of service almost equally in the two professions of teaching and the ministry and have this double classification. When the number of alumni who were both teachers and ministers is added to the number who were ministers only, the total constitutes 68.8 per cent of the 768 alumni who were ministers for a part or the whole of their professional lives.

Some of the alumni entered upon "general religious work", by which is meant all service rendered in the capacity of editor of a religious periodical, secretary to a Home or Foreign Mission Board, or other administrative denominational or interdenominational activity. There were seventy-one, or about one-tenth of the total, who did this type of work. By virtue of their positions these men entered largely into the official history of their denominations, although they did not necessarily give any greater service or make any greater name for themselves than did their colleagues in other forms of Christian work.

The school sent out only twenty-nine men to the foreign missionary field during this period. The probable reasons for this small percentage of alumni who served in this capacity will be noted in the discussion of Home and Foreign Missions in Chapter XII.

Sixty-two of the alumni did not enter upon a specifically

religious profession of any kind. Forty became business men, eighteen doctors or lawyers, and four entered governmental service. This last profession was also followed by eighteen of the ministers, in one capacity or another, as a secondary profession, usually near the latter part of their lives. The class group which had the highest percentage of students entering secular occupations was that from 1850-54, when 12.9 per cent of the student body undertook this type of work, as contrasted with only 2.8 per cent in the first five years.

It has been noted that 480, or 61.3 per cent of the 768 alumni were ministers, and that 76, or 9.8 per cent were teachers. Table V shows the places where these ministers and teachers located after leaving the Theological Department of Yale College.[10] It is of some interest to see that 130, or 27.0 per cent of these, became residents of Connecticut. The percentage of those who remained in Connecticut varied from 18.5 in the years 1845-49 to 40.5 in 1850-60.

The highest percentage of ministers who settled in New England is found in the first five years, when thirty out of forty-four, or 68.1 per cent of the students of those years remained in that section of the country. Only six went to the "West", by which is meant the states west of Pennsylvania and New York, principally Ohio and Illinois. With the class of 1830 began the "Illinois Band",[11] and beginning with the class-groups of 1830-34 the percentage of ministers

------

10. See next page.
11. See pp. 383-389.

TABLE V — GEOGRAPHICAL DISTRIBUTION OF MINISTERS AND TEACHERS WHO WERE STUDENTS IN THE THEOLOGICAL DEPARTMENT OF YALE COLLEGE DURING THE YEARS 1822-1858; ARRANGED BY CLASSES

CLASS	TOTAL	MINISTERS															TEACHERS				
		CONNECTICUT		MASSACHUSETTS		OTHER NEW ENGLAND STATES		NEW YORK		NEW JERSEY		PENNSYLVANIA		WEST		TOTAL	EAST		WEST	
		NO.	PERCENT	NO.	PERCENT	NO.	PERCENT	NO.	PERCENT	NO.	PERCENT	NO.	PERCENT	NO.	PERCENT		NO.	PERCENT	NO.	PERCENT
1825-1829	44	13	29.5	5	11.3	12	27.2	4	9.0	1	2.1	1	2.2	6 / 1a / 1b	2.2 / 13.6 / 2.2 a	7	7	100		
1830-1834	64	19	29.6	6	9.3	16	25	8	12.5					11 / 2a	17.1 / 3.1 a	8	4	50	4	50
1835-1839	99	26	26.2	9	9.0	15	15.1	17	17.1	2	2.0	3	3.1	21 / 4a / 2b	21.2 / 4.0 a / 2.0 b	17	15 / 1a	88.2 / 5.8 a	1	5.8
1840-1844	102	23	22.5	17	16.6	20	19.6	14	13.7			3	3.0	28	27.4	11	7	63.6	4	37.3
1845-1849	81	15	18.5	8	9.8	19	23.4	5	6.1			1 / 1b	1.2 b	30 / 1c / 1a	37.0 / 1.2 c / 1.2 a	15	13	86.6	2	13.3
1850-1854	53	19	34.7	3	5.8	5	9.8	3	5.8	2 d	3.7 d	1 / 1a	1.8 / 1.8 a	14 / 1a	26.4 / 1.8 a	7	6	85.7	1	14.2
1855-1860	37	15	40.6	3	8.1	7	18.8	5	13.7					7	18.8	11	5 / 1a	45.5	5 / 1a	46.5 / 9.0 a
1825-1860	480	130	27.0	51	10.6	98	20.4	66	11.6	3 / 2a / 1b	.6 / .4 a / .2 b	8 / 2c / 1d	1.6 / .4 c / .2 d	117 / 1c / 1a	24.2 / .2 c / .2 a	76	57	7.5	17 / 2a	23.3 / 2.6 a

a. minister or teacher in the South
b. minister in Canada
c. minister in Europe
d. minister in several Eastern States
e. minister in Russia

who located in the "West" increased rapidly with each succeeding class-group until the peak, 37.0 per cent, or thirty of the 81 men who became ministers, was reached in the years 1845-49.

It is interesting to compare Table II, which shows the distribution of the birthplaces of the students, with Table V which shows where those who became ministers settled after leaving the school. Taking into account the totals of all the class-groups from 1825-1860, we find the following facts: 380, or 46.6 per cent of the students were born in Connecticut; 130, or 27.0 per cent of those who became ministers, settled in that state. One hundred and fifty or 18.4 per cent of all students were born in Massachusetts; 51, or 10.6 per cent of the ministers, located there. The other states in New England, Maine, New Hampshire, and Vermont, were represented by 69 students and received back as ministers 98, or 20.4 of all those who became ministers. New York sent 113 of her sons to the school and took back 56 as ministers. The "West", which sent only eighteen men, received back 117, or 24.2 per cent of all those who became ministers. These figures show clearly the scattering to the "West" and to the northern states of New England of the students born in Connecticut and Massachusetts. These figures refer only, of course, to the alumni who became ministers; the ratio is little changed when those who became teachers are also taken into account.

Considering only the places in which they located, and without regard to the states in which they were born, we find that of the 480 students of the Theological Department who became ministers, a little over one-fourth settled in Connecticut; over half settled in all of the New England states; a little more than one-tenth in New York, and almost one-fourth in the West. Of the seventy-six alumni who entered the teaching profession, exactly three-fourths taught in the East; one-fourth in the West, and the remainder, 2.6 per cent, taught in the Southern States.

Denominational Affiliations of the Alumni

An historical sketch of the relationships between Presbyterianism and Congregationalism during the years 1775-1852 should aid in the understanding of the factors which influenced the denominational distribution of the alumni of the Theological Department in Yale College of the period 1822-1858.

Before the Revolutionary War a widespread fear of the establishment of Episcopacy in the colonies led to an increased friendly attitude between the Presbyterian and Congregational Churches. This was true especially in Connecticut. Annual joint conventions of representatives of the Synod of New York and Philadelphia and the Associations of Connecticut met during the years 1766 to 1775.[12] The effect of these joint meetings was a closer feeling of denominational kinship

---

12. Minutes of the Convention of Delegates from the Synod of New York and Philadelphia, and from the Associations of Connecticut 1766 to 1775, Hartford, 1843. 63 pp.

which found expression in such declarations as that of the Hartford North Association, which declared that Congregationalism was in all essentials in unity with Presbyterianism.[13]

It was just at this time when the Presbyterians of the Middle States and the Congregationalists of Connecticut felt themselves so much one, that a home missionary problem of hitherto unknown importance arose, affecting both bodies, and seeming to make coöperation desirable. In the westward movement of the people of New England into New York and Ohio, the Congregational ministers had found themselves working side by side with the Presbyterians. In 1790 the General Association of Connecticut voted that a further degree of union with the Presbyterians was desirable, and a committee of correspondence was appointed to secure this result.[14] The Presbyterian General Assembly was more than willing;[15] in 1791 a joint committee representing it and the Connecticut Association met at New Haven and provided for united representation at each of the separate annual meetings.[16]

The coöperation of the two bodies increased with each year until in 1800 the General Association of Connecticut appointed Jonathan Edwards the Younger and Jonathan Freeman, who were delegates from the General Assembly, and Nathan

---

13. Record printed in George Walker's History of the First Church in Hartford, 1633-1883, (1884) p. 358.
14. Records of the General Association of Connecticut, 1738-1799, published by order of the Association (1888), p. 133.
15. See Minutes of the General Assembly, 1791, pp. 29, 33.
16. The Minutes of this meeting are given in the Records of General Association, op. cit., pp. 189-191.

Williams of Tolland, and Nathan Strong of Hartford who were trustees of the Connecticut Missionary Society, as a Committee to prepare a report on the subject of further coöperation between the two denominations in the work of Home Missions.[17] Out of the report of this Committee came a resolution, which was passed by the General Association, to the effect that a Committee be appointed to represent the General Association to confer with a Committee to be appointed by the General Assembly of the Presbyterian Church, "to consider measures proper to be adopted both by this Association and said Assembly, to prevent alienation, to promote harmony and to establish as far as possible, an uniform system of Church Government, between those inhabitants of the new Settlements, who are attached to the Presbyterian form of church government, & those who are attached to the congregational form."[18]

Having thus the support of the Connecticut Churches, the proposition for agreement came before the General Assembly of the Presbyterian Church in May, 1801. This body appointed a committee on the subject.[19] The report of this committee, the celebrated "Plan of Union", made provisions whereby the ministers of either denomination were acceptable in the other church group.[20] This "Plan of Union" was passed by the General Assembly, and was presented to the

---

17. <u>Records of the General Association of Connecticut</u>, 1800, pp. 204, 205.
18. Ibid., p. 208.
19. <u>Minutes of the General Assembly of the Presbyterian Church</u>, 1801, pp. 212, 221.
20. Ibid., pp. 224, 225.

General Association of Connecticut at its meeting in Litchfield, June 16, 1801. It was ratified by this body without alteration.[21]

This agreement appears to have been entered into with good faith and cordiality on both sides. However, certain factors worked against its continuance. In practice many of the churches in the West which should have been Congregational in view of their New England heritage, became Presbyterian. The Congregational ministers who went to Ohio and neighboring states joined Presbyteries. That this was the fact was largely due in part to Congregational apathy, and in part to geographical consideration. The Presbyteries of Pennsylvania were friendly and close at hand, and New England seemed far away indeed. A second factor worked against Congregationalism in that when a church once joined a Presbytery it could not readily relinquish the connection. On Congregational principles a church may by majority vote carry itself and its property into a willing Presbytery; but on the Presbyterian principles no church can withdraw from an unwilling Presbytery by majority vote.

Although the "Plan of Union" thus added to the number of Presbyterian Churches, it by no means satisfied all Presbyterians. The stricter Presbyterians had long looked upon many of the "New Divinity"[22] as of questionable orthodoxy, and this feeling became intensified when the teachings

---

21. Minutes of the General Association of Connecticut, 1801, p. 5.
22. For a short description of this group, see pp. 314-321.

of Professor Nathaniel W. Taylor at the Theological Department in Yale College began to cause serious division in Connecticut Congregationalism and led to the founding, in 1834, of a more conservative theological seminary at East Windsor, Connecticut.

These disputes were transplanted to that part of the Presbyterian body which had been largely drawn from New England,--the portion formed under the "Plan of Union". For example, Dr. Lyman Beecher of Cincinnati seemed heretical to the more conservative Presbyterians, while the churches of New York and Ohio largely looked upon him as a champion. The trial of Dr. Beecher[23] on charges of doctrinal unsoundness increased the bitterness between the "Old School" and "New School" factions in Presbyterianism, and with the rise of the "heretical" Oberlin Theology, which savored of "Taylorism", the "Old School" group began to distrust any theology which came from New England. The animosity grew until the two factions in Presbyterianism were separated as a result of the action of the "Old School" group, which was in the majority, at the General Assembly in May, 1837.[24] The "Plan of Union" was abrogated and some of the Presbyteries of "New School" sympathy were excluded. The General Association of Connecticut took no definite action on the question of the continuance of the "Plan of Union", and the "New

---
23. Charles Beecher, ed., Autobiography, Correspondence, etc., of Lyman Beecher, Vol. 2, Chapter XXXVII
24. Minutes of the General Assembly, 1837, passim.
25. Proceedings of the General Association of Connecticut, 1837, pp. 5, 9; 1838, p. 8.

School" Presbyterians continued to work as formerly under the "Plan".[26]

But while these events were in progress, Congregationalism began to awaken to a degree of denominational self-recognition. Signs of a quickening sense of its own value appeared in the organization of State Associations in what had been fields of missionary effort under the "Plan of Union". Such an organization was effected in New York in 1834, in the Western Reserve in 1836, in Iowa in 1840, Michigan in 1842, Illinois in 1844, all of Ohio in 1852. On October 5, 1852, there gathered at Albany, New York, the first meeting of a synodical character, representative of Congregationalism as a whole, which had assembled since the Cambridge body in 1646-1648. This Convention took steps whereby the "Plan of Union" was rejected, and the strengthening of Congregational Churches in the West was assured.[27]

The denominational affiliations of the alumni of the Theological Department in Yale College were greatly influenced by that portion of American Church history which has just been briefly reviewed. This series of events explains the fact that about one-tenth of the alumni served in both Presbyterian and Congregational Churches, and gives the reason for the rapid decrease of those alumni serving Presbyterian Churches

---

26. Minutes of the General Assembly of the Presbyterian Church in America (New School), N.Y., 1838. passim.
27. Proceedings of the General Convention of Congregational Ministers and Delegates in the United States held at Albany, N.Y., on the 5th, 6th, 7th, and 8th of October 1852. New York, 1852. 95 pp. passim.

in the classes of 1855-1860 as compared with the earlier class-groups.[28]

One hundred and twenty-four of the students never became ordained in any denomination. When this number, added to the eleven who died at an early age, is subtracted from the 784 about whom we have information of this kind, there remain 649 students who were ordained. Of this group the Congregationalists constituted 424, or almost two-thirds, the Presbyterians 91, or about one-seventh, those who served in both of these denominations, 81, or a little less than one-seventh, the Episcopalians, 20, or about one twenty-fifth, and the Baptist, 9, or 1.3 per cent. The remaining thirteen alumni served in various denominations.[29] All those who were Congregationalist at some time in their lives including those of the miscellaneous group who were temporarily Congregationalists, constituted almost four-fifths of all those who were ordained. Alumni who served at least one Presbyterian or one Congregational Church made up 93.2 per cent of the entire group who were ordained.

Honorary Degrees Obtained by the Alumni

Of the 815 students who were in the classes of 1825-1860, 150, or 18.4 per cent, received honorary degrees at some time subsequent to their graduation. There were 204 honorary degrees, in all, given to these students; the chart

---

28. See Table VI on the next page.
29. See footnotes a-m with Table VI.

TABLE VI DENOMINATIONAL DISTRIBUTION OF THE ALUMNI OF THE THEOLOGICAL DEPARTMENT OF YALE COLLEGE WHO WERE STUDENTS DURING THE YEARS 1822-1858; ARRANGED BY CLASSES

CLASS	TOTAL	CONGREGATIONAL		PRESBYTERIAN		CONGREGATIONAL AND PRESBYTERIAN		EPISCOPALIAN		BAPTIST		MISCELLANEOUS		DIED AT AN EARLY AGE		UNORDAINED	
		NUMBER	PERCENT	NUMBER	PERCENT	NUMBER	PERCENT	NUMBER	PERCENT	NUMBER	PERCENT	NUMBER	PERCENT	NUMBER	PERCENT	NUMBER	PERCENT
1825-1829	65	41	63.0	2	3.0	10	15.3	2	3.0	1a	1.5			2	3.0	7	10.7
1830-1834	111	63	56.7	11	9.9	14	12.6	3	2.7	1	.9	2e 1f	1.8	5	4.5	12	10.8
1835-1839	152	64 2b	42.1	21 1c 1b	13.8	25 1b	16.4	9 1b	5.9	1	.6	3b 1f 1k	1.9			29	19.0
1840-1844	169	91	53.8	24	12.4	11	6.5	5	2.9	2	1.1	2h 1k 1a	1.1	3	1.7	31	18.3
1845-1849	134	71	52.9	21	15.6	16	11.9	3	2.2	3	2.2	2j 1k	1.4	1	.7	17	12.6
1850-1854	91	55 1b	60.4	10	10.9	7	7.6	3	3.2	1	1.0	1e	1.0			14	15.3
1855-1860	62	39 1b	63.8	2	3.2	2	3.2	1	1.6			4d 3m 1k	6.4			14	22.5
1825-1860	784	424	54.0	91	11.6	85	10.8	26	3.3	9	1.1	14	1.7	11	1.4	124	15.6

a. Congregationalist & Baptist. b. Congregs. & Episcopalian. c. Presbyterian & Epis. d. Congregs. & Presby. & Epis. e. Evangelist c. Presby. & Congregs. f. Swedenborgian g. Congregs. & Epis. & Catholic Apostolic h. Dutch Reformed. i. Disciples of Christ. j. Methodist & Congregs. & Presby. k. Lutheran

on the following page shows that a number of men received two or more degrees. The degrees were of various kinds: 129 Doctors of Divinity, 34 Masters of Art, 41 Doctors of Law, and a scattering of Ph.D.'s, Litt.D.'s, S.T.D.'s, and L.H.D.'s. The degrees given by Yale, Harvard and Princeton have been listed separately on the chart. It is rather interesting to note that over one-half of the 204 degrees were Doctors of Divinity given by forty-two colleges and universities other than Yale, Harvard and Princeton, showing the widespread influence of the alumni of the seminary. Amherst College honored ten, Hamilton nine, and Middlebury eight, of this group of alumni in this way. It was noted above that only seven Harvard graduates came to Yale for theological training during this period, this being only .8 per cent of the total student body concerning whom this information is available. Table VII shows that Harvard granted seven D.D. degrees, three LL.D. degrees and one S.T.D. degree upon the alumni of the Theological Department in Yale, this being 3.2 per cent of all the honorary degrees received. Yale College granted thirty-seven degrees to men, which is more than the number given by any other college or university.

The percentage of students in each class-group who received honorary degrees does not vary a great deal. The lowest is 13.1 for the years 1835-39, and the highest is 22.1 for the years 1850-54. The gradual decrease in student attendance during the last half of the period from 1822-58 is not paralleled by a decrease in the percentage of these

TABLE VII HONORARY DEGREES GRANTED TO MEMBERS OF THE THEOLOGICAL DEPARTMENT OF YALE COLLEGE WHO WERE STUDENTS DURING THE YEARS 1822-1858; ARRANGED BY CLASSES

CLASS	TOTAL	D.D.						M.A.						L.L.D.						OTHER DEGREES		ALUMNI OBTAINING DEGREES	
		YALE	PER CENT	HARVARD	PER CENT	PRINCETON	PER CENT	MISCELLANEOUS	PER CENT	YALE	PER CENT	PRINCETON	PER CENT	MISCELLANEOUS	PER CENT	YALE	PER CENT	HARVARD	PER CENT	PRINCETON	PER CENT	MISCELLANEOUS	PER CENT	NUMBER	PER CENT	NUMBER	PERCENT
1825-1829	12	⓪	8.3					ⓢ	5.0	1	8.3											②	16.6			10	16.6
1830-1834	21	②	4.7					⑥⑥⑥⑥③	57.1	1	4.7					ⓞ	4.7			③		③	14.0			18	15.3
1835-1839	33		3.0					14 ⑥③③⑥③	54.5	⑥ 0	9.0					ⓞ	3.0					⑥⑥⑥③	21.2	⑧ P.H.D. N.Y.U.	3.0	23	13.1
1840-1844	46	3⑥	10.3					17 ⓞ③③⑥④	62.1	0 1	4.3			ⓞ④ 4	13.0			③	6.3			⑥② 7	13.0	1 P.H.D. /⑤ S.T.D.–HARVARD / LITT.D.– / AMHERST	6.5	37	21.3
1845-1849	34	2⑥	5.5					13 ⓞⓞ⑥②	70.5	⑥	2.9											⑥ 2	14.7	/ LITT.D. ⑥ P.H.D.– PRINCETON	5.5	28	20.7
1850-1854	39	② ⑥ ⑥	12.5			⑥	2.5	7 ③ ⑥ ⑥ ② ⓞ ⓞ	43.5	ⓞ ⓞ	1.5	② ⑤	2.5	1	1.5	ⓞ ②	1.5					⑥ ⑥ 1	7.8	1 P.H.D.– LAFAYETTE 1 P.H.D.– BELOIT	5.1	22	22.1
1855-1860	19	ⓞ ⑥	10.5					4 ⓞ ⑥	34.5	2	10.5			⑧	5.2	1	5.2					⑥ ⑥	21.0	L.H.D.– HAMILTON ⑥ L.H.D.– COLUMBIA	10.5	12	19.4
1825-1860	204	17	8.3	4	1.9	1	.4	107	52.5	15	7.3	3	1.4	8	3.9	5	2.0	3	1.4	3	1.4	30	14.2	10	4.9	150	18.4

a. Each numeral in a circle in each class group represents an individual. For example the "2" which is found in seven positions opposite "1850-1854" (Class group) represents the degrees received by Professor George P. Fisher, whose degrees are named in the text on p. 146.

alumni obtaining degrees. In fact, as just stated, the class-group having the highest percentage was that of 1850-54, and the later groups were not far behind. If the obtaining of honorary degrees by the alumni is evidence of their quality as students, perhaps the students of the last ten years of this period, as compared with the previous ten classes, supplied in quality what they lacked in numbers.

Among those who were exceptionally honored, Professor George P. Fisher of the class of 1851, received seven degrees, as follows: M.A. (Hon.) Yale, 1867; D.D., Brown, 1866, Edinburgh, 1886, Harvard, 1886, Princeton, 1896; LL.D., Princeton, 1879, Yale, 1901. Professor Noah Porter of the class of 1836 was honored with the following: D.D., New York University, 1858; LL.D., Western Reserve, 1870, Trinity College (Connecticut), 1871, and Edinburgh, 1886.

Even though this study is chiefly concerned with the members of the Theological Department, while they were students there, it should not be unfitting at this point to refer to a few of the alumni of the institution of the period under review (1822-1858) who have been outstanding in their contributions, each in his own field of service. Several devoted their lives to Yale. There have been inducted into office since the founding of the Theological Department in the year 1822 three Presidents of Yale College and Yale University who were ministers. All three of these men were students in this Department during the period under review. Theodore Dwight Woolsey of the Class of 1826 was President of Yale College, 1846-1871; Noah Porter of the Class of 1826, President, 1871-1886; Timothy Dwight of the Class of 1853,

President, 1886-1899. Each of these gentlemen had been a Professor in Yale College prior to his election as President, and Timothy Dwight was the leader in the work of reconstruction for the Theological Department during perhaps the most trying period of its history, 1858-1871. W. A. Larned, Class of 1834 was Professor of Rhetoric and English Literature in the Academic Department of Yale College during the years 1839-1862; James Hadley, Class of 1846, was Assistant Professor and Professor of Greek Language and Literature in the same Department, 1848-1872. Two of the students of this period (1822-1858) became Professors in the Theological Department and Deans of the Yale Divinity School. George P. Fisher, Class of 1851, Professor of Ecclesiastical History, 1861-1901, Dean 1895-1901; George E. Day, Class of 1838, Professor of Hebrew Language and Literature and Biblical Theology, 1866-1891, Dean 1888-1895. Professor Fisher had previously held the Chair of Divinity in Yale College 1854-1861, and Professor Day was chiefly responsible for the establishment of the Missions Library of the Yale Divinity School which bears his name. Wyllys Warner of the Class of 1830 was the Treasurer of Yale College during the years 1832-1852.

In the field of Foreign Missions perhaps the name of Peter Parker (Class of 1834) is best known. Among the alumni who had a part in the building of the "West", three of the members of the "Illinois Band" and of the Class of 1830, Theron Baldwin, Julian Monson Sturtevant, and Asa Turner, are best remembered. Perhaps of the many preachers and theologians among the alumni the most outstanding are Horace Bushnell

(Class of 1833) and his able disciple Theodore Thornton Munger (Class of 1855).

CHAPTER V

ADMINISTRATION OF THE THEOLOGICAL DEPARTMENT

ADMINISTRATION OF THE THEOLOGICAL DEPARTMENT

Relation to Yale College

It has been noted in an introductory chapter (Chapter I), that the Collegiate School of Connecticut was founded by ten trustees, all of whom were ministers.[1] The chief administrator of this school, the Rector, was chosen from the group of trustees, but his executive powers were limited. However, in the year 1745, through the efforts of the Rev. Mr. Clap, a new charter was obtained by Yale College from the General Assembly of Connecticut. This document recognized the chief administrator of the College as a leading member of the Corporation, and gave to him the title of "President" rather than "Rector".[2] Subsequent to the obtaining of this charter, however, President Clap became increasingly unpopular until the General Assembly refused to grant further funds for the support of the College.[3] Finally, in 1792, when substantial aid seemed absolutely essential to the life of the institution, on the favorable report of a committee which had conferred with the Corporation and had been given every means for a full knowledge of College affairs and their management, the Legislature of the State of Connecticut adopted a plan suggested by the Hon. James Hillhouse, the Treasurer of the

---

1. p. 7.
2. Thomas Clap, Annals of Yale College (MS. first Edition 1847 pp. 48, 49.
3. See pp. 28, 29.

College, by which in return for a grant of money from the State Treasury, the Governor, the Lieutenant-Governor, and the six senior members of the Upper House for the time being became ex-officio members of the Corporation. The new arrangement took effect by the ratification of the old Corporation in June, 1792.[4]

With the coming of Timothy Dwight to the presidency in 1795, the laws for students were revised in such a way as to recognize for the first time as a vital part of the government of the College the action of the Faculty, i. e., of the Professors and Tutors sitting in consultation with the President.[5] The influence of the Professors was more potent beginning with the presidency of Jeremiah Day, who was of the same generation with the Professors, and was their former colleague under the dominant leadership of President Dwight. Theodore Dwight Woolsey, who in 1846 followed Jeremiah Day as President of Yale College, in his inaugural address spoke of the common ground on which the President met with the Faculty as a teacher, and further stated that:

> "this equality has led in this College and ought to lead, to a theory of government which precludes everything arbitrary on the part of one man, and divides the labors and the responsibilities of administration among the whole faculty. To have carried out this theory in almost perfect harmony, is the boast of this College; is the secret of its success, and a pledge of what it may accomplish hereafter."[6]

---

4. President Stiles, Literary Diary, June 27, 1792. MS.
5. Chapter I, Statute I, III-V.
6. Discourses and Addresses at the Ordination of Theodore Dwight Woolsey to the Gospel Ministry, and at his Inauguration into the Presidency of Yale College (1846), pp. 99, 100.

The professional schools in Yale College during the period 1822-1858 appear to have been recognized as secondary appendages to the Academic Department. This idea of relationship was the natural one in view of the history of Yale College. The Academic Department received priority in view of its long history. On the other hand the professional departments began as professorships or as a series of lectures which were added to the college curriculum. In the year 1801 a Professorship of Law was instituted, with the Hon. Elizur Goodrich, of New Haven, late member of Congress, as the incumbent, with a small salary. The design of the Professorship was to provide for the Senior Class some general instruction by lectures on the principles of Natural and International Law and on the Constitution of the United States It was not expected to furnish undergraduates such instruction as would qualify them for the bar.[7] The Law Department began its work as a separate Department in Yale College in the year 1824. The Medical Department in Yale College began to function in the year 1813, when four professors were appointed. "The professorship of chemistry in the college made any new provision for this science unnecessary."[8] The establishment of the Theological Department in the year 1822, as has been noted in an introductory chapter (Chapter II), began with the raising of funds for one professorship, which came

---

7. James L. Kingsley, "A Sketch of the History of Yale College in Connecticut", American Quarterly Register, vol. 8 (February, 1836), p. 202.
8. Ibid., p. 203.

to be called the Dwight Professorship of Didactic Theology.

In a series of articles which appeared in the New Englander for July and October 1870, and April, July and October 1871,[10] Professor Timothy Dwight[11] in speaking of the College declares:

> "The first and the most important work to be done in the years immediately before us is, as we believe, a work of unification. . . . .
> . . . . The history of. . . .the past shows that the development in this, as in other similar institutions in our country, has not been a development of all parts together. It has been, on the contrary, a growth for a hundred years of one department alone by itself, and then an addition to this one department of others, which, from their later origin, have seemed to be gathered around it as their center. The life and vigor of our American Colleges--even where they have widened into Universities, as at Yale and Harvard--have continued largely at this center; and the governing powers have regarded the academical department as the object of their peculiar and almost their sole care. The institutions have thus, with all their enlargement and success, been, after all, rather colleges with certain outside sections than universities made up of coördinate and coequal branches. . . . . If they (professional departments) are left to provide for themselves altogether--in the expressive phrase of recent years, "hanging on the verge of government"--they may succeed, for a while, through the power and self-devotion of the members of their faculties, but, when these men are called away or die, the institutions will prove to have little or no independent life of their own."[12]

---

9. See p. 75.
10. Vol. 29, pp. 448-470, 602-621; vol. 30, pp. 312-334, 506-527, 637-658.
11. Professor Dwight's connection with Yale College was as follows: He was a graduate of Yale College in the year 1849, tutor in the Academic Department, 1851-55, student in the Theological Department 1851-53, Professor of Sacred Literature in the Theological Department 1858-86, President of Yale University 1886-99.
12. New Englander, vol. 29 (July, 1870), pp. 448-451.

In spite of the ambiguity resulting from the use of the term "Yale College" with reference to the Academic Departments, and also with reference to the institution with all its component parts, the name "University" was not officially adopted until the year 1887.[13] Hesitation in adopting this term appears to have been largely due to the fact that many institutions of an inferior order had adopted the title.[14]

Relation to the President and Fellows of Yale College

The President and Fellows of Yale College constituted a body of men which was final in its authority with regard to the major problems of the institution. This body received and disbursed the finances of the College. It engaged instructors for the several departments, and fixed the amount of their salaries. The President and Fellows gave the final judgment in regard to any changes in the course of study, in regard to the erection of buildings, and all matters of policy concerned with the direction of the institution.

The Faculties of the several Departments made their

---

13. Acts of the General Assembly of Connecticut with Other Permanent Documents Respecting Yale University. (Printed for the Use of the Corporation, not Published. 1901) p. 18
14. In his address at the Inauguration of Theodore D. Woolsey into the Presidency of Yale College (1846), President Day derides the action of smaller institutions in that they have assumed the name of "university", and are hardly more than the Gymnasia of Germany. He seems to glory in the venerable name of "Yale College". Timothy Dwight, in the series of articles cited above, remarks: "There has been a sort of satisfaction, we confess, in the minds of the friends of this institution that it has always had the name of College." New Englander, Vol. 29, p. 466.

desires known to the President and Fellows by means of petitions addressed to the entire group, or to its Prudential Committee, or to the President of the College. These "Memorials" or "Petitions" were concerned with all the problems of the institution. The Professors petitioned the President and Fellows concerning the financial needs of the institution, the plan of the course of study, the selection of instructors, and in fact all problems of importance, including the amount of their own salaries. The Faculty appears to have been a group which was free to advise concerning all matters of policy, and its recommendations were respected by the President and Fellows. The latter body, however, reserved for itself the major legislative powers.[15]

In the year 1832 the President and Fellows appointed a committee of three of their number to[16] visit the Theological Department and to make a report concerning its needs. This committee reported[17] that the Professors of this Department "feel the need of some stated medium of communication with this body, by a Committee which shall from time to time examine into the state of the department".[18] In conformity with this request the committee recommended that an annual Examining Committee be chosen from the members of the Corporation. It appears that except for the issuance of

---
15. Minutes of the President and Fellows of Yale College, 1798-1874. MS. See especially the records of 1817, 1835, 1856.
16. Noah Porter, Aaron Dutton, Mathew Noyes.
17. Report of the Examining Committee, December, 1832. MS. 4 pp.
18. Ibid., p. 4.

laws for the governance of the Theological Department (which were now to be revised), the President and Fellows had largely allowed the Department to follow an independent course.[19]

Relation to the President

According to the Principles and Regulations of the Theological Department in Yale College[20] adopted by the President and Fellows (1833), the Theological Faculty consisted of the President of the College and the Professors engaged in Theological instruction. The next statute states that "the President of the College shall preside in all meetings of the Theological Faculty."[21]

Mr. Jeremiah Day, President of Yale College, 1817-1846, said in his address at the inauguration of his successor, Theodore Dwight Woolsey:

> "But whether we have, or have not, in New Haven, a claim to the title of a university, the labors and responsibilities of the President are almost wholly confined to the College proper. This is his appropriate sphere of action, though as a member of the Borad of Trustees, he may have a nominal relation to the professional departments.
> What then is the specific object at which the President of a college, not a Chancellor of a university should aim, in discharge of the duties of his office? Is it not to <u>begin</u> the education

---

19. Report of the Examining Committee, December, 1832. MS. pp. 3, 4.
20. 11 pp. MS. In Sterling Memorial Library, Yale University.
21. Principles and Regulations of the Theological Department, Chapter III, pp. 1, 2.

of students?"[22]

Professor Timothy Dwight in his "Yale College: Some Thoughts Concerning Its Future"[23] writes:

> "The President of Yale College is the presiding officer of the Board of Trustees, and is the head of the faculty of each and every department. . . . In the practical working of the institution, however, the theory is not fully carried out. The institution. . . . began as a collegiate school, with its presiding officer as one of its teachers. When in subsequent times, other schools were added to the original one, new bodies of instructors were appointed to their peculiar work, but the President did not extend his teachings into new departments. In this respect he has always been limited, (except, indeed, in the giving of a few lectures, in special cases of late years,) to the college or academical branch of the institution. He has met with the faculty of that branch only, in their regular meetings, and his work has been mainly in association with them. Having so many duties in that department, more, even, at times, than ought to be imposed upon any single man--he has scarcely been able to take upon himself similar duties in other departments. The necessities of the case have made him, in reality, the president of one faculty only, while, in name, he has been head of all. If we look back thirty or forty years,[24] we doubt whether the College President ever, (except in the most extraordinary emergencies,) sat in session with the officers of the professional schools."[25]

---

22. *Discourses and Addresses at the Ordination of Theodore Dwight Woolsey Into the Gospel Ministry and his Inauguration Into the Presidency of Yale College* (1846), pp. 59, 60.
23. *The New Englander*, vols. 29, 30, pp. cit., footnote 10.
24. Professor Dwight wrote in 1870; thirty or forty years back (1830 or 1840) would include almost all of President Woolsey's administration (1846-1871) and part of President Day's administration (1817-1846).
25. *New Englander*, vol. 29 (July, 1870), p. 461.

Administration by the Faculty of the Theological Department in Yale College

Every candidate for admission to the Theological Department in Yale College was required to furnish the Professor of Didactic Theology with "satisfactory testimonials of his piety and talents for usefulness; and (unless in special cases, deemed proper to be made exceptions by the Theological Faculty) of his having completed a course of liberal education, and of his intention to engage in the ministry of the Gospel."[26] Such credentials were addressed to Professor Taylor by administrators or professors of colleges or seminaries, and by the clerks or pastors of churches.[27]

The "Board of Theological Professors" (which did not according to the statutes[28] include the President of the College), decided which students should be admitted to advanced standing;[29] and whenever a student was allowed to preach before his Senior year, this Board made possible such an exception to the rule.[30] The annual examinations, which took place on the last Thursday and Friday of the second Collegiate term, were administered in accordance with the

---

26. Principles and Regulations of the Theological Department in Yale College, Chapter II, p. 2.
27. Among the "Divinity Papers" are forty-eight recommendations for students from Churches or ministers, forty-three from the Seminaries, and two from Colleges. MS. 93 pieces.
28. Principles and Regulations, op. cit., Chapter III, p. 1.
29. Ibid., Chapter II, 3.
30. Ibid., Chapter IV, 6.

wishes of the Professors.[31] Whenever a student became negligent in the pursuit of his scholastic duties it was the duty of the Professors to advise and counsel him on the subject.[32]

According to the rules of the Theological Department whenever a student failed to attend a lecture it was his duty to present his excuse to the Professor who presided "at the given lecture or recitation."[33] The situation was such that one year, "when the class, consisting of two or three, omitted to ask for the lectures, and Professor Fitch, from his usual modesty, forebore to offer their delivery",[34] the course in Homiletics was entirely neglected. On September 15, 1861, at the inauguration of the professors who were to replace the faculty of the Theological Department during the years from 1822-1858, President Woolsey remarked in his address that "our Institution hitherto has been singularly destitute of regulations: each of the professors being content with so much attendance on his instructions as the students voluntarily gave, without demanding that punctual observance of duties which is imperative in other seminaries."[35]

The Theological Department in Yale College, therefore,

---

31. Principles and Regulations of the Theological Department in Yale College, Chapter IV, p. 7.
32. Ibid., Chapter III, p. 10.
33. Ibid., Chapter II, p. 4.
34. L. W. Fitch, Letter to the President and Fellows of Yale College, New Haven, July 24, 1861. MS., 3 pp.
35. Addresses at the Inauguration of the Professors in the Theological Department, September 15, 1861. p. 8.

during the period under review (1822-1858) seems to have been largely left to itself in the matter of administration by the President and Fellows as a body, and by the President himself. And in regard to the administration of the Department by the theological Faculty, the outstanding feature appears to have been a lack of any efficient direction or plan. No minutes of the meetings of this Faculty, nor any reference to any such records, have been discovered.

Administration of Finances

It is to be remembered that the Theological Department in Yale College was made possible through the gifts of many individuals as a result of a campaign for funds, carried on principally in the city of New Haven. Professors Goodrich and Fitch were leaders in this undertaking. This was the method in general use by the officials of Yale College during this period to satisfy the various needs of the institution.[36] The Theological Department was particularly dependent upon such means of financial support since no tuition or room rent was charged of its students.[37] Whenever the need for a new Professorship was recognized, individuals were asked to subscribe their names to a statement similar to the following:

> "We the undersigned agree to pay to the Treasurer of Yale College the sums assigned to our names on the first day of January 1829, & the same again on the

---

36. Major campaigns include those for funds for the Academic Department in 1831-1832, and in 1854, 1858, 1871, etc.; for the Cabinet of Minerals, 1825; for the Library, 1843.
37. The Catalogue of Yale College, any year, 1826-1858.

first of January 1830 & 1831 for the Professorship of Sacred Literature in the Theological Department, unless by some change in our circumstances we should be unable to pay the same."(38)

Four years after its establishment, the Theological Department received a heavy loss in the failure in June, 1826, of the Eagle Bank of New Haven.[39] An invitation was immediately given by the officials of Yale College to the "ladies and gentlemen of New Haven" to meet "at the Lecture Room in Orange-street," in order to devise means whereby the Department could "continue its existence."[40]

The first fund belonging to the Theological Department, that which was raised for its establishment, was known as the Dwight Professorship Fund. The fund for the Professorship of Sacred Literature was begun in 1829 and increased by the contributions of 1829-1831. The Pastoral Professorship Fund was instituted in 1839. The general fund known as the "Theological Fund" was largely derived from the monies which had been subscribed in the campaign of the year 1832, mainly carried on in the interest of the Academic Department. It is evident from the Illustration on the next page that little effort was made to increase these funds, since they remained

----

38. The heading of such a paper is here quoted; below are the names of the subscribers, most of them for less than five dollars.
39. The Eagle Bank of New Haven, Records of the Meetings of the Directors January 1812-June, 1826, and of the Committee of Stockholders, June 1826-May, 1834. MS. folio.
40. Circular, Yale College, July 27, 1827. 1 p.

ILLUSTRATION 1. THE FUNDS OF YALE COLLEGE,

1833, 1838, 1848, 1858, 1861.[a]

	1833	1838	1848	1858	1861
Academic Dep't. Total of Funds	$139,043.17	$132,983.92	$224,034.14	$409,941.50	$413,751.17
Theological Dept.					
General Fund	1,340.44	1,772.97	10,461.79	17,651.19	55,731.66
Dwight Professorship	20,132.44	20,503.44	20,721.08	20,428.22	22,878.00
Sacred Literature Professorship	11,092.50	11,972.38	11,972.38	11,951.38	11,820.00
Pastoral Professorship			5,000.00	6,800.00	6,578.63
Theological Accum'l Fund				11,718.11	12,165.01
Medical Dep't.	10,900.00	11,657.00	11,900.00	14,400.00	17,100.00
Law Dep't.	Balance due to the College		2,118.15	3,451.26	3,526.20

a. Based on the Reports of the Treasurer of Yale College, For The Years Given.

almost static throughout the period under observation, (1822-1858). As soon as some efforts were made, during the years 1858-1860, the Theological Fund was greatly increased.[41]

The funds for the Professorships of Sacred Literature and of Pastoral Charge were entirely inadequate for the payment of the $1200 annually due as the salary for each of the incumbents of these chairs. The actual income of the Professorship of Sacred Literature averaged yearly, 1843/44-1848/49, only 874 dollars.[42] Professor Gibbs seems to have had difficulty in obtaining all of his salary almost from the first.[43] "Estimates of Income of Theological Funds, for the Acad. Year 1851/2"[44] are given in Illustration No. 2.[45] This account represents the financial interests of the Department, and reveals the typical method whereby the salaries of the Professors were paid during this period. When the President and Fellows voted on August 14, 1849, that the "existent deficiency in the salary of the Professor of Sacred Literature be made up from the General Theological Fund, and the same be done for the Professor of Pastoral Charge",[46]

---

41. Statement of the Recent Donations to Yale Theological Seminary up to December 25th, 1859. not published, 10 pp. See also Illustration I, on the preceding page.
42. Note among the "Divinity Papers", MS., 1 p.
43. Note among the "Divinity Papers" (written by Professor Gibbs), August 25, 1830, September 7, 1830, telling of his conferences with the Prudential Committee and with Governor Tomlinson in regard to collecting arrearages on his salary.
44. MS., 4 pp.
45. See pp. 168-170, at the end of this chapter.
46. Minutes of the President and Fellows of Yale College, August 14, 15, 16, 1849. MS.

this body appears to have been following the usual procedure.
The manner in which it was suggested that the salaries of
Professors Gibbs and Goodrich be met is evident from the
following penciled note appended to the report of June 30,
1849:[48]

Prof. Gibbs		Prof. Goodrich	
745	Sacred Lit. (fund)	600	his fund and Mr. Bidwell[49]
54	for teaching Hebrew	120	Mrs. S.
800		301	Bonds & notes of Theol.
75	surplus of Dwights (fund)	1021	Fund; including minor of
875	/average	200	deficiency. This is
120	Kimberley house (rent)		covered by rent of rooms
1095			in Theol. Seminary.
132	Stocks of unexpended income		
1127	interest of		

The Report of the Committee appointed by the President and Fellows in the year 1832 for the purpose of investigating the needs of the Theological Department mentioned the first "embarrassment of the school as a lack of funds for the support of indigent students."[50] If any efforts had been made to meet this situation, they had not succeeded before 1852/53. The Catalogues of Yale College previous to this year invariably contained the following statement:

> "No funds have as yet been granted to this department for defraying the expenses of indigent students. In addition to the usual aid which may be derived from the American Education

---

47. See also the Minutes of the President and Fellows, July 26, 1853, July 25, 1854; President Woolsey's Minutes for business before the President and Fellows, MS., 1849, 1851.
48. MS., 2 pp.
49. Mr. Bidwell gave $300 a year for 5 years. His note, dated January 14, 1839, is among the "Divinity Papers".

Society,[51] there is an Association in this city whose object it is to assist those preparing for the Ministry."

The "Association" referred to above was most probably the "Charitable Society for the Education of Indigent Pious Young Men for the Ministry of the Gospel",[52] which was founded in New Haven, September 14, 1815. Hon. Tapping Reeve was elected President, Rev. Samuel Merwin, Vice President, Rev. Nathaniel W. Taylor, Secretary, Mr. Stephen Twining Esq., Treasurer, and Mr. Charles Sherman, Auditor. President Timothy Dwight, Professors Day, Silliman and Kingsley, and Messrs. Taylor and Merwin composed the Committee of Appropriations.

---

51. The American Education Society was incorporated under the laws of the Commonwealth of Massachusetts in the year 1816. According to its Constitution, the object of the Society was "to educate pious young men for the gospel ministry". One could become a member of the Society by subscribing to its Treasury, at one time, one hundred dollars. (Article I). A permanent fund, consisting of bequests, legacies, and donations, given for this special purpose, was formed by the Directors. (Article II). In 1850 the parent Society had twenty-six auxilaries, including the Connecticut Education Society, which was established in 1826. Young men, who, according to a designated group of men, were qualified in scholarship and character, were aided in the pursuit of their education for the ministry throughout their college and seminary courses if necessary, usually receiving a scholarship of seventy-five dollars a year, although the average sum per student was lower. During the academic year 1850/51 the number of students aided by the parent Society and its auxiliaries was four hundred. The report of 1852 reveals that the Connecticut Auxiliary sent $1,081.21 to the parent Society, and received appropriations to the amount of $3,110.00. The Societies did not include in their reports the names of the students, or the total number of students aided in a given institution.
52. Connecticut Charitable Education Society, Constitution and Records. MS.

Rev. Lyman Beecher was chairman of the Committee of Supplies. Twelve neighboring Associations of Congregational Churches each had two representatives in the Society. This Society confined its efforts to those students who were preparing for the ministry at Yale College.[53] The organization held an annual meeting and elected officers for the ensuing year.

The number of students rendered aid is not reported in the minutes of the Society until the meeting of December 6, 1876 when $391 was divided among seventeen academic students, and $400 among four theological students. The next session is the last one to be recorded, at which time (December 4, 1877), $450 was appropriated to students of each of the two departments.

Even though the obtaining of funds for indigent students appears to have been begun by the officials of the Theological Department in the year 1852, the total annual income had reached the sum of only $570 by the year 1867.[54]

Another financial problem which was faced by the Theological Department in the later years of this period was the need of funds for erecting a building more suitable to the requirements of the school than was the "Divinity College". When the President and Fellows had decided in 1835, to build a structure for the use of theological students on the College square and in line with the buildings of the Academic Department, it was agreed that when the expansion of this department

---

53. Connecticut Charitable Education Society, Constitution and Records. MS. Article 1.
54. Memorial of the Professors of the Theological Department to President and Fellows of Yale College, 1867. MS. p. 4.

demanded the site, the "Divinity College" should be removed.[55] Such a demand was made in the year 1856.[56] The very evident inadequacy of the building to meet the needs of the students of the Theological Department will be noted in a succeeding chapter.[57]

In a Memorial to the President and Fellows of Yale College, July 20, 1867, Professor Dwight, writing for the theological Professors, made an estimate of the financial needs of the Theological Department.[58] He stated that at least a sum of $15,000 was needed for the endowment of Professorships,[59] between $50,000 and $70,000 for funds for indigent students, and about $75,000 for a new building. In the introduction to his Memorial he stated that the funds of the institution totaled about $50,000 at the time of Professor Taylor's death in 1858, and the condition of affairs was such that an annual campaign was necessary for the supplying of the deficiency in the Professors' salaries.

The administration of the finances of the Theological Department appears to have been characterized by the same lack of efficient direction that, as was noted above, was a feature of the administration of the Department in general.

---

55. Minutes of the President and Fellows, January 7, 1835.
56. *Ibid.*, July 29, 1856.
57. Chapter XI; pp. 356, 357.
58. MS. 7 pp. Professor Dwight wrote in 1867, and the financial condition of the school had improved since 1858. See Illustration No. 1.
59. This is a modest sum; throughout the period 1858-1871 the faculty of the Theological Department sacrificed their salaries to the needs of the school.

ILLUSTRATION 2. ESTIMATES OF INCOME OF THEOLOGICAL FUNDS, FOR THE ACAD. YEAR 1851/2[a]

1851/2   Theological Fund

Receipts

Bills Pble. $10,418.68, of which $4000 at 7 per cent		280.
6418 " 6 " "		385.
Stocks 650.20 $36.& $21.		57.
Rent of house		120.
Rent of rooms in Theol. Bdg. occupied by Acad. students, &c. about		100.
Entrance Fees about		100.
From C. M. Fund	185.50 or	159.
		$1201.

Expenses

Insurance on Theological Building	30.. ..	
Sweeping and cleaning "	200.. ..	
Repairs say	50.. ..	
Locating Officer	25.. ..	
Rent of Lecture Room	50.. ..	
Mrs. Minor's Annuity	240.. ..	
Fuel and Lights about	30.. ..	
Income of Elliott fund		
1 p. c. invested		
5 p. c. spent in bks.	60.. ..	685..

Sacred Literature Prof. Fund

Receipts

Bills Pble. $10,900, of which $3200..at 7 per. cent		224..
7700.." 6 " "		462..
Stocks, $1141.		84..
From C. M. Fund.	113.. or	114..
		884..

Expenses

Salary of Professor Gibbs

---

a. In this Illustration an attempt has been made to reproduce a manuscript record found among the "Divinity Papers" in the Sterling Memorial Library of Yale University.

ILLUSTRATION 2. ESTIMATES OF INCOME OF THEOLOGICAL
FUNDS, FOR THE ACAD. YEAR 1851/2. (Continued)

Dwight Professorship Fund

Receipts

```
Bills Pble.        $13,900..@ 6 per cent  $834.
  Deduct int. on $700.. notes of
  J. C. Leffingwell, on which
  interest has not been paid for
  several years                              42.    792..

Prof. Fitch's subscription                         100..
Stocks $4443   22 sh. N. Haven Bk    198
               18     Middletown "   108
                4     Phoenix    "    36
                7     Cheshi. Turnpike 15          357
From C. M. Fund                                     60
                                                  1309.
Salary                                          $1200.
```

(Besides the foregoing Funds, there is a surplus
of Income unexpended, amounting to about $1000,
on wh. no interest is allowed.)

Pastoral Professorship Fund

Receipts

```
Bills Pbls.  $7100.62, of which $6000 at 7 per cent 420.
                                1100  " 6 "    "     66.
                                                    486
Miriam's subscription, if continued                 200
                      (not pledged)
                                                    686
                                             Salary
                                             $1200. ?
```

The income of the Salter Fund (of $120.. per annum, or
$94. if the fund is taken at its original sum of $1566.67.) for
"cultivating, encouraging & promoting the study of the Hebrew
language, and other Oriental Languages in Yale College." may
perhaps be applied towards the support of the Professor of
Sacred Literature. It is supposed that since about A. D. 1825,
this income has been expended, excepting four payments of $50
each, 1845-47 = $200..

ILLUSTRATION 2. ESTIMATES OF INCOME OF THEOLOGICAL FUNDS, FOR THE ACAD. YEAR 1851/2. (Continued)

Summary

Rects.		Expenditures	
Genl. Theol	1201.-	685.	
Sacr. Lit	884.-	1200	?
D. P.	1309.-	1200	
P. P.	686.-	1200	?
	$4080	$4285	

PART III

FACILITIES FOR INSTRUCTION

Chapter VI   Purpose and Plan of the Course of Study

Chapter VII   Administration and Content of the Course of Study.

Chapter VIII The Libraries.

Chapter IX   The Student Societies

CHAPTER VI

PURPOSE AND PLAN OF THE COURSE OF STUDY

PURPOSE AND PLAN OF THE COURSE OF STUDY

By the purpose of the course of study is meant those designs and aims which the leaders of the Theological Department served in the construction and execution of that course of study. For the purpose of discovering these aims, the official statements of the College officers on the subject will be examined at this point. The more detailed expression of that philosophy in practice will be investigated in connection with the contents of the course of study.

On September 11, 1827, the President and Fellows took cognizance of a demand, made by the undergraduate students, that the "dead languages" be left out of the course of study in the Academic Department, by passing a resolution that the Governor of the State, the President, and three Fellows[1] of the College should constitute a committee "to enquire into the expediency" of so altering the regular course of instruction. This Committee later requested the Faculty to express their views. A treatise, entitled "Reports on the Course of Instruction in Yale College, by a committee of the Corporation and the Academical Faculty", followed. This report was accepted by the Corporation and ordered published.[2]

---

1. His Excellency Governor Tomlinson, Rev. President Day, Rev. Dr. Chapin, Hon. Noyes Darling, and Rev. Abel McEwen.
2. Minutes of the President and Fellows of Yale College. September 9, 1828. MS. The Report was printed by Hezekiah Howe, New Haven, 1828. 56 pp.

The same was republished in the American Journal of Science and Arts, in 1829.[3] A portion of the article was included in the 1829/30 Catalogue of the College and retained its place therein, in its original form, until the issue of the Catalogue for the year 1854/55. The Corporation's order to publish, the inclusion in the Journal of Science, and finally in the College Catalogue, all indicate that this report had official sanction. Excerpts from the Catalogue follow:

> The object of the system of instruction to the undergraduate in the college is not to give a *partial* education, consisting of a few branches only; nor, on the other hand, to give a *superficial* education, containing a little of almost everything, nor to *finish* the details of either a professional or practical education; but to *commence* a *thorough* course, and to carry it as far as the time of the student's residence here will allow. It is intended to maintain such a proportion between the different branches of literature and science, as to form a proper *symmetry* and *balance* of character. In laying the foundation of a *thorough* education, it is necessary that *all* the important faculties be brought into *exercise*. When certain mental endowments receive a much higher culture than others, there is a distortion in the intellectual character. The powers of the mind are not developed in their fairest proportions, by studying languages alone, or mathematics alone, or natural and political science alone. The object in the proper collegiate department is not to teach what is peculiar to any one of the *professions*: but to lay the foundation which is common to them all. There are separate schools of Medicine, Law, and Theology, connected with the college. . . . With these the undergraduate course is not expected to interfere. . . . The principles of science and literature, are the common

---

3. Vol. 15, No. 2, Art. VIII, pp. 287-351. This periodical was conducted by Benjamin Silliman, M.D., LL.D., Professor of Chemistry, Mineralogy, &c. in Yale College, (see title-page); and was published in New Haven.

foundation of all high intellectual attainments. They give that furniture, and discipline, and elevation of mind,(4 which are the best preparation for the study of a profession. . . .

In a portion of the Report which does not appear in the Catalogue, these points are explained in greater detail:

The two great points to be gained in intellectual culture, are the discipline and the furniture of the mind; expanding its powers, and storing it with knowledge. The former of these is, perhaps, the more important of the two. A commanding object, therefore, in a collegiate course, should be, to call into daily and vigorous exercise the faculties of the student. Those branches of study should be prescribed, and those modes of instruction adopted, which are best calculated to teach the art of fixing the attention, directing the train of thought, analyzing a subject proposed for investigation, following, with accurate discrimination, the course of argument; balancing nicely the evidence presented to the judgment; awakening, elevating and controlling the imagination; arranging, with skill, the treasures which memory gathers; rousing and guiding the powers of genius.

In laying the foundation of a thorough education, it is necessary that all the important mental faculties be brought into exercise. . . . The mind never attains its full perfection, unless its various powers are so trained as to give them the fair proportions which nature designed. If the student exercises his reasoning powers only, he will be deficient in imagination and taste, in fervid and impressive eloquence. If he confines his attention to demonstrative evidence, he will be unfitted to decide correctly, in cases of probability. If he relies principally upon his memory, his powers of invention will be impaired by disuse. . . . . From the pure mathematics, he learns the art of demonstrative reasoning. In attending to the physical sciences, he becomes familiar with facts, with the process of induction, and the varieties of probable evidence. . . .(5

---

4. Catalogue of the Officers and Students of Yale College, 1829/30. pp. 26, 27.
5. American Journal of Science, 1st Series, Vol. 15, pp. 304, 305.

It is also urged that, "due proportion be observed between lectures,. . . . and recitations; that is examination in a textbook". It is argued that to use more than one textbook makes for a lack of definiteness, which confuses the student and allows him an excuse for his ignorance. Textbooks are not considered as necessary in the advanced studies in a professional school as they are in college. The author of the Report is of the opinion that the arguments presented, "with few exceptions, are not new and controverted points, but such as have long been settled."[6]

The Plan of the Course of Study

The plan of the curriculum for the Theological Department is provided for by the official rule of the President and Fellows in the "Principles and Regulations of the Theological Department in Yale College",[7] adopted by that body, August 21, 1833. Chapter I, a "General View of Theology as a Professional Study", explains the purpose of the school and outlines the course of study as follows:

> To meet the wants of the church and of the world, and the increasing demands of the Community for an able and efficient ministry, a full course of theological study, for those who have received a collegiate education, should embrace at least three years, and should, under favorable circumstances, extend, with more or less minuteness, over the following branches.

---

6. *American Journal of Science*, 1st Series, Vol. 15, p. 351.
7. MS. 11 pp.

I. The more important preparatory sciences, which are in a great degree anticipated in the College course, viz.
   1. Mental and Moral Philosophy.
   2. Some departments of Philology: as Latin, (2) Classic Greek, and (3) German.
   3. Ancient History.
   4. Natural Science.
II. Introduction to Theology, or, instruction respecting the nature and extent of the Science, the Method in which it should be studied, the books from which it is derived, and its history.
III. Exegetical Theology, or the knowledge which is employed in the interpretation of the Bible; embracing,
   1. The History of the Canon, or, the history of the origin, transmission, and present state of the text of those books which have been received among Christians as of divine authority.
   2. Sacred Philology; or the knowledge of the languages necessary for the interpretation of the Bible.
   3. Biblical Archaeology; or the knowledge of ancient things, either mentioned, alluded to, or implied in the Bible, viz.
      (1) Sacred Geography and Ethnography,
      (2) Sacred History and Chronology,
      (3) Natural History of the Bible,
      (4) Domestic, Political and Sacred Antiquities of the Hebrews.
   4. Sacred Criticism; or, the art of determining the true text of the Bible.
   5. Sacred Hermeneutics; or, the art of investigating and determining the true sense of the Biblical writers.
IV. Historical Theology: including,
   1. The History of theological opinions.
   2. The History of religious institutions particularly of the Church.
   3. The History of the progress of vital piety.
V. Systematic Theology; or instruction respecting doctrines and duties which are involved in the Christian System,
   1. Doctrines,
      (1) Of the Inspiration of the Sacred Volume
      (2) Of the Being and Attributes of God
      (3) Of Providence and Angels
      (4) Of the nature and character of man
      (5) Of the Savior and plan of Salvation
      (6) Of the means of Grace
      (7) Of Positive Institutions
      (8) Of the Last things, as Death, the Resurrection, the Judgment, Heaven, and Hell.

2. Duties
     (1) Toward God
     (2) Toward Fellow-beings
     (3) Toward Ourselves
VI. Applied Theology embracing,
  1. Homiletics; or, instruction concerning the Composition and Delivery of Sermons
  2. Liturgics; or, instruction concerning Devotional Exercises
  3. Catechetics; or that which relates to the instruction of the young
  4. Duty of the Pastor, (1) in his own Society, (2) as a member of Ecclesiastical bodies. (8

Chapter III gives the duties of professors, and states, besides the watching over the "spiritual interests of the Students", just which courses each professor shall teach. Chapter IV, "General Statutes" tells what courses shall be taken by each of the three classes. From the combining of these two chapters the following outline may be made:

Junior Class--

  Exegetical Theology--Professor Gibbs.

  Mental and Moral Philosophy--Dr. Taylor.

Middle Class--

  Systematic Theology--Professor Taylor.

  Exegetical Studies (cont.)--Professor Gibbs.

Senior Class--

  Applied Theology--Professor Fitch in Homiletics, and Professor Goodrich on the Pastoral Charge.

---

8. Principles and Regulations of the Theological Department in Yale College, pp. 1-4. MS.
9. It is noteworthy that even though in Chapter I the study of Church History is listed as required and in Chapter III it is stated that "the Professor of Latin Language in the College, it is expected, will instruct in Ecclesiastical History", there is no assignment of this course in the prescribed list of studies in Chapter IV. A course in Church History was not offered in the Theological Department before the appointment of Professor George P. Fisher in 1861.

Chapter IV further mentions the requirement of an entrance examination; the licensing of ministers in the Senior year;[10] and the holding of a public examination[11] of all the Classes, on the last Thursday and Friday of the "Second Collegiate" term, "at which time dissertations may also be read at the discretion of the Professor, or at such other time as the Committee from the Corporation, after consultation with the Professors should decide upon."

Chapter II, dealing with regulations concerning the students, declares that the Seminary is open to ministers of every denomination. Every candidate for admission is expected to have completed a course of liberal education, "unless in special cases, deemed proper to be made exceptions by the Theological Faculty."

In the notes of the lectures of Professor Fitch on Homiletics, in the Senior year, Mr. S. J. M. Merwin[12] records a general outline similar to the above classification of theology, and in his abridged lectures which follow, he has phrasing which is almost identical with the above. Exactly the same arrangement of subjects is given. In the Junior year, according to George E. Day's notes of the lectures of Professor Gibbs on Theological Encyclopedia, this plan of study was explained as an introductory course in theology.

----

10. Prior to the Senior year the students were not allowed to preach, except by very special permission, Statute 2.
11. An oral examination, in keeping with the method used in Yale College.
12. S. J. M. Merwin, Notes on Professor Fitch's Homiletics. MS.

The most unusual and very important feature of the classification is the use of "theology" in a very broad sense. Light is thrown upon the conception of theology as Professor Gibbs' lectures continue. He explains that Theology in the modern sense is the science of religion. "Science is an arrangement or collection of truths deduced from first principles: or, a learned and definite view of religious truth for practical purposes." He continues to discuss the difference between theology and religion. Religion is of divine origin, as old as the race of man. Theology is mere science; while Religion embraces thought, feeling and will. "The distinction between Religion and Theology is marked by πίστις and γνῶσις. Religion is for the people; Theology for the schools. Theology is difficult to obtain; Sources are in ancient and obscure books; it treats of invisible objects; it inculcates many things ungrateful to our natural feelings."

That the leaders in theological thought felt assured of the value of such a classification as the above, is apparent from the frequency of occurrence and faithfulness to the classification which has been noted. That exegetical study in the original language of the Sacred Scriptures should come first, and be followed by a Systematic Theology, which in turn was succeeded by a year of Practical Theology, seemed most logical. That this plan of the curriculum continued with hardly any changes, even of a minor nature, is apparent from the happy manner in which the notes of the students, for whatever year, fit nicely into the divisions of the studies laid down above. And when the curriculum of the School was first printed in the Yale Catalogue,[13] in the year 1850-51, this very same scheme was outlined, differing from the above plan only in a greater detail of treatment.

Guidance to the probable original source of this classification of theological studies so extensively used by the Theological Department is given by Mr. S. J. M. Merwin in his Notes on Professor Fitch's Homiletics. In the margin he indicates that the scheme of classification has been taken from the Biblical Repository, Volume I. This periodical was conducted by Edward Robinson, Professor Extraordinary in the Theological Seminary at Andover, and the volume designated by Merwin is the one for the year 1831. In the four issues for that year a series of articles entitled "Theological Education in Germany" is given, prepared by the editor.[14] After discussing "German Universities", "The Course of Study at the Universities", "Examinations, Ministerial Standing, etc.", in Parts I, II, and III, respectively, in Part IV he translates for the benefit of his readers, "Directions for theological students entering the University of Halle. Published by the theological faculty". In section 1 of this article is given a "General View of Theological Study."[15] The course of study outlined in "The Rules and Regulations of the Theological Department in Yale College" has the same general outline,

---

13. Catalogue of the Officers and Students of Yale College, pp. 38, 39.
14. pp. 1-51, 201-226, 409-452, 613-638.
15. pp. 615-625.

and differs from the above only in the smaller number of courses offered, and also in a neglect of a provision for the study of Ecclesiastical History.

CHAPTER VII

ADMINISTRATION AND CONTENT OF THE COURSE OF STUDY

ADMINISTRATION AND CONTENT
OF THE COURSE OF STUDY

The Academic Year

The Catalogue of the Officers and Students of Yale College, for November 1822, describes the school year as follows:

> There are three vacations in a year; one of six weeks, beginning at Commencement, the second Wednesday in September; the second, two weeks from the second Wednesday in January; and the third, four weeks from the first Wednesday in May.[1]

This statement continues in each annual catalogue until the issue of the year 1831/32, when a single alteration occurs whereby the commencement is changed from the second Wednesday in September to the third Wednesday in August.[2] In the Catalogue of the year 1841/42, the time of Commencement is designated as the third Thursday in August.[3] The length of each vacation remains the same throughout these years. The school year, then, during the years 1822-1831 began the latter part of October and continued with a vacation of two weeks in January and four weeks in May, until the Commencement on the second Wednesday in September.

The Catalogue for the year 1850/51 states that public Commencement is held on the last Thursday in July of each year. The calendar for that year follows:

---

1. Catalogue of the Officers and Students of Yale College, 1822, p. 25.
2. Ibid., 1831/32, p. 30.
3. Ibid., 1841/42, p. 33.

> The first term of the current year closes Tuesday, Dec. 24th, 1850; the second term opens Wednesday, Jan. 8th, 1851, and closes Tuesday, April 15th; the third term opens Wednesday, May 7th, and closes at Commencement, Thursday, July 31st. The first term of the ensuing year will open Wednesday, Sept. 17th, 1851.[4]

This custom continued through the year 1857/58. It is evident, therefore, that from 1832 to 1850 the school year began the first of October and continued until the third Thursday in August, with a vacation of two weeks in January and four weeks in April. During the years 1850 to 1858 the term of study began in September and ended in July. In all of these cases the school year was divided into three terms, the first two of fourteen weeks each, and the last term of twelve weeks.

Size of the Classes Which Met For Study

It is not difficult to determine the size of the classes which met for study with the several professors, because all courses were required, and particular studies were designated for particular classes. Thus all those in the Junior Class attended, as a group, each particular lecture required of them. The size of the Classes varied with different periods. The degree of this variation from period to period, for each class, may be learned from an examination of Table I, on page 121 (Chapter IV). The largest number belonging to any one class is that of the Middle Year for the session, 1838-

---

4. Catalogue of the Officers and Students of Yale College, 1850/51. p. 34.

1839. When the Classes are divided into groups of five years each, beginning with the term, 1823-1824, which is the year when the student body was divided into classes[5] (see Table I, page 121), the highest yearly average for the Junior Class is 22.6, from 1833-34 to 1837-38; for the Middle Class is 26.8 from 1838-39 to 1842-43; and for the Senior Class 20.2, from 1838-39 to 1842-43. It may be noted from Table I that the yearly average after the peak was reached declined very rapidly until the end of the period.

Sources For an Investigation of the Course of Study

In the investigation of the content of the course of study, and the manner in which each subject was approached by the instructor, the notes taken by students upon the lectures of these professors will constitute the sole source. The only lectures published were those of Dr. Taylor, and these subsequent to his death. The collection of student notes which is available[6] varies somewhat as to style and value. Some of them are little more than outlines. Others evidently were taken in class, with an effort to follow the professor accurately. Some must have been recopied im-

---

5. The First General Catalogue of the Theological Department in Yale College (1838) records that only two students were in attendance the first year, 1822-23, and they were in the Junior Class.
6. These manuscripts will be examined in connection with an investigation of each particular subject in the course of study.

mediately after the class, or at a later period. One or two are termed abridged notes. Some have an interesting history; for instance, the notes of Samuel W. Barnum on Professor Taylor's "Mental Philosophy" bear upon a flyleaf the following notation:

> "<u>Genealogical History</u>--These notes were taken from the revised and corrected copy of Dr. Azariah Smith. His copy was taken from L. S. Hobart's copy as far as the classification of Mental facts on page 123; the rest was copied from S. G. Whittelsey's amended edition of Rev. Mr. Cotton's improvement of Rev. Mr. Dutton's notes."

This history and the care which these students exhibited in taking and treasuring these notes is significant. First, it is an indication of the important place which lectures held in the curriculum. Secondly, it shows that the students considered them of future value. This is indicated by a habit, common to several of them, of leaving the bottom half of the page blank as space for parallel notes from other sources. Thirdly, it appears that the content of the lectures changed very little over a long period of years, else a student like Mr. Barnum would find little value in notes of previous years. The agreement of detail in these lectures is very great. That the professor made few changes in his course is further shown by an examination of Mr. Barnum's notebook. He copied the lectures on one page only, so that the left-side page was left blank for additional notes. Only very brief and scanty additions are found on these pages. Mr. David T. Stoddard writes upon the flyleaf of his volume that he bought the book from Mr. W. D. Ely. Few supplementary notes are added by him.

Although all the student notes which have been discovered are of years preceding the first printing of the plan of the course of study in the school Catalogue (1851-52), from the dates found in these notes it is evident that the order of the subjects was the same at the time (1833-1844) the notes were taken. The passing from subject to subject and from year to year in this investigation, may be followed more understandingly, therefore, by frequent reference to the statement entered in the 1850-51 Catalogue.[7]

The Course of Study

The Junior Year

The Junior year was begun with a course in Hebrew Grammar under the guidance of Professor Gibbs. The Grammar used was Roediger's Gesenius. The translation of Moses Stuart, to whom Gibbs bore the relation first of pupil and then of an assistant, was probably used the first few years. Professor Gibbs had prepared a Hebrew and English Lexicon while he was at Andover, the second edition of which was bound and published with Professor Stuart's Grammar in 1832.[8] In 1840 a translation by Professor T. J. Conant, of Rochester Theological Seminary, appeared. It was soon followed by the eleventh edition of Stuart's translation. Professor Conant published, "A defense of the Hebrew Grammar of Gesenius

---

7. See Illustration 3, on the next page.
8. New Haven, Hezikiah Howe, 1832. 236 pp.

ILLUSTRATION 3. THE COURSE OF INSTRUCTION IN THE THEOLOGICAL DEPARTMENT IN YALE COLLEGE ACCORDING TO THE CATALOGUE OF THE OFFICERS AND STUDENTS OF YALE COLLEGE, 1850/51; pp. 38, 39.

"The regular course of instruction (in the Theological Department) occupies three years, and comprises the following subjects:

JUNIOR CLASS.- Hebrew Grammar, (Roediger's Gesenius, translated by Conant,) Conant's Hebrew Exercises and Chrestomathy, Principles of Sacred Criticism and Hermeneutics, Critical and Exegetical Dissertations. Lectures by the Professor of Sacred Literature on some topics in Introduction to Theology, and in Exegetical Theology. Lectures by the Professor of Didactic Theology on Mental Philosophy including the Will.

MIDDLE CLASS.- Lectures by the Professor of Didactic Theology, on Moral Philosophy, Moral Government, Natural Theology, Necessity and Evidences of Revelation, and Systematic Theology. Exegetical study of the Scriptures and Dissertations continued.

SENIOR CLASS.- Lectures of the Structure and Composition of Sermons, on Public Prayer. Criticism of Skeletons and of Sermons, Exercises in Extemporaneous Speaking and Preaching before the Class, Lectures on Pastoral Charge, on Revivals of Religion, on the History of Modern Missions, and on Expository Preaching, Lectures on Elocution attended by the Practice and Delivery of Sermons.

There are weekly Debates in the Rhetorical Society, at which the Professor of Didactic Theology presides and in which the members of all the classes participate.

The students have access to the College Library, and to the libraries of the several literary societies in the College.

A building has been erected". . . . etc. . . . .

against Professor Stuart's Translation",[9] in which he endeavored to point out the discrepancies in Dr. Stuart's work. Conant's translation was subsequently used by Professor Gibbs in his teaching. The course presupposed former work in this branch of study in College, and, after some review in grammar, proceeded with Hebrew Exercises and Chrestomathy. The Grammatical Exercises and the Chrestomathy, which were used by Professor Gibbs, are found, included as a supplement, in Conant's Grammar.[10] The Chrestomathy was composed of Hebrew selections from the Bible, with detailed explanation and criticism, designed to strengthen one's knowledge of the language.

The student was then led into a study of Hebrew Philology and the Principles of Interpretation. A notebook of W. A. Larned[11] has been preserved which bears the caption, "Gibbs--Hebrew Philology and Principles of Interpretation". The first few lines of this work are as follows:

"On a particular meaning of the Prepositon לְ

Prepositions unite words, which stand in true relation to each other. According to Ewald, and I think him correct in his opinion, they originally point out the

---

9. New York, D. Appleton and Company, 1847, 33 pp.
10. Gesenius, F. H. W., Gesenius' Hebrew Grammar, 14th edition, as revised by Dr. F. Rödiger. Translated by T. J. Conant. To which are added a course of exercises in Hebrew Grammar, and a Hebrew Chrestomathy, prepared by the translator, New York and Philadelphia, 1846.
11. Three Brief Notes dated "Sept. 1831". W. A. Larned (Junior, Middler, Senior, 1831-34), b. Thompson, Conn., June 23, 1806; B.A. Yale 1826, M.A.; Yale (tutor) 1828-31; Theol. School, Troy, N.Y. (instr. Greek and Hebrew) 1835-37; Yale (Prof. Rhetoric and English Lit.) 1839-62, during which time he was editor of the New Englander.

relation of place--either motion or rest with respect to place. There are three principal relations of things to things expressed by prepositions of place, of time considered as moving or resting. They are prefixed to the place, or more generally the thing, from which or to which there is motion or in which there is rest . . . .

In regard to מִן, its first relation is of place.

A. to the place or thing from which something proceeds. To this belong No. 1. a.b.c.: 2 b.c.d.e.f. 3.A. in Gesenius. . . . .

B. It is prefixed to the place or thing, at a distance from which something is at rest. He sits from strife, i.e. Strife that from which at a distance he sits at rest.

C. It is prefixed to the place or thing which the Subject of the discourse is at rest and from which another thing is distant. . . . . Gesenius No. 3C.

1. It is prefixed to a place or thing from which another is remotely distant: מֵרָחוֹק : at a distance, Gen. 22.4. Abraham saw the place which was at a distance from him.

2. Under, below, as opposed to upper, upon, above
   [6 examples]
3. Before and Behind
   [8 examples]
4. On the right & On the left
   [5 examples]

. . . . (Written Sept. 1831) I see that Prof. Stuart has mistaken the meaning of מִן as a preposition of rest in his note to Gen. 1.7."(12)

"On the Genitive", he continues,

"Besides the construct state, it may be expressed by אֲשֶׁר and by לְ alone. But what is the position of these words? Can they be placed before the nouns signifying the thing possessed? as Genesis 16.2 לוֹ אִשָּׁה ? Can they be rendered grammatically for a wife of him or to him? Can they be grammatically translated a seed of thee?--I think not."(13)

The notes continue concerning the Numerals, and another preposition.

The method employed by Professor Gibbs in the "Exegetical Study of the Greek Scriptures" is indicated by further notes

----

12. W. A. Larned, op. cit., pp. 1-8.
13. Ibid., p. 9.

on his lectures, taken by Mr. Larned.[14] The lectures begin thus:

> "I shall examine the students in the following particulars--1st the usual meaning of each word and its inflection. 2. At the End of a sentence, its analysis into simple propositions and then into Subject, copula, predicate, objects direct and remote, and the mode of connection of the Simple propositions with each other. 3. Translation according to the analysis. 4. Illustration of the figures of Speech if there be any--as Ellipsis--Anacoluthon, &c.
> 5. The actual Sentiment, in declaring what explains the principles of interpretation.[15]
> In these notes I shall make Kuinoil's Commentary the basis. When I differ from Him or Rosenmueller[16] I shall here note it.
> I will note down the figures of language.
> I will illustrate the principles of Interpretation.
> 1. $T\text{o}\nu$ $\mu\text{e}\nu$ $\pi\rho\omega\tau\text{o}\nu$. The $\mu\text{e}\nu$ here is without its corresponding particle $\delta\epsilon$ which is omitted along with the whole Epidusis of the sentence. I think this a better explanation than that of Kuinoel or Ros.--"[17]

A number of examples similar to the above are followed by a review of the figures of speech, e. g. Anacoluthon and Brachylogy, found in the verses in the Bible which were under examination.[18]

Before taking up the Epistles of Paul for exegetical

---

14. This notebook contains "Commentaries on Acts, on Paul's Epistle to the Philippians, and the Introduction only to a study of the Epistle of James." 27 pp.
15. The British Museum Catalog of Printed Books lists the titles of twenty works concerning the Bible under the name of Christian Gottlieb Kuehnoel; all of these volumes are in Latin, and there is no evidence that they were ever translated. The years of publication were from 1785 to 1843.
16. There are 27 volumes listed under the name of Ernest Friederich Carl Rosenmueller in the British Museum Catalog of Printed Books; 17 titles are in Latin, six in German, and four in English. Three volumes were published in 1831 and one in 1841, and the remainder prior to the year 1820.
17. Rosenmueller, Ernst Friederich Carl
18. W. A. Larned, op. cit., pp. 4-7.

study a review of his life is given. The same type of introduction precedes an investigation of the text of the Epistle of James.

It was also the duty of Professor Gibbs according to the Regulations of the Department, to lecture on some topics in "Introduction to Theology". From the standpoint of logical arrangement, it would seem that the subject of Theological Encyclopedia probably came first in this study. According to George E. Day's notes,[19] and those of J. A. Saxton,[20] [21] the whole classification of the various fields of theology were reviewed, followed by some definitions of Theology and Religion.[22]

---

19. George E. Day (Junior, Middler, Senior, 1835-38) b. Pittsfield, Mass., March 19, 1815; B.A. Yale 1833, Yale, instructor of Sacred Literature, 1838-40; minister, Marlboro, Mass., 1840-47, Northampton, Mass., 1848-51; Prof. of Biblical Literature, 1851-66; Yale Divinity School, Prof. Hebrew Language and Literature 1855-91. Dean 1888-95; d. in New Haven, July 2, 1905. He and Mrs. Day gave to Yale Divinity School for the Day Missions Library Building, the Library Endowment and the Day Fellowship, over $118,000.
20. Only an introduction is extant, 1½ pages. It is well to remember, however, that many of these courses were very, very brief, as will be observed later in this study. This course may not have comprised more than three lectures, serving only as an orientating course--an int·oduction to the "Introduction to Theology".
21. Joseph Addison Saxton (Junior, Middler, Resident Graduate) 1836-38, 1839-40; b. Tolland, Conn., Nov. 27, 1810; B.A. N.Y. University 1835, M.A. He was ordained as a Presbyterian at Greenport, Long Island, June 7, 1843, where he was a minister, 1843-45. Minister at New River, Ascension Parish, La., 1845-50; and North Congregational Church, New Hartford, Conn.; 1851-52; and in New York State 1853-54. Teacher in N.Y. City, 1854-56. Minister at New Preston, Conn., 1856-57; and at Brookfield, Fitchville and Bozrah, Conn., 1858-59. He died in New York City, Feb. 11, 1902.
22. For a survey of the content of this course see pp. 179, 180.

- 194 -

Two courses of the nature of a Biblical Introduction followed. They were "Sacred Geography," and "Chronology". Both of these are to be found in a notebook belonging to Mr. Larned,[23] and the latter in a volume prepared by an unknown author.[24] "Sacred Geography" included a study concerning the Jews, "Domestic Antiquities--Dwellings, Nomads, Agriculture, Arts, etc.; and Political and Sacred Antiquities." "Chronology" contained lectures on the different types of Jewish sacrifice.

The notes taken by the unknown student on Chronology begin thus:

> "Chronology. . . . means a discourse or treatise respecting time. Considered as a science it treats of the divisions or measures of time & of the application of these divisions or measures of time to the purposes of well aranged & concise history--
> It may be divided into technical & historical Chronology.
> Technical Chronology comprehends the statement & explanation of the several divisions or measures of time that are used in recording events by the Historian.
> Historical Chronology comprehends the application of the several divisions or measures of time to the events recorded in history so that they may be arranged in a uniform & consistent series & their mutual connexion & dependence be discovered."([25]

Lecture I, under "Technical Chronology", reviews the

---

23. 35 pp. MS. Only the outline for "Sacred Geography" is given.
24. Although in this volume are recorded the subject, the professor, and the school, it is entirely devoid of any name or dates connected with the author. The book contains the following notation upon the flyleaf: "Found by W. W. Blackshaw in the Old Winslow House, Minneapolis, Minn., when it was being torn down to make room for the Minneapolis Exposition about 1885." The majority of the lectures are those of Dr. Taylor. "Sacred Chronology by Professor Gibbs, is found on pp. 285-299, and Historical Chronology on pp. 316-322.
25. Notes of the Unknown Student, p. 286.

natural divisions of time, including the different types of days, viz. the artificial day, natural day, siderial day, and the solar day; and the same in regard to the month, and the year. Lecture II discusses "artificial measures". Under "Historical Chronology" the number of years in each period from the creation to the coming of Christ is calculated.

Inserted in Mr. Larned's notebook on Chronology are five fragmentary pages of manuscript bearing the caption "Harmony of the Evangelists, in respect to the Crucifixion, death, resurrection, of Christ and his meetings afterwards with his apostles and followers." Professor Gibbs lectured particularly concerning the discrepancy, real or apparent, which exists between the Markan and Johannine accounts of the time when the crucifixion occurred. In an attempt to arrive at the correct conclusion, he reviews seven possible interpretations, and concludes his remarks, according to Larned, by saying, "The only plausible and probable Explanations are the 4th & 7th. Either are sufficient to rebut the charge of contradiction. I cannot make up my mind between them."

The next course required of the Juniors was, "Lectures by the Professor of Didactic Theology on Mental Philosophy including the "Will". The notes of six students on these lectures have been preserved. The students, with the dates which appear in their notebooks, are: W. D. Ely,[26] January 1,

---

[26]. Mr. Ely's notes are apparently accurate, and are quite readable. William Davis Ely (Middler 1837-38); b. Hartford, Conn., June 16, 1815; B.A. Yale, 1836, M.A.; Yale Medical School, 1837-38; Yale tutor in Natural Philosophy 1839-42, also student in the Yale Law School; Hartford, Conn. (law) 1842-56; Providence, R. I. (cotton manufacturer) 1856-1908; died there June 11, 1908.

1837; S. W. S. Dutton,[27] 1838; Chauncey Goodrich,[28] 1838; F. A. Saxton,[29] 1838; Solon C. Avery,[30] 1839; Samuel W. Barnum,[31] 1843. A comparison shows that there was practically no change in the content of the course, "Mental Philosophy", during the three years, 1836 to 1839, but that it was slightly enlarged by 1843. According to the dates, the study seems to have begun on or about January 1, the beginning of the second term, and continued from thirty-seven to forty-two

-----

27. Mr. Dutton's account is very scattered, no attempt at fullness seems to have been made. Samuel William Southmayd Dutton (Junior 1835-36, student while tutor 1836-38); b. Guilford, Conn., March 14, 1814; B.A. Yale 1833, M.A.; ordained, June 26, 1838, in North Church, New Haven, Conn., where he was a minister 1838-66, also associate editor of the <u>New Englander</u>, 1843-66; d. Millbury, Mass., Jan. 26, 1866.
28. Mr. Goodrich's work is well written.
   Chauncey Goodrich, (Junior, Middler, Senior, 1838-41, Resident Graduate, 1841-43), son of Professor Goodrich, b. Middletown, Conn., July 20, 1817; B.A. Yale 1837, M.A.; minister Malden, Mass., 1843-47, Watertown, Conn., 1849-56; d. New Haven, Conn., March 27, 1868.
29. Mr. Saxton's notes are apparently complete and are written in a legible hand.
30. Mr. Avery apparently gives a full and accurate edition. Interlinear comments are made.
   Solon Cicero Avery (Junior, Middler, Senior, 1839-42) b. Groton, Conn., April 27, 1816; not ordained; Rochester, New York, merchant until 1854; d. in that place and year, July 29th.
31. Mr. Barnum writes with fullness, in a small hand.
   Samuel Weed Barnum (Junior, Middler, Senior, 1841-44, Resident Graduate 1845-1847) b. New Salem, N.Y., June 4, 1820; B.A. Yale, M.A.; reviser of Webster's Dictionary, 1845-47; minister, in following places: Granby, Conn., 1848-50, Feeding Hills, Mass., Stamford, Conn. 1863-65; Literary work in New Haven, Conn. 1856-91; died there Nov. 18, 1891.

lectures until the end of the year.[32] No clue is given as to what days in the week the class met.

Dr. Taylor began his lectures with a review of the influence which philosophical opinions have exerted upon Theology. He examines the "sources of prejudice against mental philosophy", and follows with a discussion of "the importance of this science". He says,

> "My design is not to go over that wide field of mental philosophy,. . . ., but to discuss only some topics most closely connected with Theology & to begin our inquiries where our knowledge begins and where those fundamental principles are to be found on wh. all our conclusions in Morals & Theology are ultimately based,. . . . A complete answer to that question "What is the human mind?" would constitute a system of mental philosophy. . . . .What is to be done then is (1) To obtain an unerring knowledge of all the facts of mental science and (2) To reduce this knowledge to a perfect system of classification. Under these heads arise several inquiries wh. I propose to answer."[33]

In order that the professor's method in handling his subject might be better understood, and the general content of the course brought to light, the following general outline,[34] accompanied by a few notations is given:

----

32. S. W. S. Dutton, in his Sketch of the Life and Character of Dr. N. W. Taylor, makes the following statement concerning the course in Mental Philosophy: "He devoted to this subject a larger part of his instruction than did any other theological teacher of whom we have knowledge." New Haven, 1858, p. 10.
33. According to Avery, op. cit., pp. 5-7.
34. Based on a Symposium of all the notes taken by the above students except where the individual source is specified. Use of what was then the contemporary vocabulary is attempted.

Introduction
  I. The obtaining of a knowledge of all the facts of mental science
      A. What are the facts of mental science?
      B. This unerring knowledge is attainable
      C. How is it attainable?
          1. The nature and origin of our knowledge
          2. The knowledge of mental philosophy obtained by reflection in the specific forms of
              a. Definition
              b. Comparison
              c. Analysis
      D. The Superiority of the knowledge thus obtained
      E. The reality of that philosophical knowledge tested by common sense

  II. Classification of Mental Facts
      A. The mind as an existence
      B. The mind as an existence with a nature
      C. The mind as a substance; objections
      D. The mind as an immaterial substance
      E. The mind as a self-active substance or cause
      F. The mind as a Spiritual Substance, i. e. self-active in relation to
          1. The Intellect, perception. Perception is not belief
          2. Susceptibility
          3. The Will

(It is at this point that Professor Taylor finds a very live issue on account of the theological thought of the time, and it is here that he makes his largest contribution to that thought.)[35]

                          a. Preliminary Remarks--
                          ...."President Edwards' Inquiry into the Will I consider an excellent work--I believe it to have been the cause of the revival of Evangelical Religion both in this country and in Great Britain....I esteem Edwards quite as important a Reformer at the point where he came in as either

----

35. To be discussed in connection with his controversial writings. See Chapter X.

Luther or Calvin!
"It is not inconsistent with what I have said to remark that the Book is not perfect, and that it frequently contradicts itself-- No inspired man is so great as not to contradict himself." (36

b. Definition--
(After remarking that President Edwards' definition is not sufficiently definite, he defines the Will as the "power by which the mind can & does choose elect or prefer any one of a number of objects as apparently good or the means of good i.e. happiness") 37

  c. The terms used to denote acts or states of the Will
  d. Classification of the states of the Will
  e. The act of choosing
  f. Meaning of the Word Cause
  g. Necessity
   Edwards' views of necessity
    (1) He confounds certainty and necessity
    (2) He gives two different definitions of moral necessity
  h. Natural and Moral Inability
   ("Difference between the two-- 'Natural Inability,' is a deficiency of natural power to perform any act of moral quality, as involving volition or preference.
   'Moral Inability' respects exclusively Acts of Will, and signifies simply a Certainty that a particular act will not be!") (38
  i. Determination of the Will
  j. Are Volitions necessary?
  k. What is a free agent?
   The Word Cause
   The Word Liberty

---

36. W. D. Ely, op. cit., p. 141. The punctuation marks and underlining indicate the intonations of the speaker's voice.
37. S. C. Avery, op. cit., p. 126.
38. W. D. Ely, op. cit., pp. 173, 174.

The Middle Year

The course of study for those who were members of the Middle Class was divided into two main divisions. First, the "Exegetical Study of the Scriptures and Dissertations" was continued. No student notes concerning this course have been discovered, but it probably differed from those given in the Junior Year, only in the degree of advancement in linguistic studies. Second, the major portion of the time was given to lectures by the Professor of Didactic Theology. It appears that these lectures were divided among these several courses: Moral Philosophy, Moral Government, Natural Theology, Necessity and Evidences of Revelation, and Systematic (or Revealed) Theology. From the dates given in the notebooks of the students it is apparent that one course was given at a time and that each followed immediately after the other. S. J. M. Merwin[39] begins with Moral Philosophy and numbers the lectures consecutively without a break through all the courses up to "Systematic Theology", and calls the first discourse on that subject, "Lect. 46". These

---

39. For the Middle and Senior years Mr. Merwin's notes are valuable, particularly in that he keeps the most complete account of the dates and numbers of the lectures.
   Samuel John Mills Merwin (Middler and Senior 1842-44, Resident Graduate 1844-45) b. in New Haven, Conn., Nov. 3, 1819; B.A. Yale 1839, M.A.; Andover Theological Seminary 1840-42; minister in following cities: Southport, Conn., 1844-59, Cheshire, Conn., 1860, South Hadley Falls, Mass., 1860-67; resident of New Haven, 1884-88; d. there Sept. 12, 1888.

lectures were given five days a week throughout the Middle year.

Moral Philosophy[40] comprised a course of ten[41] lectures, which seems to find its nearest kin in the present courses of study in Christian Ethics.[42] Indeed, Mr. Ely heads his series with "Ethics" instead of Moral Philosophy. The major matters under discussion in this course were:

> Introduction
> "Definitions: Right= fitness to the end for which it was designed.....Those actions which are adapted to promote the ultimate end of acting, i.e. existence; Wrong = fitted to defeat the end. What is the peculiar quality of actions denoted by the term Moral? Applied equally to right and wrong-- Philosophers differ--all will agree--that is moral in any action which, when we contemplate it, excites feelings of self-complacency or remorse . . . .
>
> Dr. Taylor wound up with some remarks on studying, hoped we'd learn how to use our brains, said very few men now-a-days knew how to use their brains right--according to his way of thinking great want of logic--too much hodgepodgery in Theology. No man can interpret who don't understand Theol. hoped we'd draw him all out."[43]

    I.   Benevolence the source of man's highest happiness.
    II. Can man from a knowledge of himself know right and wrong?
    III. Man will determine benevolence to be right action.
    IV. What is moral obligation?
    V.   What is the standard of duty?
    VI. Is Virtue founded in Utility?
    VII. What is conscience?

---

40. For this course the lecture notes of Messrs. Avery, Merwin, Saxton and Ely are available. It appears that another student made use of Mr. Merwin's book the following year, and inserted dates for that year--which dates are quite parallel to Merwin's.
41. Therefore of only two weeks duration.
42. In the introduction Dr. Taylor remarks "The want of time will allow me to give but a brief discussion of those principles of Morals which have a bearing on Theology particularly, Natural Theology." Quoted from W. D. Ely, op. cit., p. 278.
43. Merwin, op. cit., pp. 1, 2. The outline is based upon a symposium of the notes available.

In summary, in the last sentence of the lectures, Dr. Taylor says, "We see one thing very clearly from this subject, that a Benevolent Creator has constituted us such that all our perceptibilities can be, (and are in fact,) appealed to, to persuade us to right action--our love of praise--of elevation of character, &c.,&c.[44]

The next group of lectures was given upon "Moral Government".[45] The discussion of this topic permeates Dr. Taylor's lectures on theology. He considered it a basic subject, and seems to have given it greater prominence in his lectures with each succeeding year.[46] The length and design of the lectures included in the subject designated as "Moral Government" did not change. It seemed to serve the purpose of giving an opportunity for a definition of, and explanation of, that term.[47] It continued for only five lectures and is

---
44. W. D. Ely, op. cit., p. 329.
45. The sources include the notes of Messrs. Ely, Avery, Saxton and Merwin.
46. Lectures on topics connected with the moral government of God are found in "Natural Theology", "Necessity and Evidences of Revelation", and "Revealed Theology".
47. In his definition and discussion of Moral Government Dr. Taylor was anxious to prove that under such a moral government God was given freedom to exercise his justice in harmony with his benevolence and in the interest of securing the highest happiness for man; and that under such a system man is given freedom of choice as a moral agent seeking the happiness of others and of himself. That man should seek eternal happiness was not considered selfish by Professor Taylor. In this conception of the moral government of God Dr. Taylor endeavored to keep the Calvinistic emphasis on the sovereignty of God, and at the same time to elevate the position of man. The former was done because of his devotion to the Calvinistic system, the latter, in order to meet the objection of the Unitarians that such a system degraded man's position; and most of all to make the gospel more preachable by affording man greater ability to repent and to help his own condition. This conception of Dr. Taylor's is only hinted at in this course on "Moral Government", but the whole view is necessary for an understanding of the definitions and general outline of the topic given in the several different courses in theology.

closely bound up with "Natural Theology", which immediately followed, and which continues for nineteen additional lectures, and gives much space to discussion of the moral government of God.

Moral Government

I. What is a perfect Moral Government?

    A. It implies a Moral Governor.
    B. Is an Influence on moral beings
    C. Implies the influence of authority
    D. Is exercised through the medium of law
    F. What are Legal Sanctions?
        1. Their nature
            a. not good or evil arbitrarily awarded
            b. not evil inflicted to reclaim an offender
            c. not simply natural good and evil
        2. Their necessity

II. How does the influence of Moral Government differ from the influence to secure right moral action which results from the perceived nature and tendency of things?
        a. Negatively
        b. Positively

III. What is justice in a Moral Governor?

IV. How may a Moral Governor evince the perfection of his government.(48

The course in "Natural Theology"[49] opens with the question, "Is there a Supreme Creator?", and after giving the arguments of Clarke, Kant, Cousins, Paley, Locke, Daley, Berkeley, Emmons, and Dwight, the main body of the lectures is begun with arguments, pro and con, concerning the several attributes of God. The remaining portions of the lectures deal with these topics:

-----

48. Outline based mainly on the accounts given by S. J. M. Merwin and S. C. Avery.
49. The sources are the notes of Messrs. Ely, Avery, Merwin, Saxton and of the unknown author, the last being only fragmentary.

III. The Modes of God's existence
   IV. The ultimate end of God in creation is his own blessedness
   V. The purposes of God
   VI. God as a Preserver of the World
   VII. God as Governor
       A. God's Providential Government
       B. God's Moral Government
          1. God administers a moral government
          2. God administers an equitable moral government
          3. God's rightful authority
             a. Revelation alone cannot prove God's benevolence
             b. Proof of God's benevolence. (50

The next subject bears a title varying slightly with different years. Mr. Dutton's notes[51] have the caption, "Necessity and Evidences of Revealed Religion"; Mr. Avery's and Mr. Saxton's, "Evidences of Christianity"; and Mr. Merwin's "Necessity and Evidences of Revelation". The last named is the title of the course as stated in the Catalogue of 1850-51. The course comprised thirteen lectures, beginning, in Mr. Merwin's year, November 15, and ending December 8.[52] A general outline follows:

   I. The necessity of Revelation
   II. The Nature of the Evidences which are ours
   III. The kinds of Evidence
       A. Direct evidence
       B. Indirect evidence
          1. The authenticity of History in the Scriptures
          2. Indirect arguments

----

50. This partial outline is based on one given by Mr. S. C. Avery in his notes. In his notes fifty-six pages concerning this course are given to the topics preceding "God's Moral Government" and the thirty-five remaining pages are devoted to that subject.
51. The notes of S. W. S. Dutton are incomplete on this subject.
52. This course seems to have met only three or four times a week instead of five, as did all the rest of the theological courses in the Middle year.

IV. Christianity is from God
V. Deistic Objections

That the students were interested in the subject is indicated by an entire omission of the lecture in order to allow discussion[53] on at least one occasion. In the last lecture Professor Taylor declared for "the genuineness of our copy of the New Testament", and the "credible nature of the facts recorded, especially <u>Miracles</u>"[54].

The lectures constituting the final course given by the Professor of Didactic Theology in the Middle Year were devoted to the formation of a systematic theology, based on revelation, particularly that revelation in the Bible. In keeping with this purpose the course is called "Revealed Theology" at the time when the notes under examination were taken, and is designated as "Systematic Theology" in the first appearance of the plan of the course of study in the 1850/51 Catalogue of the College. At the time when these student notes were written, the course began between "Dec. 5th" and "Dec. 9th" and continued, five days a week, until the end of the school year.

The design of the course was to bring into an organic and logical whole the true doctrines and duties of the Christian religion. To this end very many passages of scripture

---

53. Merwin, <u>op. cit.</u>, Thurs., Nov. 24. Another example of student interest is found inside the cover of Merwin's notebook. A note in pencil asks: "Have you any data for judging what will be the moral character of the <u>first act of a free moral agent exposed to temptation?</u>" Then follows, in different handwriting: "I don't see how you could--reasoning a priori."
54. S. J. M. Merwin, <u>op. cit.</u>, Lecture XLV.

were quoted as a basis for the doctrines promulgated. A review of this course in the form of a general outline follows:[55]

    Part I. <u>Doctrines</u>--
        I. God
           A. His Unity
              1. Importance of the phrase
              2. Proof
           B. The Trinity
              1. The meaning of the doctrine
              2. Proof of the doctrine (Very many Scripture passages cited in the Old Testament)
              3. Objections--and answers to the Unitarians.
       II. Christ
           A. The Divinity of Christ
              1. Proved from his names
              2. Proved from his attributes
              3. Proved from his works
              4. Proved from the worship paid him
              5. Objections
           B. The Humanity of Christ
           C. Preëxistence of Christ
      III. The Divinity of the Holy Ghost
      IV. God as Governor
           A. God's Moral Government as exhibited by Revelation

(In his introduction to this topic Professor Taylor says, "I am not aware that any writer in Theology, <u>Natural</u> or <u>Revealed</u>, or on Moral Philosophy has ever treated this as a <u>distinct</u> subject------only alluded to it,------It is a subject of very great importance and until it is understood, there will be some writers who will maintain the doctrine of physical depravity, physical regeneration, etc. making God really (though not intentionally) the "minister of sin". For these reasons I have given a great prominence to this subject in my course of moral govt. in itself &c, then the proof from the light of nature that God is administering a perf. M.G. over this world--

----

55. Based upon the notes of Mr. S. W. S. Dutton, which are very scattered, of Mr. S. C. Avery, Mr. S. J. M. Merwin, Mr. Geo. E. Day, and Mr. F. A. Saxton.

I shall now consider it in the light of Revelation.")[56]
      1. The fact that God administers a moral Government over men
      2. The nature of God's Moral Government as revealed in the Bible
         a. The sum of the requirements of God's Law
            (1) The Law of Eden
            (2) The Law of Moses
            (3) The Law of the New Testament
         b. The sanctions of God's Law
         c. Preference, expressed in God's Law, of Obedience to Disobedience
   B. Providential Government of God
      1. The Nature and Extent of God's Providential Purposes
      2. The Certainty and Manner of their accomplishment
      3. The End of God's Providential Purposes
      4. Objections to the above
V. Concerning Man
   A. His Original State
      1. Was Man created a moral agent?
      2. Was the original character of Man holy?
      3. The Temptation of Man
   B. His fallen State
      1. The fall of Man
      2. Total moral depravity
         a. Explanation of the doctrine
         b. Proof
            (1) From the Bible, with remarks on preaching the doctrine
            (2) From experience and observation

---

56. According to Merwin, op. cit., p. 37. In the Introduction to two volumes bearing the title, and containing the lectures of Professor Taylor on Moral Government, Professor Noah Porter says, "The Moral Government of God was the great thought of Dr. Taylor's intellect, and the favorite theme of his instructions in theology" (p. iii). These volumes were published the year after Dr. Taylor's death. Nathaniel W. Taylor, Lectures on the Moral Government of God, N.Y., Clark, Austin & Smith, 1859, 2 vols. xiii, 417 pp.; viii, 423 pp.

3. Native Depravity
    a. Erroneous theories refuted
    b. Dr. Taylor's Theory
        (1) Statement of the Doctrine
        (2) Vindication of the Theory
        (3) Objections to Dr. Taylor's theory
C. Man's State under Grace
    1. The Atonement
        a. The nature of the atonement
        b. The fact proved
        c. The manner of the atonement
            (1) The Orthodox view
            (2) The Unitarian argument
            (3) Objections to both theories
        d. A long series of Questions
        e. The extent of the atonement
    2. Justification
    3. Regeneration
        a. The nature and necessity of Regeneration
        b. God the Holy Spirit--the Author.
        c. The Means
        d. The Evidences
            (1) Liability to mistake Christian character
            (2) Tests of Christian Character
    4. Election (at this point Professor Taylor preached a series of sermons, usually four in number)
        a. The fact of Election
        b. Election as related to other doctrines
        c. The manner in which God executes election
        d. Objections to the doctrine of Election
        e. Usefulness of the doctrine in preaching
    5. Reprobation
    6. Adoption
    7. Sanctification
    8. Peace of Conscience
    9. The Perserverance of the Saints
    10. The Resurrection
    11. The Intermediate State
    12. The Judgment

Part II. **Duties**
- I. The Sabbath
  - A. What it is
  - B. Its Obligation
    1. From the nature of the duty
    2. From its original institution
    3. From the commandments in the Decalogue
    4. From its Observance by the Apostles
  - C. The Manner of Keeping the Sabbath
- II. The Church
  - A. What is a Church?
  - B. The Admission and Dismission of Members
  - C. The Government of the Church
    1. With whom does the power lie?
    2. The Manner in which the discipline of a particular Church is to be administered
    3. The Officers of the Church
  - D. The Ordinances of the Church
    1. Baptism
       a. Should Children be baptized?
       b. Baptism as a Covenant
       c. Direct proof of Infant Baptism
       d. Mode of Baptism
    2. The Lord's Supper

With this course in Systematic Theology the work of the Middle Year was concluded.

A volume has been found in the Yale University Library which does not bear the name of its author but which contains "Dissertations" written by a student in the Theological Department of Yale College during the years 1828 and 1829. These were based upon the theological lectures which were given by Professor Taylor in the Junior and Middle Years. One hundred seventeen dissertations are written upon nine hundred and two pages. According to the author's "Index", discussions on "Intellectual Philosophy" occupy seventy-eight pages, those on "Moral Government "are contained in thirty-four pages, and essays on topics in Systematic Theology cover seven hundred ninety pages, indicating that most of the dissertations were written in the Middle Year. It seems to have been the custom for a student to write one or more dissertations upon a certain lecture, and at a later time to read one of these essays before Professor Taylor for his approval or disapproval.[57] The student seems to follow a similar method in attacking each problem. Dissertation LIV is an example:

> "Dissertation LIV   Read to Dr. Taylor Oct. 2d, 1828
>   The Divinity of Christ continued
>   The Divinity of Christ proved from his works--
> Plan I. Creation
>   II. Did Christ create the world?
>   III. In what way does the miracles of Christ prove his divinity--
>
> Before I enter upon the main argument to prove that Christ created the world I propose to show that he who created it must be Divine & that no created being could have performed such a stupendous work by his own power. . . . . But before I answer this, I would state, we have on a former occasion shown satisfactorily, that whatever being God is, there is not another such in the universe--& further, he is a <u>cause</u> every way efficient to the production of the universe with all its glory & boundless extent. We also said that it was a principle of sound philosophy, & I would add of common sense-- <u>That we are not to suppose any more causes, to produce effects, than those effects</u> require. Here is a cause sufficient, fully so, to produce all the effects, which exist. It is absurd to say that anything more is necessary. . . ."(58

---

57. The caption for the dissertation beginning on page 91 is as follows: "Dissertation on Lect. 14th". The next dissertation is on "Lect. 15th" which was "Read before Dr. Taylor". Dissertation No. XVIII records the amount of time which is needed for the reading before Professor Taylor--"23 minutes".
58. pp. 485, 486. This dissertation is concluded on p. 494.

The Senior Year

The opportunity having been given for the students to learn the "science of the Exegetical Study of the Holy Scriptures" in the first year, and to devote their second year to the obtaining of a systematic theology, it appears to have been the design of the curriculum-builders of this period that the members of the Senior Class should be led to acquire techniques in "Practical Theology". For this reason the third year of study was devoted, almost wholly,[59] to Homiletics and kindred subjects.

A course in Homiletics[60] was given by Professor E. T. Fitch at the beginning of the Senior Year. It consisted of about twenty-six lectures, given on Monday, Tuesday, and Wednesday of each week, through October and November, and part of December.

The lectures were begun with a review of the classification of the whole field of theology in order to show the place of Practical Theology in this scheme classification of theological pursuits. Professor Fitch says, according to Merwin, "Practical Theology occupies itself with the whole circle of studies directly preparatory to the exercises to the sacred office of a Christian teacher. It, therefore,

---

59. The exceptions were two small courses in "Revivals of Religion" and the "History of Missions".
60. Lecture notes on this subject include those of S. C. Avery, W. D. Ely, S. W. S. Dutton, who calls the course "Sermonizing", S. J. M. Merwin, George E. Day, and F. A. Saxton.

presupposes a stock of knowledge already acquired, which the instruction now to be given, is to work up and bring into use."[61]

The outline of the course in Homiletics based upon the notes of students, is as follows:

Introduction (given above)

"I. The various parts of a discourse which enter into the composition of a Sermon
Introduction:
Question--Why not enter at once on the various kinds of sermons, & illustrate the parts in connection with the whole instead of taking up the parts separately?
Ans. First--Because these parts have their essential characteristics peculiar to the pulpit, in their design, method, qualities, &c. wherever they are used
Second. . . . .
Third . . . ."
  A. The Text
    1. The advantages derived from the use of the text
    2. Objections to its use
    3. Origin of the practice
    4. The qualities in a text which are to be expected
  B. The Exordium
    1. Its design
    2. Topics for exordial use
    3. The qualities of an Exordium
  C. Exposition
    1. The design of the Exposition
    2. The rules for expository preaching
    3. The qualities of Exposition
  D. The Subject
    1. Scripture texts as subjects
    2. Biographical material
    3. The Unity of a Subject
  E. The Division
    1. The propriety of division
    2. Rules for selecting the different parts of division
    3. Arrangement of the parts of a discourse
    4. Subdivisions
  F. Discussion
    1. Explanatory
    2. Argumentative
    3. Persuasive form of discussion

---
61. p. 24.

       G. Transition and Recapitulation
       H. Application
          1. Its source
          2. Its design
          3. Manner of introducing application
          4. Modes of Conclusion
  II. The Different Kinds of Sermons
       A. Critical and Practical Lectures
       B. The Explanatory Sermon
       C. The Biographical Sermon
       D. The Argumentative Sermon
       E. The Pathetic Sermon
       F. The Persuasive Sermon
  III. The Materials of Sermons
       A. What are the original materials of a sermon?
       B. From what sources shall the preacher gather his materials?
       C. How may a preacher best obtain a supply for a given discourse?
  IV. The Composition of Sermons
       A. The Selection of the Subject
       B. Invention
          1. Requisites to good Invention
          2. The rules of Invention
       C. The Expression of Thought
          1. The selection of words
          2. The forms of expression
          3. General qualities of Style
       D. The Manner of Composition--
          Shall it be written out or delivered extemporaneously?

The intonations of the voice of the preacher-professor are preserved in Mr. Ely's [62] notes concerning "Invention".

"I am how to speak of Invention in regard to the selection of those particular thoughts, which make the filling up of a plan. The great principle here is that of Utility! Utility! Utility!!!
    1st adopt for the filling up solid thoughts-- those which bear the scrutiny of truth--nothing false or conceited."

That Professor Goodrich gave a series of lectures in Homiletics and in Rhetoric parallel to those of Dr. Fitch is evident from a few notes taken by Mr. Merwin on Homiletics. Merwin

----

62. p. 524. Ely's work is particularly valuable in this respect--that he endeavored to put on paper the oratorical emphases of his professors' lectures.

writes,

> "The Professor commenced by saying that it was a sensible remark of Hume's that 'Rhetoric must be taught by examples'. His object is, to follow the course marked out by Prof. Fitch in his Lectures, and make them practical; or, exemplify the Lectures on Homiletics."

Mr. Merwin's notes are the only source for the content of Professor Goodrich's course in Homiletics, and his copy gives evidence of not being completed.[63] The subject which is discussed, however, is "Exordiums", and under the following headings:

> "Whence is the matter of Exordiums to be derived?
> I. From Adjuncts or circumstances of the Text (This is the Picturesque)
> II. From the Subject Matter of the Text (This is observational)
> III. From general truths (This is also observational)
> IV. From the circumstances or situation of the speaker or audience. (This is Pathetic)"

Mr. Merwin's notes on the course in Rhetoric begin with "Lecture VI, Thursday, Nov. 2, 1843, and end with Lecture 14th, Tuesday Nov. 28th, 1843." A general outline of the notes is as follows:

> Debate in Public Assemblies, at the bar and in college Societies.
> [64]
> II. Refutation of Arguments
>   A. "Mode of detecting the errors in an Adversary while he speaks"
>   B. Considerations of replying to him
> III. Persuasive Oration
>   A. Sources of Persuasion

---

63. The lectures cease abruptly and are found on only eight pages in his notebook. The fact that "exordiums" was the only topic on which notes are found would probably indicate that the course had scarcely begun.
64. Mr. Merwin's numeral; evidently the first lectures have been lost.

        B. The influence of the personal
           standing of the orator
        C. Consideration of the character
           of the Audience
IV. Invention of matter for the filling out
    and completing the oration
V. A Study of some of the greatest English
   orators and their most successful performances
       A. Lord Chatham
       B. Charles James Fox
       C. Edmund Burke
       D. Henry Grattam
       E. William Pitt
          (etc.)
VI. American Orators
     A. Historical Introduction
     B. James Madison
     C. Alexander Hamilton
     D. Fisher Ames
        (etc.)

Professor Goodrich's courses in Homiletics and Rhetoric, which paralleled the lectures in Homiletics given by Professor Fitch, were followed by a series of discourses on "Expository Preaching" under the tutelage of Professor Goodrich. According to Merwin,[65] the lectures on this subject began "Thursday 7th Dec. 1843", and were ended on December 28, making a total of eleven lectures. The first lecture begins in the following manner:

> "Lecture 1st Thursday 7th Dec. 1843
> Quest. Whence are the materials for sermons to be obtained? Didactic Theology won't do always--change of sentiment on this subject--people tired of long-winded doctrinal sermons, want to have it enterwoven &c. doctrine-practical
> Ans. The systematic study of the word of God must be the great way--two or three hours every day, whatever else you may do, should be devoted to this systematic

---

65. S. J. M. Merwin, who has been the author of the most complete reports throughout the Middle and Senior years is the only source for this and the following course-- Missions.

>study of the word of God with reference to obtaining rich materials of thought for serm.s. Very few clergymen do this.--Albert Barnes said when he left the Serminary he determined to study in this way 3 hours every day--the three best hours--get up at ½ past four A.M. commence study at 5 & keep at it till 8, & then write serm.s two hours-- found a great advantage from it--one was, he <u>always knew what to go to work at when he got up</u>.-- great deal of time wasted for want of a definite plan of study. Another was, always had a subject for Expository Preaching. Minister should have <u>one expository lecture every week</u>."

The advantages and methods of expository preaching were then perused with a large use of examples, particularly from the Psalms and the Pauline Epistles.

Following "Expository Preaching", Professor Goodrich gave, once a week until near the middle of April at least,[66] a series of studies entitled "Expository Lectures". After an endeavor to determine whether the discourse recorded in Luke 6: 20-49 is the same as the more complete account in Matthew, Professor Goodrich divided the Sermon on the Mount into six sections and explained the different parts, and the transitions from one part to the other. An idea concerning his method may be gained from the following:

>"Here it will be useful, before examining v. by v. to cast our eyes forward and consider the gen<u>l</u> scope of this section--
>1. The <u>beatitudes</u> properly 7 in number (v. 3-9). Then follows an assurance that all this characterized the persecuted as they might expect to be, have a

---

66. The last lecture recorded by Merwin is for April 10, but the lectures may have continued. However, Merwin's usual completeness, and the fact that in that last week two lectures were given, instead of the usual one, and that that which Professor Goodrich says in his introduction he intends to do is completed, point to the supposition that this day, April 10, is the date of the last lecture.

>   great blessing (v. 10-12). This forms the key-
> stone & application rather than a distinct beati-
> tude co-ordinate with the rest--7= the no. of
> perfection among the Jews = sacred no.
>   2. A still more important remark is that
> all the 7 spring out of the 1st,--have their basis
> in one fundamental idea (v.3). The 6 which follow
> are only developments of the 1st--forming a
> beautiful chain of connected thought--that funda-
> mental idea is this--"Blessed are the poor in
> spirit"--they who truly feel their spiritual desti-
> tution wh. creates the necessity of redemption,
> and a sense of destitution is therefore the in-
> dispensible pre-requisite to obtaining redemption.
> Let us then trace the dependence of the subsequent
> beatitudes on this fundamental idea.
>   (a) A sense of spiritual want leads us to
> mourn for the cause of it = our sin. . . . .
> . . . ." 67

The entire course is composed of fourteen expositions upon the Sermon on the Mount.

There are two courses, listed in the Catalogue of 1850-51 concerning which no student notes are available and, indeed, no materials of any kind whatsoever. Whether such notes were lost, or whether these courses were added after the time when most of these student notes were taken, has not been discovered. The latter is more probably true since no provision for these subjects is made in the regulations of the Theological Department (1833) which were reviewed in Chapter VI. These two courses are "Public Prayer" and "Revivals of Religion". Both of them were undoubtedly minor subjects in the course of study, but the latter would most probably reveal interesting data concerning the revival attitudes, methods, and techniques of the time. The former possibly was given by Professor Fitch, and the latter most probably by

---

67. Merwin, op. cit., p. 208.

Dr. Goodrich, in view of his experience in that field.

Lectures in Pastoral Theology were given by Professor Goodrich near the end of the school year, totaling about twelve expositions in all. A general outline follows:

> Object--to ascertain what are the <u>exact rights</u> of a minister in this relation & what the <u>exact limits</u> of his duties
>
> I. Ecclesiastical Polity
>   Two classes--Prelacy, and ministerial parity
>   A. History of the Progress of Congregationalism
>   B. Difference between Congregational and Presbyterian Polity
> II. The Civil Relations of the Pastor
> III. The Pastor's Relation to his own church
>   A. Discipline of the Church
>   B. In Public Worship
>   C. Parochial Visits
>
> General suggestions--
> "1. When you settle, expect to remain for life & don't make too much out of every little report."
> "2. Try to get the opinion of some judicious friend as to your own condition--whether there is anything out of the way in zion."
> 3. Always attend ecclesiastical meetings.

- It appears that before the transference of Mr.

---

68. See p. 99.
69. According to Merwin they occurred from "Tuesday 28th May 1844 to Tuesday 25th June 1844, usually on Tuesdays, Wednesdays, and Thursdays".

    The notes of David T. Stoddard on these lectures are also available. Stoddard bought the notebook from W. D. Ely, and found it necessary to add these lectures of Professor Goodrich, since Ely attended the Seminary before Dr. Goodrich's transfer to the Theological Department in 1839.

    David Tappan Stoddard (student while tutor in the College, 1840-42, Resident Graduate 1842-43) b. Northampton, Mass., Dec. 2, 1818; Williams College, 1834-35, B.A. Yale 1838, M.A., Andover Theological Seminary 1839-40; Marshall College, tutor, 1838-39; Yale, tutor, 1840-42; missionary for A.B.C.F.M., to the Nestorians at Urumiah, Persia, 1843-57; d. there Jan. 22, 1857.

Goodrich to the Theological Department in 1839, Rev. Leonard Bacon was, at least on one occasion, a visiting lecturer on "Ecclesiastical Organizations", but the discourses seem to have been largely of a historical nature, and the meagreness of existent sources[70] does not merit further examination.

At the end of the Senior year, a course in the History of Missions was presented by Professor Goodrich. It extended, according to Merwin,[71] from June 26th to July 25th, meeting on Tuesday, Wednesday, and Thursday, and comprising a total of thirteen lectures. A general view of the course follows:

> Introduction
> "Reasons. 1. To show how much is done, on the one hand to repress our boasting, and on the other to encourage
> 2. to awaken Ch n respect and love for others who are laboring for us in the cause e. g. Episcopalians.
> 3. To enlarge our hearts in prayer for the efforts of all nations--study geography.
> Peculiarly important to ministers--For (1) New fields of usefulness opening (2) Perhaps you ought to enter it--(3) Too much absorbed in the West.
> Plan to exhibit the actual conditions and prospects of Missions. Subordinate I. Some slight sketch of their history. II. Geography, climate, scenery-- a picture of it."

With these aims in mind, Protestant Missions around the world are reviewed, and in conclusion "Books for Reference" are given, totaling twenty-three titles, of which three pertain to geography, two are general, one is a missionary atlas, and the remainder are Histories, Memoirs and Biographies.

---

70. W. D. Ely has preserved one page--with no date. George E. Day's notebook contains the contents of two lectures, dated March 3, and March 10, 1837.
71. These notes were taken upon stationery and loosely inserted in his notebook. 22 pp.

Professor Fitch's Sermons

A portion of the course of study, which does not appear in the Catalogue, and may not have been regarded by the officers of the school as a part of the curriculum, is found in the sermons delivered by the Rev. Mr. Fitch in the College Chapel each Sunday morning. In keeping with that which was required of him as Professor of Divinity, and in following President Dwight, Dr. Fitch preached a series of sermons of a doctrinal nature which formed, in four years, a complete theological system.

In pursuit of this aim, Professor Fitch discussed the doctrines of the Calvinistic system, following much the same outline as that used by Professor Taylor in his course in Systematic Theology. That some of the students valued them as much as classroom lectures is evident from the rather complete notes which have been preserved.[72] Dr. Fitch's own record of the preaching of his sermons is given in three manuscript volumes.

Part I consists of an "Enumeration", which bears the record of the sermons preached, listed by number, with the subject, the text and the different places in which each was delivered. Three hundred sixty-seven sermons are listed in

---

72. MS. notes of doctrinal Sermons and lectures by Dr. Fitch and others, 1829-1840, 2 v.
Ibid.--for 1845-1848, 365 pp. Also S. C. Avery has written near the end of one of his classroom notebooks, an apparently complete, and certainly detailed, outline of Professor Fitch's Sermons.

this manner, some of them being preached in sixteen or seventeen different places. For example:

6. Law magnified by Christ Is. XLII. 21 Aug. 7. 1815

        Chapel, Andover
        Parkstreet, Boston
        Dr. Morse's, Charlestown
        Mr. Taylor's, New Haven
        Mr. Swift's, Derby
        Mr. Dodge's, Haverhill
        Dr. Spring's, Newburyport
        Mr. Emerson's, Beverly
        Worcester
        Salem, evening lecture, Mr. Emerson's
        Lynn
        South Hadley
        Northampton
        Hartford   (Old South)
        Yale College   73

The first sermon was written in "Nov. or December, 1814", and the last on March 16, 1856.

Part II, entitled "Chronological Table of Preaching" records that the first sermon was delivered in 1814, before the Society of Inquiry at Andover Seminary, and the last discourse on June 6, 1858. Beginning on February 7, 1819 an account of the sermons preached in the Yale College Chapel is given. If the minister was a visitor his name is given; if Dr. Fitch preached, the number of the sermon delivered by him is recorded. A selection of the discourses pronounced by Dr. Fitch in the Chapel of Yale College was published by his son, L. W. Fitch, in 1871.[74]

----

73. Vol. 1, p. E.
74. E. T. Fitch, *Sermons, Practical and Descriptive*, New Haven, Judd and White, 1871. 365 pp.

Examinations

On August 14, 1832, the Corporation voted "that Rev. Doctor Porter, Rev. William Noyes and Rev. Aaron Dutton be a committee to examine into the state of the Theological Department and consult with the Professors of this Department upon its general interests and measures requisite to promote its greatest usefulness and report at the next meeting of the Board. This report[75] recommended[76] that an annual examining committee, consisting of three members of the Corporation, be appointed.

The examination of students in the studies reviewed above was not officially provided for until 1832, and from the insinuations[77] apparent in the recommendations of that year, they seem to have been largely neglected prior to this date. The Reports of these committees which have been

---

75. Minutes of the President and Fellows, August 14, 1832. MS.
76. Report of the Theological Committee, 4 pp. MS.
77. The last paragraph of the report reads: "It being understood that there will annually be a public examination of the school, as stated in the rules to be submitted ['The Rules and Regulations of the Theological Department' examined in Chapter IV of this study] your Committee would also suggest the following resolution viz.-- Resolved that a Committee of three from this body be annually appointed to attend the annual examination of the Theological students."

preserved [78] do not vary a great deal, the majority of them being of the type exemplified by that one bearing the date of April 17, 1845: [79]

"To the President & Fellows of Yale College

The subscribers, having attended the examination of the students in The Theological department of sd College,- have been highly gratified with their attainments, upon the various subjects, upon which they were examined, and we are satisfied from the examination and from the dissertations read by the students, that they and their teachers have been faithful.

New Haven S. R. Andrew
April 17, 1845. R. Lowry   Committee
                 L. Griggs
                 K. Olmsted"

The Committee which reported in April, 1840, gives more information concerning the method of examination:

"The examination commenced Wednesday morning April 22d at 8 o clock, with the Junior class, in the translation and exegesis of the original Scriptures, both Hebrew and Greek, conducted by the Professor of Sacred Literature. It was continued until nearly noon, and gave satisfactory evidence of the exact and thorough instruction given to the class. . . . This was followed by dissertations prepared and read by the members of the class on various topics having a common bearing on the questions respecting the double sense of certain parts of the Scriptures. These also were creditable to the class-evincive of manly and independent thought; of reverence for the Scriptures and love of truth. . . . In the afternoon of the same day commenced the examination of the Middle class, under the Professor of Didactic Theology, & was continued until night; & resumed the next day, & at one o clock was closed. It was very particular

---

78. The following reports are among the "Divinity Papers", Dec. 1832; Aug. 13, 1834; Aug. 15, 1837; Aug. 14, 1838; April 19, 1839, April 23, 1840, April, 1844; April 17, 1845; April 22, 1846; April 16 and 17, 1850; July 24, 1854 (The approximate date of the termination of studies for each of the several years is apparent from the account of these dates.)
79. MS. 2 pp.

on all the parts of the course. . . .viz. . . .
mental and moral Philosophy; natural religion; the
necessity and evidences of divine revelation; the
authenticity of the divine inspiration of the
Scriptures; the Trinity of the Godhead; the Moral &
Providential purposes of the Government of God; . .
. . The members of the class were questioned
minutely as to their views on these subjects; their
ability to maintain the truth; and the fallacy of
the opposite errors. . . . The examination each day
was preceded by prayer; & the general appearance &
conduct of the young men were such as well becomes
candidates for the sacred ministry. . . . . [80]
. . . .

Mr. E. R. Gilbert, an examiner for the year 1854, wrote:

"As one of your Committee, I attended the
examination of the Theological Department of the
College on the 4th & 5th of April last.[81] Although the sessions were long and fatiguing, yet I
was much interested in the review then had of the
course pursued by myself more than 20 years ago, &
in the evidences presented of advancement in that
department of our institution."

The course of study which was offered to students attending the Theological Department in Yale College during the period 1822-1858 remained almost entirely unchanged, even in respect to details. Evidence of the static condition of the curriculum is apparent from a comparison of the plan of the course of study as outlined in the "Principles and Regulations of the Theological Department", which bore the date of the year 1833, with the plan as outlined in each of the annual Catalogues of Yale College beginning with that of 1850/51. The manner in which the students cared for their manuscript notes of the professors' lectures and sold the copy to other students who attended the institution in later years is a

---
80. The Committee neglects to make any report concerning an examination of the Senior Class.
81. The Report bears the date of July 24, 1854.

further indication of the fact that the course of study changed inappreciably. The Junior Year was devoted almost wholly to the study of the Hebrew and Greek languages, with one course in theology; the Middle Year was almost entirely taken up with courses in theology, with the studies in "Sacred Literature" being continued; and in the Senior Year the students attended lectures in Homiletics and "Pastoral Theology". Professor Fitch preached sermons each Sunday morning in the College Chapel which in a period of four years constituted a system of theological doctrine. The examinations of the students were conducted orally by the Professors before a Committee appointed annually by the President and Fellows of Yale College. The outstanding features of the course of study during this period, therefore, were: the entire neglect of a course in Church History; the predominance of the study of theology; and the static condition of the plan and content of the course of study.

CHAPTER VIII

THE LIBRARIES

THE LIBRARIES

The Libraries which were available to the students of the Theological Department in Yale College during the first era in its history were: the College Library, and the Libraries of the Linonian, the Brothers in Unity, and the Rhetorical Societies.

The College Library

According to tradition Yale College began with the bequeathing of a collection of books rather than a dedication of a group of buildings. Although this tradition appears to lack foundation in all its details, it is indicative of the important place which the library held in the minds of the founders of the College.[1]

In keeping with the humble beginning of the School and of the Library, the office of librarian was not of great importance in the earlier years. Before 1805, the Senior Tutor acted as librarian, and in President Clap's time received therefor an additional salary of six pounds.[2] Professor James L. Kingsley was librarian from 1805 to 1824, Professor Josiah W. Gibbs from 1824 to 1843, and Mr. Edward C. Herrick from 1843 to 1858.

The most valuable accession to the library during the

---

1. See pp. 6, 7.
2. Thomas Clap, *Annals of Yale College* (1766), p. 43.

eighteenth century was the gift of Bishop Berkeley in 1733. President Clap writes, "The Number was near 1000 Volumes (including those which he had sent before) whereof 260 were Folios, and generally very large. I judge that this Collection cost at least 400 Pounds Sterling."[3] Prior to the year 1742 "there had never been any perfect Catalogue of the Books in the Library." In that year the books were arranged in order upon the shelves, "(but in Honour to the Rev. Dr. Berkeley, for his extraordinary Donation, his Books stood by themselves, at the South End of the Library)"[4].

The Library grew very slowly following the gift of Bishop Berkeley, and actually decreased during the Revolution.[5] A bequest for theological works, made by Rev. John Elliott of Guilford, Connecticut, in 1824, was allowed to accumulate until in 1834 it reached the stipulated amount of $1000. In 1823, the date of the last printed catalogue of the Library, the number of volumes was six thousand five hundred; in 1835, ten thousand. In 1845, the income of the library having been for some years husbanded with this object in view, purchases to the amount of $8,000 were made by Professor Kingsley in Europe. A new building for the use of the Library, which surpassed in size and beauty all other structures on the College Square, was just then ready for

---

3. Thomas Clap, op. cit., p. 42.
4. Ibid., p. 43.
5. President Clap says that the number of books in the Library was about four thousand in 1766. The Catalogue of 1791 records the titles of two thousand four hundred volumes.

occupancy. This improvement, taken in connection with the fact that the librarianship, which had hitherto been attached to some other and more engrossing college duty, became, with the appointment of Mr. Herrick, an independent office, forms a marked era in the history of the Library. In 1849, the number of volumes had risen to 20,515.[6]

The service which the library was designed to render finds expression in the Laws of Yale College for the different years. According to the edition of 1829:[7]

> "I. No person, except the President, Fellows, members of the Faculty, resident Graduates, Junior and Senior Sophisters, shall have the liberty of drawing books out of the Library, but by permission of the President and professors. . . .
> II. The Library shall be opened on Thursday of each week, vacations excepted, between the hours of two and three in the afternoon. No Student shall be allowed to draw books from the Library oftener than once in a fortnight; . . . graduates may attend the Library every Thursday, at the time above specified. . . . [8]
> No persons, except the members of the Faculty, may have more than three books at a time.
> III. . . . . no Student, Graduate or Undergraduate, shall carry a book belonging to the Library out of the city of New Haven, on a penalty, in each of the cases aforesaid, of being deprived of the privilege of borrowing books for a time not exceeding six months, or of paying a fine not exceeding one dollar, at the discretion of the Faculty.
> V. Resident Graduates and Undergraduates, and such persons as have special license to borrow books from the Library, should pay at the rate of 12 cents every month for a folio volume, 8 cents for a quarto,

---

6. Report of the Librarian of Yale College to the President and Fellows, July 2, 1849. MS. 2 pp.
7. Chapter IX, Of the Library.
8. The Library of the Theological Seminary in Andover, according to the Laws of that institution, was open from 2 to 4 P.M. on Saturday, before the legislation of 1837. After this date the doors were open for one hour and a half, during the Winter term, and two hours, during the summer term, on the afternoon of each week day.

6 cents for a octavo or lesser volume, and double the sum for every book that is recited. And if the book be not returned within a month from the time it was borrowed, double the sum should be paid, every month until it shall be returned."

Noteworthy features in these laws are that the use of the Library was limited to those students who had an academic standing above the Freshman and Sophomore Classes; that the Library was opened for one hour each week, and then only for the withdrawal of books; that such books which were withdrawn were subject to a stated fee varying in amount with the size of the volume.

These rules remained unchanged until the legislation of [9] 1848. The Laws of that year permitted the Library to be opened five hours each secular day of the week. However, Juniors and Seniors in the Academic Department had the liberty of drawing and consulting books of the Library on Monday and Thursday only, and no other restrictions concerning the use of the Library were removed.[10]

The type of books possessed by the Library and the proportion of them which would probably be used more extensively by theological students may be ascertained from the following compilation arranged in the order of the greatest number of titles under each of the divisions given, and based on the Catalogue of the Library for the year 1823:[11]

---

9. The Laws of Yale College, Chapter IX, The Library, for the Years, 1833, 1839, 1843.
10. Ibid., (1848).
11. Catalogue of Books in the Library of Yale College, New Haven, 1823. 100 pp.

Theological Works and Treatises	540	Titles
History	359	"
Greek and Latin Classics	276	"
Natural Philosophy and Astronomy	199	"
Annotations on the Bible	185	"
Chemistry, Mineralogy and Natural History	185	"
Sermons	162	"
Mathematics	153	"
Miscellanies	151	"
Geography, Voyages and Travels	149	"
Bibles, Introduction to the Bible, etc.	128	"
Law, State Papers, Statistics, etc.	103	"
Poetry and Plays	100	"
Anatomy, Physic, Surgery	98	"
Ecclesiastical History	82	"
Systems of Divinity	79	"
Dictionaries and Lexicons	78	"
Philology and Rhetoric	78	"
Logic and Metaphysics	69	"
Evidences of Revelation	68	"
Fathers	66	"
Biography	60	"
Antiquities	47	"
Grammars and Rudiments	44	"
Translation of the Learned Societies, the Arts, etc.	33	"
Ethics	23	"
Natural Religion	21	"

A very noticeable feature of this catalogue of books is that in very few cases does the Library possess two or more copies of the same title.

With the purchase of books in Europe, beginning in 1840, the proportion of works of a theological nature grew less with each year. Besides Professor Kingsley, Professor George E. Day, an alumnus of the Theological Department, and now a Professor of the Lane Seminary, and Professor Noah Porter of Yale College, were active in obtaining suitable volumes for the Library.[12] From the manuscript Catalogue used by the

---
12. George E. Day, Letter to E. C. Herrick respecting books for the Yale Library. Walnut Hills, O. April 18, 1857. MS. 1 p. Noah Porter, Three Letters to E. C. Herrick, Berlin, and Paris, 1853, 1854, MS. 4; 2; 2 pp.

Librarian during the years 1844-1895, it is evident that the Library of Yale College grew not only in numbers but also in variety of subjects and in fields of interest during the years 1844-1858.[13]

The Extent to Which Theological Students Used the College Library

According to the "Principles and Regulations of the Theological Department in Yale College", the Library was "open to all Theological students to take such books as are prescribed by the Professors free of taxation; but no student shall take more than two volumes at a time nor retain them longer than four weeks."[14]

In the "Day Books"[15] of the Librarian of Yale College were recorded the volumes withdrawn by the students of the Theological Department along with other members of Yale College. Unfortunately those volumes containing the records for the years 1824/25-1833/34 have not been found. From the existent records one may ascertain with accuracy not only the number of books read by each and every student, but also the author and title of each of the volumes taken from the Library.

---

13. Catalogue of the Yale College Library, 1844-1895. MS. 579, (65, 53) pp.
14. Chapter IV, Statute 5 (1833) MS.
15. Nine Volumes, 1817-1824, 1834-1869. MS.

The Number of Students Using the Library

Twelve of the fifteen students who were registered in the Theological Department in Yale College in the first two years of its history withdrew books from the College Library.[16] The remaining academic years of this period concerning which we have record, 1834/35-1857/58, have been divided into periods of five years each. The largest number of students to use the Library in any one of these periods is 211, for the period 1834/35-1838/39. However, the largest percentage of students withdrawing Library books was reached in the period 1849/50-1853/54, when a little over nine-tenths of the students used the Library. In general, it appears that the opportunities afforded by the College Library were enjoyed by a larger part of the student body of the Theological Department during the last years of the period 1822-1858 than during the first years.

The Number and the Type of Books Withdrawn

The average number of books withdrawn per student per year varies with each five-year period from 0.2 to 11.3. The average number of books read by each student each year, when all the years of which we have record are considered is 9.2. The number of books read by a student in one year varies from 1 to 54, with the median number being 7.5. Since the average number of books per student per year is 9.2, and the

---

16. See Table VIII on the next page.

TABLE VIII. NUMBER OF STUDENTS OF THE THEOLOGICAL
DEPARTMENT WHO USED THE LIBRARY OF YALE COLLEGE
AND THE NUMBER OF BOOKS WITHDRAWN

Academic	Total number Students in School	Total number of Students using Library	Percent of Students using Library	Total No. of Books withdrawn	Average No. of Books withdrawn
1822/23 1823/24	15	12	80	104	8.6
1834/35 1838/39	347	211	67.9	2289	10.8
1839/40 1843/44	340	188	55.5	1193	6.3
1844/45 1848/49	272	192	70.5	1203	6.2
1849/50 1853/54	192	175	91.1	1180	6.7
1854/55 1857/58	115	81	70.4	919	11.3
1822/23 1823/24 and 1834/35 1857/58	1281	859	66.5	7888	9.1

median 7.5, it is evident that a small group of students read a great many books.

In order to determine what was the major interest of the books read by the student, the following plan has been arranged. The different books recorded as withdrawn in the Day Book of the Librarian during one year by one student will be called hereafter a "List of Books". When the books contained in this list are chiefly concerned with subjects of a theological nature, to the extent that all the volumes, with perhaps one, and never more than two exceptions, bear titles which mark them as theological books, e.g., "Jonathan Edwards' Works", or "Cogan on the Passions", then that list of books will be known as a "Theological" type of list. The lists of books withdrawn by the theological students from the College Library during the period fall into four other "types" of lists, besides the "Theological" type. These are: "Theological-Text"--a list is so described when all of the books, with perhaps one exception, are devoted to theological subjects, a portion of which have been designated as text-books by the professors of the Theological Department in Yale College; "Theological-German"--theological books in the German language, for the most part; "Theological Varied"-- a number of books on various topics with the majority being of a theological nature; "Varied"--volumes on several subjects, including perhaps a few dealing with theological questions. Examples of each of these types are given in Illustrations 4-9, to be found on the pages at the end of this Chapter.

Of the total number (859) of students using the Library each year during the period under examination, 570, or almost exactly two-thirds, withdrew a list of books annually which was devoted almost wholly to theological subjects.[17] This very great emphasis upon the reading of theological books only is probably largely due to the statute of the Theological Department, quoted above, which stated that students should withdraw from the Library those books which were prescribed by the Professors free of taxation. Evidently this prescription limited the students to those books which had a direct bearing upon the course of study, and it appears that little provision was made by the professors whereby collateral reading could be done on various subjects. In general, however, the proportion of the "Theological" type of lists seems to decrease with each succeeding group of five year periods.

The next most popular type of lists is that which has been termed the "Varied";[18] 160 annual lists, during the entire period for which we have records, being of this type. The remaining three types are ranked thus: "Theological-Varied", 55; "Theological-Text", 47, and the "Theological-German", 11.[19] The last type, constituting works read in German, would from the nature of the case, be enjoyed by a very small group of the students. Six of the eleven annual lists of this type occurred in one five-year period,

---
17. See Table IX, on the next page; and Illustrations 4 and 9, pp. 260, 268.
18. See Illustration 8, p. 266.
19. See Illustrations 5-8, pp. 262-266.

TABLE IX. TYPE OF BOOKS WITHDRAWN BY STUDENTS OF THE
THEOLOGICAL DEPARTMENT FROM THE YALE COLLEGE LIBRARY

Academic Years	Total No. Students using Library	No. of Students per Type	Type	Number of Books		
				Low	Median	High
1822/23	12	7	Th.	1	5	18
		3	Th. Text	7	12	23
		0	Th. Ger.			
		0	Th. V.			
1823/24		2	Varied	3		9
1834/35	211	132	Th.	1	7	36
		8	Th. Text	6	18	22
		0	Th. Ger.			
		20 a	Th. V.	3	19	71
1838/39		51 b	Varied	1	10	54
1839/40	188	124	Th.	1	5	19
		7	Th. Text	2	7	27
		1	Th. Ger.		8	
		8	Th. V.	3	13	25
1843/44		48 c	Varied	1	4	19
1844/45	192	139	Th.	1	5	20
		14	Th. Text	1	10	17
		3	Th. Ger.	3	3	44
		5	Th. V.	4	10	33
1848/49		31 d	Varied	1	4	28
1849/50	175	129	Th.	1	7	38
		7	Th. Text	3	16	26
		6	Th. Ger.	15	22	33
		15	Th. V.	3	11	46
1853/54		18 e	Varied	1	9	25
1854/55	81	55	Th.	1	7	35
		8	Th. Text	1	6	22
		1	Th. Ger.		11	
		7	Th. V.	7	19	33
1857/58		10 f	Varied	2	10	28
1822/23 1823/24 and 1834/35 1857/58	859	586	Th.	1	6	38
		47	Th. Text	1	12	27
		11	Th. Ger.	3	10	44
		55	Th. V.	3	13	71
		160	Varied	1	8	54

a. Including two students, each of whom read theological and Latin books, with emphasis on the latter. b. Including three students - one who read 51 books dealing with the Latin language; two others who read books in English literature. c. Including Two students, one reading in English literature and the other reading Latin works. d. Including one student who read miscellaneous volumes in German. e. Including five students - two reading theological and English works; one Latin books; one theological works in Latin; one theological works in Greek. f. Including four students - two reading theological books and works in English literature; one reading in English literature; and one theological works in Latin.

that of 1849/50-1853/54.

Books Most Often Consulted by the Students

The twenty volumes which were most often withdrawn from the Library by the students of the Theological Department, during the years 1834/35 to 1839/40, are given in Illustration 9, which may be found at the end of this Chapter. Only one of these twenty books is concerned with a topic other than theological, and it stands fourteenth in rank on the list. The "Works" of Jonathan Edwards, the originator of the "New England Theology" is in first place, and was consulted almost twice as often as its nearest rival, "Mosheim's Ecclesiastical History". The fact that this latter work holds second place in the frequency with which the books were withdrawn, is remarkable in view of of the fact that no provision for the subject of Church History was made in the course of study of the Theological Department in Yale College until after the close of the period under review (1822-1858). The remaining eighteen works are concerned with the writings of theologians, with the exception of a volume entitled, "Young Ministers' Companion".

A list of the twenty works most often consulted by the students of the Theological Department during the decade 1839/40-1848/49[20] differs from the group just reviewed in the following particulars: "Mosheim's Ecclesiastical

---

20. See Illustration 12, at the end of this Chapter, p. 275.

History" has fallen from second to eighth place in the list, and although "Edwards' Works" still holds first place it does not surpass so much as before its nearest competitors, "Dwight's Works", and "Reid's Works". "Porter's Homiletics" is now one of the twenty books listed, and holds fourth place. The outstanding difference between the books most often withdrawn in the last period reviewed and those consulted in this period, is that three periodicals are found in this list, with the "Biblical Repository" in fifth place, the "Quarterly Christian Spectator" in the twelfth position, and the "Biblical Repertory" immediately following the latter.

The list of twenty books most often withdrawn during the years 1849/50-1857/58 [21] differs from that group just reviewed in the following particulars: "Edwards' Works" has been supplanted in first place, by a slight margin, by the "Preacher's Guide". More recent works, such as "Whateley's Peculiarities of Christianity", "Campbell's Systematic Theology", "Campbell's Four Gospels", have come to join the volumes of such propounders of the "New England Theology" as Edwards, Dwight, and Emmons. This is indicative of a new emphasis upon the study of the Bible, which was beginning at this time, and was characteristic of a later period.[22] The beginning of the influence of German theologians upon the study of theology is seen in the fact that such works as

---

21. See Illustration 13, p. 277, at the end of this Chapter.
22. For a discussion of the change from a theological to a Biblical emphasis see Chapter XIII, pp. 409-416.

"Hegstenberg on the Psalms", "Goethe's Werke", and "Schiller's Werke" were often being consulted by the students of this period. If the list of twenty books were extended to twenty-five, "Baumgarten's Pentateuch", and "Hagenbach's History of Doctrine" would be included in the group.

In the list of twenty books most often consulted by the students of the Theological Department during the period 1858/59-1867/68,[23] a decade subsequent to the period under review in this study (1822-1858), the outstanding features to be noted are the following: The works of Edwards, Hopkins, Emmons, and Dwight, are still being read, but have lost their former preëminence. The works of Horace Bushnell are now being read more frequently. The volumes published from the pen of Dr. Taylor after his death are being consulted. Of the twenty books listed, four of them are texts in Church History. The added interest in this subject is undoubtedly due to the appointment of Professor George P. Fisher to the Chair of Ecclesiastical History in 1861. A more intensive study of the Bible and the influence of German scholars in this field is evident from the presence of such popular books in the list as "Hengstenberg on the Psalms", "Hagenbach's History of Doctrine", "Olshausen on the Gospels", and the same author on "Philippians", and "Meyer's Commentary".

---

23. See Illustration 14, p. 278, at the end of this Chapter.

The Libraries of the Several Societies

The Libraries which were supported almost wholly by the undergraduates, but which were open to some theological students, were those belonging to the Linonian, the Brothers in Unity, and the Calliopean Societies.

The Linonian Library, which is younger by sixteen years than the society itself, was according to tradition, commenced in 1769, when Timothy Dwight, Nathan Hale, and James Hillhouse made the first contribution of books.[24] The example thus set was soon followed by the Brothers in Unity, but for half a century the progress of both libraries was exceedingly slow. About 1825, the advance became more rapid, but slackened again after 1850, when the interest in the societies began to decline.[25] The number of volumes in the Linonian Library has been as follows: in 1800, four hundred seventy-five; in 1811, seven hundred; in 1822, twelve hundred; in 1831, three thousand five hundred; in 1841, seven thousand five hundred; in 1846 ten thousand one hundred; 1860, eleven thousand three hundred.[26] The

---
24. The records of the proceedings of the Society for the year 1769 have been lost, but in the preface to the Catalogue of books in the Library (1860) it is affirmed that in the records for the year 1769 the gratitude of the members of the Society is expressed to the three men who made the first contribution of books at that time.
25. In recording the Minutes of the Society or of its Committees, often there is comment upon the "prosperity" of the Society. See Linonian Society, Records of Meetings, 1845-1863, 3 vols. MS.; Treasurer's Accounts, 1822-1842, 1 vol. MS.; Standing Committee Accounts, 1833-1852, 1 vol. MS.; Prudential Committee Records, 1858-1861, MS. Brothers in Unity, Records of Meetings, 1816-1828, 1 vol. MS.
26. See the various Catalogues published in these years.

Brothers' library ran an almost parallel course, the mutual rivalry suffering neither to get far in advance of the other. The Calliopean Society, organized in 1819, gathered a library which at the time of its dissolution in 1854, amounted to six thousand volumes.[27] Before they were removed to the College library in the year 1844 these three libraries occupied together the second floor of the Athenaeum. The importance of these libraries to the students in the Academic Department is indicated by the following statement, written by the College librarian, Mr. Addison Van Name, in 1879: "For the last fifty years, the undergraduate students have been accustomed to look for the supply of their ordinary needs less to the college library than to those most useful auxiliaries, the libraries of the public societies".[28]

Each of these libraries was open for the patronage of those theological students who were graduate members of any one of the Societies, and who paid an annual fee of one dollar a year, and to those students who had been elected honorary members of any one of the Societies.[29] There is no evidence that the Calliopean Library was consulted by the students of the Theological Department. It has been noted that the great majority of the students of this Department came from New England. The members of the

---

27. Report of the Librarian to the President and Fellows of Yale College, July, 1854, MS., 3 pp.
28. "The Library", Yale College, a Sketch of its History, ed. by W. L. Kingsley, Vol. I, p. 168.
29. Linonian Library Register, 1842-1845. MS.

Calliopean Society were almost entirely from the South, and "by a long established custom. . . . but few of the inhabitants of the New England states. . . . offered themselves as candidates for admission" to this Society.[30]

According to the Catalogue of the Library of the Brothers in Unity Society,[31] this group possessed in September 1832 one hundred seven different titles under the category "Divinity". The emphasis of selection was upon "Poetry", "Novels and Romances", and "Biographies", but the works in "Divinity" appear to be well selected. Books taken from the Library were required to be returned within two weeks, encyclopedias within one week.

The Catalogue of the Linonian Library for October, 1831,[32] lists one hundred sixteen titles under "Divinity". This group of books appears to be about equal in the quality of its selection to that of the Brothers' Library. The larger part of this Library is also devoted to "Poetry", "Novels and Romances", and "Biographies".

Use Made of the Linonian Library

"Registers" which record the withdrawal of books from the Linonian Library are available for the years 1822/23-1831/32, and 1842/43-1852/53.[33] Those for the years 1832/33-1841/42, and those subsequent to the year 1852/53

---

30. Catalogue of the Calliopean Society (1839), p. 4.
31. Brothers in Unity Society, Catalogue of Books, 49 pp.
32. Linonian Society, Catalogue of Books in the Libraries of the Linonian Society, New Haven, 55 pp.
33. Ten volumes, MS.

appear to have been lost. When the years for which we have record are divided into four periods,[34] the percentage of the students registered in the Theological Department who used the Library, varies from about one-fourth to one-third (24.4 to 35.4). The highest percentage of students who withdrew books from the Linonian Library is found for the last period for which we have record, 1847/48-1852/53.

The 269 lists of annual withdrawals averaged 9.4 books per student per year. The average for the number of books taken from the College Library was 9.2 books per student per year.

The method used in recording the withdrawal of books from the Linonian, the Brothers in Unity, and the Moral and Rhetorical Libraries, was as follows: The last name of the borrower was written at the top of the page; under this name were three columns just wide enough to include the number of the volume, the month, and the day. The titles of the works are not given. A manuscript catalogue of books, arranged alphabetically and numerically, was used by the Librarian for the purpose of the identification of the books. These catalogues were frequently revised. Three such catalogues have been preserved.[35] Unfortunately only one of them, that one for the year 1831 and 1832, coincides in date with the records of withdrawals which are extant.

---

34. See Table X on the next page.
35. These Catalogues bear no dates. From a comparison with the printed catalogues, and the date of the last books recorded in them, they may be identified as those catalogues in use about 1831, 1834, and 1840 or 1841.

TABLE X   USE MADE OF THE LIBRARY OF
THE LINONIAN SOCIETY BY THE STUDENTS OF
THE THEOLOGICAL DEPARTMENT IN YALE COLLEGE.

Academic	Total No. of Students in School	Total No. using Library	Percentage Students using Library	Number of Books			Total No. of Books With Drawn	Average No. of Books per Student
				Low	Median	High		
1822/23 1826/27	87	29	33.3	2	7	24	245	8.4
1827/28 1831/32	245	60	24.4	1	6	58	629	10.4
1832/33 1841/42			Records Lost					
1842/43 1846/47	325	90	27.6	1	10	42	872	9.6
1847/48 1852/53	254	90	35.4	1	8	60	784	8.7
1822/23 1831/32 and 1842/43 1852/53	911	269	29.5	1	8.2	60	2530	9.4

In Illustration 15 [36] is given an example of a typical annual withdrawal of books by a student of the Theological Department. The numbers and dates are from the "Register", the titles of the works from the manuscript catalogue, and the information contained in brackets has been obtained from other sources.[37]

Although the number concerning whom we are able to gain this information is comparatively small (15), it appears that most of the students withdrew a list of books which, in view of an interest in several subjects, would be classified as "Varied" in its nature.

Use Made of the Brothers in Unity Library

The years for which records are available concerning withdrawals from the Library of the Society of Brothers in Unity are: 1832/33-1833/34,[38] 1841/42, 1847/48-1857/58. According to data obtained from these records about one-fifth to one-third (18.3 per cent to 32.0 per cent) of the students registered in the Theological Department used the Library.[39] It is significant that the highest percentage is that of the first period (1832/33-1833/34), and the

---

36. See p. 281.
37. These sources are: the printed catalogue of the Library, and the General Catalogue of the Theological Department in Yale College (1836).
38. One volume which appears to record withdrawals previous to 1832 has defeated every effort at solution. No names are given. Numbers appear at the top of each page. Evidently each member was given a number and the key to the code has been lost.
39. See Table XI on the next page.

TABLE XI. USE MADE OF THE LIBRARY OF THE SOCIETY OF BROTHERS IN UNITY BY THE STUDENTS OF THE THEOLOGICAL DEPARTMENT IN YALE COLLEGE.

Academic	Total No. of Students in School	Total No. using Library	Percentage Students using Library	Number of Books			Total No. of Books With Drawn	Average No. of Books per Student
				Low	Median	High		
1832/33 1833/34	104	34	32.6	1	8	55	370	10.8
1834/35 1840/41			Records	Lost				
1841/42	59	19	32.5	2	7	30	216	12.0
1842/32 1846/47			Records	Lost				
1847/48 1851/52	217	48	22.1	1	8	71	543	11.3
1852/53 1857/58	158	29	18.3	1	7	20	224	7.0
1832/33 1833/34 and 1841/42 and 1847/48 1857/58	538	129	25.2	1		71	1353	10.4

lowest is for the last period (1852/53-1857/58). There seems to have been increasingly less dependence, for the withdrawal of books, upon the Library of the Society of Brothers in Unity by the students of the Theological Department.

The average number of books read per student per year by the theological students who were borrowers from this Library (10.4) compares favorably with the average number per student per year from the College Library (9.1) and the Linonian Library (9.4).

Illustration 16, and Illustration 17 [40] constitute typical examples of two lists of books withdrawn by two students from the Library of the Society of Brothers in Unity. The information contained therein was obtained in the same manner as that which was reviewed above in connection with the records of the Linonian Library.

The Moral and Rhetorical Library

The origin of the Moral Society, and its evolution, first into the Moral and Theological Society in 1828, and finally into the Rhetorical Society in 1843, will be reviewed in the next Chapter.[41] In the year 1822 the number of volumes in the Library of the Moral Society was 433.[42] These works were entirely devoted to theological subjects.

This Library was inherited by the Moral and Theological

---

40. See pp. 283, 285.
41. Chapter IX, first section.
42. Catalogue of Books belonging to the Linonian Brothers' and Moral Libraries, Yale College, September 1822, New Haven, 39 pp.

Society of the Theological Department in Yale College. No catalogue of the Society was published subsequent to the year 1822. However, according to the attestation of the Librarian in a manuscript Catalogue of the Library, there was a total of 719 volumes in the year 1844, and a sum of 772 volumes on April 20, 1849.

On December 3, 1857, the books of the Moral and Rhetorical Library were deposited in the Yale College Library.[43] Besides a "number of pamphlets, bound or unbound, broken sets of periodicals, etc." there were 331 volumes deposited at this time. The first editions of one hundred nine of these books were of dates prior to the year 1800; 150 bore dates of the years 1800-1825; and seventy-two dates of the period 1826-1850. The following periodicals were also deposited at this time:

```
"Biblical Repository 1st Series v. 1-12, 1831-8
                     2nd Series v. 1-12, 1831-44
                     3rd Series v. 1-5,  1845-49
                          Index
Biblica Sacra  v. 1-9, 1844-52
Biblical Repertory  v. 1-3 and 7-23, 1829-31 and 1835-51
Christian Spectator  v. 1-10, 1819-28
Quarterly Christian Spectator  v. 1-10, 1829-38
Christian Examiner  v. 5-39, 1829-45
Christian Review v. 6-12, 1841-7
Christian Observer  v. 1-3, 10-20, 22-26, 1802-26
Missionary Herald  v. 17-48 (some nos. wanting)
Panoplist  v. 8-14, 1813-18
New Englander  v. 1-10, 1843-52
North British Review  v. 1-5, 1844-6
Literary and Theological Review  1834-8"   (44
```

According to the Constitution of the Rhetorical Society

----

43. Yale College Library, Register of Donations to the Library, 1852-1870. MS.
44. Ibid.

of the Theological Department in Yale College, the Library was opened twice a week for the delivery of books.[45] Each member was taxed fifty cents per year, and a portion of these funds was applied to the needs of the Library.[46] The Society was also the recipient of books given to the Library by friends of the group.[47]

The Society became greatly concerned about the neglect of its Library in the year 1841, and drafted a new constitution to insure its future.[48] To this end the Librarian was required to "keep two complete Catalogues of the books belonging to the Society: one of them <u>numerical</u>, the other <u>alphabetical</u>."[49] The Standing Committee selected the books to be purchased and examined the Library at the regular periods when the books were called in.[50] The Librarian had exclusive care of the Library with the coöperation of an Associate, and was held responsible for every book which was lost during his term of office.[51] Following the account of these requirements in the Constitution, Sections 3 to 15 inclusive are concerned with rather elemental, but very rigid, rules concerning the use of the books.

For the next three or four years the records of

---

45. Book D, Constitution of 1834, Article VI, Section 1. MS.
46. The Rhetorical Society, Treasurer's Book, see especially the entry for October 7, 1839. MS.
47. Book D, Minutes, August 3, 1842, MS. The members express their gratitude for the books given to the Society by Professor Goodrich and Mr. Forrest Shepherd.
48. Book B, Minutes, March 10, 1841.
49. Book D, Constitution of 1841, Article III, Section 5.
50. <u>Ibid.</u>, Section 6.
51. <u>Ibid.</u>, Article VI, Sections 1 and 2.

withdrawals from the Library were kept in better order,[52]
but this renewed interest seems to have been short-lived.
The last record of withdrawals is for the year 1843/44, the
last date in the manuscript catalogue of the Library is 1849,
and, as has been noted, the books were deposited in the
College Library in 1857. Probably the small returns from
the annual fee of 50 cents per student were not sufficient
for the purchase of the new books needed for the Library.
An examination of the Treasurer's Book[53] reveals that a
major part of the income of the Society was dedicated to the
regular running expenses of the Society exclusive of the
Library.

Use Made of the Moral and Rhetorical Library by Students

From about one-half to three-fourths of the total number of students registered in the Theological Department in Yale College withdrew one or more books annually from the Moral and Rhetorical Library in each of four five-year periods, 1823/24-1842/43.[54] The highest percentage (78.6) was reached in the period 1828/29-1832/33. This percentage decreased rapidly in the two subsequent five-year periods to the lowest figure of 51.4 per cent. However, the students in the last years of the entire period 1823/24-1843/44 surpassed, in the average number of books read per student per year, those who withdrew books in the early years of

---

52. Register of the Moral and Rhetorical Library, 1841-1843. MS.
53. The Rhetorical Society, Treasurer's Book, 1835-1853. MS.
54. See Table XII on the next page.

TABLE XII. USE MADE OF THE LIBRARY OF THE MORAL AND RHETORICAL SOCIETY BY THE STUDENTS OF THE THEOLOGICAL DEPARTMENT OF YALE COLLEGE

Academic	Total No. of Students in School	Total No. using Library	Percentage Students using Library	Number of Books			Total No. of Books Withdrawn	Average No. of Books per Student
				Low	Median	High		
1823/24 1827/28	122	58	48.3	1	8	49	608	10.4
1828/29 1832/33	244	192	78.6	1	7	54	1842	9.5
1833/34 1837/38	329	229	69.5	1	6	37	1985	8.6
1838/39 1843/44	348	179	51.4	1	9	55	2185	12.2
1843/44	66	39	59.0	1	20	64	811	20.7
1823/24 1843/44	1109	697	62.8	1	7.5	64	7431	10.6

the period. In other words, although the number of those
reading decreased rapidly during the period, the smaller
number of students at the end of the period averaged more
books per year. The average number of books read per student
per year (10.6) surpasses the number withdrawn per student
per year in each of the three other Libraries reviewed.
These volumes inevitably dealt with theological subjects
since that was the only type contained in this Library.[55]

Comparative Use of all the Libraries
by the Students

More students used the College Library than any other
Library in each five-year period with the exception of one
period. Two hundred twenty-nine members of the Theological
Department withdrew books from the Moral and Rhetorical
Library during the years 1833/34-1837/38. In a parallel
period, 1834/35-1838/39 two hundred eleven students read
books from the College Library. When all the records are
considered, a little over two-thirds (66.5 per cent) used the
College Library, a little less than two-thirds (62.8 per cent)
the Moral and Rhetorical Library, and about one-fourth of the
students used each of the Libraries of the Linonian and
Brothers in Unity Societies. The trend at the end of the
period, however, was in the direction of a much greater
number of the members of the Theological Department consult-

---

55. See Illustrations 18 and 19 for examples of books withdrawn from the Moral and Rhetorical Library; pp. 287, 288.

ing the Yale College Library, and an increasingly smaller group using each of the three other Libraries.

It would be of benefit to this study if information could be obtained concerning the number of students who used all four of the Libraries. Unfortunately as a comparison of Tables VIII-XI[56] will indicate, although records for several years are available in the case of each Library, at no point do the years of the records for all four Libraries coincide. And for a comparison of the use of three Libraries, only the years 1842/43 and 1843/44 are to be had; these three are the College, the Linonian, and the Moral and Rhetorical Libraries. It has been noted above that the Library of the Society of Brothers in Unity was, of the four Libraries, used least by the members of the Theological Department.

During the academic years 1842/43 and 1843/44, forty-one students withdrew books from the College Library only, twenty-six from the Linonian Library only, and forty-four from the Moral and Rhetorical Library only. Five students made use of both the College and Linonian Libraries; twenty-five of the College and the Moral and Rhetorical Libraries; six of the College, Linonian, and Moral and Rhetorical Libraries; and one of the Rhetorical and Linonian Libraries. Of the 148 students consulting Libraries in these two years, 111 (exactly three-fourths) consulted the books in only one Library, thirty-one used two, and six used three Libraries.

---

56. See pp. 234, 237, 245, 247.

Plans for the Improvement of Library Facilities

It has been noted above that not until subsequent to the year 1843 was the College Library open for more than two hours each week, and then only for the withdrawing of books. The Library of the Moral and Rhetorical Library permitted the borrowing of books two days each week. No evidence has been found which would indicate that a reading room was in existence in any Library of the College prior to the year 1829, in which year such a room was instituted by students of the Theological Department. In fact, as late as 1848, the Laws of the College rather discouraged the use, as reading rooms, of those rooms which had been granted to the Linonian and Brothers Societies for the housing of their Libraries:

> "It shall be the duty of the several societies, to whom rooms may be assigned in the Library building, through their Librarians or other officers, to afford all facilities for the inspection of their rooms and libraries as the Corporation or Faculty may direct. . . . The rooms so assigned to the several societies may be occupied by them until needed for the College Library, or so long as the President and Fellows shall see fit. Such rooms shall be used for Library purposes and no other. No meetings of the Societies shall be held in them, nor shall they be used as reading rooms except under the direction of the College Inspector or Prudential Committee."(57

The Librarian of Yale College in his Report to the President and Fellows for the year ending July 1866 stated that

---

57. The Laws of Yale College, 1848, Chapter IX, ...

it was "expedient" to establish a reading room in connection with the College Library, and pointed out that the necessity of uniting the student Libraries and the expense of the plan had thus far interfered with its execution.[58] In 1867 a reading room, "well-furnished" with newspapers and periodicals, American and English, was opened in South Middle College, four rooms having been thrown into one for the purpose.[59]

The Theological Atheneum

The steps which were taken by the students of the Theological Department in Yale College whereby a reading room in connection with that Department was begun appear to have proceeded as follows, in the customary form of the organization of a Society. At the meeting of the Society for Christian Research, December 20, 1828, a "Committee was appointed to report at the next meeting as to the expediency of establishing a reading room".[60] No mention of the report of this committee is found in the subsequent minutes of this Society. However, it appears that a larger number of the students of the Theological Department than were members of the Society for Christian Research were gathered to hear the report of the Committee. The establishment of the

---

58. Minutes of the President and Fellows, July 24, 1866.
59. Addison Van Name, "The Library", Yale College, a Sketch of its History, ed. by W. L. Kingsley, Vol. I, p. 189.
60. Society for Christian Research, Constitution and Records of Meetings. MS.

"Theological Atheneum" is recorded as follows:

"At a meeting of the Theol. Students in Yale College, Jan. 1829, the committee appointed at a previous meeting to consider the subject of establishing a reading room in connexion with the Theol. Department, reported in favor of it. The report was accepted."(61

According to the constitution which was adopted, the Secretary of the Society was to have charge of the reading room. Any graduate could become a member of the Society by paying annually the sum of two dollars. Any other person by paying a like amount, could become one of the group. Fifty-one subscribers signed their names to the Constitution.

The publications taken by the Society were:

      Foreign Quarterly Review
      North American Review
      Theological Repertory
      Christian Advocate
      African Repository
      German Lutheran Magazine
      Sunday School Magazine
      Christian Examiner
      Spirit of the Pilgrims
      Recorder and Telegram
      Christian Register
      Christian Watchman
      Catholic Miscellany
      Moravian Magazine
      Tract Magazine
      Journal of Science
      United States Journal of Commerce
      Free Press

According to the accounts of the Treasurer for the years 1831-1832 [62] about fifty dollars were expended each year in the interest of the reading room for periodicals

---

61. The Theological Atheneum, Records, MS.
62. Theological Reading Room, Treasurer's Account Book, Yale College, November 15, 1831. MS.

which belonged to the Society. Even though no evidence of the continuance of the reading room subsequent to the year 1832 has been found, the Society appears to have been well represented as to the quality of its members and well supplied as to funds, and may have existed for some years after 1832.

As was previously noted, Professor Gibbs was librarian of the College Library from 1824 to 1843. In October, 1845, he drew up "A Plan of a Reading Room for Periodicals."[63] Each subscriber was to pay for one magazine. For each dollar spent by a subscriber, the Library was to invest two dollars for subscriptions. Each member would be allowed to use the particular magazine, for which he had deposited funds, in his room for a period of time not exceeding a week. There is no evidence that the plan was carried into execution.

A Group of Illustrations

A group of Illustrations to which frequent reference has been made in this Chapter are to be found at this point. For the sake of clarity and greater usefulness to the reader they have been divided into divisions, each with a common interest.

---

63. MS. 3 pp.

ILLUSTRATIONS 4-19

Division I - Illustrations 4-10

In Division I are contained Illustrations 4-10, which constitute individual examples of the different types of lists of books withdrawn by one student in one year. It will be recalled that a "Theological" List of Books (Illustrations 4, 9) includes titles which are concerned, with one or perhaps two exceptions, with subjects of a theological nature. A "Theological-Text" type of List (Illustration 5) is made up of titles of books dealing with theological topics a large portion of which have been designated by the Faculty as textbooks to be used in the course of study. A "Theological-German" List (Illustration 6) contains the titles of books, with perhaps one exception, which are devoted to theological works written in German. A "Theological-Varied" Type of List (Illustration 7) contains titles of books, some of which are concerned with theological subjects and some which have been written upon a variety of topics. A "Varied" Type of List (Illustration 8) is made up of titles of books written upon a variety of subjects.

ILLUSTRATION 4. AN EXAMPLE OF A "THEOLOGICAL" LIST OF BOOKS WITHDRAWN FROM THE LIBRARY OF YALE COLLEGE. [a]

Blakeman P.

1838

Oct	4	Tappan's Sermons 8 vo	Oct	11
Oct	11	Edwards V 8 vo	Nov	1
Oct	11	Dren on the Resurrection 8 vo	Oct	25
Oct	11	Emmon's Sermons 8 vo	Oct	25
Oct	25	Massillan's Sermons Vol. I 8 vo	Nov	8
Oct	25	American Preachers 8 vo	Nov	1
Nov	1	Pascal's Thoughts 8 vo	Nov	22
Nov	1	Smith's Sacrifice &c. of Christ 8 vo	Nov	22
Nov	8	Fuller's on Deism 8 vo	Nov	22
Nov	22	Brown's Sermons 8 vo	Dec	6
Nov	22	Goldsmith's Roman History Vol. I and II, 8 vo	Dec	6
Dec	6	Goldsmith's Roman History Vol. II, 8 vo	Dec	20
Dec	6	Do.'s History of England Vol. I and II, 8 vo	Dec	27
Dec	20	McWhoter's Sermons 8 vo	Dec	27
Dec	27	Stow's Biblical Theology I, II 8 vo	Jan	17
Dec	27	Wilberforce' View of Chr. 12 vo	Jan	17
Jan	17	Stow's Biblical Theology Vol. II 8 vo	Jan	31
Jan	17	Dwight's Theology Vol. II and III 8 vo	Feb	7

a. An effort has been made in each of the Illustrations 4-10 to reproduce the record of withdrawals for a particular student for one academic year as it is found in the Day Book of the Library of Yale College.

ILLUSTRATION 4. AN EXAMPLE OF A "THEOLOGICAL" LIST OF BOOKS WITHDRAWN FROM THE LIBRARY OF YALE COLLEGE. (continued)

Jan	31	Campbell's Lectures Vol. I 8 vo	Feb	7
Feb	7	Dwight's Theology Vol. III and V, 8 vo	Feb	21
Jun	14	Edwards works Vol. IV 8 vo	Jul	4
Jun	19	Dwight's Theology Vol. I 8 vo	Jul	4
Jul	4	Dwight's Theology Vol. II 8 vo	Aug	8
Jul	11	Westminster Review Vol. II and 14 8 vo	Jul	18
Jul	19	McWhorter's Sermons 8 vo	Aug	8

ILLUSTRATION 5. AN EXAMPLE OF A "THEOLOGICAL-TEXT"
LIST OF BOOKS WITHDRAWN FROM THE LIBRARY OF YALE COLLEGE

W. C. Foot

			(1836-37)	
Oct	8	Edward V	Mar	17
Oct	8	Roseum N. T. II	Apr	20
Oct	8	Kinnoel II	Apr	20
Dec	3	Campbell on Miracles 2 vols. 8 vo	Dec	17
Feb	3	Newcome's Harmony 8 vo	Apr	20
May	3	Treat on Revelation 8 vo	Jul	4

ILLUSTRATION 6. AN EXAMPLE OF A "THEOLOGICAL-GERMAN"
LIST OF BOOKS WITHDRAWN FROM THE LIBRARY OF YALE COLLEGE.

Cyrus Pitts (Theol.)

1843				1843	
Oct	25	Die Psalmen: Mendelsohn, 12 vo		Dec	7
	26	Justis Harfenklange 8 vo Ren		Dec	19
	26	Hug: Einleitung in das Neue Test. Vol. 2, 8 vo		Nov	23
Nov	23	Neander: Gesch. der Christl Relig. &c. Bd. I Theol. I 8 vo		Dec	11
				1844	
Dec	7	Bible in German Vol. I, 8 vo		Feb	7
				1843	
	11	Theologische Studien Und Kritiken Bd. I, 8 vo		Dec	9
	22	Reid's Inquiry into the Mind 8 vo		Feb	5
1844					
Jan	6	Bell's Divine Mission of Christ 8 vo		Feb	5
Nov	26	Hug: Einleitung Vol. 2		Dec	27
Nov	26	Paley's Horae Paulinae 8 vo		Dec	27
1845					
Feb	6	Outramus de Sacrificous, 12 vo		Feb	13

ILLUSTRATION 7. AN EXAMPLE OF A "THEOLOGICAL-VARIED"
LIST OF BOOKS WITHDRAWN FROM THE LIBRARY OF YALE COLLEGE.

S. Denison Peet (Theol.)

1851				
Oct	10	Olmsted's Philosophy 8 vo	Nov	15
		Selen's Biographical Dictionary	Oct	15
	15	Mosherm's Eccl. Hist. trans. Murdock Vol. I	Oct	15
		" " " " " Vol. II	Nov	15
		Rosenmillevi Scholia in Neve. Test. Vol. V 8 vo	Nov	7
Oct	17	Bruder: Concordentia Neve. Test. Vol. V 8 vo	Oct	20
	20	Frisbie's works 8 vo	Dec	6
	29	Beecher: Baptism, its Import and Modes	Nov	15
	31	Roseumiilevi Scholia in Neve Test. Vol. V 8 vo	Nov	7
			1852	
Nov	7	Kuinoel: Com. in Neve Test. Vol. IV 8 vo	Jan	13
		Clarke's Commentary Vol. IV to VI	Dec	6
	15	Coleridge's Aids to Reflection 8 vo	Dec	13
Dec	11	Prince: Chronology of New England 8 vo (E.C.H.)	Dec	22
			1852	
	22	Gieseler: Eccl. Hist. Vol. 2 8 vo	Jan	28
1852				
Jan	13	Kuinoel: Com. in Neve Test. Vol. 5, 8 vo	Mar	9
Jan	15	Hopkins: Lowell Lectures 8 vo	Mar	9
	28	Browne: Ordo Seclorum 8 vo	Feb	17

ILLUSTRATION 7. AN EXAMPLE OF A "THEOLOGICAL-VARIED" LIST OF BOOKS WITHDRAWN FROM THE LIBRARY OF YALE COLLEGE. (continued)

Feb	3	Locke's Essays 3 Vols. 12 vo (Benev.)	Mar	27
		Hebrew Bible pt. I 8 vo (Benev.)	Feb	17
	7	Cousin's Psychology 8 vo	Mar	27
	9	Lynch's Exped. to Dead Sea 8 vo	Apr	12
May	8	Sparks Amer. Biography Vol. 24	May	11
	15	U. S. Explor. Expedition Vol. I 8 vo	Jul	2
	29	Neander: Planting & Training 8 vo	Jul	19
Jun	17	Edwards on the Will (1754) 8 vo	Jul	22
Jul	2	Clarke's Commentary Vol. 2, 8 vo	Jul	19

ILLUSTRATION 8. AN EXAMPLE OF A "VARIED" LIST OF BOOKS WITHDRAWN FROM THE LIBRARY OF YALE COLLEGE.

W. H. Collins (Theol.)

1850

Oct	18	Ford's Plays, Vol. 1, 8 vo 1850	Oct	26
	28	Spenser's Poems Vol. 1, 8 vo	Oct	31
	28	DeFoe's System of Magic 12 vo	Nov	7
	31	Scheller: Werke Vol. 1 8 vo	Nov	7
		Barry Cornwall's Poems 12 vo R	Nov	7
Nov	7	Scheller: Werke Vol. 7 8 vo 1851	Jan	1
	8	Middletown in the Greek Article 8 vo 1850	Nov	12
		Sharp " " " " 12 vo 1850	Nov	12
	26	Smith's Scrip. Testimony Vol. 1, 8 vo	Dec	20
Dec	28	Montargnes' Essays, Vol. 1, 8 vo 1851	Jan	11
1851				
Jan	9	Schiller: Werke Vol. 9, 8 vo 1851	Feb	5
	11	Montargnes' Essays, Vol. 2, 8 vo, 1851	Jan	23
	23	Buffier's First Truths 8 vo	Feb	8
Feb	5	Schiller: Werke Vol. 8, 8 vo R	Mar	3
		Channing's works Vol. 5, 8 vo	Feb	19
	8	Locke's Essay Vol. I 12 vo (Benev.) 1857	Mar	7
	19	Cousin's Psychology by Henry 8 vo	Mar	28
Mar	7	Locke's Essay Vol. 2, 12 vo (Benev.)	Apr	1
	19	Robert Hall's Works Vol. 5, 8 vo	Mar	28
		Cousin's Psychology by Henry 8 vo	Apr	1
Mar	28	Edwards Works Vols. 2, 8 vo	May	17

ILLUSTRATION 8. AN EXAMPLE OF A "VARIED" LIST OF BOOKS WITHDRAWN FROM THE LIBRARY IN YALE COLLEGE. (continued)

Apr	4	Fichte Werke Vol. 2		Apr	8
Apr	8	Goethe's Werke Vol. 19, 20 1840		May	10
	14	Hall R. Works Vol. 1 8vo 1843		May	8
May	10	Schiller: Werke Vol. 2 8 vo		Jun	10
			renewed	Jun	30
Jun	5	Bacon's Works Vol. 2 fol		Jun	9
	24	Mackintosh Works Vol. 1 1846 8 vo		Jul	16
	30	Goethe Werke Vol. 13, 14 18 vo		Jul	24
Jul	16	Macknight on the Epistles Vol. I 8 vo		Sep	18
Aug	25	Schiller Werke Vol. 10 8 vo		Oct	6

ILLUSTRATION 9. AN EXAMPLE OF A "THEOLOGICAL" LIST OF BOOKS WITHDRAWN FROM THE LIBRARY OF YALE COLLEGE (A LARGE LIST).

Oliver S. Taylor (Theol.)

1856

Sep	17	Winn's Grammar 8 vo	Oct	18
	26	Neander's Life of Christ 8 vo	Oct	18
	26	Edwards Works (N. Y. '29) 8 vo Vol. 3	Oct	18
Jan	22	Doddridge Epos. f N. T. Vol. 3, 8 vo	Jan	26
	26	Hengstenberg on Psalms Vol 8 8 vo	Jan	29
Feb	27	Dwight's Theol. 8 vo Vol. 2	Mar	10
		Wardlaw's Discourses 8 vo	Mar	10
Apr	11	Princeton Theology Essays, 8 vo Rhet.	Jun	23
Jun	10	Campbell's Gospels Vol. 1, 8 vo	Jun	29
	10	Hawley Congregationalism and Methodism 12 vo	Jun	29
	23	Campbell's Gospels Vol. 1, 8 vo	Jun	29
	23	Campbell's Gospels Vol, 3 and 4 583, 582, 8 vo	Jun	29
	29	Mayce's Discourses 8 vo	Jul	14
Jul	2	Calvin's Institutes 3 vols. 285-6-7 Thwb. Lib.	Jul	9
	9	Paine's Works 8 vo (Rhet. Libry)	Jul	14
		South on Isaiah 8 vo (Rhet. Libry)	Jul	14
		Griffin on the Atonement 12 vo (Rhet. Libry)	Jul	24
	14	Hill: Saints Inheritance 12 mo	Jul	24
Jul	14	Crosby: Second Advent 12 mo	Jul	24
	14	A Layman: Sufferings of Christ 12 mo	Jul	24

ILLUSTRATION 9. AN EXAMPLE OF A "THEOLOGICAL" LIST OF BOOKS WITHDRAWN FROM THE LIBRARY OF YALE COLLEGE (A LARGE LIST). (continued)

Sep	19	Porter's Lectures on Homiletics	Oct	12
Oct	3	Divine Inspiration (4) Ed. Henderson 12vo	Oct	23
Oct	12	Neander's Church Hist. Vol. 6, 8vo	Jan	9
Dec	2	Campbell's Gospels Vol. 1 and 2	Jan	9
Feb	26	Palmer's Eccles. Hist. 12 vo	Mar	5
Mar	2	Beecher: Baptism its Import and Modes 12 vo	Mar	11
	2	Facts and Evidences on Baptism in Three Letters 8 vo	Mar	5
	2	" " " " " " " additional 8 vo	Mar	5
	2	Hall: Terms of Communion and View of Baptists and Paedobaptists 12 vo	Mar	5
	5	Wall's Hist. of Infant Baptism 2 Vols. 8 vo	Mar	11
	5	Halley: The Sacraments, Pts, 1, &2, (Congreg. Lectures X & XI) 12 vo	Mar	11
	11	Wise Hist. of Israelitish Nation Vol 1. 8 vo	Mar	26
	11	Carson and Cox on Baptism 12 vo	Mar	20
	20	Etheride: Syrian Churches and Gospels 12 vo	Mar	28
	28	Hamilton on Rewards and Punishts 12 vo	Apr	5
	28	Davidson's Eccles. Policy of N. Test. 12 vo	Apr	5
Apr	3	Ranchs' Inner Life 12 vo	Apr	5
	5	Steinmetz Hist. of Jesuits 2 Vols. 8 vo	Apr	5
Apr	5	Ripley's Sacred Rhetoric 12	Apr	13

ILLUSTRATION 9. AN EXAMPLE OF A "THEOLOGICAL" LIST OF BOOKS WITHDRAWN FROM THE LIBRARY OF YALE COLLEGE (A LARGE LIST). (continued)

May	6	Noyes' Translation of Prophets 3 Vols. 8 vo		May	24
	7	Smith's, Not Paul but Jesus 8 vo		"	24
	24	Barrow's Sermons &c. 2 Vols. 8 vo		"	31
	24	Bushnell's, Christ in Theology 12 vo		"	31
	31	Milman's Hist. of Latin Xy Vols. 4,5,6		Jun	15
Jun	15	Do. Do. Do. " " 2		Jun	30
Jun	23	Coleman's Christian Antiquities 8 vo		"	30
	23	Smyth on Ecclesiastical Republicanism 12 vo		"	30
	23	Puncharu's Hist. of Congregationalism 12 vo		"	30

ILLUSTRATION 10. BOOKS WITHDRAWN FROM THE LIBRARY IN YALE COLLEGE DURING THE THREE YEARS OF THE THEOLOGICAL COURSE.

Charles F. Hutchins (Theol.)

1850				
Nov 11	Paley's Horae Paulinae 8 vo 1850	Dec	4
21	Gambier on Moral Evidence 12 vo 1851	Jan	3
1851			
Jan 15	Gieseler's Ch. Hist. 2 Vol.	Jun	3
Feb 1	Tholuck's Epos. of Sermon on the Mount 2 Vols. 12 vo	Mar	20
Oct 11	Day on the Will 12 vo	Nov	22
14	Barnes: Enquiry on Slavery 12 vo	Oct	20
	Bowdich: Slavery and the Constitution (pamph.)	Oct	20
Dec 8	Bushnell's sermon on "Politics under the Law of God 8 vo F.C.H. 1852	Jan	22
1852			
Feb 18	Watt's Logic 8 vo 1755	Jul	28
Mar 24	Norton: Statement of Reasons 12 vo	Apr	9
	Wukefield's N. Testament 8 vo	Apr	9
Aug 26	I. Taylor's Works Vol. 3 8 vo	Sep	9
	Mason's Works Vol. 2 8 vo	Sep	9
	Griffin's Sermons Vol. 1 8 vo	Sep	9
	German Selections 8 vo	Sep	9
1853			
Jan 10	Waddington Ch. Hist. 8 vo	May	5
Mar 29	"Preachers Guide" 8 vo	May	12
May 5	Kollock's Sermons Vol. 3 8 vo	May	9
	Mussillons Sermons Vol. I 8 vo	May	9
	Greenleaf		

DIVISION II - ILLUSTRATIONS 11-14

Each of the Illustrations numbered from 11 to 14 inclusive contains a list of the twenty books most frequently withdrawn by the students of the Theological Department from the Library of Yale College in a certain period, in the order of greatest frequency. By a comparison of one Illustration with another, one is able to learn the increase or decrease in popularity, according to the rank in frequency of withdrawals of a certain book, from period to period. It will also be noted that the type of books most frequently consulted changes from period to period.

ILLUSTRATION 11. TWENTY BOOKS MOST FREQUENTLY WITH-
DRAWN FROM THE LIBRARY OF YALE COLLEGE BY THE STUDENTS OF
THE THEOLOGICAL DEPARTMENT DURING THE YEARS 1834/35-1838/39.

(Total number of students using the library
in these years - 211)

	Number of annual withdrawals
1. Edwards, Jonathan, Works,. . .1808...8 vols.	63
2. Mosheim, J. L. , Ancient and Modern Ecclesiastical History. Translated by Murdock, 1832, 3 vols.	36
3. Dwight, Timothy, Theology Explained and Defined 1818. . . 5 vols.	24
4. Edwards, Jonathan, Enquiry Respecting the Freedom of the Will....1775	22
5. Rosenmuller, E. F. K., Scholia in Novum Testamentum, 1806-1810..5 vols.	19
6. Hopkins, Samuel, Works, 3 vols.	18
7. Leighton, Robert, Works, 1835	18
8. Yates, James, Reply to Wardlaw's Vindication of Unitarianism. 1816	16
9. Leland, John, View of Deistical Writers of England 1757	15
10. Wardlaw, Ralph, Discourses on the Socinian Controversy, 1815	15
11. Butler, Joseph, Analogy of Religion to Nature 1809	14
12. Chalmers, Thomas, Discourses on the Authority of Christian Revelation, 1816	12
13. Blaire, Henry, Sermons, 1781	11
14. Hume, David, History of England, 1810	10
15. Reid, Thomas, Works, 1813-15. 4 vols.	10
16. Cogan, Thomas, Treatise on the Passions, 1821	9
17. Stewart, Dugald, Philosophical Essays, 1811	8
18. Young Minister's Companion, 1813	8

ILLUSTRATION 11. TWENTY BOOKS MOST FREQUENTLY WITHDRAWN FROM THE LIBRARY OF YALE COLLEGE BY THE STUDENTS OF THE THEOLOGICAL DEPARTMENT DURING THE YEARS 1834/35-1838/39 (continued)

(Total number of Students using the Library in these years - 211)

	Number of annual withdrawals
19. Brown, Essays	7
20. Massillon, J. B., Sermons 1803	7

ILLUSTRATION 12. TWENTY BOOKS MOST FREQUENTLY WITHDRAWN FROM THE LIBRARY OF YALE COLLEGE BY THE STUDENTS OF THE THEOLOGICAL DEPARTMENT DURING THE YEARS 1839/40-1848/49

(Total number of students using the library in these years-- 380)

	Number of Annual Withdrawals
1. Edwards, Jonathan, Works 1808, 8 vols.	91
2. Dwight, Timothy, Theology Explained and Defined, 1818 5 vols.	65
3. Reid, Thomas, Works 1813-15, 4 vols.	61
4. Porter, Ebenezer, Analysis of Rhetorical Delivery, 1827	58
5. Biblical Repository (current issues)	55
6. Emmons, Nathaniel, Works, 1842, 6 vols.	47
7. Loath, Robert, Lectures on Hebrew Poetry, 1815	32
8. Mosheim, J. L., Ancient and Modern Ecclesiastical History, 1832, 3 vols.	29
9. Clarke, Adam, (Commentary on) The Holy Bible, 1825-26 6 vols.	27
10. Stewart, David, Philosophy of the Human Mind, 1793	25
11. Quarterly Christian Spectator	25
12. Edwards, Jonathan, (The Younger), Works 1842, 2 vols.	24
13. Biblical Repertory (current issues)	22
14. Sturtevant, S., Preacher's Manual, 1838	21
15. Hume, David, Essays and Treatises, 1860	21
16. Kinnoel, C. G., Commentarius in Libras Novi Testimenti Histoicas, 1816-18 4 vols.	20
17. Preacher's Guide	19
18. Paley, William, Horae Paulinae, 1824	16

ILLUSTRATION 12. TWENTY BOOKS MOST FREQUENTLY WITHDRAWN FROM THE LIBRARY OF YALE COLLEGE BY THE STUDENTS OF THE THEOLOGICAL DEPARTMENT DURING THE YEARS 1839/40-1848/49 (continued)

(Total number of students using the library in these years--380)

		Number of Annual Withdrawals
19.	Stuart, Moses, Commentary on the Epistle to the Hebrews, 1834	16
20.	Yates, James, Reply to Wardlaw's Vindication of Unitarianism, 1816	15

ILLUSTRATION 13. TWENTY BOOKS MOST FREQUENTLY WITHDRAWN FROM THE LIBRARY OF YALE COLLEGE BY THE STUDENTS OF THE THEOLOGICAL DEPARTMENT DURING THE YEARS 1849/50-1857/58

(Total number of students using the library in these years--256)

	Number of Annual Withdrawals
1. Preacher's Guide	61
2. Edwards, Jonathan, Works, 1808, 8 vols.	56
3. Biblical Repository	44
4. Emmons, Nathaniel, Works, 1842, 6 vols.	38
5. Hall, Robert, Works, 1830, 2 vols.	32
6. Mosheim, J. L., Ancient and Modern Ecclesiastical History, 1832, 3 vols.	29
7. American Biblical Repository (current issues)	23
8. Porter, Ebenezer, Analysis of Rhetorical Delivery, 1827	19
9. Dwight, Timothy, Theology Explained and Defended, 1818, 5 vols.	18
10. Whateley, Richard, Peculiarities of Christianity, 1831	18
11. Campbell, George, Systematic Theology, 1810	17
12. Neander, August, History of the Christian Religion and Church, 1842, 2 vols	15
13. Channing, W. E., Works, 1841, 5 vols.	15
14. Mason, William, Works, 1811, 4 vols.	15
15. Campbell, George, Translation of the Gospels, 1837, 3 vols.	13
16. Melville, Sermons	14
17. Hengstenberge, E.W., Commentary on the Psalms, 1846-8, 3 vols.	12
18. Neander, August, Planning and Training of the Church, 1842, 2 vols.	12
19. Schiller, Franz, Saemmtliche Werke, 1838	11
20. Goethe, J. W., Works, 1828	9.

ILLUSTRATION 14. TWENTY BOOKS WITHDRAWN FROM THE LIBRARY OF YALE COLLEGE BY THE STUDENTS OF THE THEOLOGICAL DEPARTMENT DURING THE YEARS 1858/59-1867/68

(Total Number of Students Using the Library in these years--234)

	Number of Annual Withdrawals
1. Neander, August, History of the Christian Religion & Church, 1842, 2 vols.	29
2. Edwards, Jonathan, Works, 1808, 8 vols.	23
3. Hopkins, Samuel, Works, 1852	21
4. Gieseler, J. K. L., Ecclesiastical History, 1854	20
5. Taylor, N. W., Lectures on the Moral Government of God, 1859, 2 vols.	19
6. Mosheim, J. L., Ancient and Modern Ecclesiastical History, 1852, 3 vols.	18
7. Henystenber, E.W., Commentary on the Psalms	18
8. Hagenbuck, Karl Rudolph, Compendium of the History of Doctrine, 1847-50, 2 vols.	17
9. Olshausen, Herman, Commentary on the Gospels, 1847	17
10. Meyer, H. A. W., Commentary on the Bible, 1834-59, 17 vols. in 7	16
11. Conybeare, W.S. & J.S. Howsen, Commentaries on the Life and Epistles of St. Paul, 1866, 2 vols.	151
12. Bushnell, Horace, Nature & the Supernatural, 1859	13
13. Hodge, Charles, Systematic Theology, 3 vols.	12
14. Emmons, Nathaniel, Works, 1842, 6 vols.	12
15. French, Parables	11
16. Taylor, N. W., Revealed Theology, 1859	11

ILLUSTRATION 14. TWENTY BOOKS WITHDRAWN FROM THE LIBRARY OF YALE COLLEGE BY THE STUDENTS OF THE THEOLOGICAL DEPARTMENT DURING THE YEARS 1858/59-1867/68 (continued)

(Total Number of Students Using the Library in these years--234)

	Number of Annual Withdrawals
17. Dwight, Timothy, Theology Explained & Defended, 1818, 5 vols.	10
18. Edwards, Jonathan, Works, 2 vols. (the Younger)	9
19. South, Robert, Sermons, 1715	9
20. Olshausen, Herman, Commentary on the Philippians, 1852	8

DIVISION III - ILLUSTRATIONS 15-19

In each of the Illustrations numbered from 15 to 19 inclusive an attempt has been made to reproduce the record of the Librarian of each of the Societies in regard to the books withdrawn by a student of the Theological Department in Yale College. In each of these Illustrations, with the exception of the one numbered 18, the information given below the last name of the student was obtained from the ledger used by the Librarian in recording withdrawals, and the remainder of the data recorded in these Illustrations has been gathered from other sources, chiefly the manuscript catalogues of the Library. Illustration 18 is the reproduction of the Librarian's record of withdrawals, which is unusually complete. The procedure almost invariably followed was that which is evident from Illustrations 15-17, and 19: the number of the book, the day and month of withdrawal were listed in three columns below the student's last name.

ILLUSTRATION 15. BOOKS WITHDRAWN FROM THE LINONIAN LIBRARY BY A STUDENT OF THE THEOLOGICAL DEPARTMENT IN YALE COLLEGE

[Henry] Gleason
[1831 - 32]

Biographie des Contemprains, New York, 1813	1293	Nov	11
British Classics [Series, Vol. 4, Spectator]	1569		11
Selections from Fenelon, [Archbishop]a	1753		11
[Archbishop]a Tillotson's Works, [Edinburgh, 1760]	1731		22
The Bee b [Edinburgh, 1791, Vol. 12]	1361		"
[S. C. Wilkes'] Wilkes' Christianb Essays, [Boston, 1829]	1755		"
[Thomas] Dick's Philosophya [of Future State, Vol. 2]	1605		25
[Archbishop] Tillotson's Works,a [Edinburgh, 1760]	1731	Dec	5
The Beeb [Edinburgh, 1791, Vol. 12]	1361		"
[Thomas] Dick's Philosophya [of Future State, Vol. 2]	1605		"
Memoirs of Jackson [Waldo's Life of Andrew Jackson, Hartford, 1819]	3164		12
Jonathan Edwards against Chaunceya [1790]	479	Dec	21
[Thomas] Dick's Philosophya [of Future State, Vol. 2]	1605		26
[Blaise] Pascal's Provincial Letters,b [New York, 1828]	2383		2

---

a. Under the classification of "Divinity" in the printed Catalogue of 1831.
b. Catalogued under Miscellanies in the printed Catalogue of 1831.

ILLUSTRATION 15. BOOKS WITHDRAWN FROM THE LINONIAN LIBRARY BY A STUDENT OF THE THEOLOGICAL DEPARTMENT IN YALE COLLEGE (Continued)

[Henry]		Gleason	
[Pres. Timothy] Dwight's Theology [Explained and Defended, Vols. 1 & 6]	1841 45	Jan	28
Universal History [Vol. 1. The Flood, Egypt, Moab, Midian, Canaan, & Syrians]	2794	Feb	2
[Walter] Scott's Novels, [Vol. 8, Ivanhoe]	2822	"	16
Tales of My Landlord, Robert of Paris & Bishop [New York, 1817]	3545	"	24
Universal History [Vol. 1. The Flood, Egypt, Moab, Midian, Canaan, & Syrians]	2794	"	16
[Thomas] Newton on the Prophecies, [London, 1771]	236	"	
[Richard] Savage & John Dyer, [Poems]	2410		10
[Walter] Scott's Novels [Vol. 2 Guy Mannering]	2828		17
Edinburgh Encyclopedia [Vol. 13] [New York]	1796		29

ILLUSTRATION 16. BOOKS WITHDRAWN FROM THE BROTHERS
LIBRARY BY A STUDENT OF THE THEOLOGICAL DEPARTMENT IN YALE
COLLEGE

[Edward Osborn]	Dunning	
	1832	– 33
Chalmers' Discourses [a]	91	10.5
[F.] Gibbon's Rome, [Decline and Fall of the Roman Empire] Vol. 3rd [Dublin, 1781-8]	1891	10.11
[S.T.] Coleridge's Poems, [London, 1829 ?]	3437	10.16
Life of Byron [T] Moore's 2nd Vol.	1898	10.23
Basil Hall's Travels in North America, [Philadelphia, 1829]		10.23
[Thomas] Brown's Philosophy [of the Human Mind, Andover, 1822]	878	1.21
British Essayists Vol. XVI, Rambler, Vol. 1st	1031	
[T] Reid's Works, [with Life by D. Stewart, Charlestown, 1813]	655	1.26
North American Review Vol. 30th	2026	2.6
Museum [of Foreign Literature & Science, New Series, Philadelphia] Vol. 3rd, [1827]	818	2.16
[T.] Reid's Works [with Life by D. Stewart, Charlestown, 1813]	655	3.6
History of Rome (Vertol's) [Abbide, London, 1720]	78	3.6
[D.] Hume's [Philosophical] Essays, 1817	913	3.6
[T.] Reid's Works [with Life by D. Stewart, Charlestown, 1913]	655	
[D.] Hume's [Philosophical] Essays, 1817	913	3.18

----

a. Catalogued under "Divinity" in the printed Catalogue of
   1831.

ILLUSTRATION 16. BOOKS WITHDRAWN FROM THE BROTHERS LIBRARY BY A STUDENT OF THE THEOLOGICAL DEPARTMENT IN YALE COLLEGE (continued)

	[Edward Osborn]	Dunning	
		1832	- 33
[Sir W.]	Scott's Life of Napoleon, 2nd Vol.	874	3.18
[G.]	Campbell's Systematic Theology [Boston, 1822?]	120	3.20
[Pres. Timothy]	Dwight's Theology [Explained & Defended] Vol. 1st	2727	4.2
[Sir W.]	Scott's Life of Napoleon, Vol. 3	874	5.24

ILLUSTRATION 17. BOOKS WITHDRAWN FROM THE BROTHERS LIBRARY BY A STUDENT OF THE THEOLOGICAL DEPARTMENT IN YALE COLLEGE

[Samuel George Willard]

	[1848-49] W
Poetical Works of [J.] Thomson, [London, 1807]	106. . . . . . . " 7 308 Willard
Ernest Mattravers, [by E. L. Bulwer] Vol. 1 [New York, 1837]	" " 5116 "
Ernest Mattravers, Vol 2	" "-- 17 "
Cheveley; or the Man of Honor [by Lady L. Bulwer. New York, 1834] Vol. 1	13 4901 Willard
Cheveley; or the Man of Honor, Vol. 2	" 4902 "
[E] Young's Night Thoughts, [New York, 1818]	1014 1853 "
Cheveley, or the Man of Honor, Vol. 1	" " 4901 "
Cheveley, or the Man of Honor, Vol. 2.	" --02 "
[Sir Walter Scott] Black Dwarf - [and] Old Mortality. Boston, 1834	1014 Willard 5834 . . . .
Episcopacy Examined & Reexamined [New York, 1835]	"18 Willard 7233
Table Talk of S. T. Coleridge [New York, 1835]	" " " 5452
Littel's Museum [of Foreign Literature Science] Vol. 13 [Philadelphia, 1828]	. . . . " 21 Willard 6412
Westminister Review, Vol. 31 [London ca. 1845]	. . . . " 25 Willard 2145
[Sir Walter Scott] Waverly Novels - Tales of the Crusaders - 18 [Boston, 1834 or 1845?]	" " Willard 9562
American Review [Whig] New York 1845-51 Vol. 1	" " " 1461
North American Review, Vol. 66, [The current year, 1848]	"11 Willard 2399
[Sir Walter Scott] Kenilworth [Philadelphia, 1821]	"14 Willard 5840
[The Literary Character [I. Disraeli, London, 1839]	" " Willard 7901

ILLUSTRATION 17. BOOKS WITHDRAWN FROM THE BROTHERS
LIBRARY BY A STUDENT OF THE THEOLOGICAL DEPARTMENT IN YALE
COLLEGE (continued)

[Samuel George Willard]

[Miss Agnes Strickland] Lives of the Queens of England, [Philadelphia, 1841] Vol. 3	" 20 Willard 1336
[Daniel] Webster's Speeches [Boston, 1830] Vol. 1	" " " 6367
Electric Magazine [New York] Vol. 1 - 1844, Jan - Apr.	Dec 5 Willard 1180 " " "
Memoirs of [R]obert Morrison. London, 1839 Vol. 2	" " " 1403
Electric Magazine Vol. 2 - 1844 May-Aug.	Dec 8 Willard 1181
[E.] Burke's Works [New York, 1837] Vol. 1	" " " 1006
L. Sterne's Works London, 1783 Vol. 5	26 Willard 3437
Dr. [W.] Sewall's Lectures [on Christian Morals. London, 1844]	" " 5301
Mrs. A. Radcliffe Mysteries of Udolpho; Philadelphia, 1821 Vol.1	27 Willard 2263
[Mrs. A. Radcliffe] Mysteries of Udolpho; [Philadelphia, 1821] Vol.2	" " 2264
[Mrs. A. Radcliffe] Mysteries of Udolpho; [Philadelphia, 1821] Vol.3 [3 volumes in the set]	" " 2265
British Essays [ed. by F. Ferguson; London 1823. 40 vols.] Vol. 19. The Idler	3(-)1. . . . . " "Willard 337
[T.] Moore Loves of the Angels [Baltimore, 1823]	" "Willard 4615
[W.E.] Channing's Works [Boston, 1841-3, 6 vols.] vol. 1	B.14. . . . . . " " Willard 7640
[W.E.] Channing's Works [Boston, 1841-3, 6 vols.] vol. 2	. . . . Aug 4

ILLUSTRATION 18. BOOKS WITHDRAWN FROM THE MORAL AND RHETORICAL LIBRARY BY A STUDENT OF THE THEOLOGICAL DEPARTMENT IN YALE COLLEGE

Thomas Jefferson Bradstreet

1836-37

Oct. 27	576	Theo. Review v. 3 (Fine 6¢)	Nov. 13
Nov. 3	575	" " " 2	Nov. 13
Nov. 13	576	Theo. " v. 3	" 24
" 27	520	Stewarts Journal X	29
Dec. 11	540	John's Heb. Com.	29
Jan. 29	96	Chalmers Dis	Feb. 10
Feb. 26	118	Hopkins Sam Dr	
March 9	288	5 points	Apr. 8
March 25		Ct. Spectator vol. 2 No X	Apr. 8
March 29		Theo. Review No. 2 1	
April 8	589	Note History of C E ?	Apr. 19
April 12	459	Cowpers Poems	19
June 3	322	Warburton	Returned
June 3	573	Spirit of Pilgrims	Returned
10	65	Dwights Theo	Returned

ILLUSTRATION 19. BOOKS WITHDRAWN FROM THE MORAL AND RHETORICAL LIBRARY BY A STUDENT OF THE THEOLOGICAL DEPARTMENT IN YALE COLLEGE

[Samuel John Mills]

Merwin
1833-34

390	11	15	Smyth's Lectures on the Apostolical Succession
691	11	25	Methodist Quarterly Review Vol. 24
512	11	29	Chalmer's Works
390			Smyth's Lectures on the Apostolical Succession
567	12	6	Lowman on Revelation
671	12	9	New Haven Theology
567	12	23	Lowman on Revelation
670			Biblical Repertory, 1841 Vol. 13
515	12	30	Lowman's Civil Gov't of Hebrews
567			Lowman on Revelation
671			New Haven Theology
575	1	13	McKnight on the Epistles [vol.] 2
567			Lowman on Revelation
671			New Haven Theology
Chr.Ex for Jan.	2	21	Christian Examiner [Jan. 1834]
Chr.Rev for Jan.	2	24	Christian Review [Jan. 1834]
Chr.Ex for Sept.	3	31	Christian Examiner [Sept. 1833]
236	2	24	Chauncey Lees Sermons
Chr.Ex for May	4	7	Christian Examiner [March, 1834]

ILLUSTRATION 19. BOOKS WITHDRAWN FROM THE MORAL AND RHETORICAL LIBRARY BY A STUDENT OF THE THEOLOGICAL DEPARTMENT IN YALE COLLEGE (continued)

[Samuel John Mills]

492	6	9	Hengstenberg's Christology of Old Testament Vol. 1
N.Eng. for Apr.	6	23	New Englander April, 1834
684	6	23	Emmon's Works Vol. 1
684			Emmon's Works Vol. 1
500	7	7	Warburton's Divine Legation Vol. 1
502			Vol. 3

CHAPTER IX

THE STUDENT SOCIETIES

THE STUDENT SOCIETIES 1822 - 1858

The students of the Theological Department in Yale College found their greatest opportunity for the exercise of initiative and the free expression of opinion in the organization and the support of Societies. These Societies were known as The Rhetorical Society, The Society of Inquiry Respecting Missions, and The Society For Christian Research.

The Rhetorical Society

Among the organizations existent during the years 1822-1858, the Society which could claim the most venerable and continuous history was known for the greater part of this period as the Rhetorical Society of the Theological Department in Yale College. It began, as the Moral Society of Yale College, during the Presidency of Timothy Dwight. It was founded by twenty-five students, three of whom were graduates, twelve seniors, six juniors, and four sophomores, April 6, 1797.[1] No member of the faculty was concerned in its inception, nor was any instructor connected with it till November 2, 1815, when Tutor Fisher, after much discussion by the students on the expediency of such a step, was

---

1. Records of the Moral Society, Book A. MS.

offered the presidency, and accepted.

The preamble to the constitution, which reveals the design which its founders purposed to foster, was as follows:

> "Since morality is essential to happiness in this life, and in that which is to come, and since it is equally necessary to the usefulness and respect of all human institutions; the formation of a society for its promotion in this Seminary must be considered an object of high importance.-- Influenced by these considerations, the undersigned do hereby form themselves into a Society for the promotion and Preservation of morality among the members of this University; to be known by the name of the "Moral Society of Yale College"; for the regulations of which the following constitution is adopted."

In order to be a member of the Society one was required to be a professor of religion, and was asked to take the oath of secrecy.[2] Each member promised to regulate his conduct by the rules of morality contained in the Bible.[3] "If any member shall be guilty of using profane language, or playing cards, or of intoxication, or any immoral conduct, he shall be convicted of the same, for the first offense, read to the Society a written confession, and for the second be expelled."[4] At the meetings, held every three weeks, exercises were held on "moral subjects".[5] The library consisted of "such books as treat of moral and religious subjects".[6]

---

2. Records of the Moral Society, Book A, Constitution, Article I, Section 1.
3. Ibid., Article I, Section 7.
4. Ibid., Article II, Section 2.
5. Ibid., Article V
6. Ibid., Article VIII

As the majority of the students came to be those from the Theological Department,[7] the name of the Society was changed, July 17, 1828, to that of the "Moral and Theological Society". Since the morals of the students had improved during the last years of President Dwight's administration (1795-1817), the Society appears to have been gradually developing into a debating society, with an emphasis upon discussion of general topics of a religious nature. The minutes of the meetings were, during this period, briefly noted in outline form; for example a page in "Book B" is as follows:

Disputants for November 13, 1828

Apthorp Apthorp Ball	Barnes Brooks	A. Baldwin

Ques--Have religious publications in such numbers as they exist at the present day a beneficial influence in the formation of Christian character?

	Disputants for November 11th		
Seniors	Middlers	Juniors	Academics
Brismade Chestnut	Baldwin Curtiss Gelston	Crocker Curtiss Foster	Dury Dutch

Ques--Is there evidence in the providence of God or scriptures that a church will not dwindle under a competent and faithful pastor.

---
7. At the meeting of July 17, 1828, (BookB) sixteen theological, and eleven academic students were present. At the session held, Nov. 13, 1828, forty-five theological students, and no undergraduates were present. A few academic students were present at the next meeting, however.

With the adopting of a new Constitution,[8] on October 22, 1834, this Society experienced further development. The chief changes made were in regard to the name of the Society, and concerning who should constitute its membership. It was now called the "Rhetorical Society of the Theological Department of Yale College".[9] "Any graduate or Theological Student residing at this College may become a member of this Society".[10] The making of changes in the Constitution appear to have followed the natural developments noted above,--namely, the tendency to an exclusively theological membership, and from a Society for the propagation of good morals to one of a general rhetorical purpose. In this general form the Society continued to function throughout the remainder of this period, 1822-1858. The only development of any importance, arising from a new constitution adopted March 10, 1841,[11] was one of further limiting the membership to those with theological interests. According to this document, "theological graduates" and "ministers of the gospel. . . . connected with the college", instead of the former "graduates" were eligible for membership.[12]

The chief executive powers were vested in a "Standing Committee of five", who acted as general overseers of the

----

8. Recorded in Yale College Moral Society, Book B. MS. 1820-1841.
9. Constitution of the Rhetorical Society, Records of the Moral Society, Book C. MS.
10. Article III.
11. In the Rhetorical Society Book D. MS.
12. <u>Ibid.</u>, Constitution, 1841, Article II, Section 1.

work of the Society.[13] The most important single office, and also the most burdensome, was that of Librarian. Article III, Section 5, describes his duties in general, and Article VI, composed of fifteen sections, gives in detail the rules and regulations governing the performance of his work.

In accordance with the records embodied in the constitutions and in the minutes of the Society, it appears that the customary procedure was as follows:

The time of meeting was every Wednesday evening.[14] The members were expected to be in their seats within "five minutes after the ringing of the bell."[15] The Society was called to order by the President, which office was held by Dr. Taylor from 1833 until ill health forced his retirement in December 1857.[16] The meeting was opened with prayer,[17] and "miscellaneous business followed immediately". This consisted, at the beginning of the year, in hearing the reports of the collectors of dues for the several classes.[18] Fifty cents was the annual fee required of each member.[19] The Standing Committee,[20] and the Treasurer made annual reports at the end of the year. The money was spent mostly

---

13. Book C, Constitution, 1834, Article III, Section 2.
14. Constitution, 1834, Article IV, Section 1.
15. Book D., Constitution, 1841, Article IV, Section 10.
16. Dr. Taylor is first mentioned as chairman in the minutes under dates of July 3, 1833. On October 8, 1834 he was formally elected President. Book B.
17. Book B, Constitution, 1834, Article IV, Section 2.
18. Book B, Minutes, October, 1834.
19. Book C, Constitution, 1834, Article V, Section 1.
20. Ibid., Article III, Section 2.

for library books, and also for the Librarian's salary, and for candles.[21] At every meeting a selection of the topic for debate for the session two weeks hence was made[22] from a list of such questions previously prepared for the year by the Standing Committee.[23] However, prior to the adoption of the Constitution of 1841, disputants for the evening were selected by the volunteering of four members as their names were read in the roll call. At the next meeting the roll call began just after the name of the last person who agreed to dispute at the last meeting.[24] After 1841, the debaters were previously chosen, and the regular roll call was given simply to discover which members were present.[25] The question for the evening was then discussed by the regular disputants, after which opportunity was given for any member of the Society to express himself. A time limit of twelve minutes for the first speech, and five minutes for the second, was imposed upon regular disputants as well as the extemporaneous debaters.[26] At the end of each session it was customary for the President to give his decision concerning the question, very often substantiating his opinion by an elaborate statement, to which, on some occasions, the time of the following meeting was entirely devoted. It was constitutional for the meeting to adjourn

---

21. Treasurer's Book of the Rhetorical Society, 1835-1853.
22. Book C, Constitution, 1834, Article IV, Section 3.
23. Ibid., Article III, Section 2.
24. Book C, Constitution, 1834, Article IV, Section 3.
25. Book D, Constitution of 1841, Article IV, Section 5.
26. Book C, Constitution of 1834, Article IV, Section 6.

at nine o'clock,[27] but very often it continued until quite a late hour.

The minutes of a typical meeting as recorded by the secretary follows:[28]

> "Wed. Feby 17th '41. The Society was opened by the President. The Report of Marsh, Junior Collector for last term was rec'd. The Question for the eve'g. 'Ought Xians to commemorate the birth of the Savior' was then discussed by Messrs. O. F. Avery, Berney, Brewster, and Curtis-- also by Burr Beecher Hall Warren & Hull. Decided by the chair in the Negative--i. e. that it was absolutely wicked. Society declined voting, & adj'd.
>
> Jos. D. Hull."

The questions brought up for debate dealt with topics of a religious, theological, social, and political nature, the majority being religious and theological. Favorite questions,[29] of this last type were, Does the sinner ever perform a right moral act before conversion?; Is the Christian Sabbath a Divine Institution?; May we aim at perfect holiness with a rational anticipation of attaining it in the present life?; Are any of the evils of this life penal?; Is the inspiration of the Holy Scriptures plenary?

Social and political issues debated by the Society, with the decisions rendered, accompanied by excerpts from the Minutes of certain meetings,[30] are as follows:

---

27. Book B. This was during the period when the question was discussed the same evening in which it had been chosen.
28. Professor Nathaniel W. Taylor had been reëlected as President of the Society, August 5, 1840.
29. These questions were most frequently discussed during the years 1834-1857.
30. From MS., Book E, which contains the records of meetings from June 9, 1841 to December 2, 1857.

"19 Oct. 1842

Does the greatest good of the greatest number justify the continuance of slavery at the South? . . .

Oct. 26th--The Society continued the discussion of the subject of last meeting. . . . discussed with much warmth for two and one half hours. . . . The President then proceeded in a lucid manner to sum up and give his own views. The result of which was that. . . . In view of his present knowledge the President was rather of the opinion that the greatest good of the greatest numbers justified the further continuance of the system. The Society on the question being put to it--declined voting on either side-- and in compliance with a wish of the President to vote--<u>voted</u> that they did not <u>know</u>.

July 7, 1841

Is it a duty to abstain from all intoxicating drinks as a beverage? Dr. Taylor--negative; Society--affirmative, 8-6.

Nov. 9, 1842
Same question stated
On the opening of the debate however, it was voted that the question should not be decided but only presented, (since the President was absent) and again taken up in the presence of the President.

Nov. 16, 1842
. . . .same question. . . .
Dr. Taylor--negative; Society--negative, 9-11

Nov. 22, 1843

Does the greatest good of the greatest number justify the continuance of slavery at the South? (31 President--"perhaps it may"; The Society did not vote.

Dec. 6, 1848
(Same topic)
President--Affirmative;. . . .Society sustains him.

---

31. This is exactly the same question debated the previous year; see the first question listed in this group.

Jan. 22, 1845
Is it right to assist a slave to run away?
President, negative; Society, negative.

Dec. 5, 1849
Is it right for citizens of free States to induce slaves to run away from their southern master?
Dr. Taylor is absent, Mr. Hadley is in the President's chair
Mr. Hadley--Affirmative, Society--Affirmative, 6-2

Mar. 21, 1849
Ought Capital Punishment to be abolished?
President--negative; Society--negative.

July 10, 1850
Ought a man to obey the civil law when in his view it conflicts with the divine law?
President--affirmative,. . . .provided his view of the divine law is a false one.

Nov. 6, 1850
The Constitutionality of the law passed in the recent session of Congress with relation to the return of fugitives from Slavery.
President and Society--Affirmative.

Nov. 13, 1850
Ought the Clergy of the U.S. to attempt directly to influence political opinion farther than by the expression of their own at the ballot-box?
President--"as a general rule", negative; Society--negative

Oct. 15, 1851
Has Slavery in this country been, on the whole an evil?
President--Negative;. . .but not confirmed by the Society which seemed to be nearly equally divided in opinion. At a late hour (not far from ½ past 10 P.M.) the Society adjourned.

Jan. 27, '52
Is there any higher law than that of the Constitution of the United States?
President--negative; Society--negative

Oct. 27, '52
Is the Fugitive Slave Law contrary to the Law of God? . . . .Law and Medical students present. . . .
President--negative; Society--negative, 8-6

>   Jan. 12, 1853
>   Is Uncle Tom's Cabin a valid argument against Slavery?. . . . Ladies present. . . an honor. . . .
>   Negative--President and Society.
>
>   Oct. 12, '53
>   Ought the reform movement of the day to occupy a very prominent place in the efforts of the ministry?
>   Negative--President and Society."[32]

With the passing years the Rhetorical Society became more and more of an official literary organization of the Theological Department. It gradually became less secretive when, after 1841 any visiting minister was made welcome, and, finally any interested persons, friends of the members, were invited. The fact that a professor in the seminary, Dr. Taylor, was invariably elected president, beginning in 1841, and served until the illness of 1857, which preceded his death in 1858, furthered this general development into an official Society of the School. It had come to be expected that the entire Faculty and Student Body of the Department would be present.[33]

Professor Taylor's relations to the Rhetorical Society are evident from a review of the minutes quoted above. He seems to have been of assistance in the development of the

---

32. Even though questions of a social and political nature were in the minority greater space has been given to their examination, first, because the decisions of these issues were more variant from time to time than were the religious problems, second, in order to illustrate the part played by Dr. Taylor in the proceedings of the Society.
33. Catalogue of Yale College, 1850/51; See Illustration 3, p. 189.

rhetorical ability of each student.[34] The plan of procedure in the meetings, whereby the President gave his decision before that of the Society, tended to make his opinion one of importance with regard to the views of the students. On at least two occasions the Society refused to vote when a heated Discussion was followed by the President's negative vote, for example, on the slavery question.[35] At one meeting the Society voted not to make a decision concerning the liquor question until the President's return.[36] For several months the meetings of the Society were not held on account of the illness of Dr. Taylor.[37] The Society failed to function entirely, according to the minutes, after December 21, 1857, which was a time of failing health for Dr. Taylor. He died on March 10, 1858.

On September 30, 1861 the Society was revived and reorganized, adopting the name of "The Taylor Rhetorical Society of Yale College". A new constitution was drawn up and signed by the ten members. This constitution does not differ appreciably from its predecessor of the year 1843. In December, 1861 two new members were received, and in January, 1862 six more students joined the group. The

---

34. On several occasions he pointed out the errors in logical arrangement. The meetings of October 19, and October 26, 1842 are good examples.
35. Oct. 19, 1842, Oct. 15, 1851.
36. Nov. 9, 1842. The President and the Society had disagreed on this same question, July 7, 1841.
37. After the minutes for Feb. 19, 1851, the following is recorded: "Note. The illness of the President occasioned a suspension of meetings during the remainder of the academic year." The next minute is for Sept. 24.

manuscript records of the Society which are available stop at this point, but the annual catalogues of Yale College regularly mention the Taylor Rhetorical Society until the issue of 1870/71. Beginning in this year and continuing until the annual Catalogue of 1896/97 "debates in societies" is found in each edition. In the annual Catalogue of Yale College for the year 1896/97 and continuing until the issue of 1929/30 the activities of the "Leonard Bacon Debating Club" are described. That organization which apparently was the parent Society, the Moral Society of Yale College, as was noted above, had been begun in the year 1797.

The Society of Inquiry Respecting Missions

In the year, 1818, "A Society of Inquiry Respecting Missions" was established by a few young men who had entered the Freshman Class of Yale College in that year.[38] In 1819 the Society published and circulated the Memoirs of Simeon Wilhelm, a native convert of Western Africa.[39] The receipts of the Treasurer for the second year amounted to about three hundred dollars; a part of which came from the sale of books.[40] In 1821, "A Missionary Catechism for the use of Children: containing a Brief View of the Moral

---

38. The First Annual Circular to the Churches of Connecticut on the Subject of Missions from the Missionary Society in Yale College, p. 2
39. New Haven, 1819. 108 pp.
40. The First Annual Circular, op. cit., pp. 2, 3.

Condition of the World, and the Progress of Missionary Efforts among the Heathen" was published by the Society.[41] It contains one illustration and a map of the world. Between the years 1819 and 1834 the Society "prospered variously" and "embraced about four hundred members, many of whom" became foreign missionaries.[42]

In 1831 the more general name of "Missionary Society" was assumed by the group when the constitution was revised,[43] but it seems to have been known to its correspondents by its original name. One such letter is as follows:

"Lane Seminary, Walnut Hills, O
Feb. the 27/47

Dear Sir:

At a meeting of our Soc' of Inq' the executive com' were directed to correspond with all similar associations through't the country to the end, that we might obtain more full & satisfactory intelligence concerning the missionary spirit of the rising generation of ministers. Will you therefore be so good as to give us--1st The number in the present Senior class who expect to devote themselves to a foreign field? 2. The proportion it bears to that of the last class? 3. The number now in your Sem' who expect thus to consecrate themselves? 4. The proportion it bears to the last generation or with what it was three years ago. And oblige yours in Christ,

W. W. Wright,
In behalf of the Com'" (44

---

41. New Haven, printed by S. Converse, 1821. 54 pp.
42. First Annual Circular to the Churches of Connecticut on the Subject of Missions, p. 3.
    Mr. Isaac Bird, received a letter under the date of February 9, 1822, informing him of his election as an honorary member of the Society of Inquiry. MS. 1 p. Mr. Bird was the second graduate of Yale College to become a foreign missionary.
43. First Annual Circular to the Churches of Connecticut on the Subject of Missions, p. 3.
44. 1 p. MS.

In 1834 the Society numbered seventy members, "many of whom" had expressed their intention to become foreign missionaries. The group was also making efforts at this time to establish a "Missionary Reading-Room", and to enlarge its Library.[45]

In view of the design of the Society it is not unlikely that the letter of Mr. R. S. Cook, the Corresponding Secretary of the American Tract Society,[46] was one of many such requests received by the Society from missionary and tract societies. Mr. Cook writes in behalf of the "1,500,000 Germans in this country", and concludes his plea: "May we not rely on *your* prayers, contributions, and influence in behalf of this object!"

The order of procedure in an individual meeting was as follows:

"1st Prayer by the President
2nd Reading Record of previous meeting
3rd Disputators appointed for second or third meetings
4th Selection of question
5th Disputants volunteer
6th Miscellaneous Business
7th Dissertation by Sands [47]
8th Discussion
    Disputants McLeod [48]
            Atterbury
            Little
            Miller

---

45. First Annual Circular to the Churches of Connecticut, p. 3.
46. Feb. 7, 1844; MS. 3 large pp.
47. Probably John Drozier Sands of the Theological Department, Class of 1847.
48. Probably John McLeod, Charles Little, William W. Atterbury, all of the Class of 1847 in the Theological Department; and Benjamin Miller of the Senior Class in the Academic Department in Yale College.

9th Discussion by the Pres't
10th Do. by Society
11th Adjournment "(49

On October 4, 1852 the Society was reorganized as the "Yale College Missionary Society."[50] Under this name it met for four years, until in 1856 it again assumed the title of "Yale Society of Inquiry".[51] Beginning with the year, 1852, the Society was limited to undergraduates,[52] and was thereafter connected only with the Academic Department of Yale College.

The Society for Christian Research

This group was organized in the Theological Seminary in Yale College, November 28, 1825.[53] Its object was "to acquire and diffuse information respecting the promotion and extension of Christianity".[54] Any member of the Theological Seminary, and any Tutor in Yale College was eligible for membership in the Society.[55] The Society met on the first Tuesday in each month.[56] At these meetings the following order of exercises was observed:[57]

----

49. MS., 1 p., found among the "Divinity Papers".
50. Minutes, Yale Missionary Society; Oct. 4, 1852. MS.
51. Ibid., Jan. 8, 1856.
52. Ibid., Constitution, Article VIII.
53. Society for Christian Research Constitution, Lists of Members and Records, 1825-37. MS.
54. Ibid., Constitution, Article I, Section 2.
55. Ibid., Constitution, Article II, Section 1.
56. Ibid., By-Laws, No. I.
57. Ibid., By-Laws, No. II.

1. Prayer
2. Members and other persons present were "enquired of in turn in respect to the state of Religion."
3. Dissertations read.
4. Committees report
5. Incidental business
6. Reading of a Portion of Scripture, & Prayer

Mr. Theodore D. Woolsey,[58] was the first president of the Society. The President and Vice President constituted a committee whose duty it was to confer with the Missionary Society in Yale College.[59]

In accordance with the name and object of the Society, much time was spent in the gathering and diffusion of information concerning the promotion and extension of Christianity. To this end the following methods were used:

1. At the beginning of the school year each student reported on the "state of religion" in the localities with which he had come in contact during the summer's activities.[60]

2. A Committee on "Correspondence with Colleges, Theological Seminaries and Sister Societies"[61] was appointed, whose duty it was to exchange information concerning the progress of Christian work.

---

58. President of Yale College, 1846-1871.
59. Society For Christian Research, op. cit., Constitution, Article VI. This organization was led in its first years by Peter Parker, later a medical Missionary to China. See Constitution By-Laws, and Records of the United Band of Foreign Missions in Yale University, 1831-38; MS.; and Foreign Mission Band, The Biographical Sketch-Book, 1835, MS. - folio.
60. Ibid., the minutes for the October meetings of the years 1826-37.
61. Ibid., Constitution, By-Laws, No. III. It was voted, Dec 1828, to take up correspondence with the "London Miss. Soc., Church Miss. Soc., Miss. Soc. of Paris Theol. Sem. Basle, Theol. Sem., Gettysburg, Pa., Mr. Thurston Sandwich Islands, and Mr. Josiah Brewer."

3. Four other committees, "1. On Foreign Missions, 2. On Domestic Missions, 3. On People of Colour, 4. On Seamen", were appointed. These groups were required to gather information and to report their findings to the Society at each regular meeting, and at its annual Public Meeting.[62] On November 27, 1827, this By-Law was so amended that reports were expected at the monthly concert in the College, and a written annual report was to be furnished in July or August.[63]

Techniques used by these Committees include:

(1) Correspondence with religious leaders in different sections of the country, and abroad.

(2) The State of Connecticut was divided by counties-- one to each member of the Domestic Missions Committee, each individual being responsible for the gathering of information concerning the state of religion in that county.

(3) Several meetings[64] were spent in the formulation of a questionnaire, which was sent to the chief towns in the state of New York. The questionnaire follows, in part:

> "Questions to be asked with respect to each town in the State.
> How many religious Societies,--of what denomination and numbers?
> Names of the Ministry & how supported?
> What is the present state of religion?
> How recently has there been a revival in the town?
> Is there a Sabbath School or Bible Class?

---

62. Society For Christian Research, op. cit., Constitution, By-Laws, No. III.
63. Ibid., Amendment VII.
64. In March and April, 1826. Most of the work being done at a special meeting called for April 4, 1826.

What is the State of Morals--observance of the Sabbath?

What manufacturing establishments--what number of people in them--and what their State of Moral and Religious Institutions?

How many people of colour--and what their moral condition?"

Typical subjects for the dissertations, which were read at the monthly meetings, are, "Wherein consists the power of Public Preaching?"; "On the origin, progress, means, characteristics, doctrines, and present state of Mohammedism"; "On Persia"; "German Theology or Rationalism". The value of these dissertations, in the opinion of the members, is reflected in a vote passed by the Society requiring the Secretary to request of each "Dissertator a copy of his dissertation, with authorities consulted &c to be deposited in the Library".[65]

That the members of the Society indulged in practical work as well as "Christian Research" is evident from the reports given of the summer's activities at the meetings each Fall, and from rather frequent notations in the minutes, for example, "Revivals have been enjoyed around us extensively, and many of us have been among them".[66]

An example of the expression of the student initiative exemplified by this group is found by their assuming the responsibility for raising funds for the sustaining of the Professorship of Sacred Literature, which chair was not

---

65. Society For Christian Research, op. cit., Minutes, March 30, 1830. If this suggestion was carried out, the "dissertations" have been lost, for they are not in the Library at present. (April, 1933)
66. Ibid., April 29, 1828.

established upon a firm financial basis and often occasioned some embarrassment to its incumbent.[67] At the meeting of December 25, 1826, a Committee was appointed "to devise measures for raising a permanent fund for this purpose". On January 29, 1828, it was reported that "prospects respecting a fund for the professorship of Sacred Literature are dubious, but we hope will become favorable".[68] A plan whereby this fund could be obtained was suggested at a later meeting,[69] and in the Minutes for the last meeting of the school year it is recorded that one student "commenced his agency for the professorship of Sacred Literature a fortnight since", and another will commence a week hence.[70]

The most valuable work done by this Society, however, was undoubtedly in the pursuit of its main object--the acquiring and diffusing of information respecting the Christian enterprise. That the several members were proud of their own efficiency in this work is reflected from an incident which arose in connection with the giving of reports at the Monthly Concerts.[71] The undergraduates complained that this Society took too much time for the making of its report. The members of the group felt that this was a most pleasing compliment, that it indicated that the Society was

---

67. See pp. 163, 164.
68. Minutes for the dates cited.
69. March 25, 1828. The nature of the plan is not stated.
70. Meeting of July 1, 1828.
71. A Concert of Prayer was held each month in the academic year, beginning in January, 1827, at which time the various societies in Yale College reported on their own activities.

in a most healthy condition. However, a committee was appointed to seek ways and means of remedying this situation. This committee advised that the report of each committee be limited as follows: Foreign Missions, eighteen minutes, Home Missions, ten minutes, Seamen, seven minutes, People of Colour, five minutes.[73]

The Society seems to have had difficulties with making its meetings ones of interest during the year 1837. On November 28 of that year, a committee was appointed to devise measures to secure a fuller attendance and to increase interest in the Society. At the meeting of December 4, the committee suggested that a new constitution be adopted, and that "Discussion" be added to the regular procedure of each meeting in order to add interest to the session. At this point the Secretary writes that the new constitution has been written into a new book, in which the minutes of the meetings will henceforth be kept. This volume seems to have been lost, and no evidence of the existence of the Society in this form subsequent to the year 1837 has been found. Perhaps the Society was absorbed by the larger Society of Inquiry Respecting Missions.

It was noted in Chapter VI of this study that the course of study was largely dominated by the lecture method. At a

---

72. Society for Christian Research, Minutes, November 1, 1836
73. Perhaps the relative time allowed for each committee is evidence of the relative importance of each field in the minds of the committee.

subsequent point (Chapter XI) evidence will be presented which seems to indicate that the students had little opportunity for the rendering of practical service outside of the Theological Department. It appears, therefore, that the student societies were the chief medium for the expression of student initiative and opinion.

PART IV

CONTEMPORARY EVENTS AND CONDITIONS

Chapter X   Theological Controversies
Chapter XI   The Theological Department
               and the Community
Chapter XII   Missions: Home and Foreign

CHAPTER X

THEOLOGICAL CONTROVERSIES

THEOLOGICAL CONTROVERSIES

The theological controversies which centered around the Theological Department in Yale College during the period 1822-1858 undoubtedly greatly influenced the life of the institution. It has been noted in Chapter IV of this study that the increase and decrease in student enrollment in the Theological Department coincided with the years with the increase and decrease in the interest which the public manifested in the development of the "New Haven Theology". It was evident from an examination in Chapter VII of the course of study of the Theological Department, that theological subjects greatly dominated the curriculum, and that in the teaching of theology Professor Taylor placed a great deal of emphasis on points of a controversial nature, particularly the freedom of the will. An examination of questions which were debated by the several student societies, reviewed in Chapter IX, reveals that the students frequently discussed current theological issues. Three of the four professors of the Theological Department in Yale College of the period 1822-1858 were active in these controversies. It appears, therefore, that a review of the development of the New England Theology prior to the year 1820, an examination of the controversies which were carried on by Professor Taylor and his colleagues against their opponents, and a sketch of the subsequent influence of the "New Haven Theology", are necessary for an understanding of the Theological Department of Yale College during this period of its history, 1822-1858.

New England Theology Prior to the Year 1820

The settlers of New England were strict Calvinists. Calvinism was the creed of John Robinson, the pastor of the Leyden Church, from which the Pilgrims came over to Plymouth. It was the common faith of the colonists who planted the other New England communities, and adopted the Congregational polity. So it continued throughout the seventeenth century. In 1648, the "Cambridge Platform" was adopted by a Massachusetts synod. It sanctioned the Westminister Confession for "the Sum & Substance thereof".[1] The Savoy Confession, which the English Congregationalists had adopted in 1658, was essentially the same as to doctrine as the Westminister Creed. It was adopted, with slight changes, by the Boston Synod of 1680.[2] This creed of 1680 was approved by the Saybrook Synod in Connecticut in 1703.[3] But there was an increasing

---

1. A Platform of Church-Discipline: Gathered out of the Word of God & agreed upon by the Elders & Messengers of the Churches assembled in the Synod at Cambridge in New England, (1653), Preface, p. 1
2. A Declaration of the Faith and Order owned and practiced in the Congregational Churches in England; agreed upon and consented unto by their Elders and Messengers in their meeting at the Savoy, October 12, 1658. (London, 1659).

   A Confession of Fath Owned and Consented unto by the Elders & Messengers of the Churches assembled at Boston in New England, May 12, 1680. Being the Second Session of that Synod. (Boston, 1699) 165 pp.
3. A Confession of Faith owned and consented to by the Elders And Messengers of the Churches in the Colony of Connecticut in New England, assembled by Delegation at Saybrook September 9th 1708. (1710), p. 5.

intercourse and interchange of thought with the "mother country". The eighteenth century brought in the Arminian theology, which had spread among Dissenters as well as Churchmen in England. The works of the Arminian writers, Whitby, John Taylor, Dr. Samuel Clark, were imported and read. What was called Arminianism, coupled with tendencies toward Arian and Socinian opinions, gradually superseded the old creed in the minds and in the teachings of many, especially in eastern New England. The same decline of interest in religion that prevailed in England was experienced on this side of the Atlantic. The "Great Awakening", which began about 1740, was accompanied by the advocacy of Calvinistic doctrines and attacks upon Arminianism. The great part which Jonathan Edwards and his followers played in the religious aspect of this revival movement has been briefly noted above.[4] But these men were also active in the attempt to furnish a better basis for their preaching by giving it a firm theological foundation. They considered themselves strong Calvinists, but set out to clear the Calvinistic system of difficulties and objections that were felt both by its advocates and opponents. Jonathan Edwards the Younger lists ten improvements made in theology by his father.[5] In writing of the first improvement he remarks that the Calvinists were pressed and embarrassed by the objection of the Arminians that "the sense in which they

----

4. See pp. 60-62.
5. Works, (Andover, 1842) Vol. I, 481-492.

interpreted the sacred writings, was inconsistent with human liberty, moral agency, accountableness, praise and blame. It was consequently inconsistent with all command and exhortation, with all reward and punishment."[6]

The fundamental points in this indictment preferred by the Arminian writers, Jonathan Edwards the elder[7] took up in his two treatises, that on the "Will", and that on "Original Sin". It had been the Augustinian, medieval, and old Protestant doctrine, that the posterity of Adam were answerable for Adam's sin, and therefore both sinful and condemned at birth, because they really participated in it. The opponents of Calvinism now demanded with one voice some explanation of the imputation of a sin to the descendants of Adam, which it was confessed they had no agency in committing. Edwards meets this objection by denying the fact which it assumes, that Adam and his posterity are distinct agents.[8] He also denied that to suppose men "receive their first existence in sin, is to make him who is the Author of their Being, the Author of their depravity."[9]

The second great objection of the Arminians, which was, that according to Calvinism, men are required to do what

---

6. Works, (Andover, 1842) Vol. I, p. 482.
7. Born at East Windsor, Conn., Oct. 5, 1703, of a Welsh ancestry. His childhood was marked by a great precocity; he graduated from Yale College in the year 1720; and was installed at Northampton, Massachusetts in 1727. In 1750 he went as a missionary to the Indians at Stockbridge. He became President of Princeton College in 1758, but died on March 22 of that year.
8. Works, (Hickman ed.), Vol. I, p. 223.
9. Ibid., pp. 217-220.

they are said to have no power to do--that the freedom of the will is denied and fatalism substituted for it--Edwards particularly considers in the treatise on the Will. He endeavors to confute them on this point by his doctrine of natural ability coupled with moral inability. He defines one's liberty to be free "from hindrance or impediment in the way of doing or conducting in any respect as he wills."[10] Edwards takes Locke's definition of the Will as "a power or ability to prefer or choose."[11] He asserts that the will is determined by the motive, "which as it stands in the view of the mind, is the strongest." The Will will be induced to choose the "greatest apparent good".[12] By "natural ability" Edwards meant that one has "faculties of mind, and a capacity of nature, and everything else sufficient; nothing is wanted but a will".[13] But coexisting with this natural ability, is a "moral inability", by which is meant a fixed and habitual inclination such as renders a perseverance in evil--a perseverance of the will in its evil choice--absolutely certain.[14] He rules out contrary choice. Man is responsible because he is naturally able; he is helpless because he is morally unable. Edwards differed noticeably from the Old Calvinists in that they asserted that men since the fall are free to sin, but have

---

10. Works, (Hickman ed.), Vol. I, pp. 14, 15.
11. Ibid., p. 5.
12. Ibid., p. 6. This conception also shows the influence of Locke's philosophy upon Edwards' theology.
13. Ibid., pp. 24, 25.
14. Ibid., pp. 11, 12, 47-51.

no other freedom.

The solution which Edwards offered of the problem of original sin failed to satisfy his successors. Samuel Hopkins,[15] in certain passages seems to agree with his former teacher by asserting that all men were included and created in Adam "as one whole which could not be separated"; all being guilty in Adam's sin.[16] But in most places in his writings he teaches that men are sinners from birth through a divine constitution establishing an infallible connection between Adam's sin and their sin. But all sin consists in exercise or act. And "the children of Adam are not guilty of his sin, are not punished, and do not suffer that, any further than they implicitly or expressly approve of his transgression by sinning as he did; their total moral corruption and sinfulness is as much their own sin, as it could be if it were not in consequence of the sin of the first father of the human race, or if Adam had not first sinned."[17] Hopkins brought in the doctrine of divine efficiency in the production of sin. He considered this a legitimate deduction from the teachings of Edwards. God is the first cause to whose power the effect must be attributed. All men may sin and not be aware of that

---

15. Samuel Hopkins was born in Waterbury, Conn., Sept. 17, 1721. He graduated from Yale College in 1741, and subsequently studied theology with Jonathan Edwards for about eight months. He settled in Great Barrington, Mass. in 1743, and moved to Newport, R. I., in 1770. He published works constantly during the latter pastorate. He died there on Dec. 20, 1803.
16. Works, (Boston, 1854), Vol. I, p. 199.
17. Ibid., p. 235.

sinning.[18]

In Nathaniel Emmons,[19] Hopkinsianism reaches its greatest development. He asserts that all men become sinners by Adam. He did not make them sinners by causing them to commit his first offence. Nor did he make them sinners by transferring to them the guilt of his first transgression. "The guilt of any action can no more be transferred from the agent to another person, than the action itself."[20] Nor did Adam make men sinners by conveying to them a morally corrupt nature distinct from free, voluntary, sinful exercises. "Adam had no such nature, and therefore could convey no such nature to his posterity."[21] According to the Hopkinsian theology no individual is accountable for any sin which he does not personally commit by violating known law; that sin begins with the personal life of each man in this world, and is not the penalty of the offence of Adam. Sin, not less than holiness, was declared to be the product of the divine agency.

In more immediate relation to the theology of the Professors in the Theological Department of Yale College during the period, 1822-1858, were the tenets of President Dwight. He rejects imputation, whether it be sin, or moral actions, or holiness. "The guilt is inherent in the

---

18. Works, (Boston, 1854), Vol. I, p. 232.
19. Nathaniel Emmons was born in 1745. He was a pastor at Franklin, Mass., 1773-1827, and died in 1840.
20. Works, Vol. II, p. 590.
21. Ibid., Vol. II, p. 592.

action; and is attributable, therefore, to the agent only."[22] Nor are the descendants of Adam punished for his transgression. But we become sinners in consequence of Adam's sin, but how we cannot explain.[23] He speaks of the two-fold aspect of sin, the individual act, and the general tendency or attitude of mind. The first is of definite choosing, and is preferred to something better, since man has the power to choose otherwise. The second, which he calls "universal sin", is selfishness. "Selfishness consists in a preference of ourselves to others, and to all others; to the universe, and to God. This is sin; and all that in the Scriptures is meant by sin. In every individual sin, this will invariably "be found to be the essential and guilty character".[24] He describes the "new disposition", in the regenerate; as "Disinterestedness, Love; Good-will, Benevolence".[25] He says that "the influence which God exerts on them by His Spirit is of such a nature, that their wills, instead of attempting any resistance to it, coincide with it readily and cheerfully, without any force or constraint on his part or any opposition on their own."[26]

---

22. Theology: Explained and Defended in a Series of Sermons, (Glasgow, 1822), Vol. I, p. 254.
23. Ibid., p. 256.
24. Timothy Dwight, op. cit., Vol. I, p. 622.
25. Ibid., Vol. II, p. 8.
26. Ibid., Vol. I, p. 561.

The Controversies of N. W. Taylor and his Colleagues

The Theological controversies which centered around the Theological Department during the years 1822-1858 were a part of the development of the New England Theology originated by Jonathan Edwards. Professors Taylor, Fitch, and Goodrich pursued the same path and the same practical ends followed by their predecessors, viz., to render Calvinism defensible theoretically, and to remove practical difficulties and objections on the side of the ordinary hearers of the Gospel, who sometimes claimed that the doctrines of original sin and the impotency of the will delivered them from responsibility and rendered it useless for them to attempt anything for their own salvation.

A Growing Sense of a Need for Change

As early as January 14, 1819, Mr. Taylor wrote to the Rev. Mr. Lyman Beecher:

> Dear Brother,--I am sorry that you are not here. I came from Woodbury to see you and to talk about Edwards. I expect, however to leave your house before you will be here, and think I may as well tell you some of my thoughts, hoping to obtain some of yours in return.
> I think, in the first place, it will be impossible for us to write what we wish to write, and shall write if we write at all, and give entire satisfaction to our brethren. I am well satisfied that something should and may be done toward settling points which Edwards did not aim to settle, and which will, to some extent, change the current of theological sentiment. The dissatisfaction which might be occasioned by speaking out would, I think, render it expedient that we

should communicate as correspondents what we write, and exempt the "Spectator" from responsibility for our opinions. We may continue our communications in several numbers, the plan of which may be as follows:

    I. The object of the author, viz., to demolish Arminianism. . . .

    II. That he (Edwards) accomplished his object: show that he did, and how he did it. . . .

    III. The great utility of the work;. . . .

    IV. The imperfections of the work: these consisting generally in the fact that the writer went no farther into the nature of moral agency; that he left some points. . . .unsettled, and almost untouched.

    V. The effects of these imperfections. . . . he left a loophole for Emmonsism. . . .

    VI. Attempt to supply his defects, and to give to the world that desideratum which shall show that good sound Calvinism, or, if you please, Beecherism and Taylorism. . . .

    I will now give what I think are some of Edwards' defects, that you may keep them in your eye as you read.

    The first defect is his definition of moral agency and free will. . . .

    In the second place, he says the will is as the greatest apparent good, and also admits that the appearing most agreeable to the mind is not distinct from choice or volition. . . . .

    Another defect is, the author does not abide by his distinctions. . . . .

    Another defect is, that the necessity between motive and volition does not prove the necessity of volition; for, although this connection be inseparable, yet the necessity of the motive, as it is the necessity of that which causes the agreeable appearance, on which all depends, must also be proved. . . . .

    But I have no time to write more. . . . I am obliged to go to New Milford today, so farewell. (27

In one of his lectures to the students of Yale College, Professor Goodrich made a statement which seemed "to imply the denial of original sin--nothing sinful in infants".[28]

In answer to a letter written by Dr. Beecher enquiring

---

27. Printed in *Autobiography and Correspondence, etc., of Lyman Beecher*, Vol. 1, pp. 384-388.
28. Ibid., Vol. 2, p. 157.

concerning this incident Professor Goodrich writes[29] that he has meant to maintain that "previous to the *first* act of moral agency, there is nothing in the mind which can *strictly* and *properly* be called sin--nothing for which the being is accountable to God." He further quotes Dr. Beecher's statement to himself: "That they (infants) have accountable dispositions neither you nor I believe."[30]

On July 30, 1826, Professor Eleazer T. Fitch delivered before the students of Yale College two discourses on "The Nature of Sin". These were subsequently published.[31] The proposition asserted by Professor Fitch in this discourse was that "*sin, in every form and instance, is reducible to the act of a moral agent in which he violates a known rule of duty.*"[32] He based his arguments upon "the operation of our consciences", the manner in which a person is judged before a court of the law, and "*the views of God* as expressed in his *law*, his *judgment*, and his direct *testimony*."[33] He affirmed that there is not a *sinful heart*, in any moral agent, distinct from his own *sinful choices, determinations,* or *preferences.*"[34]

These discourses were reviewed and opposed in the "Churchman's Magazine" in its issue of November, 1826.[35]

---

29. January 6, 1822.
30. Letter printed in Autobiography and Correspondence, etc., of Lyman Beecher, Vol. I, pp. 469-471.
31. New Haven, 1826. 46 pp.
32. E. T. Fitch, op. cit., p. 4.
33. Ibid., pp. 6-12.
34. Ibid., p. 19.
35. Vol. V, pp. 248-253.

Professor Fitch endeavored to defend his position in the Christian Spectator for January 1827,[36] restating more emphatically the chief points in his former treatise.

Taylor's Concio ad Clerum

The event which precipitated the misunderstandings of the opposing theologians, and was the occasion for the beginning of the controversies which centered around the Theological Department in Yale College during this period was the delivery by Dr. Taylor in New Haven, in 1828, of a sermon upon moral depravity, as the "Concio ad Clerum".[37] The proposition maintained in this discourse was "that the entire moral depravity of mankind is by nature". In it Professor Taylor maintained, among others, the positions that moral depravity is sinfulness; that this is not created in man, nor does it consist in acting Adam's act; that it is not a disposition or tendency to sin which is the cause of all sin; that it is "man's own act, consisting in a free choice of some object rather than God, as his chief good; -- or a free preference of the world and of worldly good, to the will and glory of God. In support of this doctrine he appealed to "the testimony of the most able divines, of Apostles, and of common sense."[38] The "divines and Apostles" were John Calvin, Dr. Bellamy, President

---

36. Vol. 9, pp. 17-21.
37. New Haven, 1828, 38 pp.
38. N. W. Taylor, op. cit., p. 8.

Edwards, St. Paul, and St. James.[39] He then advances to the proposition that this moral depravity of man is by nature.[40] In the applicatory "remarks" of the sermon he said again that "guilt pertains exclusively to voluntary action."[41]

On these points, Taylor appears to have been of the opinion that he was defending the doctrine of his predecessors.[42] Nevertheless, the new freedom with which he clothed his conception of the will aroused the suspicions of the more conservative theologians. The chief point of his departure from what was commonly conceived as the teachings of the Fathers of "New England Theology" was presented by Taylor in a note added to the sermon. In an endeavor to meet the objections of the Unitarians who argued that the Calvinistic doctrine of universal moral depravity is inconsistent with the moral perfections of God, Taylor opposed the teaching which was held by most Calvinists, that sin was the necessary means to the greatest good. He sought to substitute for it the supposition that, owing to the nature of moral agency, God could not prevent sin, or at least the present degree of sin, in a moral system. In such an argument lay the germ for a new freedom for the will of man, making him no longer a mere automaton in the hands of God.

Three controversies followed the appearance of this

---

39. N. W. Taylor, op. cit., pp. 8-10.
40. Ibid., p. 8.
41. Ibid., p. 13.
42. In a note on the flyleaf of the published "Concio ad Clerum", Professor Taylor denies any knowledge of his own heresy, and claims to follow his "revered instructor" (President Dwight).

sermon, of which two sprang directly from it, the third indirectly.

1. The controversy with Harvey.

Within a few months, Mr. Joseph Harvey, pastor of the Church at Westchester, Connecticut, reviewed Professor Taylor's sermon in a pamphlet of forty pages. He affirms that Dr. Taylor's proposition is not in keeping with the teachings of President Edwards, and his followers, and that it is "irrational and unbiblical".[43] He says that Professor Taylor is like a man who attempts to cross a river standing on two boats, in that he has one foot on Calvinism and the other on Arminianism.[44]

The following June of the same year (1829), both pamphlets were discussed in the "Quarterly Christian Spectator".[45] It is argued that Harvey had attempted to stand upon the untenable ground of Edwards, where the latter had remained after rejecting imputation. It is declared necessary either to go back to the doctrine of the imputation of sin or forward to the position that all sin is actual.[46] The defects of his theory of the will are reduced to his failure to distinguish between the three faculties of the mind.

Mr. Harvey made his defense in his "Examination".[47] He seems to add little to his former argument. In "An Inquiry

---
43. A Review of a Sermon, Concio ad Clerum, p. 14.
44. Ibid., p. 28.
45. By Professor Goodrich, pp. 343-384.
46. Ibid., p. 362.
47. Hartford, 1829, 53 pp.

into The Nature of Sin",[48] Taylor replied to Harvey by reviewing President Dwight's position on the subject of sin and defended himself from the charge of departure from Dr. Dwight. In discussing the points brought forward in the "Examination" he recalled Harvey from the point which that gentleman had stated as the true issue, "Are men sinners from their birth?",[49] to the true point as he conceived it, the nature of sin. He closed his remarks by comparing Harvey's and Taylor's position with President Dwight's views and asked the reader which of the two former is in keeping with the latter.[50]

2. The Controversy with Woods.

Dr. Leonard Woods, of Andover, had previously been active in a controversy with the Unitarians,[51] Professor Woods had stood on the conservative ground of his predecessors without improving the Calvinistic position. It is not surprising, then, that he was led to an unfavorable estimate of Dr. Taylor's "Concio ad Clerum", and to reply to it at considerable length.[52] In his first "Letter" Professor Woods

---

48. New Haven, 1829, 43 pp.
49. Examination, p. 13.
50. An Inquiry into the Nature of Sin, p. 21.
51. The Controversy was carried on chiefly by means of the following pamphlets: William E. Channing, A Sermon delivered at the Ordination of the Rev. Jared Sparks.... May 5, 1819. Baltimore, 1819, 53 pp. Leonard Woods, Letters to Unitarians occasioned by the sermon of the Reverend William E. Channing at the ordination of the Rev. J. Sparks, Andover, 1820. 160 pp. Henry Ware, Letters addressed to Trinitarians and Calvinists, occasioned by the Dr. Woods' Letters to Unitarians; Cambridge, 1820. 150 pp. Leonard Woods, Letters to Unitarians; and Reply to Dr. Ware, second edition, with an Appendix. Andover, 1822, 351 pp.
52. Letters to Rev. Nathaniel W. Taylor, Andover, 1830. 114 pp.

points out the dangers of too much emphasis upon a "philosophy of religion" and a discussion of controverted points in theology, and declares for the importance of conforming exactly to the word of God.[53]

The letters are principally confined to Professor Taylor's suggestions as to the prevention of sin. Professor Woods seems to misunderstand Taylor. Whereas the latter's idea was that it was impossible for God to prevent sin while maintaining the moral system in which agents are inalienably able to sin, Woods infers that he meant that God had no power to prevent it "in the literal and proper sense".[54] President Woods contends that the existence of sin is a mystery. "The incomprehensible God, for reasons which lie beyond human intelligence, taking a perfect view of his own attributes and of the whole system of created beings, saw it best not to prevent the existence of moral evil" and "chose to admit it into the universe"; and "will make it a means of glory to his name and of good to his kingdom."[55] He is led to believe that Taylor's scheme would tend "towards a denial of all divine power and influence in the conversion of sinners except such a kind of power and influence which we have over the minds of our fellowmen".[56] Dr. Woods, in connection with each of these points, seems to be in danger of denying that human beings have any free agency. He

---

53. Letters to Rev. Nathaniel W. Taylor, Andover, 1830. pp. 7-17.
54. Ibid., p. 27.
55. Ibid., pp. 37-38.
56. Ibid., p. 47.

endeavors to prove in his last "Letter"[57] that the practical influence of Professor Taylor's opinions upon the Christian life and work in general will be detrimental.

A reply was made in the "Quarterly Christian Spectator."[58] The reviewer endeavors to prove that Professor Woods "conceded the great principle maintained by Dr. Taylor. . . . by affirming that <u>all</u> the nature of the case admits of our saying is this: that God for wise and good reasons decided to permit the existence of sin".[59] This method of claiming agreement with an opponent, a favorite in public debate, must have been rather aggravating to Woods. Meanwhile this controversy was soon lost in the stir occasioned by a greater one.

3. The Controversy with Tyler.

It had been of constant interest to the leaders in revival preaching, since the time of Edwards, to discuss the methods of exhorting sinners, and of the proper use of the "means" of regeneration. The appearance of a new work upon the subject in the form of a pamphlet published, in 1827, by the Rev. Gardiner Spring, pastor of the Brick Church, New York, entitled "A Dissertation on the Means of Regeneration",[60] was in the regular course of things. He defines the means as "whatever is adopted to arrest the attention of men to moral and spiritual objects", including the Bible,

---

57. Leonard Woods, <u>op</u>. <u>cit</u>., pp. 94-110.
58. Vol. 2 (1830), pp. 540-576.
59. <u>Ibid</u>., p. 542.
60. New York, 50 pp.

ministry, word of God, sabbath, sanctuary, etc. Unregenerate men make only an insincere and wrong use of the means,[61] and the question arises how such a use of means is connected with regeneration.[62] Mr. Spring denies that these means are helpful in appealing to an unholy heart.[63] Thus sinners are put entirely outside of the moral government of God, and must be brought to righteousness under a government of force.

Dr. Taylor, who as a preacher and evangelist, had found that the freedom of the will which he had supported in his "Concio ad Clerum" allowed the gospel to be preached to sinners with greater force, could not remain silent with the appearance of this reversion to the old doctrine of the inability of men to repent. Taylor opposed these "errors" in the four numbers of the "Spectator" for 1829, and at great length.[64] In order for Dr. Taylor to prove his point it was necessary for him to find some point in the sinful will of man to which the appeal of the gospel could be made. He finds this in "a desire for happiness", which is constitutional in man, and hence unalienated by the course of sin in which the unrepentant man has lived. His usual designation for this was "self-love", which was an unhappy term, because of its association with "selfishness"

---

61. Gardiner Spring, op. cit., p. 13.
62. Ibid., p. 16.
63. Ibid., pp. 17-24.
64. A total of 132 pp.; pp. 1-44, 209-235, 481-509, 691-712.

in common parlance, and particularly in Samuel Hopkins' writings.[65] This gave rise to much misunderstanding, which hindered the acceptance of his views. But Taylor, later in answer to Dr. Bennet Tyler, shows that by "self-love" he means the inherent human desire for happiness in preference to misery. When man, by the exercise of this "self-love" chooses that happiness which is found in God, and does choose Him, then regeneration has begun in his heart.[66] The agent of regeneration is the Holy Spirit, who acts as such in _presenting_ these motives. Here then is freedom, the neutral ground to which appeal can be made in the will, and the divine government, preserved by the theory of the divine action through motives.

So anxious was Dr. Bennet Tyler, then minister in Portland, Maine, to refute the views set forth in Taylor's review of Spring's dissertation, that he wrote his pamphlet[67] before all of Taylor's arguments had appeared. In the preface to this work Tyler attests to his friendship for the reviewer of Spring's pamphlet; however, he states that

---

65. Samuel Hopkins' Works, with a Memoir of his life and character, (Boston, 1852), Vol. III, p. 29: "All sin consists in self-love and what is implied in this. Self-love is, in its whole nature and every degree of it, enmity against God."
66. "Review of the Strictures" (Tyler's), Quarterly Christian Spectator, March, 1830, p. 15.
67. Strictures of the Review of Dr. Spring's Dissertation, Portland, 1829, 64 pp. The volume which is used as the source in this study has written upon it, "Rev. Dr. Taylor, with the respect of the author".

"recent publications, and particularly the article noticed in the following sheets, have produced the conviction, that in some things, he has swerved from the faith of our pilgrim fathers". In the main body of the pamphlet Tyler declares that "to my mind it is plain that if sinners use the means of regeneration, they must use them with a holy heart, or an unholy heart, or no heart at all; that is with right motives, or wrong motives, or no motive at all.[68] He thus denies that there is any volition, such as fixing the desire for happiness on some object, of a morally neutral character. Tyler then accuses Taylor of denying total depravity, because if the means are used without motive, the heart is then not under the dominion of depravity, which is therefore not "total".[69]

Dr. Tyler's "Strictures" were reviewed in the "Spectator" for March, 1830,[70] probably by Taylor himself. The review is keen and meets Tyler's sharp distinctions with others equally sharp. Concerning orthodoxy, the writer points out that Tyler himself differed from many of his predecessors. Taylor then goes to the main question, "What is a free moral agent?"[71] In seeking an answer to this question Taylor takes up the meaning and application of certain terms which have been in common use during this controversy. In regard to "regeneration", Taylor points

---
68. Bennet Tyler, op. cit., p. 8.
69. Ibid., p. 8.
70. Vol. 2, pp. 147-200.
71. Ibid., p. 150.

out that "regeneration" does include some act on the part of man for his own salvation even though the Spirit of God may be the first and most efficient cause in this process.[72] Taylor then redefines what he means by "selfishness", and the distinction between self-love and selfishness. He says, "Mere self-love is only the love of happiness, and aversion to misery; and so far from being sinful, is an essential attribute of a rational and even a sensitive nature."[73] "Selfishness enters when one's self-love is directed toward the fulfilment of his own interest and appetites."[74] He asserts that Dr. Tyler's theory, whereby the individual before regeneration can act with selfish motives and none other, results in a doctrine of physical depravity.[75] He further states that if there is no neutral quality in the will of man, such as "self-love", then the preaching of the Gospel of repentance to sinners is almost entirely worthless.[76]

In the year 1830 Dr. Tyler published a "Vindication of the Strictures on the Review of Dr. Spring's Dissertation on the Means of Regeneration",[77] in which he restates his former arguments, and declares with greater forcefulness that the sinner cannot possibly have any motive but a selfish one.[78] A "Brief Notice of Dr. Tyler's Vindications

---

72. Bennet Tyler, op. cit., pp. 155, 156.
73. N. W. Taylor, op. cit., p. 159.
74. Ibid., p. 161.
75. Ibid., p. 163.
76. Ibid., p. 165.
77. Portland, 63 pp.
78. Bennet Tyler, op. cit., p. 17.

of his Strictures" appeared in the "Christian Spectator"
of June, 1830.[79] In this article Dr. Taylor's arguments
are briefly restated by Professor Goodrich.

In 1832 Dr. Joel Hawes joined in the controversy by
requesting Taylor to give a statement of his views.[80]
Taylor took this occasion to affirm his belief in election,
in total depravity, in the necessity of the atonement, and
other "orthodox" doctrines, and declared himself to be a
strict Calvinist.[81] Tyler, thereupon published his
"Remarks",[82] in which he showed that he was far from satisfied with Professor Taylor's soundness in the faith.
"Examinations" and "Reply's" followed one after the other
while the controversy lasted for seven more years. No
points of major importance were introduced into the argument during these years. In one[83] of these later papers
Taylor followed the practice which he had used in the controversy with Woods, noted above, by writing one elaborate
letter to show that, "on the basis of Dr. Tyler's last
statements and explanations, all controversy between us may
be terminated in an entire agreement on the chief points at
issue."[84]

---

79. Vol. 2, pp. 380-384.
80. "Correspondence between Rev. Dr. Taylor and Rev. Dr. Hawes", Connecticut Observer, (Monday, February 20, 1832) Vol. 8, p. 30.
81. Ibid.
82. Remarks on Rev. Dr. Taylor's Letter, Boston, 1832. 12 pp.
83. "Letter to the Editor from the Rev. Dr. Taylor", Quarterly Christian Spectator, Vol. 5, pp. 448-469. (September 1833)
84. Ibid., p. 449.

Dr. Tyler published in the year 1837 a pamphlet entitled "Letters on the Origin and Progress of the New Haven Theology".[85] These letters were professed to have been written to a gentleman in the South in answer to his queries concerning the New Haven Theology. Tyler reviews the controversy, including his own contributions and makes it evident that he has not changed his opinion concerning the controverted issues.

The Establishment of the Theological Institute of Connecticut

The division of the ministers of Connecticut into two opposing factions had reached such proportions, at the height of the controversy in 1833, that one group of clergymen, behind closed doors, had formed themselves into a "Pastoral Union". In this same year, 1833, the Theological Institute of Connecticut was formed, at East Windsor, to resist the influence of the Theological Department in Yale College, and Dr. Tyler was made its president.

In a personal letter,[86] under the date of June 12, 1834, Dr. Tyler wrote to President Jeremiah Day[87] that "the propagators of the new Seminary at East Windsor are not enemies

---

85. New York, Robert Carter and Ezra Collier, MDCCCXXXVII. iv, 180 pp.
86. 4 pp; 3 in MS.
87. In the nine letters among President Day's "Papers", written during the years 1826-1846, there is no indication that any appreciable difference arose between Professors Tyler and Day.

of Yale College, but of the "New Haven Theology". The first page of the letter is in the form of a printed circular, in which it is affirmed that the founders of the new institution are "dissatisfied with the Theological Seminary at New Haven for the following reasons:

> "1. It is an appendage to the College. . .and gives the College a sectarian aspect.
> 2. The Trustees of Yale College are not a suitable body to have control of a Theological Seminary. Eight members of this Board are. . . . political men. They not unfrequently belong to other denominations and may be decided opposers of evangelical religion.
> 3. There is no creed in the Seminary at New Haven which the Professors are obliged to subscribe.
> 4. The Theological Seminary at New Haven is without any printed laws or regulations by which the Christian community can ascertain how its concerns are managed.
> 5. There is no public examination of the theological students. All that the public can know of what is taught by the Professors, and the manner in which it is taught, must be learnt from their publications and from the preaching of their students.
> This theology. . . . has given great and extensive dissatisfaction. Not that it is regarded as <u>positively heretical</u>, but its tendency is believed to be dangerous. Those who are engaged in the establishment of the new seminary do honestly believe that the New Haven Theology, if not checked will lead to fundamental error."

The Dow Incident

At the Theological Department in Yale College the Committee appointed for the purpose of attending the examination of the students by their professors in the several branches of study and with no apparent relation to the theological controversy, made its report under the date of August 13, 1834.[88]

---
88. 3 pp. MS.

One of the committee, in an appended note, states that he "cheerfully concurs in the above statement in part", since the examination in Biblical Literature was very satisfactory, "but in the branches of Moral Philosophy and Theology, the primary object of a Theological Institution, it appeared that the Instructor" teaches doctrines which "are not in accord..nce with the articles of Faith on which this College was founded, and are equally repugnant to the Holy Scriptures".[89]

On August 19 the President and Fellows received the report of the examiners and appointed a committee "to enquire and report concerning the sense in which the assent of faith required[90] of Professors in this College, has been understood."[91] In the meantime Dr. Taylor, having received a notification from the Corporation concerning the report of the examining committee, had answered in a statement[92] defending his actions, and protesting that the accusations which were brought against him were general, with no specification, nor quotations.[93] He points out that he had

---

89. Signed by "Daniel Dow". Mr. Dow was a Fellow of the Corporation of Yale College at this time, having been elected to that office in September, 1824. He was one of the principal founders of the Theological Institution of Connecticut at East Windsor in 1833, and remained an important supporter of this school the rest of his days.
90. The requirement was voted into effect, July 22, 1817.
91. Minutes, August 19, 1834. MS.
92. 4 pp. MS.
93. This type of general and indefinite allegations appears to have greatly irritated him.

given his assent to the same creed that President Dwight and others adhered to.[94] He follows this letter with another[95] of the same date, August 19, containing similar statements.

Three days later,[96] the Committee appointed to enquire into the sense in which the assent of faith required of the professors had been understood, reported that beginning with President Stiles the belief in the Assembly's Catechism and Confession had not been one "strictly interpreted, but only in respect to the substance of the doctrine". They quoted President Dwight's remark, "that he had not assented to it in any other way". Among the "Divinity School Papers",[97] there is a small bit of paper written on both sides. On one side it bears a quotation of a motion, voted by the Corporation, to the effect "that Mr. Dow be requested to inform this board whether he intends to prefer charges against Doct. Taylor", etc. On the other side of the paper a statement, signed by "Daniel Dow", states that "I will withdraw the report" (of the examination), and that in view of the Corporation's explanation of the requirement of the College as to a "Subscription to articles of faith", "no charges are preferred by me against the

---

94. There is existent what is apparently the original statement, bearing Dr. Taylor's signature. MS. 1 p.
95. MS. 5 pp.
96. It was Commencement time, and the regular session of the President and Fellows.
97. Rare Book Room, Sterling Memorial Library, Yale University.

didactic professor".[98] However, Mr. Dow seems not to have been entirely satisfied by this explanation since a pamphlet[99] opposing the New Haven Theology was perhaps written by him and certainly published[100] after the events of August, 1834. He endeavors to condemn this "'Neology' in its own language" by citing many passages from the writings of its defenders, and by following these quotations with editorial comments of a critical nature.

The Wider Influence of the New Haven Theology

The influence of Dr. Taylor and the "New Haven Theology" did not terminate with the Taylor-Tyler controversy, nor with the death of these two men in the same year, 1858. One of the best known theologians who sat in Professor Taylor's classroom, was Horace Bushnell. He revolted against his

---

98. Aug. 21, 1834. It appears possible that the motion of the Corporation may have been copied down on this paper, and then presented to Mr. Dow, for the statement on the other side has every appearance of the original. At one place the writer seems to have started to word his statement in one way, scratched out five important words, and then proceeded along the line of an entirely different thought. A copyist would not have made this type of mistake. The signature also compares very favorably with the one subscribed to the report on examinations.
99. Daniel Dow, New Haven Theology, alias Taylorism, alias Neology; in its own language, with notes appended, Thompson, Conn., 1834. 56 pp.
100. In the appendix Mr. Dow tells of the incidents which occurred at the Commencement, referring to himself as "a member of the Corporation".

teacher's rigid formulae and definitions[101] and approached the problems of theology from the standpoint of a preacher connected with the problems of practical living.[102] He stood on the ground won by Dr. Taylor in regard to sin, and human deprivity in order to build the doctrine for which he is best known, that of "Christian Nurture".[103]

The influence of the "New Haven Theology" was also felt in Presbyterianism and in connection with the relations of the Congregational and Presbyterian denominations. In 1801 an agreement, called the "Plan of Union" was entered into between the General Association of Connecticut and the General Assembly of the Presbyterian church, whereby the ministers of each denomination were acceptable in the churches of the other religious group.[104] The factors which worked against the successful continuance of this agreement have been reviewed in an earlier chapter.[105] It was noted in that connection that one of the most important of these factors was a growing distrust on the part of the more conservative group in Presbyterianism of the "New England Theology", particularly as it was developed under the leadership of Taylor. The antagonism increased until in 1837

---

101. T. T. Munger, Horace Bushnell, Teacher and Theologian, pp. 40, 41.
102. Ibid., esp. p. 401.
103. Discourses on Christian Nurture, Boston, Massachusetts, Sabbath School Society (1847), esp. pp. 22-25.
104. Minutes of the General Association of Connecticut, 1801, p. 5.
105. Chapter IV, see pp. 139-141.

it culminated in the abrogation of the "Plan of Union",[106] to be followed in 1838 by the separation of the "new-school" group,[107] and the formation of the "New School" Presbyterian Church.

Among the "Old School" Presbyterians, Professor Charles Hodge of Princeton College was probably most determined in his opposition to the New England Theology.[108] When in 1868, a plan for the reunion of the two groups of Presbyterians was discussed, Professor Hodge brought forward as one of his objections the assertion that ministers in accord with the theological opinions of Dr. Taylor were received into the pulpits of the "New-School" Presbyterian Church. This objection he fortified by opposing the theology of Dr. Taylor.[109] Professor George P. Fisher, a Professor in the Theological Department in Yale College, wrote a reply

---

106. *Minutes of the General Assembly of the Presbyterian Church in the United States of America*, 1837, pp. 420-422
107. *Minutes of the General Assembly of the Presbyterian Church in the United States of America*, 1838, pp. 33-37.
108. In his *Systematic Theology* Professor Hodge opposes Dr. Taylor at many points in his Chapters on "Sin" and "Free Agency" (Chapters VIII and IX, Volume II); and expressly states his differences with Professor Taylor on pp. 11-14 in Vol. III.
109. "Presbyterian Reunion", *Biblical Repertory and Princeton Review* (Professor Hodge, editor), Vol. XL, (January 1868), pp. 53-83. He gives specific points on which he differs from Dr. Taylor's theology on pp. 61-81.

in the "New Englander" for April, 1868,[110] in which he endeavored to point out that Dr. Taylor was in a direct line of development with prior New England Theology, including that of Jonathan Edwards and President Dwight. The "Princeton Review" and the "New Englander" indulged in several controversial articles during this period.[111] In the issue of the "New Englander" for April, 1869, the editors of that periodical state:

> "We are happy to agree with the "Princeton Review" whenever we can; and we certainly do concur with that journal in its professed willingness to submit the questions at issue between it and the "New Englander" to the judgment of candid men. . .
> . . . .
> The "animus" of the "Princeton Review" in this discussion is plain. Its Conductors have been anxious to prevent the reunion of the two branches of the Presbyterian Church. . . . Hence they have raised the cry of "Taylorism", painted this type of thought in the blackest colors, and striven thus to rally a party of proscription and intolerance."[112]

In the subsequent development of the New England Theology Professor Charles G. Finney of the Oberlin Theological Seminary may be designated as the true successor of

---

110. "The 'Princeton Review' on the Theology of Dr. N. W. Taylor", The New Englander, (Professor Fisher, an editor), Vol. XXVII (April, 1868) pp. 284-368.
    Professor F. H. Foster, in his A Genetic History of the New England Theology deems this essay "one of the finest monographs in the department of the history of doctrine ever written." Footnote 62, p. 392.
111. In addition to Professor Fisher's defense of Dr. Taylor's theology against the attacks of Dr. Hodge, Professor Timothy Dwight took occasion to criticize the methods of exegesis used by Professor Hodge. His "Review of Dr. Hodge's Commentary on Romans V, 12-19" (New Englander, July, 1868, Vol. XXVIII, pp. 551-603), is especially severe in its criticism. Two articles reviewing "Princeton Exegesis" also appeared in the New Englander in January and in April, 1869.
112. The New Englander, Vol. XXVIII (April, 1869), pp. 406, 407.

Dr. Taylor. Professor Finney had enjoyed personal contact with Professor Taylor and had discussed with him "the great theological questions".[113] He had as his colleagues in the Oberlin Seminary Professors John and Henry Cowles, who were fresh from the classes of Dr. Taylor in the Theological Department of Yale College.[114] Professor Finney became the founder of the "Oberlin Theology", which agreed in its major tenets with the theology of Nathaniel W. Taylor.[115]

In his concluding Chapter in "A Genetic History of the New England Theology"[116] Professor F. H. Foster says, concerning the New England Theology:

> At the beginning of the year 1880 it was in control of all the theological seminaries of the Congregational denomination, with possibly a single exception, and of some of the Presbyterian. At Andover the chair of theology was occupied by Park,[117] at Yale by Harris,[118] at Oberlin by Fairchild,[119]

---

113. G. F. Wright, Charles Grandison Finney, p. 179.
114. Henry Cowles, Theological Department of Yale College, 1826-1828, John P. Cowles, Theological Department of Yale College, 1826-1829.
115. G. F. Wright, op. cit., pp. 196, 213-215.
116. Chicago, University of Chicago Press, 1907. xv, 568 pp.
117. E. A. Park, Professor of Theology at Andover Seminary, 1847-1881. He carried on a controversy with Professor Charles Hodge of Princeton Seminary, stating his position for the most part in his "The Theology of the Intellect and that of Feelings".
118. Samuel Harris, Professor of Systematic Theology in Bangor Theological Seminary, 1855-1867; President of Bowdoin College, 1867-71, Professor of Didactic Theology in the Theological Department of Yale College, 1871-1899. Professor Harris was greatly desired as the successor of Dr. Taylor in 1858, but could not be obtained until 1871 on account of the financial condition of the Theological Department.
119. James H. Fairchild, the immediate successor of Mr. Charles G. Finney as Professor of Systematic Theology in the Oberlin Theological Seminary. He was President of Oberlin College, 1866-1889 and Professor of Theology, 1858-1895.

at Chicago by Boardman. Fifteen years later these teachers had all been replaced, and in no case by a man who could be considered as belonging to the New England school. It had endured more than 150 years; it had become dominant in a great ecclesiastical denomination; it had founded every Congregational seminary: and as it were, in a night, it perished from off the face of the earth. For this remarkable and almost unprecedented phenomenon there must be some instructive explanation.[121]

In pursuit of the solution he states (1) "that it failed when it sacrificed freedom to the Calvinism of the old system";[122] (2) the system was defended by reasoning which was still *a priori* in character; (3) it failed to do that which it was a pressing necessity it should do: "1. Abandon the Calvinistic conception and use of the sovereignty of God in favor of a new recognition of the facts of human nature; 2. Readjust itself to an evolutionary view of revelation and of human history; 3. Introduce the new idea of a living, and not an abstract, God into its Christology".[123]

A more recent student of the New England Theology, Mr. Joseph Haroutunian,[124] marks Professor Foster as one of a number who have examined this movement "from a strictly theological point of view, in the light of their own theological opinions, and have sought to criticize it by pointing

---

120. A. N. Boardman, Professor of Rhetoric and English Literature, Middlebury College, 1853-59; Pastor, Presbyterian Church, Binghamton, New York, 1859-71; Professor of Systematic Theology Chicago Theological Seminary 1871-93.
121. F. H. Foster, op. cit., p. 543.
122. Ibid., p. 549.
123. Ibid., pp. 551, 552.
124. In Piety Versus Moralism, The Passing of the New England Theology, New York, Henry Holt and Company, 1932. xxv and 329 pp.

out philosophical misconceptions and logical errors."[125] Mr. Haroutunian is of the opinion that the New England Theology passed away because it was based upon a medieval philosophy, culture, and social order, and therefore could not live in the modern world of thought and human relationships. The new order demanded an anthropocentric theology, and since the New England Theology was basically Calvinistic, and an anthropocentric Calvinism is impossible, that system of doctrine fell before the demands of a piety which was in keeping with the new social order.[126]

---

125. In Piety Versus Moralism, The Passing of the New England Theology, New York, Henry Holt and Company, 1932. pp. xxii, xxiii.
126. Ibid., pp. xv-xx.

CHAPTER XI

THE THEOLOGICAL DEPARTMENT AND THE COMMUNITY

THE THEOLOGICAL DEPARTMENT AND THE COMMUNITY

The City of New Haven 1820 - 1860

A contemporary engraver gives the following description of New Haven, the home of the Theological Department of Yale College, as it appeared in the year 1825:

> "New-Haven, the semi-capital of Connecticut, is situated at the head of a bay which sets up about 4 miles from Long Island Sound, 424 rods wide. It lies 76 miles N.E. of the city of New York, and 134 S.W. of Boston.
>
> The city is built on a large plain, about 2 miles from N. to S.; 3 miles from E. to W.; and is encircled on all sides, except those occupied by water, by hills and mountains of every variety of form. . . .
>
> The city is divided into two parts, called the Old and New Townships. The old town was originally laid out in nine squares, 52 rods on a side, separated by streets four rods in width, forming a Public Square in the centre. Most of these squares have been since divided into four smaller ones.
>
> The houses are generally two stories high, built of wood, in a neat, handsome, but not expensive style. Many of those recently erected, however, are elegant and stately edifices of brick and stone. Most of the houses are furnished with a piece of ground in the rear, sufficiently large for a good garden and fruit trees: these, with rows of trees, with which many of the streets are ornamented, give the city a rural and pleasant appearance.
>
> The public edifices are, the College buildings; five handsome Churches, viz. two Congregational, one Episcopal, one Methodist, and one Baptist; a Tontine, now erecting; a Court-House, Jail, two Banks, and a Custom-House. Besides these, there are three Academies, two Seminaries

---

1. Views in New-Haven and its Vicinity: with a particular Description of each View. Drawn and Engraved by I. W. Barber. New Haven, 1825. 11 pp; VI plates.

for the education of Young Ladies, a Grammar School, and a number of Boarding Schools; two Insurance Offices; five Printing Offices, from which are issued three weekly newspapers, one weekly and two monthly religious publications, and the American Journal of Science and Arts, conducted by Professor Silliman.

New-Haven contained in 1820, 8,326 inhabitants."(2

The town had been incorporated for about forty years, but it had as yet very few of the characteristics of a city. It had no paved streets or sidewalks, no street lights or sewers or running water. The ornamental feature of the place were the elms, which had been planted a number of years before on many of the streets by Senator Hillhouse. On the "Green", a large public square in the center of the city, were situated four churches, First or Center Church, in the middle of the square, North Church to the north of the First Church, both of these being Congregational, and Trinity Church to the south, which was Protestant Episcopalian. In the north-west corner of the Green stood the newly built Methodist Church. Business had reached out a little along the water front on the easterly side, into a section known as the New Township, but otherwise the city was almost entirely confined to the original area of the settlement.

New Haven, though small, was by far the largest place in Connecticut, and after Boston and Providence, the largest in New England. It was the market town for most of southwestern Connecticut. It was, with Hartford, joint capital

---

2. *Views in New-Haven*, op. cit., pp. 3-5.

of the state. Moreover, its population was quite homogeneous. The people were almost wholly of English descent. In 1820 there was said to be one Roman Catholic in town.[3] The rest were largely Congregationalists, with Episcopalians next in importance. Not until the years 1820-22 were places of worship erected by the Methodists and Baptists.

The pleasure which a college student derived from the rural atmosphere which characterized the New Haven of the first three decades of the last century is recounted in "Sketches of Yale College":

> The air, untainted by the obnoxious exhalations of a large city, partakes of the purity and elasticity of the country. . few minutes' walk in almost any direction brings one to the suburbs. In short, it is possible for any one to enjoy here every advantage--the quiet and social intercourse, the retirement and the general information, the refinement and rural pleasure of the "rus in urbe".[4]

New Haven, like other communities, was changed from a rural town to a small city during the period 1822-1858. Of the towns in Connecticut Hartford and New Haven were the largest. New Haven had the advantage over the former in its foreign commerce, which began to revive after the Revolution. Her Long Wharf, three thousand five hundred feet in length, product of lotteries, private enterprise and state aid, was finished in 1802, and was the headquarters of an extensive foreign trade.[5] Laws had been enacted making it illegal for one to permit horses and cattle to wander about

---

3. T. D. Bacon, Leonard Bacon, A Statesman in the Church, p. 69
4. (E. P. Belden), op. cit., p. 69.
5. New Haven as it Is, 1845, p. 13.

the town and upon the public Green,[6] and the citizenry were beginning to take pride in the beauty of their city.

In 1818, Chauncey Jerome began the manufacture of brass clocks in Plymouth, Connecticut, and in 1844 he moved to New Haven. His successful business led to the establishment of the New Haven Clock Company. The manufacture of firearms was begun in 1798 by Eli Whitney at Whitneyville, near New Haven. In 1858, this company was absorbed by the Winchester Arms Company. The leading industrial development in New Haven in the earlier part of the period under observation was the building of carriages. The company was first organized for their construction by Mr. James Brewster, Esq., and was later sold to Robert H. Starr and Company.[7] The New Haven Gas Company was chartered in 1847, and 253 public lamps lighted the city. Facilities of transportation were also greatly improved when four railroads began their service in and out of New Haven during this period. The New Haven and Hartford Railroad commenced running cars to Meriden in 1839, and to Hartford in 1840. The first train on the New York and New Haven Railroad ran in August, 1848. The first passenger train between New London and New Haven ran July 22, 1852. The Canal Railroad established connection with Northampton, Massachusetts in 1856.[8]

The census figures for New Haven for the decades 1820 to

---

6. By Laws of the City of New Haven, January, 1822, pp. 10-11.
7. New Haven as It Is, (1845) pp. 14, 15.
8. City Guide to New Haven (1860), J. W. Barber and L. S. Punderson, p. 33.

1860, were as follows: 1820, 8327; 1830, 10678; 1840, 14370; 1850, 22529; 1860, 39267. The homogeneity of population and of religious affiliation which marked the beginning of the period was fast passing away near the close of the era. Where there had been perhaps one Catholic person in the town in 1820, in 1860 three Catholic churches were found in the city. The Protestant group now comprised three Methodist-Episcopal, two Baptist, ten Congregational, one Universalist, and seven Episcopal congregations.[9]

The College Square 1820 - 1860

The buildings belonging to Yale College were situated on a square adjacent to the northwest side of the "Green", and the majority of them faced this public square.[10] The structure which could claim the most venerable history among those standing during the period 1822-1858 was built from the funds gained from a lottery granted by the State of Connecticut in 1745. It was constructed of brick, three stories high, and contained thirty-two rooms. A fourth story was added in 1798. At that time it was known as "Connecticut Hall", but was later designated as South Middle College. The "Old Chapel" was begun in 1761 and finished in 1763. Over the audience room was the "philosophical chamber" which was used as a lecture room. With the erection of the Lyceum, the structure of the "Old Chapel" was

---

9. *City Guide to New Haven*, (1860) op. cit., pp. 17-19.
10. See Illustration 20, on the next page.

ILLUSTRATION 20.   PLAN OF THE COLLEGE SQUARE
(about 1845)

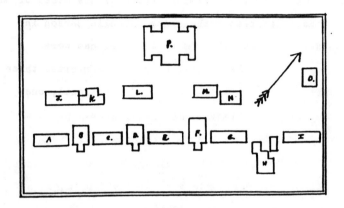

Key to the above plan:

A.	South College	H.	President's House
B.	Athenaeum	I.	Divinity College
C.	S'th Middle College	J.	Wood Yard
D.	Lyceum	K.	Chemical Laboratory
E.	North College	L.	Mineralogical Cabinet
F.	College Chapel	M.	Trumbull Gallery
G.	North College	N., O.	Coal Yards

P. New Library

Note a: This plan is based upon that given by E. P. Belden in "Sketches of Yale College", pp. 71, 72.
Note b: Buildings A-I inclusive faced the New Haven "Green".

altered and the building was called the Athenaeum. In 1782 a brick Dining Hall was built; one story in height, and in the rear of the other buildings. After 1819 it was used as a chemical laboratory. In 1803-4 the Lyceum was erected. It contained recitation rooms and accommodations for the professors. Berkeley Hall, later known as North Middle College, was also erected at this time. In 1819 a new Dining Hall was built, of two stories, with a basement for a kitchen. When the Commons were abandoned in 1843 the principal floor was used for lecture-rooms. In 1822, North College, another dormitory for college students, was built. In 1824 the Chapel, which was the immediate predecessor of Battell Chapel, was erected. Until 1843 the library was kept in the attic of this building. In 1831 Trumbull Gallery was finished and served as a depository of the works of art of Colonel Trumbull until the School of Fine Arts building was completed in 1867. The "Divinity College", occupied principally by Theological students, was erected in 1835 and 1836, and stood near Elm Street on a line with the other college buildings. A Library building was commenced in 1842. It contained the books of the College Library and those volumes belonging to the Linonian and Brothers' Societies. It was the most pretentious building on the campus during the period under observation. The Graduates' Hall was built in 1852 of Portland free-stone, the same material which was used for the library building, and was situated near the northwest corner of the college square. The president's house was erected for President Dwight and was also occupied by President Day. After the latter's resignation in 1846, the structure housed the Analytical Laboratory.

The accommodations provided for the students of the Theological Department during the first years of its history appear to have been exceedingly limited. "The two instructors, Dr. Taylor and Professor Gibbs, with the students, occupied rooms over the .... College Chapel, where also the lectures and recitations of the school were held."[11] The rooms occupied by students were six in number. In the Catalogue of the Faculty and Students of Yale College,[12] they bear the numbers: 137, 139, 140, 141, 142, 143. Rooms number 139, 142, and 143 appear to have been fitted for two students, the others accommodating only one person. Therefore, until the completion of the Divinity College in 1836, all but nine young men were compelled to live with some family in the city of New Haven. The rent charged of the students for the use of these rooms in the "third loft of the new Chapel" was thirty dollars a year for each of the corner rooms and twenty-five dollars a year for each of the middle rooms.[13] During the first year in these quarters the students were in great discomfort on account of smoke-filled

---

11. George E. Day, "Historical Address", *Addresses at the Laying of the Corner Stone of the Divinity Hall of the Theological Department of Yale College, Sept. 22, 1869*, p. 12.
12. In the Yale Catalogue the address of each student is given opposite his name.
13. Minutes of the President and Fellows, Aug. 24, 1827. MS.

rooms due to a faulty chimney and a petition was sent to the Prudential Committee of the President and Fellows.[14] The President and Fellows voted that one-half of the rent for the first two terms of the college year be refunded to these students.[15]

Steps were taken in January 1835 to prepare to erect a "Divinity College" "to be placed on the ground north of the President's home and in line with the College buildings."[16] This edifice was designed to accommodate theological students, with no charge being made for room rent, and any unused rooms were to be let to undergraduates at the customary rate charged of college students.[17]

The building was very limited in its accommodations, in keeping with the custom of the period. People, in general, were poor. They had few comforts at home and did not expect their children to have them at school. Sanitation had scarcely been thought of for home or institution. Cleanliness was generally neglected and often opposed. "Even bath tubs were opposed on religious grounds, largely because they were thought to encourage self-indulgence and a liking for luxury. The idea of making school buildings attractive was entirely beyond the majority of people. The heating, lighting and ventilation of buildings received scarcely any

---

14. 3 pp. MS.
15. Minutes of the President and Fellows, Mar. 1, 1825.
16. Ibid., January 21, 1835. This site was that of the present Durfee Hall, which was the immediate successor in 1870-71 to the "Divinity College".
17. Discrimination of this sort probably did not contribute to the mutual understanding of the two groups.

consideration."[18]

In the erection of the "Divinity College" no provision was made for lecture-rooms. The divinity classes met in the Chapel, as formerly, in a room called by Mr. S. J. M. Merwin,[19] the "Theological Chamber". It was situated on the second floor in the Chapel building, being a large room at the west end of that floor. This place had been so constructed in 1804, after the removal of the Library to the Lyceum. It was occupied by Dr. Dwight, during the remainder of his presidency, as the room where he gave his instructions to the Senior class in the College. "Here, it is said, on some of the cold days of winter, he would sit in front of the fire-place at the north end of the room, with his back to the students and his feet to the fire, and hold them as glad listeners to his instructions from the ringing of the bell at eleven o'clock till they were called to dinner at one."[20] At a later time, during the period under observation, a single lecture-room was provided for by means of a slight enlargement of one of the ordinary study-rooms designed for students. This room was only eight feet in height, twenty feet long, and thirteen feet wide.[21] There was no apartment in the building adapted to the purposes of

---

18. J. F. Messenger, An Interpretative History of Education, p. 302.
19. Notes on Professor Goodrich's course in Elocution. MS.
20. W. L. Kingsley, "The Lyceum", in Yale College, A Sketch of its History, ed. by W. L. Kingsley, Vol. I, p. 466.
21. Memorial of the Theological Faculty to the President and Fellows (1867), MS.

a library; no meeting-place for the student body; and according to Professor Timothy Dwight,"nothing which could, in any measure, give a home-like character to the daily life of the young men".[22] It was situated in a direct line with the other college buildings, and was of a simple design, four stories in height, very much resembling the other dormitories on the campus. This building, therefore, probably contributed very little to the engendering of any "school spirit", and seems to have been little more than a place for study and for sleep.

Relations between the College and the Town

The citizens of New Haven contributed to the establishment of the Theological Department in Yale College. The manner in which New Haveners supported the institution in its financial vicissitudes has also been noted in a preceding chapter.[23] However, the unofficial relations between some of the inhabitants in the town and the members of Yale College, particularly the undergraduates, were at times antagonistic. Groups of young men of the town and groups of college students at times met in what were tantamount to pitched battles. In one of these encounters a "huge knotty club" was wrested from the leader of the "town boys" by one of the students. "This token of personal courage was preserved--the organization perpetuated, and the Bully Club

---

22. Memories of Yale Life and Men, p. 281.
23. See pp. 73, 74; and pp. 160, 161.

was every year, with procession and set form of speech, bestowed upon the newly acknowledged leader."[24] These struggles were particularly frequent during the years 1820-1830, and the town group was usually lead by some "hardy tars" from the water-front. Perhaps these incidents influenced the Society for Christian Research in adding a "Committee on Seamen"[25] to the four committees which were instituted with the inauguration of the society. The largest and most tragic battle between the town and student groups took place on the night of March 17, 1854. In the struggle which ensued several were injured and one of the young men of New Haven was killed. An enraged mob turned a cannon on the college buildings, but fortunately the weapon had been spiked by an alert policeman.[26]

City missionary work was probably hampered, if not made entirely impossible, by these strained relations between the town and the college. Certain it is that Yale had very little to do with the outlying districts of the city during the period under observation.[27] Mr. Samuel H. Fisher states, in *Two Centuries of Christian Activity at Yale*, that "the idea that students could be of help to townspeople was

---

24. E. P. Belden, *Sketches of Yale College*, p. 171.
25. Society for Christian Research, Constitution, By Laws, No. III. For a description of these committees, see pp. 306, 307.
26. *The Riot at New Haven between the Students and the Town Boys*, on the night of March 17, 1854. New Haven, 1854. 47 pp.
27. H. B. Wright, in *Two Centuries of Christian Activity at Yale*, ed. by James B. Reynolds, Samuel H. Fisher, and Henry B. Wright. (1901) p. 82.

entirely foreign to that period and is a development almost entirely of the last few decades."[28]

If student religious efforts in the city of New Haven were directed by any organization connected with the student societies, the existent records do not reveal them. Those who officially directed the activities of the members of the Theological Department in Yale College appear to have made no efforts in sponsoring student initiative in this direction. In fact, in accordance with the "Rules and Regulations of the Theological Department",[29] leadership in religious work on the part of the students was probably discouraged by the regulation that a student was not given a recommendation for an application for a license to preach until the month of May in the final year of study.[30] The avenues of Christian activity which were open to the students of the Theological Department at this time were, therefore, limited to participation in Sabbath School teaching, or, in a limited number of cases, leadership in a young people's society, and personal work in the revivals of religion which were relatively frequent during this period in the College and in the town.

----

28. S. H. Fisher, in Two Centuries of Christian Activity at Yale (1901), p. 255.
29. MS. 12 pp. 1833.
30. Rules and Regulations of the Theological Department in Yale College, Chapter IV, Statute 6.

Sunday Schools in New Haven and
Yale College 1820 - 1858

The years 1817-1860 witnessed a rapid growth of the Sabbath School movement in the United States. The attitude of the churches had changed from one of antagonism to that of sponsoring societies for the moral betterment of the children of the community. At the beginning of the second decade of the nineteenth century the churches began to take a definite interest in establishing Sabbath Schools within their own organizations, and "unions" and "societies" grew rapidly.

The Philadelphia Sunday and Adult School Union, the parent society of the American Sunday School Union, was organized in May, 1817, and incorporated in January 1819.[31] The American Sunday School Union was established in Philadelphia, May 25, 1824.[32] This union had as its object: "to establish and maintain Sunday Schools, and to publish and circulate moral and religious publications". The first state Sunday School union was organized at Londonberry, New Hampshire, September 9, 1824.[33] Connecticut formed a similar union the following month. This

---

31. Second Report, 1819, p. 49.
32. The Seventh Report of the Philadelphia Sunday and Adult School Union: read at their Annual Meeting....May 25, 1824, with an account of the formation of the American Sunday School Union. Philadelphia, 1824, 97 pp. passim.
33. First Report of the American Sunday School Union, 1825, p. 7.

organization numbered "thirty auxiliaries" at the end of its first year of service.[34] Professor Nathaniel W. Taylor was elected president, the Rev. Mr. Lyman Beecher, secretary, and others of the officers were Mr. Timothy Dwight of New Haven, the Rev. Mr. Joel Hawes of Hartford, and the Rev. Mr. Samuel Merwin of New Haven. This organization held a general annual meeting, alternately at New Haven and Hartford, on the first Thursday, preceding the first Wednesday of May in each year.[35] The objects of the Union were:

> "to promote the opening of new, and the increase of old schools within the limits of this State; to form depositoris for supplying the schools with suitable books on the lowest terms possible; to stimulate and encourage each other in the instruction of children and others, and to correspond regularly with the American Sunday School Union in Philadelphia."[36]

The report of the Treasurer for the year 1830 states that $371.92 has been devoted to the "Expenses and services of eleven agents visiting and establishing Schools".[37] It was agreed that one who subscribed ten dollars to the Union became a "Life Member" of the organization.[38] Dr. Nathaniel W. Taylor was made such a member through the subscription of "Theological Students in Yale College", and Professor E. T. Fitch was similarly honored "by students in Yale College".[39]

---

34. *First Report of the American Sunday School Union*, 1825, p. 8.
35. Constitution, in the *Annual Report of the Connecticut Sunday School Union*, 1827, p. 38.
36. Constitution, Article II, op. cit., p. 38.
37. *The Annual Report*, 1830, p. 13.
38. Constitution, Article III, op. cit., p. 38.
39. *Annual Report*, 1830, p. 39.

Dr. Taylor was elected president for the first six years of the existence of the organization.[40]

In the city of New Haven a union Sunday School was established by the Congregational Churches of New Haven in the year 1822. In 1827 it numbered sixty-two teachers and 404 scholars.[41] In 1825 four Sabbath Schools were formed in New Haven and its vicinity. A "Baptist Society" had fifteen teachers and eighty pupils in 1827; an "African School" had twenty-six teachers and ninety-two scholars; "Hotchkisstown", eight teachers and fifty-nine pupils; and "Fair-Haven", sixty-three scholars.[42] In three years, (by 1830), the total number of teachers and scholars in New Haven and its environs had increased from 965 to 1252.

In view of the lack of any organization by the students or by the faculty for the directing of student activity in the churches of New Haven, the services which were rendered by the students of the Theological Department in Yale College during this period appear to have been of an individual and sporadic nature. Consequently records of such activities are scanty. There is evidence, however, that some students performed services of this type. Mr. Peter Parker taught a "Bible Class" of "twenty-three or twenty-four" young men from November 2, 1831 to August 25, 1833. His scholars appear to have been youths who were connected with the First Church of Christ in New Haven,

---

40. Annual Reports, 1827, 1828, 1830.
41. Annual Report of Connecticut Sunday School Union, 1827, p.7.
42. Ibid., The number of teachers in the Fair Haven organization is not given.

and who were about sixteen or seventeen years of age.[43]

A small piece of paper has been discovered,[44] which bears the caption "Weekly Report of Class No.___ in the African Sabbath School, Aug. 30, 1835", and the name of Mr. Samuel G. Buckingham as a teacher of a group of negro boys. Mr. Buckingham was a student in the Theological Department of Yale College during the years 1833-1836.[45]

On February 6, 1854 the "Young Men's Association of the First Ecclesiastical Society of New Haven" was organized. Its purpose was to afford young men of New Haven an opportunity for social fellowship of a Christian nature. The president of the society was Mr. Jonathan L. Jenkins, who was a student in the Theological Department in Yale College during the years 1852-1855.[46] The first annual report of the Association was made in 1855,[47] and Mr. Jenkins recounts the activities enjoyed by the group. These consisted mainly in the use of a library of religious books which had been given to the organization, and in recreational pursuits enjoyed by the society.

The first Bible Class in the annals of Yale College

---

43. George B. Stevens, The Life and Letters of the Rev. and Hon. Peter Parker, p. 69. The letter which Mr. Parker wrote to his Mother, under the date of August 25, 1833, is quoted in this volume.
44. The fragment was found with similar class reports with the Third Annual Report of the African Improvement Society of New Haven, August, 1829. 16 pp.
45. A General Catalogue of the Theological Department in Yale College (1838), p. 16.
46. A General Catalogue of the Divinity School in Yale College (1873), p. 95.
47. New Haven, 12 pp.

was organized by a group of converts of the revival of religion in the college which occurred in the year 1821. This group was instrumental in bringing about the revival of 1822.[48] There is no evidence that this class survived its college generation. In the year 1830, another Bible Class grew out of a similar situation. Some of the students were deeply concerned religiously and

> "on the 21st of November a meeting was held to form an association, to be called the Bible class of Yale College. . . .At an adjourned meeting the whole college assembled in the Chapel. . . . and a committee was chosen to confer with the faculty concerning the expediency of introducing the Bible as a regular study of the college".[49]

Professor Goodrich was chosen as the teacher of the class. The class was very well attended and was instrumental in bringing about the revival of 1831.

A Bible Class of academic students was established and continued by the efforts of Mr. David T. Stoddard, a student of the Theological Department during the years 1840-1843. He was also tutor in the academic department for two years, 1840-1842.[50] In a letter to an intimate friend, he writes, under the date of February 24, 1841:

> "I commenced soon after my arrival here, a Bible class, which has prospered far beyond my hopes. My division room is crowded every Sabbath (say by fifty students), who manifest a serious

---

48. C. A. Goodrich, "Revivals of Religion in Yale College", American Quarterly Register, Vol. 10 (February, 1838), p. 305.
49. Ibid., p. 307.
50. A Triennial Catalogue of the Theological Department of Yale College (1844), p. 26.

and inquiring spirit. I trust it is not with them mere curiosity, or a desire to speculate about the truth: but that many of them, at least, have a true love for the Bible. Two of these Bible class scholars have recently indulged a hope, though I have not evidence that is a direct result of their instruction on the Sabbath."(51)

Three sheets of paper to be found among Professor Gibbs' "Correspondence",[52] each bearing the title "Academic Bible Class", the date and the names and addresses of the students is evidence that Professor Gibbs conducted a Bible Class among the college students during the years 1850-1852. On November 1, 1850, his class was composed of seven young men, on February 9, 1851, nine students, and on February 8, 1852, twenty-four students.

Revivals of Religion in Yale College
and in New Haven

According to Professor Goodrich, from "the great revival of 1741", to the year 1837, "twenty distinct diffusions of the Holy Spirit" visited Yale College, seventeen of them in the nineteenth century.[53] The revivals of 1741 were the

---

51. J. P. Thompson, Memoir of Rev. David Tappan Stoddard, p. 80.
52. Rare Book Room, Sterling Memorial Library, Yale University.
53. "Revivals of Religion in Yale College", American Quarterly Register, Vol. X (Feb. 1838), p. 310. Professor Goodrich, who in the introduction to this article gives evidence that he is in a position to speak with authority on this subject, is the chief, and almost the only authority for the history of revivals in Yale College prior to the year 1838. It was noted in Chapter III that Professor Goodrich, more than any other one man was responsible for these revivals during the period 1817-1858.

outgrowth of a spiritual awakening which had occurred in New Haven in the year 1735. The students of Yale College worshiped with the congregation of the First Church of Christ in New Haven at that time. A revival occurred in the Yale College Church in 1757 under the leadership of its pastor, Dr. Naphtali Daggett; and another in 1783 under the guidance of President Stiles.

After observing the religious awakening of the churches in New Haven and elsewhere some of the most concerned of the students under the leadership of a member of the Senior Class, one Jeremiah Evarts, were influential in bringing about a revival of religion in 1802. The preaching of President Dwight was efficacious in causing a distinct "diffusion of the Holy Spirit" in 1802. In the winter of 1812-13, Elias Cornelius, a student in the College, became greatly concerned with his sinful state and experienced a notable conversion, and twenty of his fellows, most of whom were of the Senior Class "gave evidence of a genuine change of heart". The reading of a tract by a member of the Senior Class precipitated religious feelings which resulted in a revival in April, 1815.[54]

The years 1820, 1821, 1822, 1823, and 1824 were each marked by a revival of religion. Each of the first two "was intimately connected with a powerful work of grace" which had recently commenced in the city of New Haven. As has

---

54. C. A. Goodrich, "Revivals of Religion in Yale College", American Quarterly Register, Vol. X (Feb., 1838), pp. 295-302.

been noted above the revival of 1822 came as a result of a Bible Class which had been organized by the converts of the 1821 awakening. Concerning the causes and the fruits of the revivals of 1823 and 1824 little is known.[55] However, the total number of converts in these five religious movements must have been considerably over one hundred and fifty.[56]

Such a long series of "visits of the Holy Spirit among them" made for an attitude of expectancy. The questions regularly in the minds of the most earnest Christians were: What is the state of religion? Is it declining or improving? Will the Lord send his Spirit among us this time? The statement--"State of religion much the same as when we last met"--[57] often occurs in the minutes of the Church Committee of Yale College. The attitude of mind which was dominant in the Church Committee is also reflected in the following record:

---

55. C. A. Goodrich, "Revivals of Religion in Yale College", *American Quarterly Register*, Vol. X (Feb., 1838), p. 305.
56. This estimate is based upon the numbers for each revival given by Professor Goodrich, op. cit., pp. 303-305.
57. Minutes and Records of the Church Committee, Feb. 28, 1847. MS. The personnel of the Church Committee was composed of two students from each undergraduate class in the College. They were later known as "Class Deacons". For a history of their activities, see *Two Centuries of Christian Activity at Yale*, ed. by James B. Reynolds, Samuel H. Fisher, and Henry B. Wright; Chapter X, pp. 181-208.

"Sabbath Dec. 21st 1844
How little do we know of the future of the inscrutable ways of Providence? Since we met a few weeks since with our young brethren of the Freshman Class one of them and our number has been taken from us. John D. Lockwood a young man of Superior talents and devoted piety has been called by his Heavenly Father at the very beginning of his course to a higher and happier state of Existence. While this dispensation has cast a gloom over our course and caused all who knew the deceased to mourn, we of the Committee feel it to be a Special Warning to us to labour with our Might while it is called today. May its Author Grant that this Affliction may be the occasion of a rich outpouring of His special spirit in our midst. Our Friday Evening Meetings have increased in numbers.

Thos. Kennedy

Sc (ty)"

In the spring of the year 1825, there was another and more extensive revival; Professor Goodrich writes:

"One who was then a member of the senior class, has since informed me, that the commencement of that better state of feeling in the church, which led to this revival, may be traced to the humble and persevering exertions of a single individual, of but little standing and influence in college. . . . God smiled on his humble labors. Some of the leading members of the church were reclaimed from their backslidings, and a spirit of fervent supplication was given them from on high."[58]

Another revival occurred in 1827, being preceded by an "unusual spirit of prayer, and uncommon zeal in the discharge of Christian duties, on the part of the church."[59]

---

58. C. A. Goodrich, op. cit., pp. 305-6.
59. Ibid., p. 306.

> "The year which followed, was one of more than common prevalence of spiritual feeling. That eminent young servant of Christ, James B. Taylor, was then a member of the theological school, and his labors were blessed to the conversion of many souls in New Haven and the neighboring towns. In the spring of 1828, the college was again visited with a revival, of about the same extent as the preceding year." (60

The revival of 1830-31 was the greatest of all those which occurred during the period under examination, (1822-1858). Of this spiritual awakening Professor Fitch writes in a personal letter to a friend:[61]

> "There is in the revivals now taking place, a power and extent of divine influence, it appears to me, unexemplified since the primitive age. Christians are deeply humbled, & so burdened at heart for the cultivation of souls that they can not rest till they welcome the last sinner, for whom they pray, as a joyful penitent into the kingdom of their Lord. And sinners in great numbers are escaping for their lives from the city of sin and destruction, without looking back, or tarrying, hasting to the mountain of safety & confidence. . . . Think of more than a hundred in College within five weeks rejoicing in the Savior, and giving, as far as they can do it in so short a time, evidence that they have passed from death to life. The chapel yesterday presented as solemn and deeply affected an assembly, I think as ever I witnessed: and if you could have seen the anxious countenance, the falling tear, the various indications of melting hearts that characterized the assembly, you would have said that God the Spirit was with us of a truth. . . ."

---

60. C. A. Goodrich, op. cit., p. 306.
    Professor H. B. Wright in <u>Two Centuries of Christian Activity at Yale</u>, on p. 81, makes the statement that "the revivals of 1820 to 1830 owed much to the active and devoted work of the students in the Theological School". For an account of the revivals of this period he follows Professor Goodrich's account very closely, and gives no other authority for this statement.
61. To Rev. Seth Bliss, March 21, 1831, New Haven, MS., 3 pp.

According to Professor Goodrich the emotional element was not overdone in this revival:

> "Religious meetings were not greatly multiplied during this revival: To the ordinary exercises with which the year commenced, a sermon was added on Sabbath evening; and at first one meeting for inquiry, and afterwards a second, in the course of the week. These meetings rarely exceeded an hour in length. The amount of study during the term, was very little if at all diminished by the revival; and in many instances, there was an immediate and marked improvement in scholarship, among those who were subjects of the work. Much of the success which attended the labors of the brethren, was owing to an uncommon degree of delicacy and tenderness in their intercourse with the unconverted, and of mutual concession and fervent love among themselves. . . . The work has been characterized by perfect decorum, insomuch that even the infidel could not gainsay. Little of animal excitement or mere sympathy has been witnessed."(62

Professor George P. Fisher states [63] that not less than seventy-four were added to the College Church, and the number of converts in every denomination in the city of New Haven, which also was greatly stirred at this time, was estimated at nine hundred. He also quotes the statement of Mr. ... W. S. Dutton, at that time a student in the college, which in part is as follows:

> "Among the theological students whom I remember as having an excellent influence in the conference meetings, and in private conversation, were Albert Hale,. . . .Edwin Stevens,. . . .Amos Pettengill, Horace Bushnell and William Carter. The four last were Tutors.
>
> But specially worthy of mention were the labors of Professor Goodrich, Mr. Taylor and Dr.

---

62. C. A. Goodrich, op. cit., p. 306.
63. A Discourse Commemorative of the History of the Church of Christ in Yale College, during the First Century of its Existence (1858), p. 35.

Fitch. Professor Goodrich and Dr. Taylor were resorted to by a large number of inquirers for the way of salvation. . . . Dr. Taylor frequently preached in the evening in the Rhetorical Chamber with great solemnity and power. His discourses were admirably adapted to convince of sin, and to lead to repentance and faith. Dr. Fitch's sermons in the Chapel on the Sabbath and at meetings in the city, were wonderful examples of ingenuity, earnestness and eloquence."(64)

The revival of 1835 resulted in about fifty conversions in the College. It started from the efforts of a group of five Seniors in the Academic Department who met every evening in prayer and increased their number gradually to fifteen as men caught their spirit. President Day sent a personal invitation to every member of the College Church to attend a special meeting in the interest of a spiritual awakening. The revival began the following week and continued to the end of the winter term.

The revival of 1835, as well as the less effective ones of 1836 and 1837, aroused some opposition. The annual recurrence of revivals in connection with the day of prayer in February of each year caused much comment by those unsympathetic with these movements.

The minute as recorded in the Church Committee Records for January 21, 1838 is as follows:

"In consequence of revivals having occurred in this term for several years past successively, the impenitent in many instances are forward to reproach Christians as concerted together to get up a revival again during the present term."

In the year 1841, Elder Jacob Knapp came to New Haven

---

64. George P. Fisher, op. cit., pp. 86, 87.

to conduct a six-weeks' evangelistic campaign in the city. The meetings were held in the Baptist Church, and Christians of all denominations, students of Yale College, and Dr. Taylor, attended them.[65] Mr. Knapp took occasion to attack publicly and expose the frequenters of a notorious gambling-house in the city, several of whom were students. The young men whose names he had published, thirty-eight in number, banded together to break up his meetings and almost accomplished their purpose on one occasion. According to Elder Knapp, two of the band were afterwards converted and both of the proprietors of the gambling-house became deeply interested in religion.[66] Inasmuch, however, as a large number of the students were not influenced by Elder Knapp's preaching[67] the Rev. E. N. Kirk of Boston was invited to conduct evangelistic services in the College Chapel.[68] He and Dr. Nathaniel W. Taylor preached on alternate nights daily for three weeks. Inquiry meetings were held daily, and every evening after supper there were half-hour prayer-meetings in the students' rooms. Between seventy-one and seventy-five students were converted as a result of the

---

65. Elder Jacob Knapp, *Autobiography*, p. 115.
66. Ibid., pp. 116-118.
67. This lack of influence on the part of Mr. Knapp was probably largely due to the hyper-emotional methods used by him in his work and the "mean apparel" in which he appeared. See the testimony of a Yale student in *A Statement of Facts in Relation to the Case of Rev. Jacob Knapp*, especially pp. 18-21.
68. D. O. Mears, *Life of Edward Norris Kirk*, p. 155.

combined efforts of Knapp, Kirk, and Taylor.[69] In contrast to the opposition which he had aroused at the beginning of his labors in the city, it may be noticed that Elder Knapp was presented by the students with a purse of $120 and a testimonial signed by nearly seventy names on his departure from New Haven.[70]

Mr. David T. Stoddard, who was a Tutor in the College, and also a student of the Theological Department in preparation for foreign missionary service, was active in aiding students with their religious problems during this revival. In two letters written to "intimate friends", Mr. Stoddard says that three students came to him for personal conferences with this purpose in mind. He himself appears to have been greatly impressed and most happy with the fruits of the revival.[71]

The next and final revival of this period (1822-1858) did not occur until the year 1858. It was a part of the "Prayer Meeting Revival" which swept the country during the two years 1857 and 1858.[72] Professor Goodrich's influence was largely felt in this religious movement, even as it was in the awakenings of 1825, 1827, 1830-31, and 1835.

----

69. Elder Knapp, in his Autobiography, p. 115, gives the number as seventy-one. The number is given as seventy-five in Mears' Life of Kirk, p. 157.
70. Elder Knapp, Autobiography, p. 115.
71. The letters bore the dates: March 1, and April 1, 1841 J. P. Thompson, Memoir of Rev. David Tappan Stoddard, pp. 80-82.
72. Daniel Dorchester, Christianity in the United States, pp. 693, 694.

President Woolsey, and Dr. George P. Fisher the successor of Eleazer T. Fitch as Professor of Divinity, were also prominent in the work. No special church services were held. There were early morning entry prayer groups, and large numbers of students took part in the morning meetings held in Center Church by the townspeople.[73]

It would be most peculiar, in the light of the importance of such movements in the religious life of the time, and in view of the proximity of these movements, if the revivals of religion which occurred periodically in New Haven and its environs were not of interest and concern to the students of the Theological Department in Yale College. Undoubtedly they took a more prominent part in the support of these awakenings than may be gathered from the existent source materials. The Records of the Society for Christian Research[74] tell of the joy felt by its members at hearing of unusual religious awakenings at Milford, Humphreyville, and Hamden Plains. These students were among some of these revivals, either as witnesses or helpers.[75] That some of the students did preach, even though the laws of the school forbade them to be licensed before their Senior year, appears evident from a report of one of the Examining Committees.[76] It had been complained that students "were licensed too early--earlier than in other Seminaries". The

---

73. H. B. Wright, in *Two Centuries of Christian Activity at Yale*, pp. 93, 94.
74. Society for Christian Research, Records, 1828-1837. MS.
75. April 29, 1828.
76. December, 1832, 4 pp, MS.

Committee found that this had been done so that indigent students could support themselves, and made no recommendation that the condition be altered. The methods used in revivals of a better type were accepted, used, and urged upon the students by their professors. It has been noted that a course in "Revivals of Religion" was offered by the school at least beginning with the year 1850-51.[77]

---

77. The course of study for the Theological Department first appears in the Yale Catalogue in that year, and this subject is one of the group listed.

CHAPTER XII

MISSIONS: HOME AND FOREIGN

MISSIONS: HOME AND FOREIGN

Organizing For Home Missions

The General Association of the Pastors of the Consociated churches of the Colony of Connecticut convened by delegates at the house of the Rev. Mr. Daniel Welch, in Mansfield, June 2d, 1774. The group appears to have been the first organization to take into consideration the religious plight of the sparsely settled communities to the westward. This association thought "it advisable that an attempt be made to send missionaries among them, and for obtaining a Support for such Missionaries", recommended "it to the several Ministers in this Colony to promote a subscription among their people for this purpose".[1] At this same meeting the Association through its Committee, prepared a draft of a letter to the ministers of Boston, in which the Association expressed its sympathy for the sufferings which were brought upon the town of Boston by the British Parliament.[2] At the subsequent meeting of the Association, September 15, 1774, two missionaries were appointed "to go upon this business", of aiding the people to the westward, "next Spring".[3] These men were named at the

---

1. Records of the General Association of Ye Colony of Connecticut, June 20, 1738--June 19, 1799. Printed by order of the Association (1887), p. 76.
2. Ibid., p. 77.
3. Ibid., p. 85.

meeting on June 20, 1775, but in view of "the perplexed and melancholy State of public Affairs" few collections had been brought in, and the commissioning of the missionaries was postponed.[4] The meeting of the next year appears to have been entirely given over to thoughts of war.[5]

In October, 1792 new efforts in missionary service were begun by the General Association of the Congregational Churches of Connecticut. Ezra Stiles, Jonathan Edwards the Younger and Nathan Williams, were appointed as the committee to whom contributions should be made.[6] These three gentlemen made plans in the home of Mr. Edwards in New Haven, whereby nine pastors were commissioned for service in New York and Vermont.[7] They were sent for a period of two months in each State "to gather Churches, catechize children, ordain ministers, administer sacraments and discharge all ministerial duties as occasion might require",[8] and "to make draughts or maps of the settlements, that the Committee and the General Association may have the most particular and accurate accounts of the New-settlements for their future direction and assistance.[9]

In 1794-1796 a larger company went out to the new

---

4. Records of the General Association of Ye Colony of Connecticut, op. cit., p. 65.
5. Ibid., pp. 68-96.
6. Report of the Committee, June, 1793, 4 pp. MS.
7. Minutes of the Committee, under the dates of June 20, July 2, July 16, September 11, October 30, 1793. MS.
8. Minutes of the Doings of the Committee of the General Association of the State of Connecticut, relative to the Missionaries to be sent into the New Settlements; under date of June 20, 1793. MS.
9. Minutes of the Committee, July 16, 1793. MS.

settlements. The missionaries were in most cases settled pastors of churches, the best that Connecticut could afford, and were paid in 1793 "four dollars and a half a week, over and above the four dollars for the supply of their pulpits during their absence."[10] These ministers gave their services for a period of two or four months. In 1795 the honoraria were raised one half of a dollar per week.[11]

In view of the expanding frontier these methods soon became inadequate, and at its session of June 19, 1798, the general Association of the State of Connecticut established the Missionary Society of Connecticut. With the inception of this society organized efforts in the interests of "Home Missions" began. The preamble to the constitution of this society reveals the spirit of its founders:

> "The General Association of the State of Connecticut, impressed with the obligations on all the friends of Christianity, to propagate a knowledge of its gracious and holy Doctrines; Also encouraged by the zealous exertions for this End, in sundry Christian Bodies, cannot but hope, the time is near, in which God will spread his truth through the whole Earth.--They also consider it as a thing of great importance, that some charitable assistance be extended to new Christian Settlements, in various parts of the United States. The salvation of these souls is precious. The happiness of the rising generation, and the Order and Stability of civil Government are the most effectually advanced by the Diffusion of religious and moral sentiments, through the preaching of the gospel. In deep feeling of these truths having by prayer sought the direction of God, in fear of his great Name, they have adopted the following Constitution of a Missionary Society."

---

10. Records of the General Association of Ye Colony of Connecticut, June 18, 1793.
11. Ibid., June 16, 1795.
12. Ibid., June 20, 1738--June 19, 1799, p. 177.

The Massachusetts Missionary Society was organized in Boston, May 28, 1799, for the purpose of "diffusing the knowledge of the Gospel of Jesus Christ among the heathen, and others in remote places where the benefits of the Christian ministry and Christian ordinances are not enjoyed." The Society confined its labors for the most part to those "in remote places" on the frontier in Maine, New Hampshire, Vermont, New York, and states further West.[13]

It is to be noted that although these societies have the names of their respective states, they were designed to be national in their efforts. They were influential in civilizing and Christianizing the "West" during the first quarter of the nineteenth century. Progress in the conquering of this large region had, before 1820, moved very slowly however. The settlement of Ohio had been begun in the eighteenth century, and had been prosecuted during the first twenty years of the nineteenth, but under great difficulties. Illinois and Indiana had been admitted to the union, but with little promise of rapid growth in population and in wealth. The products of the Mississippi Valley could only reach the Atlantic seaboard in wagons, and at an expense greater than their value in the Eastern markets would repay. The unwieldy flat boat, dependent chiefly on the current for moving power, was their only means of conveying these products to the Gulf of Mexico. But in the decade,

---

13. Annual Report of the Trustees of the Massachusetts Missionary Society, May 27, 1823, pp. 3, 4.

1820-1830, the Erie canal was completed, and easily brought the agricultural products of the large regions adjoining the lake to the mouth of the Hudson; and steam had demonstrated its power to contend with the current of the Ohio, the Mississippi and the Missouri, and to bear on those rivers the products of the great Valley to the markets of the world. "The problem was solved, and it was thus made apparent to the dullest intellect, that the resources of a mighty empire were to be added to the American Republic in a single century."[14]

An added stimulus to the westward movement for the purposes of seeking new homes and new wealth resulted. But there were many who were incited to activity, not by commercial interest, but by a belief that "unless the vast populations which were soon to dwell in that valley should be pervaded and controlled by the gospel of Christ, they would be incapable of American liberty; that if they should come under the superstitions of Popery, they would soon fall into anarchy and degradation, and by their prepondering weight drag down with them our liberty and our religion. It was distinctly seen that the valley of the Mississippi must be filled with an enlightened Christianity, or there could be nothing great or good in the future of our country."[15] The result was an increased zeal in Home Missions. The

---

14. Paper, prepared by Rev. J. M. Sturtevant, "Yale Theological Seminary and Home Missions", read at the Semi-centennial Anniversary of the Yale Divinity School, p. 66.
15. Ibid., p. 66.

necessity of united efforts in the cause of Christianizing the West was recognized by religious leaders, and a group of them met in a convention in the city of New York, and on May 12, 1826, organized the American Home Missionary Society. The Congregational, the Presbyterian, the Dutch Reformed, and the Associate Reformed religious groups united their efforts in this organization.[16] According to an Article of its Constitution, "The great object of this Society" was "to assist congregations that are unable to support the Gospel Ministry, and to send the Gospel to the destitute, within the United States".[17]

The Theological Department and Home Missions

The Theological Department in Yale College was established near the beginning of the decade in which a new awakening to the needs of the new territory arose. The "Appeal of the West" was the first wave of missionary enthusiasm which visited the institution.

The societies organized by the students, especially the Society for Christian Research, and the Society of Inquiry Respecting Missions, were actively interested in the opportunities offered for Christian work in the West. At the meeting of the Society of Inquiry of December, 1828, Theron Baldwin of the Middle Class in the Theological Department,

---

16. American Home Missionary Society, First Report, 1827, pp. 58, 61.
17. Ibid., p. 3.

read an essay, "On the motives, or rather encouragements, to active individual effort in the cause of Christ, derived from the example of eminent Christian philanthropists and the present state of the world". One of those present at the meeting, Mason Grosvenor of the Junior Class, on his way home asked himself the question--What can I, as an individual do? "A plan which on some previous occasions had been faintly before his mind, now rose distinctly into view. Believing that education and religion must go hand in hand to the conversion of the world he proposed to himself the formation of an association of pious students (to be increased from year to year) to go into some one of the Western States and found a literary institution, having a preparatory and collegiate department."[18] Mr. Grosvenor met Mr. Baldwin later the same evening and suggested such a plan to him. J. M. Sturtevant of the Middle Class in the Theological Department, who had had experience on the frontier,[19] was then enlisted by them.

On December 30, 1838, Mr. Sturtevant read an essay before the Society for Christian Research, "On certain considerations which often influence a Theological student in selecting his field of labour". According to the Minutes of the Society he discussed the "Climate, State of Society and the means of intellectual improvement. The first con-

---

18. Theron Baldwin, Historical Sketch of the Origin, Progress and Wants of Illinois College, pp. 3, 4.
19. Mr. Sturtevant, was born (1805) in Warren, Connecticut but spent his boyhood in Tallmadge, Ohio.

sideration worthy of regard, the second unworthy, and the third not to be wholly neglected."[20] Theron Baldwin had also read a dissertation before the Society for Christian Research at its November meeting, but the title of his essay is not recorded by the secretary of the Society.[21]

Very shortly after Mr. Grosvenor's suggestion, and evidently while the members of these two societies, and especially the inner circle with whom Grosvenor had shared his plan, were thinking these thoughts, there appeared in the December issue of the "Home Missionary"[22] the following communication:

> ". . . .At least five or six Missionaries are imperiously needed in Illinois.
> A SEMINARY OF LEARNING
> Is projected, to go into operation next fall. The subscription now stands at between 2 and $3,000. The site is selected in this county, Morgan, and the selection made with considerable deliberation, by a committee appointed for that purpose; and is one in which the public sentiment thoroughly coincides. The half quarter section purchased for the site, is certainly the most delightful spot I have ever seen. It is about one mile north of the celebrated Diamond Grove. . . .
> The object of the Seminary is popular, and it is my deliberate opinion that there never was in our country a more promising opportunity for any who desire it, to bestow a few thousand dollars in the cause of education, and of Missions. The posture of things now is such, as to show to all the intelligent people, the good effects of your society, and to secure their coöperation in a happy degree in all the great benevolent objects of the day, IF SUCH AID CAN NOW BE AFFORDED in the objects above mentioned."(23

---
20. Society for Christian Research, Constitution and Records of Meetings, MS., Minutes, December 30, 1828.
21. Ibid., November 25, 1828.
22. Organ of the American Home Missionary Society, monthly, May, 1828--March 1909. It merged with the American Missionary in 1909.
23. The Home Missionary, vol. 1, (December, 1828) p. 136.

This letter had been written by the Rev. Mr. J. M. Ellis, who was a minister in the employ of the American Home Missionary Society, to the Corresponding Secretary of that organization. Mr. Ellis had been appointed by the Society to make a tour through the northern counties of Illinois to preach in destitute places and report to the Society such facts as might be useful in directing their appointments there.[24]

Mr. Grosvenor immediately wrote to Mr. Ellis and suggested that the association--that group of students gathered together by Grosvenor--might be disposed to choose Illinois for its field, and assist in the establishment of the proposed seminary--"should its aims and purposes be found in harmony with our plans". It took, at that time, two months to convey a letter to Illinois and to obtain an answer. In the meantime others in the seminary were contemplating making a decision concerning their life-work by joining the association of students. An affirmative reply was received and the young men signed the following compact, which bore the complimentary endorsement of President Day and Professors Taylor and Gibbs:

> "Believing in the entire alienation of the natural heart from God, in the necessity of the influences of the Holy Spirit for its renovation, and that these influences are not to be expected without the use of means; deeply impressed also with the destitute condition of the Western section of our country and the urgent claims of its inhabitants upon the benevolent at the East, and in view of the fearful crisis evidently approaching, and which we believe can only be averted by speedy and energetic

---

24. The Home Missionary, vol. 1, (July, 1828) p. 49.

measures on the part of the friends of religion and literature in the older States, and believing that evangelical religion and education must go hand in hand in order to the successful accomplishment of this desired object; we the undersigned hereby express our readiness to go to the State of Illinois for the purpose of establishing a Seminary of learning such as shall best be adapted to the exigencies of that country--a part of us to engage in instruction in the Seminary--the others to occupy--as preachers--important stations in the surrounding country--provided the undertaking be deemed practicable, and the location approved--and provided also the providence of God permit us to engage in it.

       Theron Baldwin, John F. Brooks,
Mason Grosvenor, Elisha Jenny, William Kirby,
   Julian M. Sturtevant, Asa Turner, Jr.

Theological Department of Yale College, Feb. 21, 1829."[25]

A plan for the proposed institution was drawn up under the supervision of President Day. According to the constitution proposed the institution was to be controlled by ten trustees, seven of whom were to be the men who signed their names to the above declaration. The remaining three trustees were to be elected by the subscribers to the fund which had already been raised in Illinois. The Yale group, which now came to be known as the "Illinois Band", promised to procure $10,000 for the work. The plans were presented by Mr. Sturtevant to the American Home Missionary Society. The body approved of the proposal. The urgency for the immediate beginning of work, in the minds of the supporters of the movement, was so great that Mr. Baldwin and Mr. Sturtevant were sent to Illinois, ahead of the rest of the group, before either of

----

25. J. M. Sturtevant, Autobiography, pp. 138, 139.

them had finished his last year in the Theological Department of Yale College.

The institution in Illinois commenced its operations with nine students on the first Monday in January, 1830. It had previously received the name of Illinois College by a vote of its patrons, who were assembled in the walls of its first, and then unfinished edifice. "Only about thirteen months had elapsed since the first idea of this institution entered. . . . the mind of a student at Yale College."[26]

The first president of Illinois College was Mr. Edward Beecher, who had joined the Society of Christian Research in 1825, when he was a tutor in Yale College. Mr. Sturtevant was for fifty-six years connected with the institution as teacher, professor, and president. Mr. Baldwin served two years in the pastorate at Vandalia, the capital of the state of Illinois at that time, five years as an agent of the American Home Missionary Society, and six years in the principalship of Monticello Seminary. He was then instrumental in organizing, in the city of New York, June 30, 1843, the "Society for the Promotion of Collegiate and Theological Education at the West".[27] Mr. Baldwin served as the Corresponding Secretary of this organization, the design of which is expressed in its name, from its inception in 1843 until his death in 1870. The receipts of the

---

26. Theron Baldwin, Historical Sketch of the Origin, Progress and Wants of Illinois College, pp. 7, 8.
27. First Annual Report, 1844, p. 7.

Society were a little over seventeen thousand dollars[28] during the first year of its existence. The Society served most in raising funds for endowments, for the securing of new professorships, and for aiding indigent students in western colleges.

Another of the "Illinois Band", Asa Turner, of the Class of 1830, did not remain in Illinois, but pushed on into Iowa. His work was of such a pioneer nature, and his leadership was so greatly depended upon by those who entered the territory at a later date, particularly the "Iowa Band" from Andover Seminary,[29] that he came to be known as "Father Turner".[30]

The "Iowa Band" of Andover Seminary was organized in the year 1843.[31] A few years previous to this date a similar group came together in the Theological Department in Yale College. Mr. Reuben Gaylord, a student of the Class of 1839 in this Department wrote the following to the Secretaries of the American Home Missionary Society:

---

28. i. e. $17,004.71. Annual Report, 1844, p. 16.
29. George F. Magoun, Asa Turner, A Home Missionary Patriarch, and his Times; especially Chapter XX.
30. See the dedicatory page of The Iowa Band, by Ephraim Adams. Boston, Congregational Publishing Society, 1870. 184 pp.
31. Ephraim Adams, op. cit., pp. 23, 26.

"Yale Theological Seminary, New Haven.
March 1, 1838.

    A few young men, members of this seminary, have become deeply interested in that section of our country lying west of the Mississippi, commonly known as the "Iowa District", or "Black Hawk Purchase". Seeing its destitute condition, both as respects education and religious institutions, and learning that the District is filling up with a rapidity unparalleled in the history of our country, we feel a strong conviction that, if a way be opened, it is our duty to plant our feet west of the Father of Waters. . . . Our object will be two-fold--to preach the gospel, and to open a school at the outset, which can soon be elevated to the rank of a college. Knowing that such an enterprise cannot be accomplished by individual effort, the following brethren are ready to associate and pledge themselves to engage in the work, if a way can be opened so as to warrant the undertaking: J. P. Stewart, M. Richardson, H. D. Kitchel, A. B. Haile, R. Gaylord, J. A. Clark, M. Mattocks. . . . It is our purpose to enlist one or two more of the right stamp. . . . One of our number, Stewart, was educated at the west, and has traveled extensively in the Iowa District. The writer of this has spent two and one-half years as teacher in Illinois College, at Jacksonville, so we are not acting without such knowledge as will enable us to come to an intelligent decision. . . . .
. . . .
. . . . Funds will be provided to support one or two of us as teachers. The others will devote themselves to preaching, and will be under the necessity of looking to you for a partial support. . . . .
. . . . In behalf of these brethren, I am,

                      Very respectfully yours,

                      Reuben Gaylord" [32]

Mr. Gaylord wrote to Miss Burton, his fiancee, March 17, 1838: "Our Iowa enterprise is succeeding admirably at length. Our number, seven, consists of some of the most enterprising young men in the seminary". [33] A letter of

---

32. Printed in, Life and Labors of Reuben Gaylord, by his wife (Mrs. Mary M. Welles Gaylord), pp. 82-84.
33. Life and Labors of Reuben Gaylord, op. cit., p. 84.

May 26 tells of further progress.[34] The following month he writes to Miss Burton:

"New Preston, June 18, 1838.

My Dear Sarah:

I have been at length set apart to the work of the gospel ministry. Last Tuesday, June 12, I was licensed to preach by the South Consociation of Litchfield county, which met at Litchfield. . .
. . . .
A letter has been received from Stewart, who is safe at Denmark, Iowa. . . . Clark I suppose is on the ground before this time. Haile will leave in the fall and occupy some one of the important points."(35

From the Theological Department in Yale College, under date of July 4, 1838, Mr. Gaylord expressed, to the Secretaries of the American Home Missionary Society, his purpose to leave for the West "immediately after the close of this term,[36] or not far from the 20th of next month".[37] His letter of July 27, to Miss Burton, tells of his acceptance by the Missionary Society, and of his appointment to Mt. Pleasant, Iowa, on the salary of four hundred dollars a year.[38] The subject of his next message is the rigors of the journey to the West.[39] Mr. Gaylord served as a minister in Iowa and in Nebraska; and as an agent in Nebraska and Western Iowa for the American Home Missionary Society.

Of the seven young men who were named by Mr. Gaylord

---

34. Life and Labors of Reuben Gaylord, op. cit., p. 88.
35. Ibid., p. 89, 90.
36. The end of his Middle Year.
37. Life and Labors of Reuben Gaylord, op. cit., p. 90.
38. Ibid., p. 92.
39. To Miss Burton, Cincinnati, September 3, 1838, op. cit., p. 93.

in his letter of March 1, 1838 to the Secretaries of the American Home Missionary Society, quoted above, all but J. P. Stewart have been identified as members of the Theological Department. James P. Stewart was a member of the Resident Graduate Class of the Academic Department in Yale College. He was a graduate of Illinois College of the year 1836. Information concerning him has not been found in any of the General or Biographical Catalogues of Andover Seminary, Princeton Seminary, the Theological Department of Yale College, or the Register of Graduates of Yale College (1701-1924). His home is given as the "Iowa District" in the annual Catalogue of the Officers and Students of Yale College for the year 1838/39. In his letter of June 18, 1838 to Miss Burton, quoted above, Mr. Gaylord writes that Stewart "is safe at Denmark, Iowa". It is probable that he settled in this his home state. Besides Mr. Gaylord, J. A. Clark also reached Iowa. He was active there during the years 1839-1849 in establishing churches at Burlington, Dubuque, and Keokuk. H. D. Kitchel served as a pastor in Michigan, 1848-1864, and in Illinois 1864-1866, and returned East to become President of Middlebury College, 1866-1873. John Mattocks was a minister in the state of New York, 1839-1856, and in Minnesota 1857-1875. Two of the group did not become pastors in the "West", but remained in Connecticut, Haile as a physician, and Richardson as a minister.

The influence which the "Appeal of the West" had upon the students of the Theological Department, and the extent to which such activities in the school as have been recounted above held a place in the life of those students, is perhaps most concretely shown in the fact that almost one-fourth of the alumni of the Theological Department in Yale College of the period 1822-1858, who served as ministers, rendered such service in the Western States.[40]

Organizing for Foreign Missions

The American Board

The first organization which was formed in the United States for the purpose of carrying the Gospel to lands across the seas was incorporated by the state of Massachusetts in the year 1812, with the title of "American Board of Commissioners for Foreign Missions".[41] The series of events which culminated in this incorporation began in the year 1808 with the "Hay-Stack Prayer-Meeting" led by Samuel J. Mills, then a student at Williams College. A society was formed, through his efforts, called "The Brethren". It had as its object "to effect, in the persons of its members, a mission or missions to the heathen". This society was transferred to the Seminary at Andover

----

40. See Table V, p. 134.
41. Constitution, Laws, and Regulations of the American Board of Commissioners for Foreign Missions (published by the Board), pp. 3-6.

when Mills entered that institution in the fall of the year, 1809.[42] At the meeting of the General Association of the Congregational Churches of the state of Massachusetts, June 28, 1810, four students from the Seminary at Andover, Adoniram Judson, Samuel Nott, Samuel J. Mills, and Samuel Newell, presented a Memorial to the Association in which they offered themselves to serve as foreign missionaries.[43] As a result a "Board of Commissioners for foreign missions" was appointed by the Association.[44] When the organization finally obtained its charter the word "American" was prefixed to this title.

In an "Historical Discourse",[45] pronounced on the evening of October 3, 1860, Dr. Mark Hopkins, the President of the American Board of Commissioners for Foreign Missions, made the following statement concerning the services rendered by this organization during the first fifty years of its existence:

> It has collected and disbursed, with no loss of defalcation, and no suspicion of dishonesty, more than eight millions of dollars. It has sent out four hundred and fifteen ordained missionaries, and eight hundred and forty-three not ordained; in all twelve hundred and fifty-eight. These have established thirty-nine distinct missions, of which twenty-two now remain in connection with

---

42. *Memoirs of American Missionaries formerly connected with the Society of Inquiry Respecting Missions in the Andover Theological Seminary: Embracing A History of the Society;* published under the direction of the Society, pp. 14, 15.
43. *Minutes of the General Association of Massachusetts Proper,* June 27, 1810, pp. 60, 61.
44. Ibid., pp. 61, 62.
45. In *Memorial Volume of the First Fifty Years of the American Board of Commissioners for Foreign Missions,* pp. 13-38.

the Board; with two hundred and sixty-nine stations and out-stations, employing four hundred and fifty-eight native helpers, preachers, and pastors, not including teachers. They have formed one hundred and forty-nine churches. . . . It has under its care three hundred and sixty-nine seminaries and schools, and in them more than ten thousand children. It has printed more than a thousand millions of pages, in forty different languages. It has reduced eighteen languages to writing, thus forming the germs of a new literature. . . . It has done more to extend and to diffuse in this land a knowledge of different countries and people, than any or all other agencies, and the reaction upon the churches of this foreign work has been invaluable.(46

In view of the fact that the American Board of Commissioners for Foreign Missions was the official agent of the Congregational churches, it is natural that this society should be of greatest influence upon the students of the Theological Department of Yale College, since the Professors of this seminary and most of the students, during the period under observation, were Congregationalists.[47] Of the thirty-two students in attendance at the Theological Department in Yale College during the years 1822-1858 who became foreign missionaries,[48] twenty-eight served under the American Board of Commissioners for Foreign Missions, two with the Morrison Education Society, one with the American Bible Society, and one with the Foreign Missionary Board of the Methodist Episcopal Church.

---

46. In Memorial Volume of the First Fifty Years of the American Board of Commissioners for Foreign Missions, pp. 18, 19.
47. See Table VI, p. 143.
48. See Table IV, p. 131, and the Eighth General Catalogue of the Yale Divinity School, which is the only general Catalogue of the School which gives complete information concerning these alumni.

The Morrison Education Society

Not long after the death on August 1, 1834 of the Rev. Robert Morrison, a pioneer missionary to China, a paper containing some suggestions for the formation of an association, to be called the Morrison Education Society, was circulated among the foreign residents in China, particularly in the city of Canton. This paper bore the date of January 26, 1835. On the twenty-fourth of the next month, twenty-two signatures having been obtained, and the sum of $4860 collected, a Provisional Committee--consisting of Sir George B. Robinson, bart., Messrs. William Jardine, David W. C. Olyphant, Lancelot Dent, J. Robert Morrison, and the Rev. E. C. Bridgman, was formed for the purpose of ascertaining the best method of carrying into effect a proposed plan of education.[49] Under their direction a constitution was written, and adopted by the Society, November 9, 1836. Article 2 of this constitution states that the object of the Society "shall be to improve and promote Education in China by schools and other means".[50] The Board of Trustees, five in number, were to be residents in China. The Society had no official connection with a foreign mission society of any religious body, and its membership was largely composed of British and American commercial men, resident in China. The Society supported a school for the education of Chinese

---

49. Proceedings Relative to the Formation of the Morrison Education Society, pp. 3-5.
50. Ibid., p. 5.

youth of either sex, preferably "young children six, eight, or ten years of age"; [51] and a Library which on January 1, 1838, consisted of 4542 volumes. To this Library were admitted members of the Society, and any other person who contributed ten dollars per annum to the funds of the Society. [52] The school and the Library were located in Canton from 1841 to 1845, and were then removed to Hongkong, where interruptions due to political disturbances were less frequent. The Society also gave funds for the support of students in other schools in China.

In view of the fact that the trustees of the Society were residents of China, provision was made for the appointment in the United States of "Corresponding Members" who were to act as a committee in the interest of obtaining funds and instructors for the Society. Professors Josiah W. Gibbs, Benjamin Silliman, and Chauncey A. Goodrich, were named as such a Committee. Professor Gibbs received a formal invitation to become a corresponding member in a letter written by Mr. J. Robert Morrison, from Macoa, under the date of January 1, 1836. [53] An examination of Professor Gibbs' "Correspondence" [54] reveals that forty-five letters have been preserved which were written or received by him relative to the business of this Society. On January 1, 1837

---

51. Proceedings Relative to the Formation of the Morrison Education Society, By-Laws. Section I, p. 7.
52. Catalogue of Books of the Morrison Education Society, Canton, January 1, 1838, esp. p. 35.
53. MS. 1 p.
54. Deposited in the Rare Book Room of the Sterling Memorial Library of Yale University.

Mr. E. C. Bridgman, the Corresponding Secretary of the Society, wrote to the committee in New Haven soliciting their efforts in obtaining an instructor for the Chinese children under the care of the Society. After making efforts to comply with this request, which efforts were repeatedly unsuccessful,[55] Professor Gibbs writes that the committee is endeavoring to train a young man for the post.[56] Meanwhile Mr. S. W. Bonney was sent to China in October of the year 1844. Mr. William A. Macy, the young man who had been in training for the post, and was a member of the Junior Class of the Theological Department in Yale College, began his journey soon after October 15, 1845.[57] Mr. Bonney returned soon after Macy's arrival, and the latter remained for four years in service at the school of the Morrison Education Society. Macy then came to New Haven to finish his seminary course during the years 1850-1852, and finally returned to Shanghai in 1854.[58] He died there in 1859.

---

55. Minutes concerning eight young men who are prospective teachers for the Morrison Education Society. In Professor Gibbs' "Correspondence". MS. 1 p.
56. To the Trustees of the Morrison Education Society, October 10, 1844, 4 pp.
57. A letter of introduction, a letter of recommendation, and a third letter telling of Mr. Macy's personal characteristics, were sent to the Trustees of the Morrison Education Society, each bearing the date of October 15, 1845. 1 p., 2 pp., and 1 p. respectively.
58. Four letters from William A. Macy to Professor Gibbs, from Hongkong, March 16, 1845, from Morrison Hill, July 31, 1846, from New Haven, August 20, 1850, from Shanghai, August 21, 1858.

Evidences of Interest in Foreign Missions
Manifested by the Students

The Society of Inquiry Respecting Missions was established primarily in the interest of the Christian enterprise in foreign lands. While its membership was not limited to those who had definitely chosen the foreign field as a future place of service the Society was proud of the "many" of its members who had become foreign missionaries.[59] The members of the society felt themselves "bound together by a common interest, and for the promotion of a common object, viz. THE SALVATION OF A PERISHING WORLD."[60]

The Society for Christian Research was more varied in its interests than the Society of Inquiry Regarding Missions. This is indicated by the fact that its major work was carried on through five committees, viz., "Foreign Missions", "Domestic Missions", "People of Colour", "Seamen", and "Correspondence".[61] However, in the records of this Society the committee on "Foreign Missions" always is given first place in the reports before the Society. Also the relative importance of the five interests of the Society is probably indicated in the time given each committee for its report at

---

59. *The First Annual Circular to the Churches of Connecticut on the Subject of Missions, from the Society of Inquiry in Yale College*, pp. 2, 3.
60. Ibid., p. 3. The work of this Society and the Society for Christian Research has been reviewed in Chapter IX.
61. Society for Christian Research, Records of Meetings, Constitution, By-Law III. MS.

the Monthly Concerts: "Foreign Missions", eighteen minutes; "Home Missions", ten minutes; "Seamen", seven minutes, "People of Colour", five minutes.[62] On December 30, 1828 (the same evening when Mr. Sturtevant, who was interested in the "West", read his dissertation "on certain considerations which often influence a Theological student in selecting his field of labour"), the following correspondents of the Society are recorded by the secretary: "London Missionary Society, Church Missionary Society, Missionary Society of Paris, Theological Seminary, Basle; Theological Seminary, Gettysburg, Pennsylvania; Mr. Thurston, Sandwich Islands and Mr. Josiah Brewer, Palestine".[63] Mr. Brewer was a charter member of the Society for Christian Research, a member of the first graduating class of the Theological Department in Yale College, and the first student of that institution who became a foreign missionary. Mr. Thurston was a graduate of Yale College.

Another member of the Society for Christian Research, Peter Parker, was, in the year 1831, the organizer of the "United Band of Foreign Missions in Yale University".[64] Membership in this society was limited to undergraduates,[65] Mr. Parker being the only exception. Perhaps in anticipation of the service which each was expected to render,

---

62. Society for Christian Research, Records of Meetings, November 8, 1831.
63. Ibid., December 30, 1828.
64. Constitution, By-Laws, and Records, 1831-1838. MS.
65. Ibid., Constitution, Article 3.

the life-history of each member was entered in a Biographical Sketch-book.[66] Every member therein expressed his desire to become a foreign missionary. It is the only one of the group of societies existent at this time which limited its membership to those who were "volunteers" for foreign missions. The names of forty young men are recorded in the book of records for the years of its existence 1831-1838. After a fitful struggle during the academic year 1837-1838 the secretary declared the Society "perished".[67]

At the celebration of the Semi-centennial Anniversary of the Theological Department in Yale College, held May 15 and 16, 1872, Dr. Charles P. Bush read a paper entitled "Yale Theological Seminary and Foreign Missions".[68] Mr. Bush was a graduate of the school of the Class of 1840, and in 1872, the District Secretary of the American Board of Commissioners for Foreign Missions. In his concluding remarks he made the following statements:

> "We only wish that the proportion of foreign laborers from this Seminary had been larger. It does not compare favorably with other Seminaries. Here it is only one to twenty-eight; in Princeton one to eighteen; in Andover and in Union one to sixteen."[69]

---

66. 1835, MS. folio.
67. United Band of Foreign Missions in Yale University, Constitution, By-Laws and Records, June 1836.
68. All but two of the missionaries whose services he reviewed belonged to that group of students which attended the Theological Department during the years 1822-1858.
69. Charles P. Bush, op. cit., p. 63.

At the close of this address, the Rev. Mr. Samuel G. Buckingham (Class of 1836) called attention to the comparison between the Theological Department in Yale College and some other seminaries in respect to the number of its alumni who have engaged in foreign missionary labor and said that it seemed due to the Institution and to the early professors to make an explanation of what might otherwise show a lack of missionary spirit:

> "Almost from the first, the "Illinois Band", so called, with their devotion to Home Missions, and their favorite project of founding a New England College at the West, enlisted the students in that enterprise and that field of labor. Then after Dr. Beecher removed to the West, he never came to the East without visiting New Haven, and appealing to the students to come to the West. And his appeals,[70] and the admiration felt for him here, and the peculiar friendship that existed between him and the Professors of this Seminary,[71] had their influence, and no doubt diverted some missionary spirits from the Foreign to the Home field. . . .
> It should also be said, that while Dr. Taylor did not urge his students to become Foreign Missionaries in preference to Home Missionaries, or to occupy important positions at the

---

70. For an account of Dr. Lyman Beecher's efforts in raising funds for western schools, and urging young men to come to the West see his Autobiography, Correspondence, etc., edited by Charles Beecher, especially Vol. II, Chapter XXV. His best known address on this subject is An Appeal for the West, which was published and widely circulated. Cincinnati, Truman and Smith, New York, Leavitt, Lord & Company, 1835. 190 pp.

71. This friendship of Dr. Beecher and the professors of the Theological Department is evident in the correspondence between them in regard to theological questions, some of which is quoted in Chapter X ("Theological Controversies") of this study. The deep personal friendship which existed between Drs. Taylor and Beecher is most intimately pictured in Personal Reminiscences and Memorials of Rebecca Taylor Hatch (Professor Taylor's daughter), esp. pp. 27-53.

East, he appreciated and loved Foreign Missions as well as his friend Dr. Beecher. . . . But he was accustomed to attach more importance than most men to positions and places as furnishing facilities for the Gospel. . . . And so he deemed it of the first importance that our own country should be cared for, and important positions in it be occupied by able and devoted ministers, and thus the most aid be secured toward the grand result."(72

At this same meeting a paper which had been prepared by Rev. J. M. Sturtevant (Class of 1830), who was unable to be present, was read [73] to the alumni and friends of the institution. In this treatise on "Yale Theological Seminary and Home Missions", President Sturtevant wrote:

"A more fervent faith in the truth and certain triumph of the gospel has seldom existed in modern times than in the young men under Dr. Taylor's instruction. He himself rather discouraged their going into distant fields of missionary effort. He felt himself to be environed with peculiar difficulties, and wanted his pupils, as speedily as possible, to come to his rescue, by filling at least some of the prominent pulpits in New England. But they were not greatly impressed with the necessity of this. They had full faith in the ability of their admired teacher to fight his own battles without any of their help, and were quite ready to try the temper of the weapons with which he had furnished them upon any human material, however refractory."(74

Professor Goodrich in his course on "Missions" intimated that the reason more of the students did not enter foreign missionary service was because they were "too much absorbed in the West."[75]

---

72. S. G. Buckingham, op. cit., pp. 63, 64.
73. Mr. Sturtevant's paper, therefore, could not have been influenced by the extemporaneous remarks of Mr. Buckingham.
74. The Semi-centennial Anniversary of Yale Divinity School p. 68.
75. S. J. M. Merwin, Notes on Professor Goodrich's lectures.

PART V

CRITICAL EXAMINATION
AND SUMMARY

CHAPTER XIII

THE CLOSE OF THE PERIOD

THE CLOSE OF THE PERIOD

There was a marked decline in the attendance of students at the Theological Department in Yale College in the last decade of the period under review, 1822-1858. The peak in attendance during this period was reached during the five academic years 1838/39 to 1842/43, when the sum of the annual registrations was 348. For the academic years 1843/44 to 1847/48 this sum was 293; for 1848/49 to 1852/53, 215; and the final five-year period suffered an even greater decline, when the total number of annual registrations was 121.[1]

The two Seminaries which were the leading rivals of the Theological Department in Yale College, the Theological Seminary at Andover, Massachusetts, and the Theological Seminary at Princeton, New Jersey, did not suffer such a decline in student attendance. The number of persons belonging to the Classes[2] of 1845-1849 of the Seminary at Princeton was 299.[3] The number in the next five classes constituted a decrease of 7.6 per cent to 276, and the

---

1. See Table I, p. 121.
2. By "Class" is meant that group made up of students who were expected to graduate in a certain year. Each student is counted, however, whether he graduated or not. The total number of members in the classes is here compared rather than the total number of registrations, which is true of Table I.
3. See Table XIII on the next page.

TABLE XIII. COMPARISON OF THE PERCENTAGE OF INCREASE
AND DECREASE IN THE NUMBER OF MEMBERS IN THE CLASSES OF
THE SEMINARIES AT ANDOVER AND AT PRINCETON AND THE
THEOLOGICAL DEPARTMENT IN YALE COLLEGE DURING THE PERIOD
1825-1874, IN GROUPS OF FIVE CLASSES EACH

Classes	YALE		ANDOVER		PRINCETON	
	Number of Students	Percentage Increase or Decrease	Number of Students	Percentage Increase or Decrease	Number of Students	Percentage Increase or Decrease
1825-1829	66		239		243	
1830-1834	111	84.5+	272	13.3+	234	3.7-
1835-1839	167	50.4+	288	5.8+	285	21.7+
1840-1844	169	1.1+	288	0.0	218	23.4-
1845-1849	140	17.1-	215	25.3-	299	37.1
1850-1854	95	32.1-	182	15.1-	276	7.6-
1855-1859	58	38.9-	226	24.1+	225	18.4-
1860-1864	68	17.2+	263	16.3+	331	32.0+
1865-1869	57	16.1-	194	26.2-	307	7.2-
1870-1874	119	108.7+	183	5.6-	238	32.5-

number (225) in the next five classes (1855-1859) was 18.4 per cent less than that of 1850-1854. The five-year class-group, 1860-1864, totaled 331 students, 32.0 per cent more than the preceding five classes.

In the Theological Department of Yale College 140 young men were members of the Classes of 1845-1849. The number of students in the next five classes was 95, a decrease of almost one-third (32.1 per cent). The number of students (58) in the last five classes in this period (1822-1858) was 38.9 per cent less than the number (95) in the preceding five classes. The number of members in the last class-group (58) had fallen over half (58.8 per cent) from the number in the second preceding class-group, that of 1845-1849.

The Seminary at Andover suffered a decrease of 15.1 per cent from 215, the number of members of the Classes 1845-1849, to 182, the number in the Classes 1850-1854. However, the Classes 1855-1859 constituted a period which more than overcame this decrease, reaching the total of 226, an increase over the preceding class-group of almost one quarter (24.1 per cent).

The attendance of students at the Theological Department in Yale had decreased to such a degree that only twenty-two students attended the institution during the academic year 1857-1858,[4] five being in the Junior Class,

---

4. Catalogue of the Officers and Students of Yale College, with a Statement of the Course of Instruction in the Various Departments, 1858-59, p. 6.

eight in the Middle Class, four in the Senior Class, and three were Resident Graduates. What were the causes for this diminution in the number of students seeking training at the Theological Department of Yale College?

1. Financial Difficulties

The first reason for this decline in student attendance probably lay in the fact that the Theological Department in Yale College was limited by its financial condition. Evidence of repeated financial difficulty has been noted in Chapter V of this study. The Institution appears to have been unable to compete with other Seminaries in providing scholarships for indigent students.[5] The prospective student would probably also be influenced adversely by the poor accommodations afforded by the Divinity College, the building occupied by theological students at Yale College.

2. Religious Thought Changed from a Theological to a Biblical Emphasis

It has been noted in Chapter IV that the Theological Department in Yale College received its largest groups of students during the years when the theological controversies

---

5. According to Article XVII of the <u>Constitution</u> and <u>Statutes of the Theological Seminary, Andover</u> (1839), "The necessary expenses of indigent Students. . . ." were "defrayed out of funds, appropriated to this purpose". The same is found in the edition of 1857, Chapter II, 1.

between Professor Taylor and his colleagues and their opponents were at their height. Perhaps with the subsidence of these debates on metaphysical issues, it was natural that a decline in student attendance should follow. The interest in theological definitions and in the fine points of metaphysics had also materially waned. This change of attitude is illustrated in the sermon[6] Rev. Leonard Bacon preached, March 10, 1850, on his twenty-fifth anniversary as pastor of the First Church in New Haven. He says:

> "As I attempt to recall the outline of my intellectual history for the period under review, I see that my views have been in many respects continually though gradually changing. Within that period some great controversies have agitated the religious public--controversies which have had their day, and the value of which remains only in the effect which they have produced on the prevalent modes of representing and preaching the Gospel as related to the wants of man. . . . The age in which we now live is in many respects an age of advancement; and however the theologians of the schools may contend for the immutability of their traditions or of their metaphysical inventions, theology itself, as held by practical, earnest men, cannot but partake to some extent in the general advancement of human knowledge. The progress of inductive science is continually exhibiting in new lights the connection between the Christian revelation and the works of God in nature and providence,. . . . The altered position too, of the Churches, especially in this age of freedom, of moral conflict, and of evangelical enterprise and aggression, is gradually changing the prevalent habits of theological speculation and of controversy. . . . Or to speak more definitely I may say,
> 1. My theology, if I understand myself is more Biblical, than at the beginning of my ministry. What I mean is, that my views are taken less at second hand from standard systems of theology and are drawn more directly from my own study of Bible. . . .

------

6. New Haven, 1850. 27 pp.

2. I find that I have now more freedom than I had at the beginning of my ministry in preaching the Gospel as an offer from God, of which every hearer may avail himself. There was a time when I felt it necessary to argue with men on the question of their inability. . . . to become morally and spiritually new creatures. . . . I find no better way of preaching, none more Scriptural, none more truly philosophical, than to take it for granted that the Gospel brings salvation, honestly, simply, really within the reach of every hearer, and that every hearer knows it. . . .

3. I find also, as I advance in life, ... that my views on questions of theology are more enlarged and tolerant, and, in that true sense of the word, more catholic. . . . .
. . . .

5. As I grow older, and more familiar with the Scriptures, I think I find, in my habits of thought and of preaching, an increasing appreciation of those parts of the New Testament which set forth the doctrine of the Holy Spirit. I have never preached, nor have I ever felt that the only work of the Holy Spirit is to convert men, or that there is anything more signally the achievement of Divine Grace in the commencement of the Christian life than in its continuance and growth. And yet there was a time. . . . when, in sympathy with the prevailing current of New England theology, I was perhaps too much disposed to resolve all the phenomena of the Christian life into phenomena of the will. But the more I study the New Testament, the more I see and feel that the promise of the Holy Spirit, not merely or chiefly to convert the unbeliever, but still more to dwell in the believer with Divine illumination and comfort, with inward help in duty and in trial, and with an inspiration that quickens and opens the mind to discern the beauty and glory of God in Christ, is--not less than that free offer of forgiveness which it pre-supposes--the great promise of the Gospel.

6. I may say, also, that I find, in the progress of my experience and of my studies, an increasing dislike to all metaphysical dispositions of Christianity. There have been times when I was interested in the questions and theories of scholastic theology. But now the longer I live,. . . . the less disposed am I to confide in any man's theory of Christianity, made up of philosophical deductions and logical inferences.[7]

---
7. Leonard Bacon, op. cit., pp. 6-12.

This sermon of Dr. Bacon's seems to bear the influence of Horace Bushnell, his friend and contemporary [8] at the following major points.

1. A "dislike of metaphysical dispositions", and a distaste for the fine points of theological definition and debate (point 6). [9]

2. The consequential dependence upon the simple and natural revelation of God in the Scriptures and the experience of men (points 1 and 2) was also typical of Bushnell. [10]

3. The change of emphasis in regard to the person of Christ from that of argument concerning his deity to that

---

8. When Dr. Bushnell was in danger of being condemned for heresy in the General Association of Connecticut, chiefly through the agitation of the Fairfield West Association, a crisis was reached at the meeting of the former body in June, 1853. At this time Leonard Bacon offered a resolution which was so stated as to unite the less restive groups in the defense of Bushnell. Minutes of the General Association of Connecticut, June, 1853, p. 11.
See also T. D. Bacon, Leonard Bacon, A Statesman in the Church, pp. 284, 363-366.

9. This is reflected in his method of attack on any problem, and the style of his address—he thought and wrote as a preacher, and not as a scholar.
Concerning the differences between Bushnell and the leading theologians of his day see T. T. Munger, Horace Bushnell, Preacher and Theologian, especially Chapter III. Mr. Munger also writes: (p. 29) "his theological studies in New Haven chiefly served to furnish a background against which all his work and thought in after years stand out in vivid contrast".

10. See Bushnell's "Preliminary Dissertation on the Nature of Language as Related to Thought and Spirit", pp. 9-117 in his God in Christ, Hartford, Brown and Parsons, 1849. 356 pp.
See also his discussion on the topic "Piety itself limited by Dogma", pp. 343-348, op. cit.

of exaltation in the revelation of "God in Christ" as a proof of the diety, was one of Bushnell's greatest contributions to the thought of his day, and the one at which he received many criticisms.[11]

4. "I have never preached, nor have I ever felt that the only work of the Holy Spirit is to convert men, or that there is anything more signally the achievement of Divine grace in the commencement of the Christian life than in its continuance and growth" (under point 5) is a conception of thought which is very near to the thesis of Bushnell's "Christian Nurture."[12]

Dr. Bacon's grandson and biographer, in commenting on the twenty-fifth anniversary sermon "and the changed attitude of the preacher and of his hearers", writes, "Even Dr. Taylor, who had brought the development of this system

---

11. Bushnell emphasized the deity of Christ almost to the exclusion of his humanity (see his God in Christ, edition cited, pp. 119-181). It was at this point that some theologians of his day found the greatest ground for the accusation of heresy and were led to the attempt of trying Bushnell for his unorthodoxy. Remonstrance and Complaint of the Association of Fairfield West to the Hartford Central Association, New York, 1850. 35 pp. Professor Goodrich also wrote an anonymous article criticizing Bushnell's viewpoint. What does Dr. Bushnell Mean? Hartford, 1849, 28 pp.
12. Discourses on Christian Nurture, Boston, Massachusetts Sabbath School Society, 1847. (1st edition) 72 pp. See especially pp. 22-25.
    Dr. Bacon's grandson and biographer writes (p. 284) that Bacon was particularly impressed by Bushnell's Christian Nurture since this book appeared "just at the time of Benjamin's (his son) death", and was a volume "full of consolation for the reader."

of doctrine to its completion, a man of great intellectual courage and power, the champion of progressive thought, who endured fierce assaults for his boldness, came to be regarded as a kind of relic of a bygone era, who devoted his lectures at Yale Divinity School to the discussion of forgotten issues."[13]

Perhaps the best evidence of the passing of the intense interest in the metaphysical issues of the years 1828-1838, and of the subsidence of theological controversy, was the proposal in December 1855, on the part of the Trustees of the Seminary at East Windsor that this institution and the Theological Department in Yale College should be united. The former seminary had been established in 1835 in opposition to the New Haven Theology. President Woolsey addressed a private circular to the Clerical Fellows of Yale College informing them of the proposed union, and outlining the chief advantages and disadvantages of such a step. The Clerical Fellows were invited to a meeting to be held, on the first Tuesday in February, in the office of the President.[14] The representatives of the Seminary at East Windsor were also present at this time.[15]

It was the general opinion that the churches of Connecticut would be greatly aided by the healing of the division of its leaders, and that the united institution

---

13. T. D. Bacon, Leonard Bacon, A Statesman in the Church, p. 318.
14. December 29, 1855, 1 p.
15. W. Clarke, Letter to Pres. Woolsey, Hartford, January 31, 1856. MS., 1 p.

would be stronger than either of the separate seminaries.[16] However, the chief difficulty was found in the discovery of a method whereby the Trustees of the Seminary at East Windsor and the Corporation of Yale College could jointly control the united institution, and yet neither of them surrender its powers. Distrust of the "Pastoral Union", which body controlled the Seminary at East Windsor and was composed of a secret group of Connecticut ministers, was expressed.[17] Dr. Clarke wrote to President Woolsey that he had heard that Professor Taylor had been hurt by the President's silence on the question,[18] and he also stated that some of the members of the "Pastoral Union" disliked the proposed plan of union.[19] As a result of these difficulties further action concerning the projected union was remitted.[20]

In his lecture on Expository Preaching, December 7, 1843, Professor Goodrich remarked that "Didactic Theology won't do always" for a source of materials for sermons, and

---

16. Pres. Woolsey's Circular, cited above, December 29, 1855. W. Clarke, Letter to Pres. Woolsey, Hartford, February 11, 1856. MS., 3 pp. Leonard Bacon, Letter to Noah Porter, New Haven, January 15, 1856. MS., 3 pp.
17. Leonard Bacon, Letter cited. H. P. Arms, Letter to Noah Porter, Norwich Town, January 10, 1856, MS. 4 pp. J. H. Linsley, Letter to President Woolsey, Greenwich, February 4, 1856. MS. 4 pp. Noah Porter, Sr., Letter (to President Woolsey?), Farmington, March 1, 1856. MS. 2 pp. Prof. Noah Porter, (Summary of the Proposed Union), 1856, MS., 4 pp.
18. Hartford, February 11, 1856. MS., 3 pp.
19. W. Clarke, Letter to Pres. Woolsey, Hartford, February 23, 1856. MS., 4 pp.
20. E. L. Cleaveland, Letter to Pres. Woolsey, New Haven, February 29, 1856. MS., 3 pp.

Another attempt at union was made in the Spring of 1864. This effort met the same fate as that of 1856.

that there has been "a change of sentiment on this subject--
people [are] tired of long-winded doctrinal sermons". He
said the solution to this difficulty would be found in the
"<u>systematic</u> study of the <u>word</u> of God."[21] In contrast to
this opinion is the report of the President and Fellows for
the year 1851, in which it was suggested "the propriety of
certain alterations with a view to giving greater prominence
to the study of Systematic and Revealed Theology".[22]

3. The Faculty in Their Declining Years

It has been noted in a previous chapter that four
Professors constituted the Faculty of the Theological Department in Yale College during this period, all four being
connected with the institution in some manner from its inception. Professor Josiah W. Gibbs began his connection
with Yale College, in 1811, as a tutor in the Academic
Department. Professor Goodrich began his professional
career one year later in the same office. Professor Fitch
was called to the chair of Divinity in 1817. Nathaniel W.
Taylor was elected Dwight Professor of Didactic Theology in
the Theological Department in 1822. He was the senior member of the group. There appears to have been no plan during
this period whereby these men could receive the honorable
appointment of an emeritus professor. Undoubtedly the

----

21. S. J. M. Merwin. Professor Goodrich's Lectures. MS.
22. Records of the President and Fellows of Yale College, July 29, 1851. MS.

finances of the institution would not have permitted such a procedure if it had been proposed.

It would be a mistake to assert that these theological professors made no intellectual progress subsequent to the year 1850. A lack of intellectual progress may have been the case to a degree with regard to Dr. Fitch. According to Professor Fitch's own account of his sermons, five new addresses were prepared by him in 1854, one in 1855, and none during the years 1856-57, and two in 1858.[23] Three essays from his pen of a theological and religious nature were published during the years 1840-1869. One was an article in the "New Englander";[24] a second appeared in the "Bibliotheca Sacra and American Biblical Repository";[25] and the third as a Sermon in the "National Preacher".[26] He seems to have turned his attention to the subject of Music during these later years, and two articles on this topic appeared in periodicals; one in the "American Journal of Science and Arts",[27] in 1850; and the other in the "New Englander"[28] the year following his death.

----

23. Rev. Fitch's Sermons, Enumerative and Chronological, MS., 3 Vols. He died in 1872.
24. (Review of the Works of) "Nathanael Emmons, D.D.", New Englander, Vol. 12 (April, 1855), pp. 217-63.
25. "The Doctrine of Divine Inspiration", Bibliotheca Sacra and American Biblical Repository, Vol. XII (April, 1855), pp. 217-263
26. Sermon: "The mode of preaching the Gospel that is adapted to Success; Acts XIV, 1", National Preacher, Vol. 37 (July, 1863), pp. 169-185.
27. "On Perfect Intonation of the Euharmonic Organ", American Journal of Science and Arts, Vol. IX, Second Series (May, 1850), pp. 97-116.
28. "Music as a Fine Art. Its History--Its Productions--the Elements of Its Beauty. A Lecture", New Englander, Vol. 31 (October, 1872), pp. 689-725.

Only one publication of a work by Dr. Taylor appeared between the year 1833 and the year of his death (1858).[29] However, he appears to have continued to work on his beloved topic, the Moral Government of God, producing, according to Professor Noah Porter, just a few months before his death, an improvement of his statement on certain points in regard to the subject.[30]

Professor Goodrich published in the year 1852 a volume based on his College lectures and entitled Select British Eloquence. This work comprised over nine hundred pages, "embracing the best Speeches entire, of the most eminent Orators of Great Britain for the last two centuries; with sketches of their lives, an estimate of their genius, and notes critical and explanatory".[31] Only two other writings from his hand were published, and they were limited in their extent.[32] It has been noted in Chapter III that Professor Goodrich spent the last twenty years of his life editing and re-editing several editions of Webster's

---

29. He was the author of a "Reply to the President" (pp. 5-12) in The New Haven Memorial to the President, protesting against the use of the United-States Army to enforce the bogus laws of Kansas; the Answer of President Buchanan; and the Reply of the Memorialists. New Haven, 1857. 12 pp.
30. p. viii of the Preface to N. W. Taylor's Lectures on the Moral Government of God (1859) 2 Vols. xiii, 417; viii, 423 pp.
31. New York, 1852. vii and 947 pp.
32. "Review of Spragues Annals of the American Pulpit", New Englander, Vol. 15 (May 1857), pp. 169-84. A Letter to the Secretaries of the American Tract Society, New Haven, 1858. 16 pp.

dictionary.[33]

Professor Josiah W. Gibbs appears to have surpassed his colleagues in sustained intellectual endeavor. Of the seven books published under his name, three of them were of the years 1857, 1858, and 1860, and these three were much more of a contribution to philology than the first four volumes from his pen. Professor Gibbs contributed thirty-six articles almost entirely on philological subjects to various periodicals, and twenty-one of these articles appeared after the year 1850.[34]

Perhaps one test of the intellectual activity of the Professors of the Theological Department in Yale College during the last decade of the period under review would be found in the degree of participation which they enjoyed in the important issues of the day. The outstanding political question of the years which marked the close of the period 1822-1858 was that of Slavery. In 1854, when feeling ran high at the "Anti-Nebraska Meetings"[35] held in the city of New Haven, Professor Taylor addressed the gathering. He began his speech by saying: "If I could, I should like to

----

33. The last edition published during his lifetime was that of 1857. Mason Brothers, Springfield, Mass., G. & C. Merriam, 1857. xxii, 490 pp.
34. See the Annotated Bibliography of Professor Gibbs' Writings, pp. 112-118.
    In a letter of September 27, 1858, Mr. A. J. Adler, Professor of German in New York University, writes to Dr. Gibbs, congratulating him on his excellent article on Modern Philology in a recent issue of the New Englander. MS., 2 pp.
35. Speeches and Other Proceedings at the Anti-Nebraska Meetings held in New Haven, Connecticut, March 8th and 10th, 1854, 26 pp.

say the first thing, which I have to say on this subject, in capitals;--THE NEBRASKA BILL IS A MEAN ATTEMPT TO VIOLATE A FAIR BARGAIN. (Applause). Its authors know it,-- we know it--the whole country knows it".[36] In conclusion, he said in part, "Sir, if worst comes to worst, I could lay off the garments of my profession and put on a soldier's coat in the cause of freedom. (Tremendous and long continued cheering and shouts of applause)."[37] The Rev. Dr. Bacon and Professor Silliman also made addresses at this meeting.

In 1857 when a New Haven Memorial was sent to President Buchanan "protesting against the use of the United States Army to enforce the bogus laws of Kansas", and an answer was made by President Buchanan followed by a reply from the Memorialists, Professor Taylor was the author of the reply, and Professor Gibbs joined a group of citizens, and Professors at Yale College, in affixing his name to the document. The signatures of Professors Goodrich and Fitch are not found.[38]

In contrast to these two instances of definite action on the part of Professor Taylor in regard to the question of Slavery is the apparently conservative attitude which he

---

36. Speeches and Other Proceedings at the Anti-Nebraska Meetings held in New Haven, Connecticut, March 8th and 10th, 1854, p. 10.
37. Ibid., p. 13.
38. The New-Haven Memorial to the President, protesting against the Use of the United-States Army to enforce the Bogus Laws of Kansas; The Answer of President Buchanan; and the Reply of the Memorialists. Boston (1857), 12 pp.

took on this issue at the meetings of the Rhetorical Society. It has been noted that as President of that organization he habitually rendered a decision concerning the question which had been discussed. An examination of those decisions connected with the issue of Slavery reveals that Professor Taylor greatly favored a conservative viewpoint.[39] His lectures, published in three volumes by friends after his death,[40] bear no reference to slavery, even though the majority of the discussion is concerned with the moral government of God. Perhaps Professor Taylor was limited by the prevailing view of the function of the ministry. It appears to have been a popular opinion that the minister should not devote his time and energy to the political and reform movements of the day.[41]

Under the date of January 11, 1858 Professor Chauncey A. Goodrich wrote a letter to the Secretaries of the American Tract Society "in behalf of the Rev. Jeremiah Day, D.D., LL.D.,

---

39. The Rhetorical Society, Book E, Records of Meetings, June 9, 1841--December 2, 1857. MS. See pp. 297-300 of this study for a selection of the questions and the decisions rendered.
40. Lectures on the Moral Government of God; New York, 1859. 2 vols. xiii, 417; viii, 423 pp. Essays, Lectures, etc. upon Select Topics in Revealed Theology; New York, 1859. viii, 480 pp.
41. Professor Goodrich speaks of this opinion in his final Lecture on Pastoral Duties and appears to agree with it in general. S. J. M. Merwin, Professor Goodrich's Lectures, MS. At the meeting of the Rhetorical Society of October 12, 1853, Professor Taylor rendered the decision to the effect that a minister should not spend his time and energy in the reform movements of the day. MS. Book E.

Eleazer T. Fitch, D. D., and Others"[42] protesting the failure of the Society to publish articles on Slavery. It is alleged that the Society was pursuing this policy for fear of losing subscribers in the South.[43] This action was being carried on contrary to the report of a Committee which had been appointed to investigate the question, this Committee having decided that tracts concerned with the issue of Slavery should be distributed.[44] The letter written by Professor Goodrich received the signatures of eleven clergymen who resided in the city of New Haven. The names of Professors Gibbs and Taylor are not among them. The protest of Dr. Goodrich and his colleagues was to no avail, since the Publishing Committee of the American Tract Society, on March 18, 1858, adopted a resolution which dedicated it to the policy of non-publication on the issue of Slavery.[45] Dr. Goodrich had been a trustee of the Society for several

---

42. A Letter to the Secretaries of the American Tract Society, written in behalf of the Rev. Jeremiah Day, D.D., LL.D., Eleazer T. Fitch, D.D., and Others; New Haven, 1858. 16 pp. A Committee of the New York General Association reported that the American Tract Society was guilty of alteration of texts and the avoidance of the subject in order to avoid offending those persons favoring Slavery. Report, August 26, 1855, pp. 3-11.
43. Letter to the Secretaries of the American Tract Society, p. 14.
44. Ibid., p. 2. Professor Goodrich had been a member of this Committee.
45. Minute adopted on the 18th March, 1858, by the Publishing Committee of the American Tract Society, Explanatory of their Position in Relation to the Report and Resolutions of the Committee of Fifteen, as sanctioned at the Anniversary of 1857; and the Act of the Executive Committee Adopting Such Minute (New York? 1858?), 20 pp.

years, but withdrew his support on account of this "neglect of duty", and joined the Boston Tract Society.

A factor which probably influenced the decline in the attendance of students at the Theological Department in Yale College during the last eight years of this period was the fact that all four of its professors were, with increasing rapidity, failing physically. As early as 1852 Professor Fitch resigned his office as College pastor on account of ill health.[46] He was asked to continue his lectures in Homiletics,[47] with which request he complied. He served in this capacity until his final resignation in 1863.[48]

During his last years Dr. Taylor failed very rapidly. Very often his classes, which averaged between six and seven members in each of the years of this period, met with him in his room, and when he was too feeble to read his lectures, one of the students read it to his fellows, after which Professor Taylor heard their questions, and endeavored to answer them with his former energy and spirit.[49] He resigned his office as professor, July 13, 1857, on

---

46. Letter to the President and Fellows, July 13, 1852. The Professors Silliman, Taylor and Olmsted wrote him a friendly letter expressing their gratitude for the services he had rendered the College. MS. 4 pp. Dr. Fitch responded, defending his preaching at some length. MS. 6 pp.
47. Minutes of the President and Fellows, July 27, 1852.
48. July 28, 1863. MS. 1 p.
49. Benjamin N. Martin, Nathaniel W. Taylor, Yale College, A Sketch of Its History, ed. by W. L. Kingsley, Vol. II, p. 36.

account of his age and ill health.[50] He died March 10, 1858. His funeral sermon was preached, on March 12, by Rev. Leonard Bacon, in the Center Church. The following Sunday commemorative sermons by Rev. S. W. S. Dutton[51] and Rev. George P. Fisher, were heard in the North Church, New Haven, and in the College Chapel.

On Friday afternoon, February 17, 1860, Professor Goodrich returned home from a lecture delivered to his theological class, feeling quite unwell, and before that day was done he had passed away.

Professor Josiah W. Gibbs swooned a short time before his death on March 25, 1861, while hearing a recitation, "and never met his class again except to give them his parting words, in which he expressed his gratitude that he had been permitted to finish some literary work which he feared he should not live to complete, and delicately urged them, by a reference to his own feeling at the close of life to be faithful to their calling."[52]

Each one of the four professors, therefore, with the exception of Dr. Fitch, taught until very near, or on the day of his death, and Professor Fitch was responsible for only one subject (Homiletics) in the course of study.

---

50. Among the "Divinity Papers" is a single sheet of paper, on the back of which is written, "Copy of my resignation, July 13th, 1857". The paper bears the marks of the one used by him in the first writing of the resignation, words and phrases being scratched out, apparently to give way to ones which better expressed his thought.
51. The author, while a student, of a group of lecture notes used as a source in this study.
52. George E. Day, Josiah Gibbs, in Yale College, A Sketch of Its History, ed. by W. L. Kingsley, Vol. II, p. 40.

CHAPTER XIV

THE SIGNIFICANCE OF THE PERIOD

THE SIGNIFICANCE OF THE PERIOD

The Theological Department in Yale College inherited the cultural traditions of the institution out of which it grew. The charter under which the seminary began its work had been won for Yale College in 1745. The personnel of the governing body of Yale College, the President and Fellows, was agreed upon during the administration of President Stiles. The freedom of action enjoyed by the Faculty of the Theological Department in the governance of the seminary's affairs had been granted as a result of President Dwight's efforts in 1795. Perhaps of more importance, the Theological Department enjoyed the privilege of being at once a part of a venerable institution which had been established with a major purpose of the training of the ministry in the minds of its founders, had expanded its facilities for such training by establishing a Professorship of Divinity in 1755, and had as its leaders men, such as President Dwight, who were anxious for the establishment of such a school as the Theological Department came to be.

Several major factors were influential in bringing about the demand for the founding of a Theological Department at Yale College. The secularization of the course of study, notably in the introduction of mathematics with the coming of Thomas Clap to the Presidency, of English literature and Oriental literature under President Stiles, and the expansion of the natural sciences, during President Dwight's administration, had broadened the curriculum to such a degree that it became apparent that the function of the College was to give a basic preparation in several branches of study, and that professional schools in law, medicine and theology should be established for special training in these fields. The first score of years in the nineteenth century constituted a period when the number of professional schools in general, and theological seminaries in particular, grew apace. Meanwhile the churches had awakened to a new life with the success of the revival movements under Jonathan Edwards and his successors of the next two generations. Also just at this time the great expanse of the new territory to the west began to receive a large population, and Christian men and women were awakened to the need of evangelization in that section of the country. Growing out of these influences came an increasing realization on the part of those connected with Yale College, Faculty and students, that the old methods of theological instruction by a resident pastor, or by one Professor of Divinity, were wholly inadequate for the contemporary religious needs. Evidences of this dissatisfaction are to be found in President Dwight's interest in the founding of the Theological Seminary at Andover, and the attempt of a group of Yale College graduates, on their own initiative, to obtain theological instruction from four Professors in the College.

The initial step taken in the year 1822 for the establishment of the Theological Department in Yale College came in the form of a petition by students addressed to the College Faculty, requesting that they be organized into a "Theological Class". Eleazer T. Fitch, who as the Professor of Divinity, felt most responsible, presented a statement to the Prudential Committee of the Corporation supporting their petition. The Yale College Faculty substantiated his statement in a resolution addressed to the President and Fellows. The latter body, therefore, took steps to raise funds for the establishment of a Professorship of Didactic Theology. A request to the General Assembly of Connecticut for financial aid had only recently been rejected, so subscriptions were taken in the city of New Haven. Success in this endeavor was largely due to the earnest efforts of Professors Goodrich and Fitch. The Rev. Mr. Nathaniel W. Taylor was chosen as the occupant of the chair of Didactic Theology and the President and Fellows granted permission for the Theological Department to begin its sessions in the fall of the year, 1822.

The four men who constituted the Faculty of the Theological Department during the years 1822-1858 were Nathaniel W. Taylor, Eleazer T. Fitch, Chauncey A. Goodrich, and Josiah W. Gibbs. Each of these men was the possessor of many and valuable talents. Professor Taylor, in view of his dominant personality, and since the thought of the time was largely devoted to theological questions, was considered the out-

standing man of the group. He has taken his place among the
leading propounders of the "New England Theology". Professor Gibbs was a man who was in great contrast to Dr. Taylor.
Professor Gibbs was modest and unassuming, and was a scholar
who weighed carefully, sometimes so carefully as to reach no
definite decision, every question at issue. As a result,
the subject of theology, through Professor Taylor, dominated
the course of study to such an extent as to place Professor
Gibbs' subjects in the study of the literature of the Bible
in a secondary position.

After Professor Gibbs joined the Faculty in the year
1826, Eleazer T. Fitch, who was the Professor of Divinity in
the College, was responsible for only one course in the Theological Department, Homiletics. Professor Goodrich, who became a faculty member of the Theological Department in the
year 1839, by sheer ability in his field of Rhetoric and
"Pastoral Charge" greatly influenced the students in the
Senior year. However, as a whole, the seminary was almost
completely given over to the study of theology. The study
of Church History was entirely neglected in this period, no
provision being made for a Professorship in this field of
study until the appointment of Professor George P. Fisher
in the year 1861.

The construction of the curriculum in this period was
dominated by a faculty psychology, and a conception of
"mental discipline". The lecture method was used almost entirely, with student expression taking the form of the writ-

ing of "dissertations", and the carrying on of discussion subsequent to the lecture by the professor. Dr. Taylor habitually gave his students an opportunity to express their views, but the discussion took on the form of a polemic debate between teacher and pupil, and in view of his experience and ability the professor won. In this way the students of Dr. Taylor were indoctrinated with his system of theology, which theology was of a much more progressive type than could be obtained at other seminaries in the United States at that time, being regarded as heretical by some of the rival schools.

The plan of the course of study which was followed during this period appears to have been derived from one used by the University of Halle. The outstanding feature of this classification of the several fields of study was that each of the subjects was considered a part of Theology and at the same time a Science, e.g. the science of Pastoral Theology. This plan of study was followed so closely throughout the thirty-six years of this period that the course of study for the Theological Department which was printed in the annual "Catalogue of the Officers and Students of Yale College", beginning with the year 1850/51, was almost identical with the plan outlined in the "Principles and Regulations of the Theological Department in Yale College", which was adopted in 1833. Each subject in this course of study was logically placed in a certain position in the plan, with little or no value accruing from a comparison of one type of subject matter with another. For example, the Junior Year was confined almost entirely to the study of the Hebrew and Greek languages, the Middle Year was almost entirely confined to theology, and the last year to Homiletics and kindred subjects.

A course in Chronology was also given in the Junior Year. It appears that much valuable time was spent upon topics which were concerned with the several divisions of time, e.g. the day, the week, etc., and with such questions as the number of years between the Creation and the Flood. These relatively unimportant matters were made the object of technical and laborious investigation. Such an emphasis is indicative of the stern linguistic scholarship of the time, which one admires when it is applied to more important problems. The most important course in the last half of the Junior year was that of "Mental Philosophy, including the Will", in which Professor Taylor laid the foundation for the courses in theology of the subsequent year.

In the Middle Year the course, "Exegetical Study of the Scriptures and Dissertations", was continued. However, this year was almost entirely given over to the study of theology under the tutelage of Professor Taylor. The lectures were divided among the following courses: Moral Philosophy, Moral Government, Natural Theology, Necessity and Evidences of Revelation, and Systematic (or Revealed) Theology, which followed each upon the other in that order. In these lectures Professor Taylor presented his "theological system" to his students.

In the Senior Year, with the exception of Professor Fitch's "Homiletics", Professor Goodrich was responsible for the courses in "Pastoral Theology". Professor Goodrich gave lectures upon the subject of "Rhetoric" which were designed to parallel Dr. Fitch's course in Homiletics and to make the latter more practical. The lectures on "Expository Preaching" also appear to have been given in a form which should have trained the young minister in the art of sermon-making.

The conception of the ministry which was prevalent during the period under review limited that profession very largely to the "preaching of the word". In order to preach successfully one was expected to know the original languages of the Bible, possess a sound view of theology, and know how to preach. The Theological Department in Yale College, measured by this standard of its time does not appear to have been unsuccessful in training the young men who attended the institution for the ministry. In the light of this standard the point of greatest weakness, besides the complete neglect of a course in Church History, is found in the secondary position occupied by the study of the Greek and Hebrew languages. This inferior position was probably due to the dominance of theology in the thought of the times and in the curriculum. Professor Taylor, it appears, made firm disciples of the theological system which he propounded; Professor Goodrich gave practical course in Pastoral Theology. But not all of the students of the Theological Department became ministers. About one fourth of the alumni of the period under review were teachers, foreign missionaries, or were engaged in general religious work. No provision was made for the training in the special techniques needed for the successful pursuit of these vocations. This need was not recognized by the leaders of the Theological Department in Yale College, later Yale Divinity School, according to the course of study as outlined in the annual catalogues, until the year 1900.

Judged in the light of the knowledge of a later period, the institution in company with other seminaries of that day, in a greater or less degree, also fell far short in providing for the students some exercise in practical religious service. According to the statutes of the school the students were not allowed to preach until near the end of the Senior year. Perhaps it was a wise plan to require the students to wait until greater maturity would make their preaching more valuable. However, participation in religious activity on the part of the students was almost entirely limited to service in some Sunday School, or in revivals of religion in the College or in a nearby church.

New Haven, the community of the Theological Department, bore, in the period under review, the aspect of a rural village which was rapidly growing into a city. The era of city missionary work did not begin in this community until the 1860's, probably partially on account of the strained relations between the students and the "town-boys" at this time.

Although the period 1822-1858 witnessed the rapid growth of Sunday Schools in New Haven, as elsewhere in the United States, revivals of religion constituted the dominant interest in the life of the churches, and it is in these that the theological students appear to have been most active. There was no plan in the Theological Department in Yale College whereby the religious activities of the students were organized and directed in the interest of making the services which the students rendered of greater value to the churches and to the students themselves. In fact, in view of the limited possibilities for religious activity, it appears that little or nothing of a practical nature was engaged in by the students. In the discussion of the fine points of a theology which still wore some of the vestments of medieval thought, it must have been entirely too easy for the students to theorize and to become so academic as to lose all contact with the world of definite religious experience. Theology and religion were divorced in the religious thought of the times, and appear also to have been separated in the minds of the Faculty, according to Professor Goodrich's discussion of the relation between theology and religion.

The initiative of the students found its expression in the organization and maintenance of the several student societies. The Moral and Rhetorical Society was almost entirely devoted to the debate and discussion of questions of a religious and social nature, particularly the former. In its development it became more and more an official organization of the school during the last fifteen years of its history. In this period it appears to have been somewhat dominated by the perennial presidency of Professor Taylor. The Society of Inquiry Respecting Missions was chiefly devoted to the interests of the foreign missionary enterprise and was composed of both theological and academic students. The Society for Christian Research, which was composed entirely of theological students and existed during the years 1825-37, had a name and used techniques which were worthy of the twentieth century. Its interests were depicted in its committees on Foreign Missions, Domestic Missions, People of Colour, Seamen, and Correspondence. This Society was active in the gaining of funds for the Professorship of Sacred Literature in the Theological Department in Yale College in 1827. Its members were also the instigators of the "Theological Atheneum" which was founded for the purpose of establishing a reading room for periodicals to be connected with the Theological Department. Arising out of the work of the Society for Christian Research and the Society of Inquiry Respecting Missions came the movement known as the "Illinois Band" which was quite influential in the building of the state whose name it bears.

The Libraries available for the use of the students of the Theological Department in Yale College were the College Library, and the Libraries of the Linonian, the Brothers in Unity, and the Rhetorical Societies. A little over two-thirds of the members of the Theological Department during the period 1822-1858 withdrew books from the College Library, a little less than two-thirds from the Moral and Rhetorical Library, and about one-fourth of the students used each of the Libraries of the Linonian and Brothers in Unity Societies. About three-fourths of the lists of annual withdrawals from the College Library contained the names of books which were devoted to subjects of a theological nature. The trend at the end of the period, however, was in the direction of a much greater use of the College Library as compared with the other Libraries, and in the direction of a more varied type of reading by a larger number of students. The Libraries appear to have been regarded in this period as "treasure-houses", which were open only a few hours each week, for the withdrawal of books, and then by a limited number of all the students connected with the College, which favored students were required to pay a fee for the loaning of certain books. Some of the books were declared free of taxation for the theological students by their Professors. The selection of books so designated, however, appears have been almost entirely concerned with theological subjects in direct relation to the course of study, and in this way the students of the Theological Department were not encouraged in the reading of a varied selection of topics . Attempts at supplying the need for a reading room were made by the organization of the "Theological Atheneum" in the Theological Department, and by a plan formulated by Professor Gibbs for a reading room connected with the College Library.

It should be of value at this point to endeavor to determine from the data just reviewed how the student of this period in the Theological Department in Yale College spent his time. The attendance at lectures given by the Professors appears to have required between ten and twelve hours each week. "Dissertations" were written by the students on these lectures, a single dissertation probably comprising from five to ten pages. According to the one volume which is at hand four or five of these were read by the Professor each year. One examination was given each year near its close. At this time the students were orally examined for a day or a day and a half. Of the three Societies in the Theological Department, the Society for Christian Research and the Society of Inquiry Regarding Missions held monthly sessions, the Rhetorical Society met each week. The average number of books withdrawn from the Yale College Library per student per year was 9.2. About the same number were withdrawn annually per student from each of the Libraries of the three Societies. However, about three-fourths of the students appear to have used only one Library. Activities of a religious nature participated in in the community were almost entirely limited to service in a Sunday School or in a revival of religion. The customs of the day probably limited the number of social activities which were deemed becoming a theological student. Little was made of holidays and seasons. The beginning of the era of organized athletics at Yale College belongs to a subsequent period. Therefore, although it is not a question on which there is complete data, the student who attended the Theological Department in Yale College during the period under review appears to have experienced far less demand upon his time, in the matter of class attendance, writing of dissertations or essays, religious activity in the community, and social life in general, than is required of a student in the Yale Divinity School in 1933. The student of the earlier period, however, appears to have devoted a greater part of his time and energy to the preparation for and the attendance of the meetings of the various student societies, than his successor of the present era.

Theological controversy was a prevailing interest in the Theological Department in Yale College during this period. Three of the four professors were active participants in these metaphysical debates. The emphasis on theology in the course of study, the increase and decrease in enrollment parallel to the increase and decrease in the public interest of these controversies, and the extent to which current theological issues were discussed in the societies organized by the students, are evidence of the importance of these controversies to the life of the institution.

Of the entire group of students who attended the Theological Department during the period under review almost three-fourths were natives of New England. Of the alumni of this period all those who were Congregationalists at some time in their lives constituted almost four-fifths of the entire group. The institution, at this period of its history, therefore, appears to have been a seminary which was largely devoted to the training of the young men of New England for the Congregational denomination. However, the Theological Department was established at a time when the churches of New England were awakening to the needs of the "West", and were organizing for work in Home Missions. Through the activities of the "Illinois Band" and another group which went to Iowa, and still others who settled in Ohio, about one-fourth of the alumni of the Theological Department served in the "West". However, relatively few, (twenty-nine, 3.7 percent) as compared with the seminaries at Andover, Massachusetts and at Princeton, New Jersey, became foreign missionaries. The reasons for this small number appear to have been the influence of the "Illinois Band", and the fact that Professor Taylor urged his students to serve churches in New England where they could give him support against those who were attacking him on account of his theology.

The Theological Department, with the Law and Medical Departments, seems to have suffered during the period under observation from the attitude of the administrators of Yale College which looked upon the undergraduate institution as the object for their major concern, and considered the several Departments as mere additions to the venerable College, and appendages to its organization. Presidents Day and Woolsey each expressed in his inaugural address the opinion that the Academic Department was the chief concern of the President of Yale College, and each pointed out the importance of the tradition which dictated that the President should also be an instructor in this Department. Such a state of affairs was a natural result of the historical development of the several Departments, the Law Department and Theological Department having each begun with the adding of one Professorship to Yale College. The result of this attitude, however, was that each Department was left alone in its struggle for existence. The President of Yale College was supposed to meet with the Faculty of the Theological Department in their regular sessions, but according to Professor, later President, Dwight, he seldom did so. This <u>laissez faire</u> policy extended into the Theological Department itself. There was no Dean of the Theological Faculty. Each Professor was responsible for his own course of study, and for student attendance at his lectures.

The administration of finances was carried on with little or no organization or plan. The subscription of funds was made by personal solicitation, for the most part among the citizens of New Haven. The salaries of Professors Gibbs and Goodrich were continually in doubt. Perhaps during the years when the attendance of students was large and the institution prosperous to a casual observer, the friends of the school may have been deceived concerning its condition, but when it began noticeably to decline they still made no efforts to repair the financial situation of the school. As a result, at the end of the period 1822-1858, the funds of the Theological Department totaled about fifty thousand dollars.

The institution was poor financially in every respect. Its funds for the payment of the salaries of professors were entirely inadequate. The Theological Department in Yale College could not compare favorably with other institutions in scholarships offered to indigent students, and the building which housed the school did not have suitable facilities for classroom activities, for social or public gatherings, and was about to be torn down to make room for the erection of a building for the Academic Department.

It is not surprising, then, that the last decade of the period under review witnessed a sharp decline in the attendance of students in the Theological Department in Yale College. Probably the major factor, other than financial, which brought about this decline was the fact that, in the minds of progressive religious leaders, and certainly in regard to the needs of the time, religious thought had changed from a theological to a Biblical emphasis. The Professors of the Theological Department had fought and won an apparently worthwhile battle for the freedom of man in the field of theology, but now that the times had changed, probably in part on account of their own contributions, they continued to reëmphasize the old issues. The strength of the school in the early years proved to be its weakness in the later years.

Another factor which contributed to the decline of the Theological Department in the last decade of the period under review was the fact that the members of the Faculty were in their declining years. There was no provision whereby any one of them could be made an emeritus professor. Perhaps the scarcity of funds would not have allowed the execution of such a plan if it had been suggested; nor were any young men appointed as members of the Faculty to sustain the four who were in office. The result was that three of the four professors were lost to the Department in a period of three years and the fourth resigned two years later.

The effect on the subsequent period was very great. Since the school had been built around, and was dependent upon the personalities of four professors, with their passing the school was in danger of extinction. When Professor Taylor died in March, 1858, the funds belonging to the Professorship of Didactic Theology were insufficient for the obtaining of a successor. Noah Porter, Professor of Mental and Moral Philosophy in the Academic Department, was made acting Professor of Didactic Theology in addition to his first professorship. Timothy Dwight, who had been appointed in 1858 to aid Professor Gibbs in his work, received the added responsibility of the chair of Pastoral Theology when Professor Goodrich died in 1860. In 1861, after the death of Professor Gibbs, it was a question in the minds of the friends of the Theological Department as to whether its condition warranted a reorganization. This question was answered in the affirmative, however, and plans were made whereby George P. Fisher, the Professor of Divinity in the College, was to become the Professor of Ecclesiastical History, James Mason Hoppin, who had been Pastor of a church in Salem, Massachusetts, was made Professor of the Pastoral Charge, and Henry H. Hadley, an Instructor in Union Theological Seminary, the Professor of Hebrew Language and Literature. The future of the seminary was so questionable that the last named, after one year of service, took the opportunity offered him to be a Professor in the Union Theological Seminary.

Little could be done during the Civil War in regard to the raising of funds for the institution, but between the years 1866 and 1870 the financial condition of the school was greatly improved, chiefly through the efforts of Professor Timothy Dwight who regularly contributed his salary to the funds of the Department and led in its rehabilitation. A new Divinity Hall was dedicated in the year 1869, and with its erection the attendance of students almost doubled within two years. In the year 1871 President Samuel Harris of Bowdoin College was chosen for the Professorship of Didactic Theology, which Professorship had been only temporarily supplied since the death of Nathaniel W. Taylor in 1858. In this same year (1871) the Theological Department's first Library, made possible through the liberality of Mr. Henry Trowbridge of New Haven, was placed in the New Divinity Hall, and the Lyman Beecher Lectureship on Preaching was founded. The annual Catalogue of Yale College for the year 1872 speaks of "worship in the Seminary Chapel", which building was soon designated "Marquand Chapel".

In 1873 the Lowell Mason Library of Church Music was given to the Seminary; and in 1874 a West Divinity Hall was erected, which structure came to be known as Taylor Hall. These important improvements during the period 1869 - 1874 were indicative of the new life then beginning for the Theological Department in Yale College.

BIBLIOGRAPHY

- 448 -

BIBLIOGRAPHY

MANUSCRIPTS

1. Records and Reports

Benevolent Library. Records of Books Lent. 1842-1852.

Brothers in Unity Society, Yale College. Records of Meetings. July 10, 1816 - Mar. 12, 1828.

Brothers Library. Numerical Catalogue of Books. ca. 1830; ca. 1836; ca. 1847; 1848-9; 1849, 1850. 6 vols.

Brothers Library. Register of Borrowers. 1825?, 1832?, 1832/33, 1841, 1847, 1860. 6 vols.

By the Govenor in Council & Representatives of His Majesties Colony of Connecticot in General Court Assembled Newhaven: October 9th. An Act for Liberty to Erect a Collegiate School.

By the Governour and Company of his Majesties Colony of Connecticut in New England in America. An Act for the more full and compleat Establishment of Yale College in New Haven and for enlarging the Powers and Privileges thereof. 1745.

Calliopean Library, Yale College. Numerical Catalogue of Books. 1830; 1837. 2 vols.

Calliopean Library, Yale College. Register of Borrowers. 1825-1852. 7 vols.

Calliopean Society, Yale College. Catalogue of Books recently added to the Library. 1842.

Calliopean Society, Yale College, List of Officers. 1842, 1846-52. 1 p.

Church of Christ in Yale College. Records. 1757-1877. 2 vols.

Club of the Outs or Circle of Retired Clergymen and Laymen. Record. 1846-79.

Connecticut Governor and Council. Papers relating to Yale College. 1718-1721. "Transcribed carefully" by Henry Steves. 1845.

Connecticut Charitable Education Society. Constitution and Records. 1815-1877.

Connecticut Missionary Society. Miscellaneous Papers. 1793-1804.

Convention of the Congregational Ministers in Connecticut. Minutes. 1826-31.

Daggett, Naphtali. Smithtown Records and other Family Records. 16 leaves.

Eagle Bank, New Haven. Record of the Meetings of Directors, Jan. 1812 - June 1826; and of Meetings of the Committee of Stockholders and their agents with their accounts, etc., June 1826 - May 1834.

Foreign Missionary Band. The Biographical Sketch-Book. 1835.

The Laws of Yale College, made and established by the President and Fellows. 1745, 1772, 1795. 3 editions.

Leges Collegii Yalensis. 1728.

Linonia Library. Names of Donors to the Library and a Numerical Catalogue of the Library. ca. 1829.

Linonia Library. Numerical Catalogue of Books. ca. 1830; between 1831-4; 1834; after 1841; 1863. 5 vols.

Linonia Library. Register of Borrowers. 1807-1812, 1822-1831, 1842-1852. 11 vols.

Linonia Society. Prudential Committee Records. Oct. 13, 1858 - Oct. 12, 1861.

Linonia Society. Records of Meetings. Oct. 29, 1845 - April 1, 1863. 3 vols.

Linonia Society. Treasurer's Accounts. July 23, 1791 - July 1842. 2 vols.

Minutes of the Committee appointed by the General Association of Connecticut for the direction of Missionary Service in States to the Westward. 1793-1794; 1799-1801.

Moral and Rhetorical Library. Numerical and Alphabetical Catalogue of Books. ca. 1845-49.

Moral and Rhetorical Library. Register of Borrowers. 1820-1843. 5 vols.

Moral Society, Yale College. Records. April 6, 1797 - March 10, 1841. Books A, B, and C.

New Haven, Trinity Church. Protestant Episcopal Sunday School Teachers' Society. Records. 1830-40.

New Haven, Wooster Place Congregational Church. Records. 1854-57.

On the Subject of Missions, and Statement of the Funds of the Missionary Society of Connecticut for the year 1804. 12 pp.

Orders and Appointments to be Observed in the Collegiate School in Connecticut. Editions of 1718, 1720, 1721, 1727.

Philagorian Society. Constitution and Records. 1828-30.

President and Fellows of Yale College. Minutes. 1701-1874. Termed "Proceedings of the Trustees" - 1701-1745. The original minutes for the years 1701-1716 are not available; records for a few later years are also lacking. In most every case, however, official copies of the originals have been deposited in the office of the Secretary of Yale University.

Report of the Committee appointed by the General Association to collect money for Missions. Cheshire. June, 1793. 4 pp.

Reports of the Committees appointed annually by the President and Fellows of Yale College to attend the

Examination of Students in the Theological Department.
Dec., 1832; Aug. 13, 1834; Aug. 15, 1837; Aug. 14, 1838;
April 19, 1846; April 16 and 17, 1850; July 24, 1854;
May 16, 1872.

Report of the Committee of the President and Fellows
on the Inquiry concerning the sense in which the assent
to articles of faith required of Professors in Yale
College has been understood. August, 1834. 3 pp.

Report to the Presidential Committee on Funds of
Theological Department. June 30, 1849. 2 pp.

Rhetorical Society. Records. 1841-1862. Books D and E.

Rhetorical Society. Treasurer's Book. 1835-53.

Society for Christian Research. Constitution,
Minutes. 1825-37.

Theological Atheneum. Constitution and Members.
1829. 8 pp.

Theological Reading Room. Treasurer's Account
Book. Nov. 15, 1831.

United Band of Foreign Missions in Yale University.
Constitution, By-Laws and Records. 1831-38.

Yale College Church Committee. Minutes and Records.
1837-64.

Yale College, Dwight Hall. Records, Scrapbooks, etc.
1880-1921.

Yale College Faculty. Records of Meetings. April
6, 1807 - May 2, 1883. 4 vols.

Yale College Librarian's Reports to the President
and Fellows. 1827, 1845-53, 1854, 1863.

Yale College Library. Day Books recording the
withdrawal of books. 1808-1873. 12 vols.

Yale College Library. Names of Borrowers. 1846-1866.

Yale College Library. Librarian's MS. Catalogue of Books. ca. 1857-1870.

Yale College Library. Register of Donations. January 1854 - December 1871.

Yale College Missionary Society. Constitution and Records of Meetings. 1852-65.

2. Students' Notes of Professors' Lectures.

Avery, S. C. Notes on Dr. Taylor's Lectures on Mental Philosophy, Moral Philosophy, Moral Government, Natural Theology, Evidences of Christianity, Revealed Theology; on Dr. Fitch's Homiletics. Index to Sermons by Dr. Fitch. 2 vols. 522, 526 pp.

Baldwin, Elijah. Notes on a Course of Study in Theology pursued at the Theological Seminary, Andover. 216 pp.

Barnum, S. W. Notes of Dr. Taylor's Lectures in Mental Philosophy. 440 pp.

Daggett, David L. Miscellaneous Notes on Dr. Dwight's Remarks on Rhetoric. 1607. 59 pp.

Daggett, L. A.?. Heads of a Number of Sermons by Dr. Dwight. 62 pp.

Day, George E. Outlines of Professor Fitch's Homiletics; second part of Dr. Taylor's Lectures in Systematic Theology. Lectures by Rev. Leonard Bacon on Government and Discipline of the Church. Professor Gibbs on Theological Encyclopedia. 343 pp.

Dutton, S. W. S. Notes on Dr. Taylor's Lectures on the Necessity and Evidences of Revelation on Revealed Theology. Professor Fitch's Lectures on Sermonizing. 211 pp.

Dutton, S. W. S. Notes of Dr. Taylor's Lectures in Mental Philosophy. 60 pp.

Dutton, S. W. S., Notes on Dr. Fitch's Sermons.

Ely, W. D., Notes on Dr. Taylor's Mental Philosophy, Ethics, Moral Government, Natural Theology; Dr. Fitch on Homiletics; Rev. Bacon on Ecclesiastical Organizations. In the same volume: Stoddard, T. T. Notes on Professor Goodrich's Lectures on Pastoral Theology. 582 pp.

Fitch, E. T., Notes of Doctrinal Sermons and Lectures by Dr. Fitch and others. 1829-40. 2 vols.

Fitch, E. T., Notes of Chapel Sermons, Yale College. 1845-48. 365 pp.

Goodrich, Chauncey. Notes on Mental Philosophy. 330 pp.

Larned, W. A., Notes on Commentaries on the Acts, Philippians, and James; Notes on Hebrew Philology and Principles of Interpretation; Notes on Sacred Geography, Chronology. 3 vols. 27, 17, 35 pp.

Merwin, S. J. M., Notes on Dr. Fitch's Homiletics; on Professor Goodrich's Homiletics; on Dr. Taylor's Theology; on Professor Goodrich's Duties of the Pastoral Office, and Missions. 3 vols. 158, 273, 295 pp.

Notes on Dr. Taylor's Lectures on Revealed Theology, on Natural Theology; on Professor Gibbs' Sacred Chronology and Historical Chronology. By an unknown student. 324 pp.

Pierson, Abraham. Notes of Lectures attended at Harvard College. 1667.

Saxton, F. A. Notes on Dr. Taylor's Theology; on Professor Fitch's Homiletics; on Professor Gibbs' Classification of the Theological Sciences. 2 vols. 587, 581 pp.

Trumbull, Benjamen. Notes on the Sermons of Dr. Daggett preached in the Chapel of Yale College. 1755-59. 54, 12 pp.

3. Memorials and Petitions

Carrington, George, and other students. Petition to the Prudential Committee of the Corporation. 1826. 4 pp.

Daggett, Naphtali. Memorial to the General Assembly. Oct. 13, 1767. 3 pp.

Day, George E. Petition of the Theological Faculty to the President and Fellows. April 17, 1884. 3 pp.

Dwight, Timothy. Facts and Suggestions in regard to the Funds of the Theological Department. A Report submitted to the Yale Corporation by the Theological Faculty. July 20, 1867. 7 pp.

Fitch, E. T. Memorial presented to the First Church and Society in New Haven on the call of Rev. N. W. Taylor to the chair of Didactic Theology in the Theological Department of Yale College. 1822. 21 pp.

Memorial of the Theological Professors to the Yale Corporation. 1865. 4 pp.

Memorial of the Theological Faculty concerning the site of new Theological Buildings. 1866. 7 pp.

Porter, Noah. Paper concerning the Union of the Theological Department with the Seminary at East Windsor. 1856? 6 pp. 2 copies.

Proposals from the President and Fellows of Yale College to the General Association of Connecticut respecting the Examination and public approbation of candidates for the work of the ministry educated in the Theological Department of Yale College. 1861? 6 pp.

Resolution of the Faculty of Yale College to the Corporation. 1822. 6 pp.

Statement of the Present Situation of Yale College, with Subscriptions received. June, 1822. 13 pp.

Statement of the Theological Department to the Prudential Committee of the Corporation concerning the purchase of the "Hadley" lot for the expansion of the School. March 18, 1882. 3 pp.

Washburn, F. A. Petition to the Faculty of the New Haven Divinity School. Feb. 6, 1841. 3 pp.

4. Correspondence

Adler, G. J. 3 Letters to Professor Gibbs. New York: Sept. 27, 1858; July 26, 1860; Oct. 4, 1860.

Arms, H. P. Letter to Noah Porter. Norwich Town: Jan. 10, 1856. 4 pp.

Bacon, Leonard. Letter to President Day, declining the Professorship of Rhetoric. New Haven: Sept. 6, 1839. 1 p.

Bacon, Leonard. Letter to Noah Porter Sr. New Haven: Jan. 15, 1856. 3 pp.

Bacon, Leonard. Letter to President Woolsey. New Haven: July 27, 1857. 2 pp.

Baird, Robert. Letter to C. A. Goodrich. Aug. 9, 1838. 2 pp.

Brainerd, D. L. Letter to Professor Noah Porter. Lyme, Conn.: April 11, 1864. 19 pp.

Bushnell, Horace. Letter to J. W. Gibbs. Hartford: April 4, 1854. 2 pp.

The Church in Yale College. Letter to the Alumni of Yale College at Andover Seminary. New Haven: July 26, 1816. 3 pp.

Clap, Thomas. Letter to Col. Philip Livingston, in thanks for gift for the Professorship of Divinity. New Haven: April 22, 1766. 1 p.

Clap, Thomas. Letter to Joseph Bellamy. New Haven: Aug. 6, 1763. 2 pp.

Clap, Thomas. Letter to Naphtali Daggett. New Haven: March 20, 1755. 1 p.

Clarke, William. 3 Letters to President Woolsey. Hartford: Jan. 31, 1856; Feb. 11, 1856; Feb. 29, 1856.

Cleaveland, F. J. Letter to President Woolsey, New Haven: Feb. 29, 1856. 3 pp.

Conant, Thomas J. Letter to J. W. Gibbs. Rochester: Sept. 14, 1855.

Cook, R. S. Letter to the President of the Society of Inquiry. New York: Feb. 7, 1844. 4 pp.

Cox, S. H. Letter to N. J. Taylor. New York: Sept. 2, 1825.

Daggett, Naphtali. Letter to President Stiles. New Haven: Feb. 28, 1769. 3 pp.

Daggett, Naphtali. Letter to the President and Fellows. New Haven: Sept. 11, 1780. 1 p.

Day, George E. Letter to E. C. Herrick. Walnut Hills, O.: April 18, 1857. 1 p.

Dwight, Timothy. 2 Letters to Professor F. B. Dexter. New Haven: June 26, 1882. July 4, 1882.

Fitch, E. T. Letter to Isaac Bird. New Haven: May 12, 1842. 3 pp.

Fitch, E. T. Letter to a Committee of the Faculty on his proposed resignation of his Professorship of Divinity. New Haven: June, 1852. 28 pp.

Fitch, E. T. 4 letters to President Day. Concord, N. H.: Oct. 20, 1822. 1 p. Andover: Aug. 4, (4 pp.) and 19, (2pp.), 1817. New Haven: Mar. 3, 1827. 7 pp.

Fitch, E. T. 2 Letters to the Yale Corporation. Resigning his Professorship of Divinity, July 13, 1852, 4 pp.; and resigning his Professorship of Homiletics, July 28, 1863, 1 p.

Fitch, W. W. Letter to the President and Fellows of Yale College. New Haven: July 24, 1861. 3 pp.

Fisher, George P. 2 Letters to President Woolsey. Andover: June 5, 1854. 4 pp. New Haven: 1856? 10 pp.

- 457 -

Foxcroft, Thomas. Letter to Elisha Williams.
Boston: June 14, 1750. 4 pp.

Gibbs, J. W. Copies of his own letters and other scattered writings filed in his "Correspondence". 1812-1860. 266 pieces.

Gibbs, J. W. 2 Letters to President Day. Salem, Mass.: Nov. 7, 1811. 1 p. Andover: Jan. 25, 1819. 2 pp.

Goodrich, C. A. Letter to Otis Baker. Yale College: April 22, 1830. 1 p.

Goodrich, C. A. Letter to Benjamen Curtis. New Haven: April 28, 1828. 3 pp.

Goodrich, C. A. 10 Letters to President Day. Hartford: May 24, 1815. 1 p. Durham: April 13, 1816. 1 p. Hartford: June 29, 1819. 1 p. Havre: Oct. 30, 1825. 4 pp. Jan. 10, 1826. 3 pp. London: May 29, 1826. 3 pp. Aug 22, 1826. 4 pp. New Haven: Aug. 1839. 3 pp. Berlin, Conn.: Mar. 16, 1835. 1 p. Lexington, Ky.: May 5, 1835. 4 pp.

Goodrich, C. A. Letter to Mrs. M. R. Dutton. New Haven: Dec. 30, 1847. 3 pp.

Goodrich, C. A. 3 Letters to E. C. Herrick. Yale College: Feb. 6, 1844. 1 p. Bristol: Aug. 21, 1850. 1 p. Hartford: July 4, 1853. 1 p.

Goodrich, C. A. 2 Letters to Professor E. Loomis. New Haven: July 27, 1830. 1 p. Mar. 27, 1832. 2 pp.

Genger, J. H. Letter to A. L. Alexander. New Haven: Feb. 13, 1835. 4 pp.

Harris, Samuel. 2 Letters to President Woolsey. Brunswick: May 2, 1871. 4 pp. July 1, 1871. 4 pp.

Parker, Joel. Letter to President Day. New York: Jan. 29, 1839. 3 pp.

Pierson, Abraham. Circular Letter to the Trustees of the Collegiate School. Killingworth: Jan. 12, 1706.

Pierson, Deacon Abraham. Letter to President Stiles. Killingworth: July 22, 1788. 4 pp.

Porter, Noah. 3 Letters to E. C. Herrick. Berlin: Nov. 1, 1853. Paris: 1853, 1854.

Shephard, John. Letter to Jonathan Edwards (the Younger). Nov. 20, 1793.

Silliman, Benjamin: Taylor, N. W.; Olmsted, Denison. Letter to E. T. Fitch. New Haven: June 4, 1852. 2 pp.

Society of Inquiry of Lane Seminary. Letter to the Society of Inquiry of Yale College. Cincinnati: Feb. 27, 1847. 1 p.

Society of Inquiry of Yale College. Letter to Isaac Bird. Yale College: Feb. 9, 1822. 1 p.

Taylor, Nathaniel. 2 Letters to President Day. New Haven: Dec. 5, 1820. 1 p. Hartford: Jan. 20, 1826. 2 pp.

Taylor, Nathaniel d. 2 Letters to the Yale Corporation defending himself against charges of heresy. New Haven: Aug. 21, 1834. 4, 4 pp.

Tyler, Bennet. 9 Letters to President Day. Dartmouth College: July, 1826. 2 pp. East Windsor: June 12, 1834. 3 pp. Mar. 8, 1838. 3 pp. Sept. 26, 1838. 3 pp. Oct. 24, 1838. 4 pp. May 28, 184-?. 10 pp. Dec. 8, 1842. 2 pp. "Windsor Hill": Mar. 4, 1846. 2 pp. "East Windsor Hill": Mar. 12, 1846. 3 pp.

Wales, Samuel. Letter to the New Haven County Association. Milford: Sept. 13, 1780. 4 pp.

Wales, Samuel. Letter to President Stiles. Milford: May 15, 1782. 1 p.

Watts, Isaac. Letter to Elisha Williams. Stoke Newington, near London: Aug. 16, 1734. 2 pp.

Williams, Elisha. Letter to his brother Solomon. New Haven: Dec. 30, 1775. 2 pp.

Williams, Elisha. Letter to Jared Ingersoll. Wethersfield: Feb. 22, 1753. 1 p.

Williams, Nathan. Letter to President Stiles. Tollend, Conn.: May 30, 1793. 4 pp.

5. Works

Catalogue of the Library of Yale College. Compiled by President Clap. 1743.

Clap, Thomas. The Ancient and Ecclesiastical Constitution of Colleges. 1755. 32 pp.

Clap, Thomas. The Annals of Yale College in New Haven from the first founding in the year 1701 to the year 1747. 1747. 60 pp. The same extended to the year 1765. 1765.

Clap, Thomas. Brief History and Vindication of Confessions of Faith. 1761? 66 pp.

Clap, Thomas. A Discourse on the Propriety of Using Natural, not Artificial Light. 12 pp.

Clap, Thomas. The Ecclesiastical Constitution of Colleges under the Jewish and Christian Dispensations. 1757. 33 pp.

Daggett, Naphtali. Collection of Sermons. Yale College: 1755-70.

Fitch, E. T. A Useful Life Prepares for a Peaceful Death. July 18, 1825.

Gibbs, J. W. Reminiscences of Professor J. L. Kingsley. (5 pp.) and a list of his writings. (2 pp.). 1861.

Porter, Noah. The Two-Hundredth Birthday of Bishop George Berkeley; a discourse at Yale College, Mar. 12, 1885.

Smith, Ralph Dunning. Sketches of the Graduates of Yale College, 1701-1767.

Stoddard, D. T. An Outline of the Grammar of the Modern Syriac. Oroomiah. 1853-55.

Stoddard, L. T. Astronomy Notes for a Textbook. 1852-53.

Stoddard, D. T. Lectures on Theology to Nestorian Students.

Taylor, N. W. Manuscript of a Sermon "No. 226, Glorifying God". Oct. 1816. 16 leaves.

Wales, Samuel. Twenty-six Sermons. Milford and New Haven: 1771-84.

Williams, Elisha. A Sermon, March 1745/6. Fourteen fragments of several leaves each, of sermons and lectures. ca. 1721-1725.

6. Miscellaneous

Aikman, Robert. Reminiscences of Dr. Nathaniel W. Taylor. 9 pp. ca. 1900.

Bacon, Leonard. Resignation as Acting Professor of Revealed Theology in the Theological Department of Yale College. Yale College: April 12, 1871. 3 pp.

Bidwell, d. H. Subscription of Three Hundred Dollars to the Theological Department. Philadelphia: Jan. 14, 1838.

Champion, Aristarchus. Subscription of Six Hundred Dollars to Professorship of Pastoral Charge. Rochester: Dec. 17, 1838. 2 pp.

Bushnell, Horace. Remarks to his Division of Students. 1831. 15 pp.

Christian Spectator. List of Original Subscribers. 1818.

Clap, Thomas. Address to Professor Daggett at the Establishment of the Church in Yale College. Sept. 1757. 2 pp.

Clap, Thomas. An Account of the Charges of building the New College, 1748-52. 52 pp.

Clap, Thomas. College Memoirs, location of students, etc. 1740-55. 80 pp.

Clap, Thomas. Letter on the Right of Appeal of College Students. Feb. 2, 1764. 12 pp.

Clap, Thomas. Reasons why it is necessary that the Sacrament be administered in the College. 1757? 4 pp.

Cleaveland, John. Diary. Jan. 15, 1741/42 - May 11, 1742.

Cutler, Timothy. Record of Three Marriages in Poston. June 1751 - Feb. 1752.

Daggett, Naphtali. Confession of Faith. Mar. 4, 1856. 15 pp.

Day, George E. Diary. April 24, 1832 - Dec. 20, 1837. 29 pp.

Day, Jeremiah. Charge Delivered to E. T. Fitch. 1817. 2 pp.

Day, Jeremiah. Minutes on Business for Yale Corporation Meetings. 1822-1846. 25 pieces.

Day, Jeremiah. Notes for decisions of Disputes, Yale College. 1817-26. 90 pp.

Dissertations written in the Junior and Middle Years in the Theological Department of Yale College. Author unknown. ca. 1828.

Dow, Daniel. Withdrawal of Charges against Professor N. W. Taylor. Aug. 21, 1834. 2 pp.

Fitch, E. T. His own Account of his Sermons preached. 1814-1856. 3 vols. Part I Enumeration (1-367), Part II Chronological Table of Preaching.

Gibbs, J. W. Notes concerning the Salary of his Professorship. Aug. 25, 1830. Sept. 7, 1830. 1 p.

Bibbs, J. W. Plan of a Reading Room for Periodicals in the Yale College Library. Oct., 1845. 2 pp.

Gibbs, J. W. Scheme of Classification of Topics for the Library. Catalogue. 1846? 2 pp.

Goodrich, C. A. Creed at the entrance on the Professorship of Pastoral Charge in the Theological Department. Oct. 23, 1839. 4 pp.

Goodrich, C. A. and Fitch, E. T. Note promising to pay the $5,000 needed for the establishment of the Theological Department. Sept. 10, 1822. 2 pp.

A List of Books given to the College of Connecticut in New England with names of Benefactors. Collected by Jeremy Dummer. London: Jan. 15, 1712/13.

Manuscripts Relating to the College Commons. 1820-29.

Principles and Regulations of the Theological Department in Yale College. Adopted by the President and Fellows, Aug. 21, 1830. 11 pp.

Recommendations for Students entering the Theological Department in Yale College. Forty-eight Letters from Churches and Ministers; forty-three from Seminaries; two from Colleges.

Sacred Wreath. Autograph Album presented to Rev. Leicester A. Sawyer in 1840, at his departure from New Haven.

Stiles, President Ezra. Itineraries. 1760-94. 6 vols.

Stiles, President Ezra. Literary Diary. 1769-1795. 15 vols.

Stiles, President Ezra. Miscellania (or Miscellaneous Papers or Miscellaneous Manuscripts). 1755-62. 2 vols.

Subscribers and Amounts given to the Professorship of Sacred Literature. January, 1829. 2 pp.

Taylor, N. W. Declaration of Faith and Signature. Dec. 31, 1822. 1 p.

Taylor, N. W. Resignation of his Professorship of Didactic Theology. July 13, 1857. 1 p.

Theological Department. Estimates of the Income for the year 1851/52. 4 pp.

Theological Department. Estimates of Income on the Theological and the Sacred Literature Funds. 1843/44 - 1848/49. 2 pp.

Wales, Samuel. Confession of Faith. June 12, 1782. 7 pp.

Wales, Samuel. Paper relinquishing part of his salary because of his illness, May 7, 1792. 1 p.

Woolsey, Theodore D. Minutes for the business of the Yale Corporation Meetings, 1851-70.

Yale College Society of Inquiry. Order of Procedure at a regular meeting. ca. 1847. 1 p.

PAMPHLETS

1. Unpublished Circulars

"Acts of the General Assembly of Connecticut with Other Documents Respecting Yale University. (Printed for the Use of the Corporation, not Published)." New Haven: 1901. 106 pp.

American Education Society for the Education of Pious Youth for the Gospel Ministry. "Constitution". 1827? 8 pp.

American Education Society. Circular making appeal for Fund. 3 pp.

Appeal for Library Building Funds, Yale College: Oct., 1843. 1 p.

"Circular" addressed to Citizens of New Haven concerning the loss of funds by the Theological Department in the Eagle Bank failure. July 27, 1827. 1 p.

Circular appealing for Funds for Indigent Students in the Theological Department. New Haven: May, 1862. 2 pp.

Circular Letter from Treasurer's Office Yale College, Soliciting funds for the Theological Department. 1859. 2 pp.

Circular of the Yale College Faculty. Aug. 1, 1828. 2 pp.

Circular to the Donors of the Drive for $100,000 for Yale College. Dec. 20, 1832. 2 pp.

Circular to the Friends of Yale College and of American Science. 1825. 2 pp.

Cogswell, William, Secretary of the American Education Society. 4 Circular Letters to President Day. Boston: Jan. 29, 1833. 3 pp. Jan. 13, 1834. 1 p. Feb. 10, 1836. 1 p. Feb. 1639. 2 pp. Partially MS.

Day, Jeremiah. "The Case of Yale College". July 30, 1832. 1 p.

Day, Jeremiah. "To the Citizens of New Haven." July 26, 1832. 1 p.

Fisher, George P. "Theological Education in Yale College." 1862? 7 pp.

"Memorial (Confidential) of the Yale College Faculty to the Corporation concerning the Finances of the Institution." March 30, 1878. 3 pp.

"Order of Exercises at the Anniversary of the Theological Department in Yale College." 1835-49; 1851.

"Remarks on the Present Situation at Yale College for the Consideration of its Friends and Patrons." 1817. 16 pp. The Same. Jan. 1823. 16 pp.

Riddel, Samuel H. Circular Letter to Jeremiah Day. May 10, 1849. 1 p.

"Rules of the Directors" of the American Education Society. 4 pp.

"Statement of the Course of Instruction, Expenses, etc." 1821. 8 pp.

"Statement of Facts pertaining to the Case of Yale College." Dec. 1, 1831. 3 pp.

"Statement of the Funds of Yale College." July 31, 1834. 2 pp.

"Statement of the Recent Donations to the Yale Theological Seminary up to Dec. 25th, 1869." 10 pp.

"To the Friends of Yale College (Private)". New Haven: Jan. 25, 1858. 8 pp.

"Yale College Fund of $150,000. New Haven: Sept. 1, 1854. 2 pp.

"Yale College. The Needs of the University, suggested by the Faculties to the Corporation, the Graduates, and the Benefactors and Friends of the Institution." July 10, 1871. 23 pp.

"Weekly Report of Classes in the African Sabbath School." 1835. 6 pieces.

Woolsey, President T. D. Circular Letter to the Clerical Fellows of Yale College. Dec. 29, 1855. 1 p.

2. Catalogues

Andover Theological Seminary. Catalogue of Those who have been Educated there. Andover: 1821. 15 pp.

Andover Theological Seminary. Catalogue of the Library. Andover: 1819. 161 pp.

Andover Theological Seminary. General Catalogue, 1808-1908. Boston: 1808. viii, 750 pp.

Andover Theological Seminary. Library of the Porter Rhetorical Society and the Society of Inquiry. Andover: 1830. 36 pp.

Catalogue of Books belonging to the Calliopean Society, Yale College. June, 1831. 38 pp. Feb. 16, 1837. 56 pp. Oct., 1841. 84 pp. Feb., 1846. 94 pp.

Catalogue of Books belonging to the Society of Brothers in Unity, Yale College. April, 1829. 31 pp. Sept. 1832. 39 pp. July, 1851. 294 pp.

Catalogue of Books in the Linonian, Brothers, and Moral Libraries, Yale College. New Haven: 1808. 24 pp. 1814. 27 pp. Jan. 1818. 31 pp. Sept. 1822. 39 pp. Nov. 1825. 52 pp.

Catalogue of Books belonging to the Linonian Society Yale College. New Haven: Aug. 1829. 35 pp. July 1834. 50 pp. July 1837. 82 pp. Supplement to the last edition, 16 pp. Oct. 1841. 152 pp. Nov. 1846. 274 pp. June 1860. 298 pp.

Catalogue of Books of the Morrison Education Society. Canton: 1838. 136 pp.

Catalogue of Books in the Library of Yale College. 1791. 50 pp. 1808. 80 pp. 1823. 100 pp.

Catalogue of the Calliopean Society, Yale College. New Haven: 1839. 32 pp.

Catalogue of the Library of the New Haven Young Men's Institute. New Haven: 1841. 65 pp.

Catalogue of the Members of the Linonian Society, Yale College. New Haven: 1832. 31 pp.

Catalogue of the Officers and Graduates of Yale University in New Haven, Connecticut, 1701-1924. New Haven: 1924. 832 pp.

Catalogue of the Officers and Students of the Theological Seminary, Andover, Massachusetts, Jan. 1839. Andover: 1839.

Catalogue of the Officers and Students of Yale College, 1852/53. Revised Edition. Pseudo. Springfield, Mass.: 1852. 35 pp.

- 467 -

<u>Catalogue of the Officers and Students of Yale College</u>. 1813/14 - 1885/86. <u>Catalogue of Yale University</u> 1886/87 - 1932/33.

<u>Catalogue of the Yale Divinity School</u>. 1889 - 1932/33. "School of Religion." 1914/15 - 1919/20.

<u>Collegii Yalensis, Quod est Novo-Portu Connecticutensum, Statutua, a Praeside et Sociis Sancita</u>. Novo Portu: MDCCLIX. 25 pp. (part MS). MDCCLXIV. 25 pp.

<u>Congregationalism before 1800. Catalogue of an Exhibition</u>. Anna M. Monrad, compiler. New Haven: 1915. 28 pp.

<u>A General Catalogue of the Theological Department in Yale College</u>. Published by the Students. New Haven: 1838. "Triennial Catalogue". 1841; 1844; 1847; and 1850. "General Catalogue". 1873; 1889; Supplement to 1889, 1900; 1922.

<u>General Statistical Catalogue of the Theological Seminary Bangor, Maine</u>. 1820-90. Bangor: 1890. 126 pp.

<u>The Laws of Yale College, in New Haven, in Connecticut, enacted by the President and Fellows</u>. New Haven: 1774-1862. 24 editions.

Princeton Theological Seminary. <u>Biographical Catalogue, compiled by Joseph H. Dulles, 1909</u>. Trenton, New Jersey: 1909. 681 pp.

<u>Theological Seminary of Yale College Annual Circular</u>. 1862/63. 1866/67 - 1878/79. 1882/83. 1883/84. "Yale Divinity School" 1889/90 - 1898/99.

3. Celebrations and Inaugurations

<u>Addresses at the Laying of the Corner Stone of the Divinity Hall of the Theological Department of Yale College. Sept. 22nd, 1869</u>. New Haven: 1869. 48 pp.

<u>Addresses at the Inauguration of Noah Porter into the Presidency of Yale College, Oct. 11, 1871</u>. New York: 1871. 65 pp.

Addresses at the Inauguration of Professors in the Theological Department of Yale College, Sept. 5, 1861. New Haven: 1861. 29 pp.

Addresses delivered at the Observation of the 100th Anniversary of the Establishment of the Harvard Divinity School, Oct. 5, 1916. Cambridge: 1917. 104 pp.

Addresses of Rev. Drs. Park, Post, and Bacon, at the Anniversary of the American Congregational Union, May, 1854. New York: 1854. 133 pp.

Celebration of the Fiftieth Anniversary of the Appointment of Professor William Henry Green as Instructor in Princeton Theological Seminary, May 5, 1896. New York: 1896. iv, 193 pp.

The Centennial Celebration of the Founding of Yale Divinity School, held in connection with the Fourteenth Annual Convocation, Oct. 23-25, 1922. New Haven: 1922. 24 pp.

Centennial of the Theological Seminary of the Reformed Church in America, 1784, 1884. New York. 1885. ii, 525 pp.

Discourses and Addresses at the Ordination of the Rev. Theodore Dwight Woolsey LL.D., to the ministry of the Gospel, and his Inauguration as President of Yale College, Oct. 21, 1846. New Haven: 1846. 100 pp.

Fiftieth Anniversary of the First Congregational Church, Princeton, Illinois, Mar. 23, 1881. Princeton: 1881. 45 pp.

Memorial of the Semi-Centennial Celebration of the Founding of the Theological Seminary at Andover. Andover: 1859. 242 pp.

A Memorial of the Semi-Centenary Celebration of the Founding of the Theological Institution of Connecticut. Hartford: 1884. 146 pp.

Memorial Volume of the Semi-Centennial Anniversary of Hartwick Seminary, held Aug. 21, 1866. Albany: 1867. 201 pp.

Memorial Volume of the First Fifty Years of the American Board of Commissioners for Foreign Missions. Boston: 1861. xiv, 462 pp.

Proceedings connected with the Semi-centennial Commemoration of the Professorship of Rev. Charles Hodge, in the Theological Seminary at Princeton, New Jersey, April 24, 1872. New York: 1872. 128 pp.

Princeton Theological Seminary. The Centennial Celebration of the Theological Seminary of the Presbyterian Church in the U.S., at Princeton, N.J., May 5, 6, 7, 1912. Princeton: 1912. xvi, 565 pp.

The Semi-Centennial Anniversary of the Divinity School of Yale College, May 15th and 16th, 1872. New Haven: 1872. 119 pp.

4. Records and Reports

African Improvement Society. Third Annual Report, Aug. 1929. New Haven: 1829. 16 pp.

American Board of Commissioners for Foreign Missions. Missionary Papers. I - XXIII.

American Board of Commissioners for Foreign Missions. Constitution, Laws, and Regulations. Boston: 1839. 23 pp.

American Education Society. Annual Reports of the Directors. 1-44. Andover: 1816-1823. Boston: 1826-1860.

American Home Missionary Society. Annual Reports by the Executive Committees. 1-35. New York: 1827-1861.

American Sunday School Union. Reports made at the Annual Meetings. Philadelphia: 1825-1860.

Andover Theological Seminary. Constitution and Associate Statutes. Boston: 1808. 68 pp. Andover: 1817. 40 pp. Andover: 1839. 38 pp.

The Baptist Theological Seminary of the State of New York. Constitution. New York: 1818. 8 pp.

Brothers in Unity, Yale College. Constitution and Laws. New Haven: 1861. 22 pp.

Congregational Churches in Connecticut. Records of the General Association. "Records", June 20, 1838 - June 19, 1799. Published Hartford: 1888. 198 pp. "Proceedings" 1800-1833. "Minutes" 1834-64. Hartford: 1800-1843. New Haven: 1844-64.

Congregational Churches in Illinois. Minutes of the General Association. Peoria; Galva; Quincy: 1853-54; 1856; 1858-63.

Connecticut Branch of the American Education Society. First Annual Report. New Haven: 1827. 23 pp.

Connecticut Sunday School Union. Annual Reports. New Haven: 1827, 1828, 1830.

Constitution and By Laws of the Linonian Society of Yale College. New Haven: 1863. 21 pp.

A Constitution of Civil Government for the People of the State of Connecticut, framed by a Convention of their Delegates and submitted to the People. Hartford: 1818. 24 pp.

The Convention of Delegates from the Synod of New York and Philadelphia, and from the Associations of Connecticut, held annually from 1766 to 1775, inclusive. Minutes. Hartford: 1843. 63 pp.

Copy of the Laws of Harvard College 1655, with an Introduction by Samuel A. Green. Cambridge: 1876. 11 pp.

General Association of Massachusetts Proper. Minutes. 1807-09, inc. 1810; 1812-14; 1818-20.

Massachusetts Missionary Society. Annual Reports of the Trustees. Nos. 24, 26, 28-36. Salem: 1823, 1825. Boston: 1826-1835.

Missionary Society of Connecticut. Annual Narratives, with a Statement of Funds. Hartford: 1801-1827; 1829.

Philadelphia Sunday School and Adult Union. Annual Reports. Philadelphia: 1819-1824.

Proceedings of the City of New Haven in the Removal of Monuments from its Ancient Burying Ground and in the Opening of a New Ground for Burial. New Haven: 1822. 32 pp.

President and Fellows of Yale College, to the Honorable General Assembly of the State of Connecticut. Memorial and Statement, May 7th, 1822. New Haven: 1822. 4 pp.

Presbyterian Churches in the United States of America. Minutes of the General Assembly. "Acts and Proceedings" Philadelphia: 1787-1802. "Minutes". Philadelphia: 1836-41, Old School. New York: 1838-50, New School.

Proceedings of the General Convention of Congregational Ministers, Delegates in the United States, held at Albany, New York, on the 5th, 6th, 7th, and 8th of October, 1852. New York: 1852. 95 pp.

Proceedings Relative to the Formation of the Morrison Education Society. Canton: 1826. 16 pp.

The Public Records of the Colony of Connecticut, from May, 1717, to April, 1725. Transcribed and edited by Charles J. Hoadley. Hartford: 1872. Vol. 6. iv, 602 pp.

Records of the Colony and Jurisdiction of New Haven, from May, 1653, to the Union. Edited by C. J. Hoadley. Hartford: 1858. iv, 626 pp.

Records of the Colony and Plantation of New Haven, from 1638 to 1649. Transcribed and edited by Charles J. Hoadley. Hartford: 1857. vii, 547 pp.

Records of the Governor and Colony of the Massachusetts Bay in New England. Edited by N. B. Shurtleff. Vol. 1. 1628-1641. Boston: 1853.

Report of the Committee of the Connecticut General Assembly to whom was referred the Petition of the President and Fellows of Yale College. 182 . 5 pp.

Reports on the Course of Instruction in Yale College, by a Committee of the Corporation and the Academical Faculty. New Haven: 1828. 56 pp.

Report of the Doings of the Second State Convention of Sabbath School Teachers, held at New Haven, Ct., June 1, 2, 3, 1858. Hartford: 1858. 104 pp.

Society for the Promotion of Collegiate and Theological Education at the West. Permanent Documents, including Annual Reports, Sermons and Addresses. New York: 1844-1854.

Yale College. Annual Reports of the Treasurer. New Haven: 1830-1875.

Young Men's Association of the First Ecclesiastical Society of New Haven. Constitution and By-Laws. New Haven: 1854. 3 pp.

Young Men's Association of the First Ecclesiastical Society of New Haven. First Annual Report. New Haven: 1855. 12 pp.

5. Biography and History

Adams, Ephraim. The Iowa Band. Boston: 1870. 184 pp.

Bacon, Leonard. Commemorative Discourse on the Completion of Fifty Years from the Founding of the Theological Seminary at Andover. Andover: 1858. 46 pp.

Bacon, Leonard. Four Commemorative Discourses: delivered on his 63d Birthday Feb. 9, 1865; on the 40th Anniversary of his Installation, Mar 12, 1865, and on his Retirement from Pastoral Duties, September, 1865. New Haven: 1866. 66 pp.

Bacon, Leonard. Funeral Discourse Pronounced at the Interment of James Hillhouse, Jan. 2, 1833. New Haven: 1833. 15 pp.

Bacon, Leonard. Sermon at the Funeral of Rev. Lyman Beecher, Jan. 14, 1863. New York: 1863. 31 pp.

Bacon, Leonard. Sermon to the First Church and Society in New Haven on Completing the Twenty-fifth Year of the author's Service in the Pastoral Office. New Haven: 1850. 27 pp.

Bacon, Leonard. Sketch of the Life and Public Services of Hon. James Hillhouse. New Haven: 1860. 46 pp.

Bacon, Leonard. Thirteen Historical Discourses, on the Completion of 200 years from the beginning of the First Church in New Haven. New Haven: 1839. viii, 400 pp.

Baldwin, Theron. Historical Sketch of the Origin, Progress, and Wants of Illinois College. New York: 1832. 16 pp.

Barney, Frances Bishop. History of St. Paul's Parish, New Haven, 1830-1930. New Haven: 1930. 79 pp.

Biographical Sketches of the Members of the Class of 1816, Yale College. New Haven: 1867. 77 pp.

Bouton, Nathaniel. History of the Origin and Organization of the American Home Missionary Society. New York: 1860. 18 pp.

Brastow, L. O. A Memorial Address Commemorative of the Life and Services of Samuel Harris, Marquand Chapel, Dec. 14, 1899. New Haven. 19 pp.

Carver, Henry. A Sermon Preached at the Funeral of Rev. Timothy Cutler, Aug. 20, 1755. Boston: 1765.

Chapin, Calvin. A Sermon delivered Jan. 14, 1817, at the Funeral of the Rev. Timothy Dwight. New Haven: 1817. 35 pp.

Cleaveland, E. L. A Sermon, delivered at the Dedication of the Church-Edifice in Court Street, erected by the Third Congregational Society, New Haven, Dec. 7, 1841. New Haven: 1841. 23 pp.

Cleaveland, E. L. A Discourse, delivered in the Court Street Church on the Sabbath Previous to the Removal of the Third Congregational Society to a New House of Worship, Mar. 30, 1856. New Haven: 1856. 23 pp.

Cleaveland, E. L. A Sermon, delivered on the Twenty-fifth Anniversary of the Author's Ministry, July 25, 1858. New Haven: 1858. 29 pp.

The Corporation of Yale College, Historically and Practically Considered, by a Chairman of a Class Committee on this subject. Washington: 1886. 2nd Edition. 24 pp.

Croswell, Rev. Harry. Forty Years in Trinity Parish. A Pastoral Letter. New Haven: 1856. 15 pp.

Curtis, Edward L. An Address in Memory of George E. Day. Dec. 17, 1905. 13 pp.

Dana, Mrs. Henrietta Frances (Silliman). Hillhouse Avenue 1809-1900. New Haven: 1907. 16 pp.

Dutton, S. W. S. The History of the North Church in New Haven. 1742 ... to 1842. Three Sermons. New Haven: 1842. 128 pp.

Dutton, S. W. S. Sketch of the Life and Character of N. W. Taylor. New Haven: 1859?. 22 pp.

Dwight, Timothy. Theodore Dwight Woolsey .... Memorial Address before the Graduates of Yale University, June 24, 1890. New Haven: 1896. 29 pp.

Eustis, W. T. Jr. A Discourse delivered on the Twentieth Anniversary of the Origin of the Chapel Street Church and Ecclesiastical Society, New Haven, Nov. 7, 1858. New Haven: 1858. 24 pp.

Fisher, George P. Discourse, Commemorative of the History of the Church of Christ in Yale College. New Haven: 1858. 97 pp.

Fisher, George P. A Discourse Commemorative of the Life and Services of Professor Josiah W. Gibbs. New Haven: 1861. 20 pp.

Fowler, W. C. Origin of the Theological School of Yale College. 1869. 26 pp.

Hallock, Gerard. History of the South Congregational Church, New Haven. New Haven: 1865. iv, 257, 46 pp.

Jarvis, S. F. Address at the Laying of the Corner Stone of the Trinity Church of New Haven, May 17, 1814. New Haven: 1814. 15 pp.

Kent, James. An Address delivered at New Haven before the Phi Beta Kappa Society, Sept. 13, 1831. New Haven: 1831. 48 pp.

Kingsley, James Luce. A Sketch of the History of Yale College, in Connecticut. Boston: 1835. 48 pp.

Memorial Addresses concerning Timothy Dwight, delivered in New Haven, Feb. 22, 1917. New Haven: 1917. 42, 15 pp.

Memorial of N. W. Taylor, D.D. Three Sermons: by Leonard Bacon, S. W. S. Dutton, George P. Fisher. New Haven: 1858. 43 pp.

Memoirs of American Missionaries formerly connected with the Society of Inquiry Respecting Missions, in the Andover Theological Seminary: Embracing a History of the Society, etc. Boston: 1833. 365 pp.

Merwin, Samuel. A Discourse on the Completion of Fifty Years Service in the Ministry of the Gospel, North Church, New Haven, Feb. 25, 1855. New Haven: 1855. 72 pp.

Olmsted, Denison. Memoir of Eli Whitney, Esq. New Haven: 1846. 80 pp.

Personal Reminiscences and Memorials of Rebecca Taylor Hatch, 1818-1904. New Haven: 1905. xi, 111 pp.

Phelps, Dryden. A Quarter Century Sermon preached in the First Baptist Church in New Haven, Jan. 22, 1871. New Haven: 1871. 22, xii pp.

Plan of the Theological Seminary of the Presbyterian Church in the United States of America, located at Princeton, New Jersey. Elizabeth Town: 1816. 22 pp.

Plymouth Congregational Church in New Haven, 1831-1931. New Haven: 1931. 97 pp.

Popular Sketch of the Rise and Progress of Sunday Schools in the United States. Philadelphia: 185-? 48 pp.

Sawyer, L. A. An Appeal in Favor of Good Works: A Farewell Sermon, delivered to the Church of Christ in the United Society. New Haven, Dec. 3, 1837. New Haven: 1837. 24 pp.

Savage, G. S. F. Flavel Bascom, 1890? 32 pp.

Silliman, Benjamin. An Address delivered before the Association of Alumni of Yale College, in New Haven, Aug. 17, 1842. New Haven: 1842. 44 pp.

Sketch of the Rise, Progress, and Present State of the Theological Seminary of the Presbyterian Church in the United States. Elizabeth-town: 1817. 19 pp.

Statement of the Origin, History, and Progress of the New Haven Young Men's Institute, and of its Library. New Haven: 1840. 8 pp.

Sturtevant, J. M. A Sermon Commemorative of the Life and Labors of Rev. William Kirby. New York: 1852. 15 pp.

Sturtevant, J. M. Sketch of Theron Baldwin. Boston: 1875. 52 pp.

Walker, Williston. The Coming of Yale College to New Haven. An Address ...., Oct. 21, 1916. New Haven: 1917. 11 pp.

Woodruff, George W. History of Methodism in New Haven. New Haven: 1859. 24 pp.

Woolsey, T. D. An Address Commemorative of the Life and Services of Benjamen Silliman, delivered in Center Church, New Haven, Nov. 28, 1864. New Haven: 1865. 23 pp.

Woolsey, T. D. A Discourse Commemorative of the Life and Services of Jeremiah Day, delivered in the Center Church, New Haven, Aug. 26, 1867. New Haven: 1867. 35 pp.

Woolsey, T. D. A Discourse Commemorative of the Life and Services of Rev. Chauncey Allen Goodrich. New Haven: 1860. 30 pp.

Woolsey, T. D. Discourse Commemorative of Rev. W. A. Larned, delivered in the Center Church, New Haven, Feb. 6, 1862. New Haven: 1862. 56 pp.

Woolsey, T. D. An Historical Discourse pronounced before the Graduates of Yale College, Aug. 14, 1850; one hundred and fifty years after the founding of that institution. New Haven: 1850. 128 pp.

6. Controversy

Action of the Church in Franklin, Massachusetts, in regard to the American Tract Society and the American Board. New York: 1854. 8 pp.

Bacon, Leonard. The Morality of the Nebraska Bill. New Haven: 1854. 23 pp.

Bacon, Leonard. Seven Letters to the Rev. George A. Calhoun concerning the Pastoral Union of Connecticut. New Haven: 1840. 144 pp.

Beecher, Lyman. The Rights of the Congregational Churches of Massachusetts. Boston: 1827. 63 pp.

A Brief View of the American Education Society. 1826. 23 pp.

Burchard, Charles. A Statement of Facts in Relation to the Case of Rev. Jacob Knapp. New York: 1846. 45 pp.

Clap, Thomas. The Ancient and Ecclesiastical Constitution of Colleges. New Haven: 1854-56? 32 pp.

Clap, Thomas. The Answer of a Friend in the West to a Letter from a Gentleman in the East. New Haven: 1755. 18 pp.

Clap, Thomas. A Brief History and Vindication of the Doctrines received and Established in the Churches of New England. New Haven: 1757. 41 pp.

Clap, Thomas. The Religious Constitution of Colleges, especially Yale College. New London: 1754. 20 pp.

Channing, William E. A Sermon delivered at the Ordination of Rev. Jared Sparks, May 5, 1819. Baltimore: 1813. 15 pp.

Declaration of the Association and County of New Haven in Connecticut, convened at New Haven, Feb. 19, 1744, ...5, concerning the Rev. Mr. George Whitfield, his conduct and the state of Religion in his day. Boston: 1745. 8 pp.

Declaration of the Rector and Tutors of Yale College in New Haven, against the Revered Mr. George Whitefield, His Principles and Designs. Boston: 1745. 15 pp.

Defence of the Hebrew Grammar of Gesenius against Prof. Stuart's Translation, by the original translator. New York: 1847. 53, ix pp.

Dow, Daniel. New Haven Theology, Alias Taylorism, alias Neology: in its own language, with notes appended. Thompson: 1834. 50 pp.

An Examination of a Review of Dr. Taylor's Sermon on Human Depravity and Mr. Harvey's Strictures on the Sermon. New Haven: 1829. 53 pp.

Fitch, E. T. An Inquiry into the Nature of Sin. New Haven: 1827. 95 pp.

Fitch, E. T. Two Discourses on the Nature of Sin, delivered before the Students of Yale College, July 30, 1826. New Haven: 1826. 49 pp. 2nd edition. 1842. 48 pp.

Fitch, E. T. A Vindication of the Divine Purpose in Relation to the Existence of Sin. New Haven: 1832. 48 pp.

Fowler, W. C. Attack on Professor Goodrich as an editor of Webster's Dictionary. Boston: 1857. 32 pp.

Gale, Benjamen. A Calm and Full Vindication of A Letter written to Member of the Lower House of the Assembly .... New Haven: 1759. 32 pp.

Gale, Benjamen. A Few Brief Remarks on Mr. Graham's Answer, and on his Vindication of Mr. President Clap, etc. New Haven: 1760. 8 pp.

Gale, Benjamen. The Present State of the Colony of Connecticut Considered. New Haven: 1755. 21 pp.

Gale, Benjamen. A Reply to a Pamphlet entitled the Answer of the Friend in the West etc., with a Prefatory Address to the Freemen of his Majesty's English Colony of Connecticut. (xx), 63 pp.

Goodrich, C. A. A Brief Notice of Dr. Tyler's Vindication of his Strictures. New Haven: 1830. 7 pp.

Goodrich, C. A. Can I conscientiously vote for Henry Clay? New Haven: 1844. 4 pp.

Goodrich, C. A. Letter to Rev. Henry Croswell, on the subject of two Publications, entitled "A Serious Call", and "A Sober Appeal". New Haven: 1819. 12 pp.

Goodrich, C. A. What Does Dr. Bushnell Mean? Hartford: 1848. 28 pp.

Graham, John. An Answer to Mr. Gales' Pamphlet: entitled, A Calm and full Vindication, etc. in relation to Yale College. New Haven: 1759. 28 pp.

Graham, John. A Letter to a Member of the House of Representatives of the Colony of Connecticut, in Vindication of Yale College. New Haven: 1759. 19 pp.

Harvey, Joseph. Examination. Hartford: 1829. 53 pp.

Harvey, Joseph. A Review of a Sermon Concio ad Clevum, delivered in the Chapel of Yale College, Sept. 10, 1828, by N. W. Taylor. Hartford: 1829. 40 pp.

Hobart, Noah. A Congratulary Letter from a Gentleman in the West to his Friend in the East upon the Success of his letter, entitled, The Present State of the College of Connecticut. New Haven: 1755. 15 pp.

A Letter from Rev. N. W. Taylor on the subject of his late discussion with Rev. Dr. Tyler. New Haven: 1832. 24 pp.

Letters to the Members of the American Tract Society, on the Tract Controversy, by the Boston Secretary. Boston: 1858. 112 pp.

A Letter to the Secretaries of the American Tract Society, written in behalf of the Rev. Jeremiah Day, D.D. LL.D., Eleazer T. Fitch, D.D., and Others, by Chauncey A. Goodrich. New Haven: 1858. 16 pp.

Minutes adopted on the 18th of March, 1858, by the Publishing Committee of the American Tract Society, Explaining their Position in Relation to the Report and Resolutions of the Committee of Fifteen, as sanctioned at the Anniversary of 1857; and the Act of the Executive Committee adopting such Minute. New York: 1858? 20 pp.

Nelson, Levi. A Letter to the Theological Professors at New Haven, concerning their Supposition that God may not have been able to prevent Sin in a Moral System. Norwich: 1848. 87 pp.

The New Haven Memorial to the President protesting against the use of the United States Army to enforce the bogus laws of Kansas; The answer of President Buchanan; and the Reply of the Memorialists. New Haven: 1857. 12 pp.

Proceedings of the Union Meetings, held at Brewster Hall, December 24, 1850. New Haven: 1851. 48 pp.

Remarks on Propagated Depravity and Sin as a Necessary Means of Greatest Good, first published in the Quarterly Christian Spectator for Sept. 1832, as a Review of Dr. Tyler's Remarks on Dr. Taylor's Letter. New Haven: 1832. 40 pp.

Remonstrance and Complaint of the Association of Fairfield West to the Hartford Central Association: together with a Reply of the Hartford Central Association. New York: 1850. 35 pp.

Report of the Committee of the New York General Association on the Relation of the American Board of Commissioners for Foreign Missions, the American Home Missionary Society, The American Tract Society, The American Missionary Association, and the American Sunday School Union, to the subject of Slavery, Unanimously adopted, August 26, 1855. 12 pp.

Report of the Union Meeting, held in Brewster's Hall, New Haven, Conn., Wednesday, December 14, 1859. New Haven: 1860. 52 pp.

Review of Dr. Tyler's Strictures on the Article in the Christian Spectator on the Means of Regeneration. New Haven: 1830. 56 pp.

A Review of Dr. Wood's Letters to Dr. Taylor on the Premission of Sin, together with Dr. Bellamy's Remarks on the Same Subject. New Haven: 1830. 50 pp.

Speeches at the Proceedings of the Anti-Nebraska Meetings held in New Haven, Connecticut, March 8 and 10, 1854. New Haven: 1854. 16 pp.

Silliman, Benjamen. Consistency of the Discoveries of Modern Geology with the Sacred History of Creation and the Deluge. New Haven: 1833. 60 pp.

Spring, Gardner. A Dissertation on Moral Depravity. New York: 1833. 93 pp.

Spring, Gardner. A Dissertation on the Means of Regeneration. New York: 1827. 50 pp.

Taylor, Nathaniel W. Essays on the Means of Regeneration. New Haven: 1830. 92 pp.

Taylor, N. W. An Inquiry into the Nature of Sin as exhibited in Dr. Dwight's Theology. A Letter to a Friend, by Clevicus. New Haven: 1829. 43 pp.

Taylor, N. W. Man a Free Agent without the Aids of Divine Grace. New Haven: 1818. 18 pp.

Taylor, Nathaniel W. Concio ad Clevum, A Sermon delivered, Sept. 10, 1828. New Haven: 1828. 38 pp.

Taylor, N. W. Regeneration the Beginning of Holiness in the Human Heart. Also - A Review of Rev. Mr. Taylor's Sermon on Regeneration. New Haven: 1817. 40 pp.

Taylor, N. W. Reply to Dr. Tyler's Examination. Boston: 1832. 24 pp.

Taylor, N. W. Review of Professor Norton's Views of Calvinism. New Haven: 1823. 30 pp.

Taylor, N. W. Review of Rev. Gardner Spring's Dissertation on Natural Depravity. New Haven: 1833. 20 pp.

The Tract Society and Slavery. Hartford: 1859. 26 pp.

Trumbull, Benjamen. A Letter to the Honorable Gentlemen of the Council Board, for the College of Connecticut, shewing that Yale College is a very great Emolument, and of very high Importance to the State. New Haven: 1766. 26 pp.

Tyler, Bennet. Letters on the Origin and Progress of the New Haven Theology. New York: 1837. iv, 180 pp.

Tyler, Bennet. A Letter to the Editor of the "Spirit of the Pilgrims", to which are added Remarks on a Recent Letter of Dr. Taylor's in the "Christian Spectator". Portland: 1833. 40 pp.

Tyler, Bennet. Remarks on Rev. Dr. Taylor's Letter to Dr. Hawes. Boston: 1832. 12 pp.

Tyler, Bennet. Strictures of the Review of Dr. Spring's Dissertation. Portland: 1829. 64 pp.

Tyler, Bennet. Vindication of the Strictures on the Review of Dr. Spring's Dissertation on the Means of Regeneration. Portland: 1830. 63 pp.

Ware, Henry. Letters Addressed to Unitarians and Calvinists. Cambridge: 1820. 150 pp.

Woods, Leonard. Letters to Nathaniel W. Taylor. Andover: 1830. 114 pp.

Woods, Leonard. Letters to Unitarians and Reply to Dr. Ware. Second edition, with an Appendix. Andover: 1820. viii, 351 pp.

Woods, Leonard. Letters to Unitarians occasioned by the Sermon of the Rev. William E. Channing at the ordination of Rev. Jared Sparks. Andover: 1820. 100 pp.

A View of the New England Illuminati: who are Infatigably engaged in Destroying the Religion and Government of the United States; under a feigned regard for their Safety. Philadelphia: 1799. 20 pp.

7. Miscellaneous Sermons

Bacon, Leonard. The American Church, A Discourse in Behalf of the American Home Missionary Society. New York: 1852. 23 pp.

Bacon, Leonard. A Discourse on the Traffic in Spiritous Liquors, delivered in the Center Church, New Haven, Feb. 6, 1838. New Haven: 1838. 54 pp.

Bacon, Leonard. The Hopefulness of Efforts for the Promotion of Peace, pronounced at the anniversary of the Hartford County Peace Society, June 10, 1832. Hartford: 1832. 26 pp.

Beecher, Lyman. A Plea for the West. Cincinnati: 1835. 190 pp.

Cutler, Timothy. The Depth of Divine Thoughts: and the Regards due to them. A Sermon delivered in the audience of the General Assembly of the Colony of Connecticut, at New Haven, Oct. 18, 1719. New London: 1720. 2, 38 pp.

Cutler, Timothy. A firm Union of a People Represented
.... A Sermon preached before the General Assembly of the
Colony of Connecticut, at Hartford, May 9, 1717. New
London: 1717. 65 pp.

Cutler, Timothy. The good and faithful Servant and
the joy awarded to him. A Sermon, Christ Church in Boston,
June 28, 1747. Boston: 1747. 21 pp.

Daggett, Naphtali. The great and tender concern of
faithful Ministers for the Souls of their People .... A
Sermon, preached at Danbury, Sept. 9, 1770. New Haven:
1770. 32 pp.

Daggett, Naphtali. The Great Importance of Speaking
in the most Intelligent Manner in Christian Churches. A
Sermon, preached at the Installation of Rev. Nathaniel
Sherman .... New Haven, May 18, 1768. New Haven: 1768.
44 pp.

Daggett, Naphtali. The Faithful Serving of God and
our Generation the Only Way to a Peaceful and Happy Death.
A Sermon occasioned by the Rev. Thomas Clap. Jan. 7, 1767.
New Haven: 1767. 39, 7 pp.

Daggett, Naphtali. The Testimony of Conscience a
most solid Foundation of Rejoicing. A Sermon, preached in
Boston, May 19, 1773. Boston: 1773. 52 pp.

Dwight, Timothy. The Dignity and Excellence of the
Gospel. A Sermon, preached at the Ordination of N. W.
Taylor to the Gospel Ministry, April 10, 1812. New Haven:
1812. 42 pp.

Dwight, Timothy. Sermon preached at the Opening of
the Theological Institution at Andover, Sept. 28, 1808.
Boston: 1808. 38 pp.

Fitch, E. T. Liberal Christians helpers to the
Truth. A Sermon, preached at the Anniversary of the Female
Education Society. New Haven: 1829. 28 pp.

Fitch, E. T. National Prosperity Perpetuated. A
Discourse delivered in the Chapel of Yale College on the
day of Annual Thanksgiving, Nov. 29, 1827. New Haven:
1828. 34 pp.

Fitch, E. T. A Sermon preached at the funeral of
the Rev. John Elliott. New Haven: 1825. 19 pp.

Fitch, E. T. A Sermon preached at the Ordination of Rev. W. C. Fowler. Aug. 31, 1825. New Haven: 1825. 44 pp.

Hinsdale, Charles. A Discourse on Christian Education. New Haven: 1833. 32 pp.

Lockwood, John. Man Mortal: God Everlasting .... illustrated in a Discourse delivered .... after the Death of the Hon. Col. Williams .... New Haven: 1755. 48, xv pp.

Sermons preached in the interest of the American Home Missionary Society. 1847-49, 1851-55, 1857-59. Eleven pamphlets. New Haven, published by the Society.

Smith, Eli. The Missionary Character. An Address delivered before the Society of Inquiry in the Theological Seminary in New Haven, April 1, 1840. New Haven: 1840. 38 pp.

Taylor, N. W. Public Opinion, the Glory and Danger of Democracy. A Sermon addressed to the General Assembly of Connecticut, Hartford, May 7, 1823. Hartford: 1823. 43 pp.

Williams, Elisha. Death the Advantage of the Godly. A Sermon. New London: 1728. 42 pp.

Williams, Elisha. Divine Grace Illustrious in the Salvation of Sinners. A Sermon delivered before the General Assembly of Connecticut, at New Haven, Oct. 22, 1727. New London: 1728. 3, 37 pp.

Woolsey, T. D. The Ministerial Office, its Permanency and Ends. A Sermon preached at the installation of G. E. Day, Jan. 12, 1848. Northampton: 1848. 24 pp.

8. Miscellaneous Pamphlets

Barber, J. W. Views in New Haven and its Vicinity, with a particular Description of each View. New Haven: 1825. 11 pp. 6 colored plates.

By-Laws of the City of New Haven, January, 1822. New Haven: 1822. 31 pp.

City Guide to New Haven; being a Pocket Directory for Citizens and Strangers .... by J. W. Barber and L. S. Punderson. New Haven: 1860. 36 pp.

Clap, Thomas. An Essay on the Nature and Foundation of Virtue and Obligation. New Haven: 1765. 68 pp.

The Club, New Haven, Connecticut, 1838-1886. 40 pp.

A Confession of Faith Owned and Consented unto by the Elders & Messengers of the Churches assembled at Boston in New England, May 12, 1680. Being the Second Session of that Synod. Boston: 1699. 165 pp.

A Confession of Faith Owned and Consented to by the Elders and Messengers of the Churches in the Colony of Connecticut in New England, assembled at Say Brook, September 9th, 1708. New London in W. E.: 1710. 116 pp.

Dwight, Timothy. Yale College: Some Thoughts Respecting its Future. New Haven: 1871. 110 pp.

Fitch, E. T. An Account of the Meeting of the Class which graduated at Yale College in 1810, held at New Haven, Aug. 18, 1840. New Haven: 1840. 14 pp.

Fitch, E. T. Music as a Fine Art. New Haven: 1872. 36 pp.

Take Heed Words by Miss Gould. Music by Dr. E. T. Fitch. 2nd ed. New Haven. 1866? 2 pp.

New Haven As It Is. Embellished with a Map of the City and Several Engravings. New Haven: 1845. 24 pp.

Plan of the Theological Seminary of the Protestant Episcopal Church of the United States. Hartford: 1820. 23 pp.

A Platform of Church Discipline: Gathered out of the Word of God, and agreed upon by the Elders and Messengers of the Churches assembled in New England. Printed in New England and London: 1653. 30 pp.

The Riot at New Haven between the Students and the Town Boys, on the night of March 17, 1854. New Haven: 1854. 47 pp.

Yale College Society of Inquiry Respecting Missions. A Missionary Catechism for the use of Children. New Haven: 1821. 54 pp.

Yale College Missionary Society. First Annual Circular to the Churches in Connecticut, on the Subject of Missions. New Haven: 1834. 12 pp.

PERIODICALS

The American Quarterly Register. Vols. 1-18. (July 1827 - May 1846). Boston.

The Biblical Repertory and Theological Review. Vols. 1-8 (1829-1836); The Biblical Repertory and Princeton Review, Vols. 9-42 (1837-1870). Princeton; Philadelphia; New York.

The Christian Spectator, conducted by an Association of Gentlemen. Passim. Vols. 1-10 (1519-1828). New Haven.

The Home Missionary, Vols. 1-31 (1829-1859). New York. Published by the American Home Missionary Society.

The New Englander. Vols. 1-31 (1843-1872). New Haven.

The New Havener. Vols 2 and III (1836/37 - 1837/38). New Haven.

The Quarterly Christian Spectator, Passim. Vols. 1-10 (1829-1838). New Haven.

"Reports on the Course of Instruction in Yale College, by a Committee of the Corporation and the Academical Faculty." American Journal of Science and Arts. Vol. 15 (1829), No. 2, Art. VIII, pp. 287-351.

Robinson, Edward. "Theological Education in Germany." The Biblical Depository, Volume First, Nos. I-IV (1831), pp. 1-51, 202-226, 409-451, 613-637.

Taylor, N. W. and Hawes, Joel. "Correspondence" The Connecticut Observer, Vol. 8 (Monday, Feb. 20, 1832), p. 30..

(The contributions of Professors Fitch, Gibbs, Goodrich, and Taylor, to various periodicals are listed in the Annotated Bibliographies of these men to be found in Chapter IV of this study, and are not repeated here.)

COLLECTIONS OF HISTORICAL SOCIETIES

Dexter, Franklin B. "Estimates of Population in the American Colonies." Proceedings of the American Antiquarian Society, New Series, Vol. V (Oct. 1887 - Oct. 1888), pp. 22-50.

Dexter, F. B. "The Founding of Yale College." Papers of the New Haven Colony Historical Society, Vol. III (1882), pp. 1-31.

Dexter, Franklin Bowditch. "An Historical Study of the Powers and Duties of the Presidency in Yale College." Proceedings of the American Antiquarian Society, New Series, Vol. XII (Oct. 1897 - Oct. 1898), pp. 27-42.

Dexter, F. B. "The Influence of the English Universities in the Development of New England." Proceedings of the Massachusetts Historical Society, Vol. XVII (1879-80), pp. 340-352.

Dexter, F. B. "A Sketch of the Life and Writings of John Davenport." Papers of the New Haven Colony Historical Society, Vol. II (1876), pp. 205-238.

Dexter, F. B. "Student Life at Yale College under the first President Dwight." Proceedings of the American Antiquarian Society, New Series, Vol. 27 (April 11, 1917 - Oct. 17, 1917), pp. 318-335.

"New Haven Town Records, 1649-1684." Edited by F. B. Dexter. New Haven Colony Historical Society. New Haven: Printed for the Society, 1917, 1919. 3 vols. 547, 457, 457 pp.

"Some Original Papers Respecting the Episcopal Controversy in Connecticut, MDCCXXII." Collections of the Massachusetts Historical Society, Second Series, Vol. II, pp. 126-137; Vol. IV, pp. 297-301. Boston: 1816.

BOOKS

1. Biography and History

Adams, John Quincy. A History of Auburn Theological Seminary, 1818-1918. Auburn, New York: Auburn Seminary Press, 1918. 235 pp.

Bacon, Benjamen Wisner. Theodore Thornton Munger New England Minister. New Haven: Yale University Press, MCMXIII. xxiii, 409 pp.

Bacon, T. D. Leonard Bacon, A Statesman in the Church. Edited by B. W. Bacon. New Haven: Yale University Press, 1931. xv, 563 pp.

Baldwin, Ebenezer. Annals of Yale College, from its foundation to the year 1831. Appendix - to the year 1838. New Haven: B. and W. Noyes, 1838. viii, 324 pp.

Barber, J. W. History and Antiquities of New Haven from its earliest settlement to the present time. New Haven: 1831. 108 pp.

Belden, E. P. Sketches of Yale College, with numerous Anecdotes, and Embellished with more than 30 Engravings. New York: Saxton and Miles, 1843. xi, 192 pp. 4 plates.

Blake, Henry T. Chronicles of the New Haven Green from 1638 to 1862. New Haven: 1898. 280 pp.

Bush, Charles P. Five Years in China; or the Factory Boy made a Missionary. The Life and Observations of Rev. William Aitchison. Philadelphia: Presbyterian Publication Committee, 1865. 284 pp.

Bushnell, Horace. Discourses in Christian Nurture. Boston: 1847. 72 pp.

Beecher, Lyman. Autobiography, Correspondence, etc. Edited by Charles Beecher. New York: Harper and Bros., 1864-65. 2 vols. viii, 560; vii, 587 pp.

Chamberlain, Joshua, L. Yale University: its History, Influence, Equipment, and Characteristics, with Biographical Sketches and Portraits of Founders, Benefactors, Officers, and Alumni. Boston: R. Herndon and Company, 1900. 259 pp.

Clap, Thomas. The Annals or History of Yale College in New Haven .... to the year 1766; with an appendix containing the method of instruction and government. New Haven: 1766. ii, 124 pp.

Clark, Calvin M. History of Bangor Theological Seminary. Boston: The Pilgrim Press, 1916. xiv, 408 pp.

Dexter, Franklin B. Biographical Sketches of the Graduates of Yale College with Annals of the College History, 1701-1815. New York: Henry Holt and Company, 1885; 1896, 1903; 1907; 1911. 5 vols. viii, 788; 793; 725; 752; 815 pp. New Haven: Yale University Press, 1912, Vol. 6. 844 pp.

Dexter, Franklin B. Biographical Notices of the Graduates of Yale College including those graduates in classes later than 1815, who are not commemorated in the annual Obituary Records. New Haven: 1913. 411 pp.

Dexter, Franklin B. Documentary History of Yale University, under the Original Charter of the Collegiate School of Connecticut, 1701-1745. New Haven: Yale University Press, 1916. xviii, 382 pp.

Dexter, Franklin B. A Selection of Miscellaneous Historical Papers of Fifty Years. New Haven: 1918. viii, 397 pp.

Dexter, Franklin B. A Sketch of the History of Yale University. New York: Henry Holt and Company, 1887. 108 pp.

Dexter, Henry Martyn. The Congregationalism of the Last Three Hundred Years, as Seen in its Literature .... with a Bibliographical Appendix. New York: Harper and Brothers, 1880. xxxviii, 326 pp.

Dwight, Timothy. Memories of Yale Life and Men, 1845-1899. New York: Dodd, Mead and Company, 1903. 500 pp.

Edwards, Jonathan. An Account of the Life of the late Rev. David Brainerd, minister of the Gospel, missionary to the Indians .... Boston: 1749. xii, 316 pp.

Fisher, George P. Life of Benjamen Silliman. New York: Charles Scribner and Co., 1866. 2 vols. ix, 408; x, 407 pp.

Gilman, D. C. *Life of James Dwight Dana.* New York: Harper and Brothers, 1899. xii, 409 pp.

Holmes, Abiel. *The Life of Ezra Stiles, D.D. LL.D. .... President of Yale College.* Boston: 1789. 404 pp.

Kingsley, James L. *Life of Ezra Stiles.* Sparks' American Biography. New Series. Vol. VI, pp. 3-79. Boston: Charles C. Little and James Brown, MDCCCXIV.

Kingsley, W. L., ed. *Yale College, a Sketch of its History, with notices of its several Departments, Instructors, and Benefactors, together with some account of Student Life and Amusements, by various authors.* New York: Henry Holt and Co., 1879. 2 vols. xxvi, 504; xvi, 533 pp.

Knapp, Elder Jacob. *Autobiography.* New York: Sheldon and Carn, 1868. xxvi, 341 pp.

The Life and Labors of Rev. Reuben Gaylord, by his wife. Omaha: 1889. x, 437 pp.

Magoun, George F. *Asa Turner, A Home Missionary Patriarch and His Times.* Boston and Chicago: Congregational Sunday School and Publishing Society, 1889. 345 pp.

Means, D. O. *Life of Edward Norris Kirk.* Boston: Lockwood, Brooks and Company. xvi, 432 pp.

Munger, T. T. *Horace Bushnell, Preacher and Theologian.* Boston: Houghton Mifflin and Co., 1899. xiv, 425 pp.

Oviatt, Edwin. *The Beginnings of Yale (1701-1726).* New Haven: Yale University Press. 1916. xxi, 456 pp.

Pierce, Benjamin. *History of Harvard University from its Founding in the year 1636, to the Period of the American Revolution.* Cambridge: Brown, Shattuck, and Co., 1833. xix, 316, 159 pp.

Prentiss, G. W. *The Union Theological Seminary in the City of New York.* New York: Busan D. F. Randolph and Co., 1889. vi, 294 pp.

Reminiscences of Scenes and Characters in College; by a Graduate of Yale, of the Class of 1821. New Haven: 1847. 229 pp.

Reynolds, James B., Fisher, S. H., Wright, H. B., editors. *Two Centuries of Christian Activity at Yale.* New York: G. P. Putnam's Sons, 1901. xv, 367 pp.

Rice, Edwin W. *The Sunday-School Movement and the American Sunday-School Union, 1780-1927.* Philadelphia: The Union Press. 1927. 485 pp.

Sprague, William Buell. *Annals of the American Pulpit: or Commemorative Notices of Distinguished American Clergy of Various Denominations.* "Trinitarian Congregationalists". Vols. I and II. New York: R. Carter and Bros., 1857. xxvii, 723; viii, 778 pp.

Stevens, George B. *Life of Peter Parker.* Boston: Congregational Sunday School and Publishing Society, 1896. 362 pp.

Stokes, Anson Phelps. *Memorials of Eminent Yale Men.* New Haven: Yale University Press, 1914. 2 vols. xxiii, 371; 452 pp.

Sturtevant, Julian Monson. *An Autobiography.* New York: Revell and Company, 1896. 349 pp.

Thompson, J. P. *Memoir of David Tappan Stoddard.* New York: 1858. vi, 422 pp.

Tracy, Joseph. *The Great Awakening: A History of the Revivals of Religion in the time of Edwards and Whitefield.* Boston: Tappan and Dennet, 1842. xviii, 433 pp.

Trumbull, Benjamen. *A Complete History of Connecticut, civil and ecclesiastical, from the emigration of its first planters from England .... to the close of the Indian Wars.* New Haven: Maltby, Goldsmith and Co., 1818. 2 vols. 567, 548 pp.

Walker, George Leon. *History of the First Church in Hartford, 1633-1883.* Hartford: Brown and Goss, 1884. xii, 503 pp.

Woods, Leonard. *History of Andover Theological Seminary.* Boston: J. R. Osgood and Co., 1885. 638 pp.

Wright, G. Frederick. *Charles Grandison Finney.* Boston: Houghton Mifflin Co., 1891. vi, 329 pp.

2. Textbooks and Faculty Publications

An American Dictionary of the English Language. By Noah Webster. Revised and Enlarged by Chauncey A. Goodrich. Springfield, Mass.: George and Charles Merriam, 1854. Preface by the editor, x pp. lxxxix, 1367 pp.

Dwight, Timothy. The Conquest of Canaan; A Poem in Eleven Books. Hartford, New England: MDCCLXXV. vii, 303pp.

Dwight, Timothy. Greenfield Hill: a poem in Seven parts. New York: 1794. 183 pp.

Fisher, George P. Discussions in History and Theology. New York: Charles Scribner's Sons, 1880. x, 555 pp.

Fitch, Eleazer T. Sermons, Practical and Descriptive, preached in the Pulpit of Yale College. New Haven: 1871. vii, 365 pp.

Gesenius, F. H. W., Hebrew Grammar. Fourteenth edition as revised by Dr. Emil Rödiger. Translated by T. J. Conant, to which are added, a course of exercises in Hebrew Grammar, and a Hebrew Crestomathy, prepared by the translator. New York: 1846. x, 297, 64 pp.

Gesenius, F. H. W., A Hebrew and English Lexicon of the Old Testament, including the Biblical Chaldee. Translated from the German works of Professor W. Gesenius by Josiah W. Gibbs ... Andover: 1824. London: 1827. v, 656 pp.

Goodrich, Chauncey A. Elements of Greek Grammar. Taken chiefly from the grammar of C. E. Hachenbery. New Haven: Oliver Steele, 1814. vii, 317 pp.

Goodrich, Chauncey A. Exercises in Elocution. New Haven: 18--? 84 pp.

Goodrich, Chauncey A. Exercises in Public Speaking. New Haven? 183-? 16 pp.

Goodrich, Chauncey. Lessons in Greek Parsing or Outlines of Greek Grammar. New Haven: Durrie and Peck, 1857. (Twenty Seventh edition). iv, 138 pp.

Goodrich, Chauncey A. **Select British Eloquence.**
New York: Harper Brothers, 1870. vi, 947 pp.

Gibbs, Josiah W. **Formation of Teutonic Words in the English Language.** New Haven: 1860. viii, 139 pp.

Gibbs, Josiah W. **A Latin Analyst on Modern Philological Principles.** New Haven: 1858. viii, 150 pp.

Gibbs, Josiah W. **Philological Studies with English Illustrations.** New Haven: 1857. vii, 244 pp.

Gibbs, Josiah W. **Selections from the Holy Scriptures ... for Children.** New Haven: 1830. viii, 88 pp.

Kuinoel, D. Christiani Theophili. **Commentarius in Epistolan ad Hebraeos.** Lipsiae: Carolum Tauchitz, 1831. xxxvi, 544 pp.

Kuinoel, D. Christiani Theophili. **Commentarius in Libros Novi Testamenti Historicos.** Lipsiae: Johannem Ambrosium Barth, 1816-1818. 4 vols. x, 838; 716; 730; xxx, 848 pp.

Kuinoel, D. Christiani Theophili. **Observations ad Novum Testamentum ex Libris Apocryphis.** Lipsiae: Johannem Theophili Fiendium, 1818. viii, 231 pp.

Stuart, Moses. **Gesenius Hebrew Grammar.** Translated. Andover: Flagg and Gould, 1821. xii, 386 pp.

Taylor, Nathaniel W. **Lectures upon Select Topics in Revealed Theology.** New York: Clark, Austin and Smith, 1859. viii, 480 pp.

Taylor, Nathaniel W. **Lectures on the Moral Government of God.** New York: Clark, Austin and Smith, 1859. 2 vols. xiii, 417; viii, 423 pp.

Taylor, Nathaniel W. **Practical Sermons.** New York: Clark, Austin and Smith, 1858. 455 pp.

3. Theological Works

Beecher, Edward. **The Papal Conspiracy Exposed, and Protestantism Defended in the Light of Reason, History, and Scripture.** Boston: Stearns and Co., 1855. 420 pp.

Beecher, Lyman. Works. Boston: John P. Jewett and Company, 1852-53. 3 vols. ix, 425; iv, 443; iv, 456 pp.

Bellamy, Joseph. Works, with a Memoir of his Life. Boston: Doctrinal Tract and Book Society, 1853. Vol. I. viii, 540 pp.

Bushnell, Horace. God in Christ. Hartford: Brown and Parsons, 1849. vi, 356 pp.

Bushnell, Horace. Nature and the Supernatural, as Together Constituting the One System of God. New York: Charles Scribner, 1858. xii, 528 pp.

Dwight, Timothy. Theology Explained and Defended, in a Series of Sermons, with a Memoir of the Life of the author. Middletown, Conn.: Clark and Lyman, 1818-19. 2 vols. lvii, 668; 665 pp.

Edwards, Jonathan. Works. Edited by Edward Hickman. London: Ball, Arnold and Co., 1840. 2 vols. cclxxvi, 691; iii, 969 pp.

Edwards, Jonathan the Younger. Works. Andover: Allen, Morrill and Wardwell, 1842. 2 vols. xl, 518; vii, 556 pp.

Emmons, Nathaniel. Works. Edited by Jacob Ide. Boston: Congregational Board of Publication, 1860. Vol. II, xii, 838.

Hodge, Archibald Alexander. Outlines of Theology. New York: Robert Carter and Brothers, 1878. 678 pp.

Hodge, Charles. Systematic Theology. New York: Scribner, Armstrong and Co., 1877. 3 vols. xiii, 648; xi, 732; viii, 880, 81 pp.

Hopkins, Samuel. Works, with a Memoir of his Life and Character. Boston: Doctrinal Tract and Book Society, 1852. 3 vols. viii, 266, 534; viii, 770; vi, 798 pp.

Tyler, Rev. Bennet. Lectures on Theology, with a memoir by Rev. Nahum Gale. Boston: J. E. Tilton and Co., 1859. 395 pp.

4. General Works

Boardman, George Nye. A History of the New England Theology. New York: A. D. F. Randolph Company, 1899. 314 pp.

The Centennial Celebration of the Theological Seminary of the Presbyterian Church in the United States of America at Princeton, New Jersey, May fifth - May sixth - May seventh, Nineteen Hundred and Twelve. Princeton: 1912. xvi, 565 pp.

Clark, George W. A History of Connecticut, its People and Institutions. New York: G. P. Putnam's Sons, 1914. xx, 609 pp.

Davis, Ozra. The Pilgrim Faith. Boston: The Pilgrim Press, 1913. 266 pp.

The Diary of David McClure, Doctor of Divinity, 1748-1820, with notes by F. B. Dexter. New York: Knickerbocker Press. 1899. vi, 219 pp.

Dorchester, Daniel. Christianity in the United States, from the first Settlement down to the Present Time. New York: Hunt and Eaton, 1895. 814 pp.

Douglass, Truman O. The Pilgrims of Iowa. Boston: The Pilgrim Press, 1911. xiv, 422 pp.

Dwight, Theodore. President Dwight's Decisions of Questions discussed by the Senior Class in Yale College, in 1813-1814. From Stenographic notes. New York: J. Leavitt, 1833. 348 pp.

Foster, Frank Hugh. A Genetic History of the New England Theology. Chicago: University of Chicago Press, 1907. xv, 568 pp.

Fowler, W. C. Essays: Historical, Literary, Educational. Hartford: Case, Lockwood and Brainerd Co., 1876. 298 pp.

Haroutinian, Joseph. Piety Versus Moralism; The Passing of the New England Theology. New York: Henry Holt and Company, 1932. xxv, 329 pp.

Mather, Cotton. Ratio Disciplinae Fratrum Nov-Anglorum. A faithful Account of the Discipline Professed and Practiced in the Churches of New England. Boston: 1726. 210 pp.

Messenger, J. F. An Interpretative History of Education. New York: Thomas Y. Crowell and Company, 1931. ix, 387 pp.

Mitchell, Donald G. Ike Marvel. Reveries of a Bachelor, or a Book of the Heart. New York: Scribner, Armstrong and Company. 1877. 280 pp.

Professional Education in the United States. Prepared by H. W. Taylor and J. R. Parsons. Albany: University of the State of New York, 1900. 2 vols. 1353 pp.

Walker, George Leon. Some Aspects of the Religious Life of New England, with Special Reference to Congregationalism. New York: Silver, Burdett and Co., 1897. 208 pp.

Walker, Williston. Creeds and Platforms of Congregationalism. New York: Charles Scribner's Sons, 1893. 604 pp.

Walker, Williston. A History of the Congregational Churches in the United States. American Church History Series. New York: The Christian Literature Co., 1894. xiii, 451 pp.

TITLES IN THIS SERIES

1 Joseph Bellamy, "Works," Boston, 1853 (in two volumes).
2 Samuel Hopkins, "Works," Boston, 1852 (in three volumes).
3 Nathanael Emmons, "Works," Boston, 1861 (in six volumes).
4 Jonathan Edwards, "Works," Andover, Mass., 1842 (in two volumes).
5 H. Shelton Smith, "Changing Conceptions of Original Sin: A Study in American Theology Since 1750," New York, 1955.
6 George Nye Boardman, "A History of New England Theology," New York, 1899.
7 Frank Hugh Foster, "A Genetic History of the New England Theology," Chicago, 1907.
8 "The Utilitarin Controversy, 1819–1823," Bruce Kuklick, ed. (in two volumes).
9 Edwards A. Park, "Selected Essays."
10 John Terrill Wayland, "The Theological Department in Yale College, 1822–1858," New York, 1987.
11 George P. Fisher, "Discussion in History and Theology," New York, 1880.
12 Nathaniel W. Taylor, "Practical Sermons," New York, 1858.
13 Nathaniel W. Taylor, "Essays, Lectures, Etc. Upon Select Topics in Revealed Theology," New York, 1859.
14 Nathaniel W. Taylor, "Lectures on the Moral Government of God," New York, 1859 (in two volumes).
15 Horace Bushnell, "God in Christ," Hartford, 1849.
16 Horace Bushnell, "Christ in Theology," Hartford, 1851.
17 Charles Hodge, "Essays and Reviews," New York, 1857.
18 Henry B. Smith, "Faith and Philosophy." New York, 1877.
19 Earl Pope, "New England Calvinism and the Disruption of the Presbyterian Church," New York, 1987.
20 John W. Nevin, "The Anxious Bench," Chambersburg, Pa., 1844 bound with John W. Nevin "The Mystical Presence," Philadelphia, 1846.
21 Philip Schaff, "The Principle of Protestantism," Chambersburg, Pa. 1845 bound with Philip Schaff, "What Is Church History?," Philadelphia, 1846.